Administration Procedures

for

Advanced Secretarial Students

Carol Carysforth

Heinemann

Heinemann Educational Publishers
Halley Court, Jordan Hill, Oxford OX2 8EJ
A Division of Reed Educational & Professional Publishing Ltd

OXFORD   BLANTYRE
MELBOURNE   AUCKLAND
IBADAN   JOHANNESBURG   GABORONE
PORTSMOUTH NH (USA)   CHICAGO

First published 1997
99 00 11 10 9 8 7 6 5 4

A catalogue record for this book is available from the British Library on request.

ISBN 0 435 455419

Designed by Jackie Hill

Typeset by TechType, Abingdon, Oxon

Printed and bound by Biddles Ltd, Guildford

Contents

Introduction

This book has been written to introduce you to the range of administrative and secretarial duties you will face in employment as the millennium approaches. Rapidly changing technology and working practices mean that job roles today are very different from those encountered five or ten years ago. Multi-skilling, high-level information technology skills and a keen appreciation of the need to control both costs and quality in business are paramount for administrators and secretaries alike. This book therefore takes a rather different approach from that found in traditional texts.

Both tutors and students will quickly notice that the format of this book does not correspond to any particular administrative or secretarial qualification syllabus. This has been done for several reasons. Firstly, there are different schemes and awards available for administrators and secretaries. However, given that the working job roles of administrative and secretarial staff are not dependent upon an individual syllabus, this book can serve to introduce you to the subject, whichever award you are undertaking, and give you essential, up-to-date information and guidance.

Secondly, few jobs in this area comprise a majority of isolated or discrete tasks. Rather, the practising administrator or secretary has to turn his or her hand to a variety of related tasks and problems in any working day. A comprehensive knowledge and understanding of both fundamental and more involved issues is required to handle these situations effectively. Thinking across any artificial boundaries indicated unintentionally by a syllabus is therefore essential – and is reflected in the form of assessment. Whether this is by examination or by assignment, you will be required to consider *all* relevant aspects of your role to produce an acceptable response.

Finally, in many schemes there are a few nebulous or esoteric terms which may cause anxiety. An example is the modern trend towards concentrating on 'systems' and 'procedures' as tools through which administrative tasks can be controlled. It can be difficult for a 'new' student to grasp this concept. For that reason, this book integrates such concepts within the main topic areas – as well as consolidating them towards the end of the book. This will enable you to become familiar with them early in your studies and to apply them, from the outset, to the duties you will be expected to carry out.

The facts given in Section 1 show that the future for administrative and secretarial staff has rarely been brighter. In most organisations there has not only been an increase in administrative staff, which has improved job prospects for students, but also a qualitative improvement in the job role itself. This book has been written to enable you to face the future with confidence and develop your abilities to the full.

Carol Carysforth-Neild
January 1997

Acknowledgements

My grateful thanks are due to all those who have made contributions and suggestions towards this book. In particular, I would like to thank Peter Nicholson, Gabrielle Lagan and Vince Higham, whose expertise on modern computer systems is awe-inspiring and whose assistance and advice was invaluable; Jolanta Wilde (and her students) who tested out some of the early chapters; Bridget Swindlehurst for her journalistic contribution; Sue Knights for being a sounding board, and Pauline Cave who keeps me sane when the world seems to have gone mad!

Thanks must also go to those at Heinemann – Margaret Berriman who kept me on my toes and gave me inspiration on the bad days (as always!); Jan Nikolic and Susan Ross for converting my manuscript to its present form – and persisting with getting the details right across both of these companion handbooks.

Finally, thanks to my family – as ever – for being so constantly supportive and understanding.

The author and publishers would like to thank the following for permission to reproduce photographs and other copyright materials.

Airtours Holidays Ltd
Best Magazine (Gruner & Jahr (UK))
C W Cave & Tab Ltd
Esselte UK
First Impressions
Granville Technology Group Ltd
Images Colour Library
The London School of Economics
The Newspaper Licensing Agency
Novell UK Ltd
PA News Photo Library
Plain English Campaign
Railex Systems Ltd
TRIP/M. Ewing

● Dedication

Dedicated to Mona and Walter Neild. With love and affection.

● Introduction

You might think that the advertisement above is simply an advertiser's ploy to attract people towards working as an administrator or secretary. Yet all the facts given are true! Not only are the work activities undertaken by those who have a supporting role to managers varied, interesting and *essential* if an organisation is to operate successfully, but the demand for people with the requisite skills is increasing every year.

Many people who are considering taking up administrative or secretarial work as a career are unclear about the job itself. Those who talk about secretaries frequently have some very old-fashioned ideas about the type of work undertaken today. Therefore the first concern of anyone thinking about becoming an administrator or secretary should be to ascertain what the jobs entail, what skills and qualities are required and – for the ambitious – what these types of jobs may lead to in the future.

This section therefore aims to give you insight into the work of administrators and secretaries, their duties and responsibilities and the career opportunities available to them. It also gives an overview of the way in which they contribute to the overall management and organisation of the business and is written to help you to understand more about the job you aim to do.

Note: If you are taking Key Skills as a separate qualification linked to this award, or may, in the future, wish to obtain NVQ 3 accreditation for some of the work you have completed and your own personal development, then you will find this section particularly useful.

Secretarial shortages

In 1995, employment agencies were forecasting that a severe shortage of well-trained secretaries and administrators would start to plague Britain by 1996. Whereas in 1990 there had been six candidates for every job vacancy, by 1995 that had fallen to just one. The London agency Acme Employment was reportedly likening suitable secretaries to 'gold dust'.

The problem was apparently caused by the transformation of many secretarial jobs into high-status, multi-skilled roles where information technology (IT) skills for high-tech offices were essential. London salaries ranged from £14,000 for junior secretaries, to £17,000 for middle-range personal assistants (PAs) and secretaries, up to £30,000 for top PAs – with precise salaries being determined by the level and range of skills possessed by the applicant.

The problem was not confined to full-time, permanent vacancies. Temporary workers were also in high demand – particularly by companies which had struggled through the recession and were hesitant about recruiting permanent employees until their circumstances improved.

You and your job

1

● Introduction

At first sight, it is surprising how many people (especially young people) appear attracted towards a course of study without having much idea about what they will learn or where it will lead. However, this is more understandable if you consider that it is extremely difficult to obtain an accurate view of a job until you actually do it! Everyone is susceptible to those who give us their 'expert opinions' – whether or not they know anything about the job in reality. In the secretarial and administrative area there are so many misconceptions it is often better to start from scratch and find out for yourself about the work you will carry out!

Whilst opinions may differ as to the exact content of today's administrative and secretarial jobs, there are certain facts you can take as being beyond dispute.

- A knowledge of new technology and good IT skills are critical to success.

- The job is more varied and more challenging than ever – with opportunities to organise video conferencing, carry out desktop publishing, use a variety of software packages, access e-mail, web sites and the Internet.

- New skills include project management in research, administration and team administration.

- In many organisations (3M and the Industrial Society are examples) administration has been integrated into the business. The title of secretary has been abolished, and specialised skill levels have been designed for administrators.

- Other areas where expertise is required include languages, graphics packages, creating presentational materials, operating a computer help line, producing in-house journals, arranging conferences, and carrying out research to filter the vast amount of information now available.

- Computer literate, effective and efficient office workers have the opportunity to meet the challenge of the new millennium and reach career heights only dreamed of by their predecessors.

If all this seems overwhelming, then step back and think of only two things. First, you want to be on a career path which will lead somewhere. Second, you want to enjoy your time as a student. If you can do both, then you have the best of both worlds. As a starting point, this chapter has been written to guide you in the area of your choice and to give you more information on the skills you will need, the challenges you may face and the opportunities which are available.

● So you want to work in administration?

When you are planning a career, it is usual to talk to a variety of people to gain some idea of what would be involved. You are likely to want to ask questions such as

- what will I actually *do?*

- what qualifications will I need?

- what can I expect to earn?

- where will I work?

- what can this type of job lead to?

- is there anything else I need to think about?

It is regrettable that many people may be discouraged from pursuing an office-based career because they are misinformed either about the work they would be doing, or their prospects for promotion or both. Some are worried that the work may be routine or tedious, others that there will be few opportunities for promotion or advancement.

Of course it is possible to find yourself in a dead-end, boring job no matter what your chosen career. In this case most people look around for somewhere else to work. Today, in most organisations, you are far more likely to find life so hectic that you hardly have time to drink a cup of coffee, let alone become bored! If prospects are limited or non-existent, then study the job advertisements until you find one which is asking for your skills and experience. In administration you will find that no matter where you live, there are usually several organisations in your area advertising for staff.

● The role and duties of administrators and secretaries

What's in a name?

Administration and secretarial jobs are advertised under a wide range of titles. You will look at some of these in more detail in a moment. For now, let us concentrate on the distinction between an administrator and a secretary. However, be warned! Business organisations are not consistent in the way that they advertise jobs. Some companies have no secretaries – their job titles include admin assistant, deputy administrator and administrator. Others use secretarial titles. Others have a mixture. The only way to be clear about the job itself is to read the advertisement in full or, better still, the job description (usually sent to all job applicants).

The job of 'administrator' is relatively new – 10 years ago there were very few advertisements with this as a heading. The term 'secretary' is, of course, much older, but has frequently been the subject of debate. Unfortunately, mainly because of some mediocre reporting by the media, many highly qualified professional secretaries felt their role was being devalued. Terms such as the 'office wife' are not only sexist but also imply that secretaries do little more for their living than remember their (invariably male!) boss's family birthdays and collect his dry cleaning! In truth, few do either and several work for high-powered female executives. Interestingly, the term PA has suffered less from this type of publicity – most people would acknowledge that being the PA to Richard Branson or Anita Roddick would be an extremely challenging and exacting job to hold, and hardly likely to focus on dry-cleaning collection skills!

For now, think in terms of administration staff providing an office support service for a group of staff, a whole department or a company as a whole, and a secretary as providing a support service for one or two managers or directors.

What will I do?

The term 'support service' is vague and it would not be surprising if you consider it tells you little about what you would actually do. However, there are one or two other points you must bear in mind. What you will actually do depends upon the following factors.

- The **level** of job you have. Obviously you cannot start at the top of the tree, but have to gain experience and work your way upwards. Prospective employers will look at three main aspects of your application for any job, including

  - the skills and qualifications you possess
  - your ability and aptitude (which is usually assessed at interview)
  - your previous experience – for this reason, do not set your sights too high for your first job (as you need someone to take a chance on you and give you a start), but equally, do not set your sights too low in terms of your final career goal.

- The **type of organisation** you work for. You may work for a private company, a public-sector organisation (eg a hospital or local authority) or a small fledgling firm with only a handful of staff. The type of business the company is in, its size and its structure will all make a difference to your job role.

- The **type of boss** you have and his or her style of management. Some managers are keen to develop their staff, help them to progress and want to see them succeed. This type of boss is obviously the best to have! Others are less people-conscious (for a variety of reasons) and some have little interest in people management. The degree to which you can cope with this will depend upon your own personality and needs.

However, although there are variable aspects to administrative and secretarial jobs, there are some features which are usually common to most of them, given that the vast majority of businesses have as their main aim making a profit, and all are concerned with satisfying their customers' needs as efficiently and effectively as possible. For that reason the basic needs of organisations are similar, eg

- goods and equipment will need ordering and suppliers will need paying
- records, documents and other information must be produced, stored, retrieved and transmitted when necessary
- customers, other organisations and other departments within the company need their queries answered promptly
- managers need up-to-date, accurate information on which to base future decisions.

Office staff undertake all these duties – and more besides. Essentially, they have three main roles.

- **Handling information** – this may be received by mail, telephone or electronically and despatched by any of these means. It must be classified in such a way that it is easy to store and retrieve. It may need to be researched, analysed, processed, recorded in a different way or displayed in a different format. It may need to be reproduced and communicated to others either verbally or in writing.

- **Dealing with others** – clients may include external customers, suppliers, other businesses that provide a service (eg banks and insurance companies), government agencies (eg the Inland Revenue) or colleagues from another department. Requests (and complaints) need channelling to the correct person and handling promptly and efficiently. To many customers, the first person with whom they make contact effectively 'becomes' the organisation – and as such the business as a whole is judged on this person's performance and attitude.

- **Operating control systems** – virtually all organisations have internal systems and procedures to monitor their operations, from sales levels to accident records. In particular, the costs of an organisation have to be watched carefully. If these increase beyond the level of income earned from sales, then the company is in trouble!

Undertaking these duties results in a variety of office services which may be **centralised** (if administration is in a separate section) or **decentralised** (if administrative offices are a feature of each section or department) (see page 21).

Office or administrative services include

- dealing with visitors
- dealing with telephone calls
- reprographics
- mail handling
- document production (usually using IT equipment)

- document transmission
- classification, storage and retrieval of information (both on paper and electronically)
- purchasing of consumables and stock-control systems
- financial services (eg paying suppliers) and record keeping plus operation of the petty cash system
- arranging meetings and interviews
- communicating information promptly to those who need it.

Levels of jobs

As a **trainee** or **junior administrator** you would be likely to operate as a member of a team that is expected to be able to undertake all the activities listed above – either for a specific department or in a separate Administration section, using the specific systems used by your employer.

At **administrative assistant** level your range of duties would change. You would be responsible for making more decisions on your own, for helping junior staff and for assisting management more directly. You would no doubt also be expected to start to develop second sight – so that you can foresee and prevent problems before they occur (see page 17)!

In addition, administrative assistants may be involved with

- responding to correspondence
- making and monitoring financial payments
- contacting suppliers and obtaining/assessing quotations for equipment
- arranging travel and accommodation
- arranging events (eg seminars and conferences)
- making appointments
- researching information.

If, instead of being promoted to administrator, you decided to work as a secretary, then you could find yourself undertaking any of these activities, but usually for one or two specific managers or directors. This role may be more appropriate in some enterprises where, for instance, one manager or director has a particular need for this type of personal assistance.

Discussion point

Read the case study below and discuss the questions which follow with your tutor and other members of your group.

Louise had celebrated for days when she was promoted to marketing director's secretary. After four years in the general administration office she felt that, at last, all her hard work had been rewarded. However she was a little dismayed to find that, for her first week in the new job, Pamela Donalds, the marketing director, would be abroad.

On her first day Louise busied herself by going through the files to familiarise herself with the type of work carried out by Pamela and her business contacts. She carefully studied Pamela's schedule for the week and the notes made by her predecessor, who unfortunately had left the job a month before.

The following day Louise was a little worried when the telephone rang, but recognised the caller from her study of the files. Nick Johnson was the account executive at Wildings, the company's advertising agency. He needed urgent information about an advertisement being placed in the national press the following week – its size, how many insertions and which papers. Louise looked in the files, found a copy of a similar advertisement two months ago and repeated the booking.

On Wednesday Louise found herself involved in trying to check some promotional costs urgently required by Finance. On Thursday she was approached by a supplier of multimedia computer systems and made an appointment for him to talk to Pamela the following week. On Friday the managing director's secretary rang to ask if the sales figures for the past month were available. After searching the files without success, Louise looked on Pamela's desk, found some rough figures on her note pad and read these out. Pleased with herself after a good week's work, she tidied her desk and left for home.

1   Decide which of Louise's actions and decisions were correct – and identify those where you think she exceeded her authority.

2   In the case of Louise's mistakes, suggest the action she should have taken.

3 **a** To what degree do you think the organisation is at fault for not giving Louise clearer guidance on her role?

b What could her company have done to help her?

4 Imagine Louise 12 months later – an experienced secretary who knows her job well.

a Which tasks do you think she should now be able to handle on her own?

b How do you think these tasks would be affected by the degree of responsibility she is allowed by Pamela?

c What do you consider are the dangers in giving an inexperienced employee too much responsibility too soon?

Senior job roles

The two most senior job roles are generally those of a fully fledged **administrator/senior administrator** or a **PA.**

As an administrator or senior administrator you would be expected to organise the office so that everything ran smoothly, to delegate jobs to your staff and to have your own role in assisting managers in some key areas of work. This is likely to depend on the type of office you work in and the jobs being undertaken. In Finance, for instance, you may be responsible for keeping checks on all expenditure against budgets. In Personnel, you may be responsible for scheduling and organising all interviews, medicals and training sessions. In Marketing, you may be in charge of checking advertising 'proofs' and preparing materials yourself.

This leads us on to the role of a personal administrator or PA. A PA is the 'next stage up' from a secretary – just as a fully fledged administrator is the next stage up from an administrative assistant. A PA is usually employed by a senior manager, director or chief executive of an organisation, so is normally operating at a higher level in the organisation than a secretary. However, a fundamental difference between secretaries and PAs is usually the type of decisions they can make, without referring to 'their boss'. The PA therefore has more responsibility as, the greater the range of decisions individuals can make, the greater the scope of disasters they can create! In the case study above, if Louise had been employed as Pamela's PA she would fairly quickly have been expected to know about every aspect of the job – and probably even see the multimedia computer representative herself, or turn him away if she so decided.

For that reason, both PAs and senior administrators are usually experienced professionals. They are paid more because they are trusted to make decisions which, if a mistake was made, could be potentially costly to the company. These activities can range from handling important customers to managing their own budgets for expenditure. PAs are also likely to be involved in

- planning and organising events, procedures and activities

- coordinating the work of other people

- organising and allocating resources

- checking, monitoring and supplying key information to their managers

- controlling the activities which take place in their own area

- suggesting, instigating and developing systems and procedures to assist the work undertaken in their area

- 'thinking ahead' for their managers – by foreseeing potential problems and providing information ahead of time

- taking the brunt of the general administrative work and reducing the load on their managers

- acting as a 'deputy' for their manager in his or her absence.

However, there is one crucial difference. Whereas a senior administrator will be responsible for either a specific area of work or a group of administrative staff, a senior PA is likely to be involved in providing personal assistance for one very senior (and very busy) executive.

However, again a word of warning: be wary of job titles. In one organisation a 'secretary' may have more responsibility than a 'senior administrator' in another! The best guide is always the job description, which should clearly show the degree of responsibility given to the job holder.

● Preparing for employment

What qualifications do I need?

'Qualifications' can be divided into different categories. These include

- skill qualifications, such as keyboarding, IT skills or shorthand speed

- academic qualifications, such as GCSEs, A-levels, or a degree

- professional qualifications, such as the RSA Diploma in Administrative and Secretarial Procedures or the LCCI Private Secretary's Certificate or Private and Executive Secretary's Diploma

- personal qualities, ability and aptitude.

Learning the skills

Generally, the more skills you have and the higher level your qualifications in this area, the greater your potential to earn a high salary. Look back at the news item on secretarial shortages on page 4. It refers to high-level IT skills and multi-skilling. In plain English, this means turning your hand to virtually anything! In practical terms, it means fast, accurate keyboarding and a good knowledge of a whole range of IT packages.

Changing job roles

Over the past five years there has been a definite trend in many organisations towards replacing secretaries and PAs with administrative assistants and administrators. This has been caused by advances in computerisation and software packages which have meant that not only can more information be processed at any one time but also executives can now do much of the routine work themselves! They are just as capable of using a personal computer and sending e-mail messages as a secretary!

In addition, there has been a concerted drive to improve profitability by increasing sales and reducing costs. This has led to fewer managers being able to afford the luxury of a personal secretary. Broader job roles for most administrative staff have evolved in relation to processing the additional information now available, monitoring targets for both sales and costs – and providing improved customer service.

This trend has had enormous benefits for potential administrators and secretaries – mainly because there are greater career opportunities for a broad-based administrative or secretarial job role which incorporates high-level IT skills. Traditionally, ambitious secretaries found it very difficult to 'cross the divide' into management jobs. Now there is often very little difference between the work carried out by a senior administrator and a first-line manager. The downside? It depends upon whether you are male or female! Recent studies have shown a marked increase in the number of men applying for administrative jobs as opportunities have increased, giving female applicants tough competition at interview!

A list of possible skill areas – all with relevant qualifications – is shown in Figure 1.1. Do not expect to be studying all these now – it would be too much for you. However, the more you can tick off the list eventually, the better.

A useful extra is to learn (or develop) a language – particularly if you want to travel. Remember that membership of the European Union (EU) has meant that you can apply for jobs in 14 other European countries – and British administrators and secretaries are much in demand in many of Europe's capital cities. Within the UK, fluency in a second language will not only increase the range of jobs you can apply for but will also help you to command a higher salary in most organisations.

Note: If you are at present on a full-time course and want to start work in a year, you can continue to study by a variety of methods. You can attend a traditional part-time course (some colleges now operate these on Saturday mornings), through a 'drop-in' skills centre (which usually means you book

Keyboarding/text processing
Word processing
Communication
Shorthand
Audio transcription
IT skills – database, spreadsheets, word processing (eg CLAIT and IBT)
Desktop publishing
Presentation and graphics packages (eg Powerpoint)
Multimedia applications (text, graphics, sound and pictures)
Integrated software
DOS and Windows
Stand-alone PCs and networked computers
Internet
Electronic mail

Languages – particularly Spanish, French and German *or* (if you want to be different) Japanese. Community languages, eg Urdu and Gujerati, are valued by many public-sector organisations.

Relevant and related NVQs
Administration: levels 2–4
Telesales: level 2
Using IT: levels 2 and 3
Customer Service: levels 2 and 3
Accounting: levels 2–4

Figure 1.1 Skill qualifications/areas of expertise

in advance and learn at your own pace), through an adviser or trainer in your workplace or even, in a few cases, through a distance learning package!

Academic qualifications

Most employers look for a few GCSEs in their prospective office workers. English is the most important subject, given that if someone is unable to write a clear and coherent note, then there are going to be obvious difficulties at the start! If you have A-levels, then this will add to your 'employability' (almost regardless of grades). If you have not, all is not lost.

Even though you may not be interested in gaining higher level academic qualifications now, you may like to bear in mind that some of the top jobs do ask the job holder to have a degree. You can study part time, or even by distance learning through the Open University in years to come. A good route to a part-time degree is often through a Higher National Certificate – often obtaining a degree is possible through a relatively short top-up course.

Professional qualifications

If you are studying for an RSA or LCCI award, then you have the security of knowing that your final qualification will be recognised by employers throughout the country. Once you are working, a whole range of other options will be open to you. You could, for instance, take an NVQ award – such as a level 3 or 4 award in Administration – provided that you hold a job with the responsibilities commensurate to that particular scheme. Alternatively, if you work in a particular department or area, you could take a professional qualification which would help you to learn more about it. For instance, the Institute of Personnel and Development offers qualifications for trainee personnel officers, the Chartered Institute of Marketing for those working in Marketing departments and so on.

Personal qualities, ability and aptitude

It is a fact that no two people are identical. The above list of qualifications may have inspired your neighbour, but made you quite faint at the thought that you could be studying for the next few years before you reach the top! At this point, it should be said that few people attempt to obtain every qualification available in each category (unless they are workaholics!) and most people take time off from their studies – particularly if they are promoted or move to a new job. Some people are quite content to rest on their laurels and have no wish to move 'onwards and upwards'.

However, it is as well to recognise those traits within yourself which will certainly be spotted by an interviewer – and to decide whether you are happy as you are or are quite ambitious. It is no good thinking in one way and acting in another! The applicant who has learned nothing new in the past ten years is hardly going to be at the front of the queue for the next promotion!

It is always difficult to list the qualities of a good administrator or secretary. Most of these lists are very offputting as there is hardly anyone with all the attributes listed in some books. Therefore, although you obviously need to be smart, friendly, trustworthy and so on, below is a list of the attributes which distinguish the potentially excellent worker from the average.

The specialist brigade!

If you think that all secretaries work for commercial companies, then you could not be further from the truth. A whole array of administrators and secretaries work in specialist areas. Examples include parliamentary secretaries (who work for MPs), farm secretaries (who travel from one farm to another), legal secretaries, medical secretaries and those who join the armed forces!

In the Royal Navy you would be known as a 'writer' and would work at sea or on shore (at home and abroad); in the Army you would be a 'military clerk' (serving in army bases all over the world); and in the RAF a 'personnel administrator'. A variation, for those who like to travel, is to work for the Foreign Office. British consulates are located in all the major countries of the world (and some of the lesser-known areas) and have British nationals as their administrative and clerical staff.

If you're interested in these types of opportunities, then contact your local Forces Careers Office or the Foreign Office. A word of warning, however – in the Army the top PA jobs are now being given to civilians – so the work you do may be more routine than you really want. But if you want to see the world, then this might be a small price to pay!

Secretarial/administrative virtues

- **Enthusiasm** – someone who is keen and eager is a joy to work with. Someone who is a moaning misery is not. Neither is someone who complains the minute something goes wrong or he or she is given an extra job in an emergency. Therefore, if you are tempted to moan, *don't*. Wait until you get home!

- **A positive attitude** – this means always seeing a problem as an opportunity. If something needs retyping, rather than being irritated, think of it as an opportunity to make an even better job of it this time round. If there's a backlog of filing (which everyone hates) think of it as an opportunity to find that letter you were looking for, and so on.

- **Commitment and loyalty** – if you cannot stand the organisation you work for, then leave. Do not undermine everyone else's efforts to do a good job. Commitment also means looking for opportunities to do your firm a favour – remember, the more business your company does, the safer your job! Next time a customer rings when you are up to your eyes in work, remember that without such customers you may be collecting a benefit cheque. Make a good impression, eg if they have a query which may help to make a sale, then either assist them yourself or refer them quickly to someone who can help them. Make a real effort to make everyone you deal with feel *good* afterwards.

- **An eye for detail** – there is nothing worse than a sloppy administrator or secretary whose every document has to be checked.

- **A good memory** – so that next time someone asks 'Has anyone seen the report on catering I had last week?', *you* are the one who can remember.

- **Discretion** – if your boss cannot speak freely when you are around without knowing you will keep quiet, then you do not have a hope of getting on. No matter how tempting, or how juicy the gossip, keep your mouth firmly shut – or your boss will rapidly stop telling you anything

- **Reliability** – potentially good administrators and secretaries do not need watching 24 hours a day to make sure they do what they are paid to do. A lousy one will nip out to pick up some shopping the second the boss has to leave for a meeting or has a half day off. Reliability also means only having to be asked *once* to do a job it is not your boss's job to keep a list to remind you of work outstanding!

- **Being personable and humble** – so that you are just as nice to know when you are on the top of the tree as you were at the bottom!

- **Serenity** – panicking has never been a good way to solve a problem or cope in a crisis. Remember the saying 'If you can keep your head, when all about you are losing theirs' and people will know you as someone who can *cope* and who does not go to pieces when anything goes wrong.

- **Second sight** – this does not mean buying a crystal ball, and is something you will learn over time, if you work at it. What most bosses want is someone to protect them from as many minor irritations as possible and to *think for them*. This can only come with practice and is very difficult to teach. As a first step, think of any job in three stages, ie

  - doing the basic job
  - doing the basic job plus seeing if this triggers any other ideas
  - doing the basic job but seeing all other possible implications.

Try the quiz below to measure your own potential!

Test your potential quiz

1 Your colleague is writing out a telephone message from her notes and you spot her writing down one wrong digit. Do you:
  a ignore it – it's nothing to do with you
  b tell her she's incompetent
  c point it out as tactfully as possible?

2 Your boss is leaving on a short business trip this afternoon. You notice that in three days' time (the day of her return) the monthly sales update must be with the managing director. Do you:
  a keep quiet – she's busy enough today
  b remind her
  c offer to check that all the representatives' reports and sales figures have been received and to start drafting the update in her absence, using previous reports as your guide?

3 You make an appointment for your boss to see a company 100 miles away. The person you speak to warns you the place can be difficult to find. Do you:
  a say that your boss is great at finding his way around
  b scribble down a few directions
  c ask the company to fax you a map with their location marked?

4 Your boss has been trying to have a word with a particular member of staff for a week without success. The matter is getting more urgent every day. Whilst she is in a meeting the member of staff concerned calls into your office. Do you:
  a say nothing – for all you know they may have met earlier this morning
  b ask the member of staff to pop back later that day
  c make a definite arrangement for a short meeting later that day – and advise your boss immediately she comes out of the meeting?

5 A new, junior member of staff has been doing some financial calculations for your boss. When you receive them do you:
  a pass them to your boss immediately
  b quickly scan them to make sure they seem complete and sensible
  c check them to make sure he has not made any silly mistakes?

Score yourself

You may think this was the easiest quiz you have done in a long time – with the obvious answers being **c** in every case! However, the quiz was in fact designed to illustrate what is meant by 'second sight' rather than as a real test. Try to develop that skill when you are doing any assignments or practical tasks – or are on work experience. It is invaluable!

What will I earn?

Salaries for administrators and secretaries vary considerably depending upon

* the level of the job, skills required and the amount of responsibility

* the organisation concerned and its standard pay rates

* the area in which you live, eg London salaries are nearly always slightly above regional ones because of the higher cost of living in the capital

* the time when you are looking for a job – if you are unlikely to be job searching for another two years, then it is a reasonable assumption that salary levels may have increased between 2 per cent and 5 per cent.

The best way to find out about salaries – and to find out more about job roles and responsibilities is to undertake the exercise on page 19.

Not negotiable!

The worst moment of an interview for many people is if the interviewer asks 'How much do you think I should pay you?'. This *can* happen if the job is advertised with 'salary negotiable'. If you have worked before, then you can add a percentage to your existing salary. If it is your first job, then this is obviously not possible.

One young woman (this is a true story!) who was in that position had at least prepared for the problem in advance – by asking her father what he thought she should say in this situation. He replied that one answer could be that she felt she was worth £1000 a month, ie £12 000 a year. On the day of the interview, she repeated her father's words to the manager who was interviewing her. He replied that he had been considering paying her £11 000 but was prepared to split the difference and pay her £11 500.

When she returned home, she recounted this story to her parents. They were so relieved that she appeared to have obtained a job (after supporting her through several years of study) that they were horrified to learn that her reply to the offer had been that she would have to think about it. With that she had left the office. As they were discussing her action, the phone rang. It was the manager. He said he wasn't prepared to fall out with her over the question of salary – she could have £12 000 a year!

The moral of this story is that not everyone is so lucky! Negotiable *means* that you can expect to negotiate *around* a figure. Practise with someone else beforehand if the idea unnerves you!

Discussion point

1   Look at the advertisements in Figure 1.2. As a group, make a note
of the type of duties you would have to undertake in each job –
particularly those which are common to more than one.

University of Southgate

DEPARTMENT OF INTERNATIONAL HISTORY

Departmental Administrative Assistant

Salary £12,400 to £14,000 pa inc.

The Department of International History offers both undergraduate and postgraduate courses, and has approximately 30 research students. The post provides administrative and secretarial support to the department.

Candidates should have good keyboard skills and be familiar with Wordperfect 5.1/5.2 word processing packages, and possibly spreadsheets, but training and/or cross-training can be given. Excellent Interpersonal skills and a pleasant telephone manner are essential as there is a great deal of contact with students and other staff. The work-flow is varied and can range from very quiet periods to frenzied activity, as at the beginning of the academic year.

For application form and job description please send SAE to: The Recruitment Section, Personnel Services, University of Southgate, Hill Road, London N24 5AU.

Administration Assistant

As a result of its continued expansion, Fast-Track Ltd, leading UK computer supplier, is strengthening its Administration Department. The work will entail routine administration. In addition there will be considerable liaison with other departments, suppliers and customers.

In order to undertake the duties involved applicants should demonstrate accuracy and thoroughness in a Stores/Goods-In/Despatch clerical function. It would be desirable if applicants possessed experience in communicating with others by letter, telephone and fax. Keyboard skills would be an advantage.

* If you believe you have these qualities and will thrive and remain calm in a fast changing environment send your CV to the Recruitment Manager quoting Job Ref: TIAA to the address below.

 **Fast Track Ltd**

Computer House,
High Road,
Rossendale,
Lancs BB1 4ZX

SECRETARY
SKI HOLIDAYS

Based in Bristol   **Circa: £12,500**

An efficient, energetic secretary is required to provide support to the Ski Holidays Department.

Excellent secretarial skills including shorthand and WP experience are essential along with good communication, planning and organisational skills.

The successful candidate will be a smart professional, able to converse at a high level with Senior Managers, Directors and members of the Tour Operator, used to working under pressure to deadlines, with the ability to work on own initiative.

If you are able to fulfil these requirements and are interested in the above position, please write with a full CV to:

Nicola Bates, Ski Holidays, Take-a-break plc, 35–43 Sunshine Road, Bristol BS21 3LR.

Take-a-break plc

 **Premier** **Secretary/ Assistant**

Premier, one of the UK's most popular weekly magazines, seeks a well organised and efficient secretary. Reporting to the Features and Health Editors, your role will be to ensure the smooth running of two busy departments, through secretarial and administrative support.

Your duties will include copy typing, dealing with telephone enquiries, answering readers' letters and maintaining accurate filing systems. You will also be in contact with freelance contributors, PRs, travel companies and tourist offices.

You will need to be versatile and unflappable, able to prioritise and to work well under pressure. You will also need at least 2 years' previous experience, an accurate typing speed of 50wpm, and a friendly telephone manner. Shorthand would be an advantage.

Please send CV quoting current salary to:
Deena Patel, Senior Personnel Officer, Premier Magazine, 13 Writers Place, Birmingham B1 2ZZ

Figure 1.2 Job advertisements

2   As a group, collect at least 12 secretarial or administrative advertisements from your regional paper or from regional news-sheets (issued weekly) or from national papers.
    a   Note the salary range – particularly for jobs in your area.
    b   Make a list of the skills required.

3   As a group, make a final list of the skills you think you will need to compete for the jobs you have selected.

Working conditions

Where will I work?

Most secretaries and administrators can expect to work in an office – although there are exceptions (see the 'The specialist brigade' on page 15. However, offices vary. Some are large, open-plan areas, where staff are housed in acoustic 'pods'. These allow a large space to be used very effectively with people working near each other but having some privacy through the screens around them.

In others there may be one general office area – with desks for clerical staff and admin assistants. Those above this level may have their own offices.

If you work for a very small organisation, you may have an office on your own or share one with two or three other people.

There are advantages and disadvantages to sharing an office. If it is hectic and noisy, then this can be a distraction when you are trying to concentrate. However, you will not be lonely! If you have your own office, then the opposite applies. Life is more peaceful (unless there are constant visitors), but you may miss the general banter of working as a member of a group.

If you work in a general administration role, then it is likely that you will share office space in the early years of your career. If you are aiming more for a secretarial role, then you might find that you have an office adjacent to your boss – and work on your own or with only one other secretary.

Centralisation/decentralisation

Centralisation means that a large number of service functions in a large organisation are housed in one area, and used by everyone. Examples include reprographics and printing, mailroom, filing and computer services. A large building society head office, for example, will have a large filing section with expensive computerised/automatic retrieval systems and specialist staff who are responsible for continually filing and retrieving deeds and other documentation. This does not mean that there is no need for individual departmental filing of, say, personnel records, but the majority of the company's paperwork will be stored in the central system.

Centralisation is likely to narrow your job role a little as it is unlikely you would be heavily involved in any service function which is provided centrally (unless you worked in that particular area).

Advantages of centralisation
- Supervision and monitoring of activities is easier.

- Standard systems can be in place, used by everyone.

- Staff can be highly trained to offer a professional service to users.

- The service is easier to control and to cost for budgetary control.

- Expensive specialist equipment may now be a viable proposition because it will be in constant use by trained operators.

- There is an obvious promotional career path.

Disadvantages of centralisation
- There is less flexibility – users have to follow a set procedure which might be inappropriate in an abnormal situation or a crisis.

- Increased documentation – often there are forms to complete and records to keep in relation to the amount a service is used.

- Work can be boring and repetitive.

- Individual departmental managers have less control.

Other aspects to consider

Offices vary greatly in their siting, decor, equipment and facilities. An old building near a busy railway line is likely to be very different from a modern building on an industrial estate or in a town centre. Equally, a large organisation may be able to afford hi-tech computer equipment, a digital switchboard and computerised filing system whilst a small firm of two budding entrepreneurs may only possess one personal computer (PC), a small telephone system and a couple of filing cabinets! The large employer may offer you a range of facilities such as health screening and use of the company canteen, whereas the small firm is unlikely to be able to provide these.

However, people rarely obtain job satisfaction because they are in fabulous surroundings. Usually, the content of the job and the people they work with are far more important. If you are given the opportunity to go on work experience as part of your course, you should try to sample more than one type of organisation – a good idea is to try a small firm and a large company. As the surroundings, facilities and work role are likely to be different, you will gain an insight into the size of organisation you are likely to prefer.

A final consideration is hours of work. The type of organisation for which you work will affect these. You cannot expect, for instance, to be the senior administrator in a large holiday hotel, on a cruise liner or in an entertainments complex or leisure centre and work a 9am–5pm day! At a junior level you are likely to have to work a rota system, and at senior level you would expect to be available during some unsocial hours especially if there was an emergency or if it was the height of the season.

However, it is worth noting now that the higher you rise and the more invaluable you become, the greater the chance that you will be expected to be flexible with your hours and to help out by working late when it is necessary. If you want to get on and be highly regarded by your boss, do not always expect every hour you work to be compensated by time off in lieu or with an overtime payment. Counting the hours marks one down as being someone who is only doing the job for the money – and not because he or she is committed to the organisation. A small firm may not always be able to afford to pay you the extra you would like. So long as your boss is fair, appreciates your help and does not take advantage of your good nature, then you can only gain by being the type of person who can be relied upon to help when it is needed.

The 'virtual' office

Researchers in the USA and at BT's laboratory in Martlesham have developed a virtual reality office which appears on the user's PC. It is possible to move the furniture, repaint the walls, even hang different pictures! Doors lead to other offices, meetings rooms and even to the outside world. The aim is to make things easier for computer illiterates.

How? By replicating most of the normal actions in an office. Discarded documents are put in the 'virtual' wastepaper bin, files are located in the 'virtual' filing cabinets, messages can be pinned on the 'virtual' message board. Meetings can even be held in the 'virtual' meetings room and documents researched in the 'virtual' library.

One day, you may be able to work in a 'virtual' office sitting in your own home,

Discussion point

Fiona and Julie studied on the same secretarial course. Two years later, Fiona is working as a junior secretary for a consultant in a large hospital, whilst Julie is administrative assistant in a small computer firm – owned by two computer wizards in their 20s. Apart from Julie there is only one other office employee, Lesley, who is administrator/secretary.

Assuming Fiona and Julie meet for coffee one day, what do you think they would find are the main differences between the jobs that they do?

• Career prospects – upwards and onwards

What can it lead to?

At this stage of your career you may think it would be a miracle if you ever made it to administrator or PA level, let alone beyond. Yet the opportunities do exist for working above this level. For a few examples of what you could do – particularly if you wanted to specialise in a certain area, study Figure 1.3. This gives a small selection of the jobs that were advertised in *two* national newspapers and *one* regional newspaper during two weeks in August 1996. The only factor they have in common is that all the advertisers asked for administrative or secretarial experience from applicants. However, there were some surprising requirements, eg the job of assistant research officer required candidates to have keyboarding, shorthand *and* statistical skills!

Job title	Sector	Advertised salary
Health and safety administrator	Local authority	£15 000 – £21 000
Business support manager	NHS Trust	£22 000
Customer services administrator	Textile company	negotiable
Personnel assistant	NHS Trust	£12 500 – £15 000
Education and training administrator	Sports and Leisure	£10 500 – £14 600
Office manager	Health	£20 700
Assistant to personnel manager	Media	negotiable
Events assistant	Professional body	circa £15 000
Database administrator	University	£14 000 – £15 904
Community grants coordinator	Voluntary sector	£18 000 – £20 000
Assistant research officer	Public sector (police)	circa £18 000
Membership secretary	Professional body	up to £17 000
Product and marketing assistant	Greeting-card company	£12 000
Conference administrator	Professional body	£15 000 – £17 000
Sponsorship assistant	Voluntary sector	negotiable
Course administrator	University	Up to £17 000
Editorial assistant	Publishing	negotiable
IT and finance coordinator	Local authority	£18 700 – £20 000

Figure 1.3 Selection of administrative/secretarial jobs advertised in August 1996

If you ever want inspiration, look at the job advertisements in the 'Crème de la Crème' section of *The Times* (currently published each Wednesday). Here you will see a selection of top PA, secretarial and administrative jobs, with salaries of up to £30 000 a year not unknown!

A final point – if you are trying to progress and move on, then it is worthwhile looking slightly further afield than you perhaps might otherwise have done for your first job. If you live in London or the South East, then you will be familiar with people commuting quite considerable distances to their workplace. You may also be used to travelling yourself if you live in the country, several miles from your nearest college or major town. If you live in an urban area, however, you may be less used to the idea of commuting. But you are likely to limit your horizons considerably if you think that any job you have must be within a ten-minute bus ride of where you live! If the salaries in your nearest large town or city are better than those in your own area, then it might be worthwhile considering jobs there, particularly if there are good transport links or if you have your own car.

● Final considerations

Is there anything else I need to think about?

At the beginning of this chapter you considered the likely general roles of administrators and secretaries. You may be surprised to know that the Administration Lead Body (which designs and oversees Administration NVQ awards nationally) describes the administrative role as 'the establishment, operation, maintenance and evaluation of systems, procedures and services to assist organisations to achieve their objectives'.

You have spent some time looking at office services but have not yet considered 'systems and procedures'. What are these, and how will they affect you?

If you ask most secretaries and administrators about their jobs, they will probably include two areas that would not have been regarded as part of their role a few years ago. One is cost control, and the other is project management. Administrative control (see Section 6) is an area which is rapidly growing in importance in all organisations.

You have already read about 'costs' earlier in this chapter. Interestingly, the costs of running a business were seldom discussed in secretarial textbooks ten or even five years ago. Today they are absolutely critical for all organisations and as such have affected everyone's job. Systems and procedures are in place (or should be!) in all companies to *control* what happens and the actions people take. The aim is to make sure that people do things in a certain way, that checks can be made and that activities can be costed.

Complementary to this, project management is related to the planning and steering of a project from start to finish to make sure that it is completed on schedule and within budget.

Your job will be affected in that you will be expected to

- plan and schedule work and other activities realistically and to achieve predetermined objectives

- organise the work for a particular job in such a way that the plans can be fulfilled

- monitor progress to make certain that everything is going according to plan and according to budget – and deal appropriately with any variances (differences) from the plan

- identify problems which might hinder the plan and cause a delay or add to costs

- make decisions to ensure that the correct remedial action is taken.

If this seems overwhelmingly difficult, then be assured that it is not! Major systems and procedures will be in place in any company you work for, but you will need to understand why they exist and how you can contribute to them. Administrative systems and procedures are normally developed – and even instigated – by administrative staff, but you would not be expected to take an active role in this until you are familiar with the general duties carried out. When you are ready to move towards this stage, you will usually find it adds an extra dimension to the job which makes it more of a challenge and much more enjoyable.

Project management is normally learned by assisting a project coordinator initially and then by trying to manage a small, simple project yourself. However, again there is no need to worry as guidance is given in Section 6.

A final word

Hopefully, this chapter has helped to clarify some of the initial thoughts you may have had, answered some of the questions you may have hesitated to ask and made you more enthusiastic about your forthcoming career. What you do, and how far you go is now up to you – although your tutors, this book (and others) and a variety of materials are available to help you. Remember, too, that your colleagues on the course can also be a source of support and inspiration, as well as being your friends. If you are determined to succeed, you surely will.

 Questions to consider

On your own, draft out how you would like to see your career progressing over the next ten years. Set 'markers' for progress after one year, two years and five years.

Now compare your ideas with the rest of your group. Discuss those factors which would help you to achieve your goals and those which would hinder you – and talk about how you could adapt your plans if necessary.

If you want to make the exercise even more interesting you can draw up two lists each – your 'dream' plan and another, more realistic one!

Revision practice

Further revision practice questions appear at the end of subsequent sections. However, you may like to consider your answers to one of the following to review the topics you have just covered.

Short-answer questions

1   Briefly describe two key differences between the job of an administrator and a personal secretary.

2   An increasing number of men are applying for jobs as administrators. Briefly explain the reason for this trend.

3   Identify six duties routinely carried out by office staff.

4   Identify three additional responsibilities you would expect to undertake if you were promoted from being a member of the general administrative staff to assistant administrator.

5   Describe six important personal qualities needed by someone working in an administrative or secretarial position.

6   Explain two advantages and two disadvantages of centralisation.

Essay questions

1   What are the advantages and the disadvantages of providing a centralised administrative service in an organisation
    a   for the organisation itself
    b   for the individual employees?

2   Identify the qualities and qualifications you would consider appropriate for a candidate applying for the position of secretary to the marketing director.

3   You are administrator in a medium-sized organisation. How would you deal with each of the following problems?
    a   One of the junior employees regularly arrives late each morning and is impatient to leave at night.
    b   One of the managers is poor at planning and organisation and therefore frequently arrives with several very urgent jobs. He expects all the staff to drop everything they are doing to process his work quickly.
    c   Your manager is late returning from lunch when the senior executive from head office arrives unexpectedly.

4   Your workload as secretary has been increasing consistently over the past 12 months and it has been agreed that you should have an assistant to help you.

a   Identify the duties which you would expect the assistant to
     carry out
     i   immediately
     ii   after becoming familiar with the organisation and the work
          it undertakes.
b   Draft a suitable advertisement showing those qualifications and
     qualities you consider would be essential and those you
     consider would be desirable.

Case study

Sally Bracken is a friend of yours. She originally decided to study A-levels
after achieving several GCSEs including English Language grade B. She
has now changed her mind and decided she wants to work in an office –
aiming eventually for a top administrator's or private secretary's job.

a   What type of qualifications would you advise her to gain before she
     applies for a job?

b   If Sally asked you to help her to devise a five-year career
     development plan, what would you include in this and why?

c   What other advice would you give Sally to help her to advance in
     her career?

OFFICE SERVICES LTD

Let us handle all your office procedures!

- Mail processing
- Dealing with visitors
- Ordering and controlling office supplies
- Processing payments inwards and outwards
- Expenditure monitoring and control

Health, safety and security a prime consideration at all times.

SERVICE WITH A SMILE GUARANTEED AT ALL TIMES

The key question – could you apply for a position there?!

● Understanding office procedures

One of the most basic requirements for all administrative staff is a thorough knowledge and understanding of the range of office services that may be provided. You may remember that a list of these was given in Chapter 1 on pages 8–9. As a potential administrator you need to know not only the up-to-date *facts* about these services (what can be offered, by whom and how), but also a much broader appreciation of other aspects which will concern both you and your line manager. For instance, you will need to be able to organise and provide office services so that there is high quality and costs are controlled, to understand what alternatives are available in an emergency and so on. The way to achieve a consistently high service is usually by ensuring that specific procedures have been laid down which, so far as possible, take into consideration the needs of the users and guarantee that everyone will be carrying out the work in the same way.

For that reason this section not only gives you the basic information you need on office services but also develops key issues that will enable you to offer a professional administrative service in each area. The areas covered are

- processing mail

- dealing with visitors

- purchasing

- stock control

- financial matters

- security and confidentiality

- health and safety.

After you have learned the basic system which is usually in place in an organisation, and the procedures followed by staff, you will then be in a position to make decisions about how these may be changed or adapted. You should also be able to make realistic suggestions about how potential problems may be solved and improvements made.

Take each chapter at a time, note the basic facts which apply today (and how these may change) and then use the discussion points to develop the areas you would have to consider as a fully fledged administrator or secretary/PA.

Organising and processing mail

2

● Introduction

Documents and other items may be sent using a variety of methods and carriers. Most people appreciate, for instance, that there are a number of **electronic** options, such as fax and electronic mail (e-mail) for transmitting documents (see pages 173 and 176). However, there is a still a major requirement to send many items using the traditional postal services. The Royal Mail service handles about 70 million items every day. In addition, there are private courier firms and delivery and collection organisations which will transport urgent and/or important items both within the UK and internationally.

Your involvement in organising mail will depend upon several factors – primarily the size of the organisation which employs you and the type of business it operates. There is a tremendous difference between working for a large mail-order company which receives sacks full of post every day and a small estate agency which mainly deals with customers on a face-to-face basis. Most large organisations have a central mailroom which receives and distributes the mail to departments. Even a small organisation needs a nominated person to take responsibility for this key function. Usually, the processing of outgoing mail is also centralised for several good reasons, as you will see later. However, the range of services provided centrally – and/or the contribution expected from each department – can vary considerably. Again, even the smallest firm needs somebody who can be relied upon to post the mail each evening.

However, you should note that as a potential departmental administrator or secretary/PA, *you* need a clear understanding of what can be achieved and how – even if you will pass on the actual actioning of the request to a centralised section. This not only helps you to advise your boss but also means that you will not request the impossible or ask for services that do not exist!

● Incoming mail

The two key objectives for anyone dealing with incoming mail should be that

- mail is distributed as early as possible in the working day

- no mail is damaged, lost or wrongly delivered.

How these objectives are achieved will depend upon the quantity of mail you handle, the systems in place and the services, facilities and equipment which are employed.

Prompt delivery is essential. Urgent requests and important information can dramatically affect the scheduling of a business person's day. For this reason the Royal Mail has introduced a service called **Timed Delivery** which enables an organisation to request a precise delivery time for its mail. It can then arrange to process the opening and distribution of mail even before the main body of staff arrive for work. It also means that the mailroom can open earlier and staff who work there can be released for other duties as soon as the mail has been distributed.

Mail must be opened and handled carefully. Damaged documents may be unreadable, lost documents can cause needless problems – particularly if they are urgent or important – and items which are wrongly delivered may lead to delays and problems for the staff concerned. Therefore, you not only have to consider the speed of the mail distribution service but also the quality of the service. Both are important if your 'internal customers' are to be satisfied!

Royal Mail – perceptions and problems

The public view of the Royal Mail service is very good. The 1996 survey by the National Consumer Council showed that almost 9 out of 10 people are satisfied with the speed of the postal delivery service, 8 out of 10 people are happy with Post Office counter services and 7 out of 10 think the price of a postage stamp is reasonable. In addition, the Royal Mail achieved a 92.6 per cent success rate in next-day deliveries – behind Switzerland, Sweden, the Netherlands and Denmark, but ahead of many other countries in Europe and the United States.

However, foreign competitors may prove to be the biggest threat to Royal Mail in the future. A draft directive from the European Commission in 1995 outlined a proposal that all countries could be able to compete from 2001 in offering mail services. This means that a company sending a large direct-mail shot could divert its post to be despatched from the cheapest country or even through a private operator. Unless Royal Mail can offer a competitively priced and highly reliable delivery service – ahead of its European competitors – it could find itself losing a considerable amount of business in the future.

Basic issues

At some stage of your career you will no doubt be involved in 'opening the post'. The system in operation in your organisation may be

- a centralised mailroom which opens, sorts, records and distributes the mail

- a centralised mail facility which simply sorts the post departmentally, the post is then collected by departmental administrative staff and opened, sorted and distributed departmentally – in this type of organisation the mail for executives is often delivered to their secretaries unopened

- one nominated person is responsible for dealing with the incoming mail, in the case of a small firm.

Regardless of the exact system in operation, at some stage the following set of procedures must take place.

1 **Sorting and handling procedures.** A variety of mail items will be delivered every day and it is usual to start by pre-sorting these into different categories as follows.

- **Urgent items** – these may either be marked 'Urgent', delivered by special courier or sent by the Royal Mail's Special Delivery service. These items must be opened and delivered quickly, or the recipient must be notified so that the item can be collected if it arrives after the mail has been distributed.

- **Personal or private and confidential items** – these should not normally be opened, unless special instructions have been given. For instance, a manager who will be absent for any length of time should leave instructions for his or her deputy to handle such items. It is not the job of the mailroom staff to open envelopes so marked.

- **Guaranteed delivery mail** – these include Registered and Recorded Delivery items. Most organisations record these separately so that there is clear responsibility for handling and delivery.

- **Monetary items** – cheques or even cash may be received by the organisation. Some companies operate a procedure whereby these have to be recorded separately by mailroom staff to prevent discrepancies.

- **Wrongly delivered mail** – this should be reposted unopened. An appropriate note can be made on the envelope, eg 'Not known at this address'. However, do note that some customers may have misinterpreted the name of one of your staff or even the name of your company. If you *think* the item may be for you, but are not sure, then you should open it to check. If you find you are wrong, then reseal the envelope and write on it 'Opened in error' before adding any further directives to the Royal Mail service.

- **Routine mail** – this will comprise the bulk of items. First class mail is normally opened first.

- **Circulars** – these include advertising literature or other documents which may be seen by several members of staff, as well as journals and magazines which are often passed round an office or organisation. Many companies devise a 'circulation slip' to attach to such items – it is not normal to photocopy such documents because of the expense involved. If the organisation is very large, circulars and journals are normally sent to the appropriate department and then distributed to the relevant staff.

- **Parcels** – these may be delivered at the same time as the mail or at different times throughout the day. Normally, the recipient is expected to sign for them. Bear in mind that it is often wise to write 'Contents not checked' on the delivery form as the deliverer will not be able to wait whilst you check the parcel is complete and undamaged. However, if the parcel is obviously damaged on delivery, then this should be clearly noted on the form. In some organisations it is usual to open parcels; more often they are delivered to recipients unopened. In all cases urgent parcels should always be delivered immediately they are received and not left until the following day when the post is distributed. Very heavy parcels should not be lifted or delivered by office staff unless there is no alternative, in which case lifting should be carried out in accordance with the requirements of the Manual Handling Regulations (see page 118) and special equipment must be used to transport it, eg a small two-wheeled truck or trolley.

2 **Checking procedures.** The next stage is to ensure that

- all enclosures are, in fact, enclosed and attached firmly to the main document (staples are usually better than paperclips which can 'hook' other documents underneath them

- the recipient is clearly identifiable – if this is not the case, then a decision has to be made as to which would be the most appropriate department or person to receive the item

- all envelopes are empty before being discarded – many organisations operate a policy whereby envelopes are retained for 24 hours in case of any queries.

3 **Recording procedures.** Most organisations date-stamp items of incoming mail, either by using a pre-printed rubber stamp or an automated procedure. Date-stamping is useful not only if there are any queries about the date of delivery but also to indicate to staff when the item was received. Some organisations even *time-stamp* each item. Date-stamping is particularly beneficial if the document is referred from one person to another before a response can be made, as it indicates how long the sender has been waiting for a reply! You should note that it is not usual to date-stamp legal documents such as contracts, or financial documents such as cheques as this defaces the document.

4 **Distribution procedures.** Mail may be placed into baskets and await collection by individual staff or it may be delivered to departments or staff. It is usual to place mail in the following order.

- Urgent items should be placed on the top so they will be seen first.

- Personal unopened items are next.

- First class mail is placed on top of second class items.

- Circulars, journals and magazines are at the bottom.

This means that a busy executive can quickly flip through his or her mail and easily identify the most important and urgent items received that day.

Other considerations

1 **Equipment.** The type of equipment you have at your disposal may range from a paper knife or a simple mail opening machine to a more sophisticated device which can undertake a range of procedures.

- Traditionally, electric mail openers made a slit in the envelope, very close to the edge. It was up to the operator to remove the contents. The latest machines not only open the envelope on more than one side but also allow the operator to view the empty envelope as a final check. The contents of the envelope are delivered on a special tray in front of the operator.

- Organisations which receive thousands of remittances through the post daily (eg credit card companies) can benefit from a machine which can detect the presence of cheques or credit card slips and automatically process and record all the remittances received.

2 **Space.** Even in a small organisation there should be a special area for opening the post, otherwise items of mail can be easily 'lost' amongst other papers and documents. For this reason the area should be kept clear and the working surface should be large enough to contain key items of equipment, eg date-stamp and stapler.

3 **Furniture.** In addition to a large desk area or table top there must also be labelled trays, baskets or pigeon holes into which opened mail can be placed. These should be clearly labelled and are better made of wire mesh so that no items can be hidden in the darkness of enclosed shelves. Storage space will also be required for any record books (eg for remittances) and other forms or documents, eg circulation slips.

4 **Security procedures.** In high security organisations or those involved in 'risk' areas there are likely to be formalised security procedures which may even require the scanning of all incoming mail. Even in the smallest firm, the person in charge of the incoming mail should be aware of Home

Office guidelines on dealing with suspicious items. Many companies issue staff with a copy of their own guidelines as to how employees should respond if they are worried about any particular item of mail. An example is given in Figure 2.1.

MARKHAM ELECTRONICS PLC

Mailroom Security – Suspicious Items

The guidelines below have been prepared to help mailroom staff who may be faced with handling a suspicious item. It is important that you familiarise yourself with the key points. If you are doubtful about the procedure to follow in an emergency, contact the mailroom supervisor *now* – do not wait until an emergency occurs!

1 You will have no warning about a suspicious package. If you are worried about an item you have received then tell your supervisor *immediately* – do not think you will look foolish by doing so.

2 Contact your supervisor if an envelope or package shows any of the following *danger signs.*
   - a smell of marzipan or almonds
   - greasy marks on the envelope or wrapping
   - visible wiring or tin foil – especially if the package is damaged
   - an envelope or package which seems to be unusually heavy for its size
   - excessive wrapping
   - poor handwriting, spelling or typing
   - uneven weight distribution in the package or rigid contents in a flexible envelope
   - an incorrect address, unusual or foreign postmark
   - too many stamps for the weight of package
   - delivery by hand from an unknown source

3 If you are on your own for any reason, and receive a suspicious item, then the procedure you *must* follow is given below.
   - Immediately isolate the item – preferably on a table in the centre of the room, away from windows and walls.
   - Do *not* tamper with the package in any way.
   - Leave the area and *lock* the room. Telephone security on 2020 from a different area or building – as some devices can be activated when you use a nearby telephone.

Figure 2.1 A company's code of practice

Discussion point

1 You work for an organisation which has always logged remittances received in a special book by recording the date received, the name of the payee, method of payment, amount and account number. There is also space for comments if any discrepancies are noticed. Your boss is considering replacing this book with a computerised system, so that the mailroom operator can log remittances received on her PC. As a group, discuss the benefits and drawbacks of using a computerised system rather than a manual recording system.

2 Design a circulation slip which would enable a magazine to be distributed around your class and returned to your tutor after everyone has seen it. Discuss the wording you could include which might deter any member of the group from keeping the magazine for too long!

3 Read the security procedures outlined in Figure 2.1.
  a As a group, discuss the problems for administrators in
    i trying to ensure that all staff stay alert over a long period of time
    ii emphasising to staff who raise a false alarm that this will not make them appear foolish to their colleagues.
  b You work for two directors who run a small business between them. On the day you receive a suspicious item both of them are away from the office. Decide who you would contact and what information you should have available. Discuss your answer with your tutor.

Outsourcing internal mail

To reduce costs some organisations which receive large quantities of mail each day have contracted out this service to the Royal Mail. One example is the Benefits Agency. In Tyne Tees, where 27 of its 159 offices are located, over 160,000 items are received in the mail every week.

Instead of benefits staff opening the mail and directing it to different departments, all this is undertaken by a Royal Mail service and sent directly to the correct section of the Agency. Valuable items, such as cheques and customer order books, are also tracked by means of a special computer-based system. The service can even cope if customers have written the wrong address or forgotten to use the reply-paid envelope!

Administrative issues

Administrators are usually held responsible for the speed and quality of the service. This usually means ensuring that the procedure is one which achieves its objectives and that those staff who are involved do not deviate from it. An administrator may find that he or she is responsible for training junior staff to do what they are supposed to do, when they are supposed to do it! He or she will also usually be the recipient of any complaints about or problems arising from an ineffective procedure or poor service.

It is therefore important for administrators to be able to recognise the types of problem that occur which indicate the *procedure* is not working and those which simply show that someone is not doing what they should do!

To a large extent the success or failure of the system depends upon whether there is a procedure at all! However, if you know that everyone has been given guidelines to follow, then it is a simple matter to check whether you have omitted an important item of information or whether someone is ignoring them instead.

Discussion point

1. As a group, prepare a set of guidelines for your own office staff on opening and distributing the mail. Assume you work for a large organisation which receives mail centrally and sorts it departmentally. You are the administrator responsible for the collection, opening, sorting and distribution of mail within your own department.

2. Study the following complaints you have received. Discuss them as a group and with your tutor. Decide which complaints
    *   *are more likely* to identify an omission in the guidelines you prepared
    *   *are more likely* to indicate a member of staff is not following instructions.

    In each case suggest the action you should take to remedy the problem.

    a All items marked both 'Urgent' *and* 'Personal' are left unopened (sometimes for a couple of weeks) if the recipient is on holiday.
    b Several 'problem' documents addressed to the organisation but not to a specific department or person are found hidden in a drawer in the office.
    c Everyone knows about Mr Brown's overdraft because the letter from the bank was opened in error and the information spread around the building.

d A senior manager expresses concern that this week alone three items were damaged upon receipt and two important items appear to have disappeared somewhere in the building.

e Items are constantly returned to the office by recipients marked 'Not my area – sorry'.

f A manager complains that his mail is delivered in a muddle, with the most urgent items at the bottom.

g Items are routinely date-stamped over key areas of text.

3 It is a ten-minute walk from your department to the mailroom, yet your office staff seem to take at least 30 minutes to collect the post each morning. This is resulting in a variety of complaints each day because of the delay. You suspect the two staff involved go for coffee or gossip in the main office instead of coming straight back – yet when you have mentioned this to them they have denied it, saying that it takes an age for the mailroom to sort the post and they often have to hang around. You have considered sending only one person but the weight of items would be too much to carry. As a group, discuss how you would solve this problem.

Secretarial/PA issues

If you are responsible for sorting and distributing the mail to a senior executive, then there are several additional actions you should take – firstly to help your boss and secondly to keep yourself informed of current events.

- Check that the documents are sorted correctly with the most urgent items on top. Add to these any overnight faxes or urgent messages.

- Skim-read the documents as you go through them. Try to note any important information which your boss will want quickly.

- Check all items have been date-stamped correctly.

- Get out any relevant files you know your boss will need to answer incoming correspondence. Some managers like incoming documents attached to their relevant files, others prefer the files kept separate.

- Take the mail to your boss. Often a brief verbal resumé of the key items is appreciated.

- If your boss is away on business or on holiday, then make sure that
  - you note any urgent items to mention when you are in contact
  - you have an agreed procedure for handling urgent or personal items
  - you do not leave any confidential items uncovered on his or her desk for any casual callers to read.

(See also Chapter 17.)

Discussion point

You are secretary to the health and safety officer of your organisation, Joanne Townsend. She frequently circulates health and safety bulletins and updates to other managers but wants them returned to you afterwards for safekeeping. In the past three months ten bulletins have been circulated and only one returned. Discuss as a group what you would do

a to chase up the missing bulletins, assuming they were all sent out with a circulation slip

b to prevent this problem from continually recurring

c if, in a frantic rush one morning, you opened a highly confidential and personal letter to Joanne by mistake.

● Outgoing mail

The organisation of outgoing mail depends upon the amount of mail being handled by the organisation and the degree to which the tasks involved are dealt with centrally or departmentally. To take two extremes, the outgoing mail section in a small firm of accountants may be one person at a desk with a set of postal scales and a small franking machine. In contrast, any organisation which deals with high-volume mail on a daily basis (eg credit card or mail-order companies, government offices and mailing houses, which send mail-shots and special offer information to customers) is likely to have a highly automated and integrated mailroom controlled by computer!

However, all organisations have the same objectives when designing their procedures for dealing with outgoing mail. These include

- the prompt despatch of all mail

- the despatch of individual items using the most appropriate method of delivery at the most economical price

- regular information about, and control of, the costs incurred in despatching outgoing mail.

Basic issues

Either departmentally or centrally each of the following actions must be taken in good time for the despatch of mail each day. For that reason there are usually clear deadlines for the last time outgoing mail can be received at a central point in time to 'catch the post' that day.

1 **Checking procedures.** Letters must be checked to ensure they are signed; enclosures must be checked to ensure they are complete. This is

particularly important when a large parcel is being assembled containing several items.

2 **Insertion procedures.** The envelope must be of an appropriate size; documents must be folded the minimum number of times before being placed in the envelope. Care must obviously be taken that the correct documents are inserted in the right envelope! Fragile items being sent by post need protection – either by using a padded bag or, if a parcel is being assembled, by protecting the contents with the use of corrugated paper, bubble wrap or polystyrene fillers.

3 **Addressing and sealing procedures.** All envelopes should be correctly addressed and sealed. Items placed in window·envelopes need to be positioned so that every line of the address is clearly visible. Bulky items should be sealed with sticky tape for extra security; parcels should be sealed with special tape (stronger than ordinary sticky tape) and the sender's address written on the outside. Fragile items must be clearly marked (special stickers are available for this).

4 **Sorting procedures.** Mail should be sorted into the following groups.

- Special items (either of high value or high priority).
- Foreign mail.
- Routine items.
- Parcels.

Items which are being sent by a special Royal Mail service or courier must be clearly marked.

5 **Calculation and despatch procedures.** All items need to be weighed and the correct postage calculated. Forms required for special mail items should be completed and stickers attached to the items. The mail must be franked or stamped and either delivered to the post office or be ready for collection at a pre-arranged time.

Today virtually all of these procedures can be integrated and automated, so that in a highly automated mailroom the vast majority of items are processed from a central control point using a vast array of equipment. However, given that in this type of facility it is likely that specialist staff will be employed, you are more likely to find that you are involved in manually undertaking these operations in most organisations in which you work.

Other considerations

1 **Equipment.** The type of equipment in place can vary from the most basic (eg a book of stamps!) to highly mechanised or computerised equipment costing many thousands of pounds.

Usually, the components of a mechanised mailroom include the following.

- **Electronic postal scales** which weigh envelopes and automatically calculate the correct postage rate. These operate through an electronic chip which is programmed with the current postal rate. Obviously, when the rates change, the chip must also be changed. Special services and destinations can be indicated simply by depressing the relevant key(s).

- **A franking machine** which automatically prints a postal impression plus a company advertisement on each envelope. Labels are produced for bulky envelopes or parcels. Franking machines are bought, leased or rented from a commercial supplier – *not* the Royal Mail! Units of postage are purchased in advance and programmed into the machine. When the level of credit is running low, this is usually signalled by a special warning light. There are various ways of purchasing additional units – the more basic machines have a detachable section which is taken to a post office. The most sophisticated can be reprogrammed automatically by telephoning the supplier's recrediting centre.

  Some features are standard on most machines, eg disposable ink cartridges and the ability to print advertising messages. Useful refinements include the ability to print special delivery messages (eg Airmail) and a clear information display so that the user can check important information quickly. However, there is a considerable difference between the features on a basic machine and those available on more expensive models (see Figure 2.2).

  Franked post must not be posted in the normal way but placed in special pouches and either handed over a post office counter or collected by the Royal Mail.

  Franking machine operators need to take care as mistakes can be expensive. The Royal Mail has no obligation to deliver envelopes with the wrong date or a poor impression and will make the recipient pay a surcharge if the amount franked is too low – which is hardly the best thing for customer relations!

- **Folding, inserting and sealing machines.** These vary from desk-top models which undertake a single operation to linked units which automatically process a large volume of mail very quickly.

- **Addressing machines.** These are usually computerised and enable a large quantity of envelopes or labels to be printed quickly from a database of addresses.

An integrated, computerised system is one where all the machines are linked together and controlled by computer. Not only is the process

Feature	Budget model	Mid-range	Top range
Price range	£800–£2500	£2600–£6500	£6600–£16 000
Motorised	No	Varies	Yes
Motor speed (cycles per hour)	3500 – 6000	8000	10 000 – 14 000
Envelope thickness	Up to 6 mm	Up to 9 mm	Up to 19 mm
Automatic labelling	No	Optional	Yes
Automatic feeder	No	Varies	Yes
Envelope sealing	No/optional	Varies	Yes
Automatic date change	No	Varies	Yes
Batch totals	Yes	Yes	Yes
Accounting codes	No	Varies	Yes
Low-balance warning	Varies	Yes	Yes
High-value warning	Yes	Yes	Yes
Information print-out	No	Varies	Yes
Can be linked to PC	Varies	Varies	Yes

Figure 2.2 Franking machines – comparative features

capable of handling as many as 22 000 envelopes per hour but also the operator can check the costs of the mail at any point and produce detailed print-outs for management as required.

An organisation which has the requirement for many parcels and packages to be wrapped may have additional items such as a heavy-duty staple gun and a parcel-tying machine.

2   **Space.** A specific space needs to be allotted for staff processing outgoing mail. Even in the smallest office there should be a designated basket for 'the post'. It is usually better if there are separate baskets for internal mail, UK mail (special services, first class and second class) and overseas mail. Do bear in mind that envelopes will arrive throughout the day for posting from a variety of people or departments. In a small organisation, therefore, the person responsible for preparing the post for despatch can weigh and stamp or frank the envelopes throughout the day – to avoid a last-minute rush. In a large organisation with high-volume mail handling, a specially designated area will be set aside for the equipment required and there will be full-time mailroom staff.

3   **Furniture.** At the most basic, a desk and a chair are required. An operator responsible for controlling a computerised mailroom will have a special workstation conforming to current health and safety requirements (see pages 115 and 116). There should be a separate table

available if parcels and packets are wrapped in the mailroom. A filing cabinet or cupboard is useful for keeping leaflets and information on Royal Mail services. If your organisation has an account with Royal Mail, then copy invoices and statements will also have to be filed.

4 **Other requirements.** An array of miscellaneous items and materials are usually stored in a mailroom. These will include scissors, staplers, calculators and sticky tape and printed labels (for parcels), envelopes and padded bags, boxes and packing materials, Royal Mail stickers to denote special services or parcels (see page 47).

5 **Mailroom policies and procedures.** Most organisations have clear policies in effect to control the cost of outgoing mail and to prevent abuse of the system. Although costs will be carefully monitored (see page 48) prevention is always better than cure. For that reason all employees should be familiar with the way in which items are routinely handled. However, all policies should allow for some flexibility in case an exception has to be made at some time (eg a large mail-shot has to be sent or alternative methods must be investigated for urgent items during a postal strike).

An example of a typical organisational policy on outgoing mail is given in Figure 2.3.

MARKHAM ELECTRONICS PLC

Outgoing Mail - Policy and Procedures

The policy of this organisation is that outgoing mail should be processed accurately and rapidly to facilitate its despatch. To assist the mailroom staff to achieve this objective all staff are asked to adhere to the following procedures.

1 Outgoing mail must be received by the mailroom *no later than 1500 hours* for same day despatch. Urgent documents requiring transmission after this time should either be

   - faxed to the recipient
   - posted by the department. For this reason each section has its own small supply of postage stamps. A record must be kept of any such expenditure and a copy sent to the mailroom at the end of each month.

   In exceptional circumstances departmental managers may contact the mailroom supervisor to make special arrangements. Such requests will be logged and action taken if this facility is abused by any users.

2 All routine outgoing mail must be enveloped and sealed within departments with special mailing instructions clearly marked on the envelope. In the absence of other instructions all outgoing mail will be despatched by second class post.

3 Internal mail for other departments and branch offices must only be enveloped if confidential. All such mail will be batched for onward transmission by mailroom staff.

4 Departmental managers must contact the mailroom supervisor in advance if large mail shots are required. These can be prepared by the mailroom to keep costs to a minimum. However, at least two weeks' notice is required so that space and staff can be allocated effectively.

5 Any items of international mail or mail which requires special services must be despatched through the mailroom. The mailroom supervisor has the right to amend the requested service if a more appropriate or cost-effective service is available.

6 Staff must not send personal items of mail through the mailroom and only outgoing mail in printed company envelopes will be accepted unless stamped beforehand. The company reserves the right to open any official envelope where there are reasonable grounds to suspect that the contents are of a personal nature.

7 For security reasons, departmental staff delivering mail to the mailroom must not bring with them any bags or packages which are not directly related to their outgoing mail requirements.

Figure 2.3 A company's policy on handling outgoing mail

PAF and its applications

Correct addressing is a key requirement of any company sending large mail shots. Otherwise much of the money invested in expensive brochures and leaflets will be wasted. Today a variety of computerised address systems are available to help companies to manage this problem.

Most are based on the Royal Mail's Postcode Address File (PAF). This can simply check addresses or generate complete addresses from the customer's postcode and house number. The user buys the system and installs it on the company computer system. The most sophisticated handle postcode changes automatically and can 'intelligently' deal with unreadable characters and 'problem' addresses (such as flats which need additional identification). The Royal Mail will give advice to any company on the best system for its purposes.

Such systems not only ensure that addresses contain the correct information but also that they are printed in a format which is approved by the Royal Mail.

Mail distribution services

In addition to the basic first and second class postal services, the Royal Mail offers a variety of more specialised services. Some of these are available to both business and private customers, others are only available to high-volume users. In any organisation you may find that you are expected to be a mine of information on postal services and to give advice and information when it is needed. Bear in mind, however, that Royal Mail services change – so anything you read in a book (including this one!) may soon become out of date. It is for this reason that the Royal Mail issues a range of booklets and leaflets which give the latest information. Copies of the latest editions should be kept at a central point in any mailroom.

Many of these leaflets can be obtained at a local post office, but the Royal Mail customer service section can supply more specialist leaflets on all their services including

- standard services (first class, second class and Recorded)
- guaranteed services (Special Delivery, Registered and Registered Plus)
- mail receiving services
- sending mail abroad
- business services – at home and abroad.

Also included in the booklets is additional information on how to wrap parcels for the post, items which cannot be sent by post, how to cope with customs and deal with other problems you may face.

The Royal Mail division which handles parcels and packets is Parcelforce. Again a variety of booklets is available giving up-to-date information on all its services both within the UK and internationally.

Finally, there are also a large number of couriers and collection/delivery organisations in every town and city that will deal with urgent deliveries of mail and parcels all over the world.

Check it yourself

1   Write an envelope and check with your tutor whether it would be acceptable to the Royal Mail.

2   Nominate different members of the group to make the following telephone calls to obtain information for the group as a whole. Those not nominated to make telephone calls can visit their local post office to collect other leaflets on Royal Mail services.

   • Ring the Royal Mail Customer Service Centre on 0345 740 740 and request the following booklets.
     Handy Guide to Postal Services
     How to use Special Delivery, Registered and Registered Plus
     A Quick Guide to Mailing Abroad
   • Ring the Royal Mail Business information line on 0345 950 950 and ask for the following booklets.
     Postal Services for Business
     The Easy Way to Mail Abroad for Businesses
   • Ring Parcelforce on 0800 22 44 66 and ask for the following booklets.
     Nobody Delivers More Worldwide (A Complete Guide)
     UK Guaranteed Service Price Guide
     UK Price Guide Standard Service
     International Concise Guide

   When you have obtained all the above literature, make sure you can look up information quickly and easily.

3   In your local *Yellow Pages* look up the names and addresses of three private courier or delivery firms in your area and note the main services they offer and how these compare with those offered by the Royal Mail. As a group, discuss when you may be likely to use a private firm rather than a special Royal Mail service.

● Administrative issues

As an administrator, your remit in relation to outgoing mail is likely to include the following.

* Monitoring and controlling postage costs. You may do this manually (in a small firm) simply by keeping a log of special items and a record of stamps purchased. Today most franking machines have a cost reporting feature which will give this information automatically and there are sophisticated computer systems which monitor the costs of heavy-volume users. If you work at departmental level, then your boss will be more concerned that your department is not wrongly charged with postal costs which are not directly related to your own department's mailings. For this reason, large companies often install a franking machine which either allows accounting codes to be allocated to different items for despatch or have one which can be linked to a PC which can be used to obtain and process sophisticated accounting information.

* Ordering mailroom materials and supplies. This means keeping a record of stocks and usage so that nothing runs out unexpectedly (see also Chapter 5, page 68.)

* Ensuring that staff know and understand how to use the different services. The Royal Mail will train staff but this is usually only necessary for specialist mailroom staff. Usually, it is the mailroom supervisor or office administrator who is the most knowledgeable and any queries must be referred to this person.

* Making sure the equipment is used safely and correctly. This means training staff and not just 'letting them loose' to see what happens!

* Ensuring quality of output, eg letters placed in the correct envelopes, envelopes correctly addressed, all enclosures included, etc. In many organisations with a centralised mailroom this responsibility still rests at departmental level, with only sealed items being accepted in the mailroom.

* Arranging for the maintenance and repair of equipment as required. This does not just mean calling in the engineer when there is a problem, it also means regularly checking that there are enough units in the franking machine, particularly if a large mail-shot is scheduled to be sent.

* Making arrangements for 'one-off' mail-shots or special deliveries. This requires planning in advance not only because of the additional cost involved but also because additional staff may have to be drafted in to help – particularly if there is a lack of automated equipment available. The penalty for forgetting could be having to fill envelopes yourself all day to help out!

- Dealing with problems as and when they occur. This can be anything from a last-minute urgent item which arrives after the post has gone to a large, ungainly item which no one knows how to wrap correctly!

Usually, everyone will look to you for the operation to run smoothly. In other words, in many organisations, if there are complaints about the service, dozens of returned items, delayed mail or equipment breakdowns you are the person most likely to take the blame.

Again, you will need to consider any problem carefully. Has it been caused because the outgoing mail procedure is faulty, or because people are not doing what they should do? In the first case, the problem will recur time and again unless you rethink the system currently used in your organisation. If it is one person ignoring the guidelines, then you have to decide whether that person simply does not know any better (and needs careful counselling and training) or is being deliberately awkward – in which case you will probably warn the person concerned and, if this does not work, report the matter to your boss.

 Discussion point

You have a very basic franking machine at your workplace which was purchased some years ago. Lately there have been several problems.

- The new junior has forgotten to alter the date on a few occasions. Luckily you spotted the mistake quickly and refranked a zero value label for the reverse of the envelope with the correct date. You are worried about this trend as you know the Royal Mail has no obligation to accept envelopes franked with the incorrect date.

- You found four envelopes stuffed in a drawer – all franked for very large amounts in error. You are annoyed because you know these can be submitted to the Royal Mail for recrediting and have stressed this on several occasions.

- Because you were very busy last week you forgot to take the meter to the post office for recrediting, with the result that on Thursday there was a panic because there were no units in the machine. You are also fed up with carrying such a heavy and cumbersome object to the post office on a regular basis.

Reread the text on franking machines and Figure 2.2. If possible obtain up-to-date literature on several models by contacting the major manufacturers, such as Pitney Bowes (Tel: 0900 426731), Neopost (Tel: 01708 746000) and Frama UK Ltd (Tel: 01992 451122). Make sure that only *one* person from the group contacts each company.

Then prepare a list of the benefits which would be gained by upgrading the machine and decide which one you would purchase if you had a budget of £5 500.

● Secretarial/PA issues

If you are employed as a secretary or PA, then you will be more likely to be preparing outgoing mail for your boss than that for the whole organisation. However, if you work for a very small organisation, you could be doing both!

Your boss is likely to expect you to

- be a mine of information on every service which he or she could possibly want to use

- be able to cope with emergencies and urgent items quickly (so stamps in the desk drawer are essential!)

- prioritise his or her work so that all items are despatched on time – this also means preparing documents for signature *before* he or she leaves the office early to keep an appointment

- be responsible for contacting the mailroom if there are any special jobs being planned or problems with the mail

- check any costs apportioned to your boss or your boss's department by the mailroom.

Discussion point

Assume that your company operates the outgoing mail procedure illustrated in Figure 2.3 on page 45.

Discuss as a group, and with your tutor, how you would cope with each of the following problems.

a One senior executive for whom you do some work insists that all his mail is sent first class.

b A colleague who works with you is forever pleading for her personal post to be sent through the office system. On the first occasion you let her go ahead because she said it was urgent and important and she had no time to go to a post office or to buy any stamps.

c Yesterday, in a rush, you forgot to put a confidential memo in an envelope. It went to the mailroom for internal distribution and you fear several people may have read the contents.

d You have noticed the disappearance of £20 worth of postage stamps from your desk drawer.

e One of your bosses puts all the correspondence for a branch office in separate, addressed, sealed envelopes before passing them to you.

Dealing with visitors

3

Introduction

Of key importance to any organisation is the reception and handling of visitors. There are usually two major issues relating to visitors.

- Security procedures must be in place to prevent any unauthorised visitors from roaming around the building(s).

- Bona fide visitors should be looked after with care and consideration.

The second objective relates to **customer service** – an area which has been increasing in importance. All organisations today recognise the importance of giving a good service to *all* their customers so that a good business relationship is created. Customers who are neglected, ignored or dealt with in a casual or offhand manner are very likely to take their business elsewhere in future!

Normally, therefore, you have two concerns. Firstly, to make sure that the procedures for booking visitors in and out of the building are adequate and are adhered to. Secondly, to make sure your own 'people skills', as well as those of any junior staff you work with are excellent. As always, you also need to know how to cope when something goes wrong.

Basic issues

The first point to bear in mind is that there can be a variety of different types of visitors calling into your organisation or your office every day. For instance

- customers

- suppliers or their representatives

- delivery people

- trades people and maintenance workers

- colleagues from other departments or branch offices.

All must be treated with the same care and consideration – the electrician and courier deserve politeness and a prompt response to just the same extent as the organisation's managing director!

Many organisations have a separate reception area or reception desk where visitors call. For safety reasons, this is often away from any delivery area so that you are unlikely to get large parcels or goods deliveries suddenly arriving in reception. If you do, your job is to get the items moved – quickly – before someone falls over them!

The reception desk should be free of clutter and personal belongings, nothing valuable should be lying around and the whole area should be bright, cheerful, welcoming and *tidy*. Clear signs and directions to visitors are also invaluable. If visitors are often kept waiting for a few minutes there should be appropriate seating and some magazines available.

However, it is useless having an immaculate reception area if the reception staff are surly, unkempt and impolite – or make visitors wait until a job is finished before giving them any attention. All reception staff need to

- be able to communicate clearly and politely
- display good social skills
- appear friendly and welcoming
- be well-groomed
- have good organisational skills
- be able to stay calm under pressure.

All organisations will have some type of procedure for booking in visitors as part of the overall security system. Usually, there is a visitors book which records all visitors, whether they are expected or not. Typical headings are shown in Figure 2.3. Some have a duplicate slip which is given to the visitor who must hand it in again on departure. More frequently, a visitor's badge is issued which must be worn whilst the visitor is on the premises and handed in again on leaving. You should note that the record of current visitors in the building is useful if there is a sudden emergency – such as a fire alarm or bomb scare – and the security services need to check that everyone is out of the building.

As a further security precaution it is usual to ask suppliers, delivery people and maintenance workers for some form of identification before they are given access to the building *in addition* to checking that they are expected.

VISITORS BOOK

Date	Name	Organisation	Car reg number	To see	Time of arrival	Time of departure

Figure 3.1 Typical headings in a visitors book

Organisations that make regular appointments for their clients, such as doctors and hairdressers, usually have an appointments book rather than a visitors book. It is quite likely that you will have seen one of these in operation and your name has been an entry at several times in your life! You should note that this type of book only records expected visitors. If you work as a secretary, such appointments are more likely to be recorded in your boss's (and your) diary (see Chapter 19).

Other considerations

The more you know about your organisation – its business, products, services, personnel and procedures – the more likely you are to be able to offer concrete help and advice to visitors. This is particularly true if the visitor is completely unexpected or has a difficult request. Perhaps he or she does not know who to see about a particular matter, wants information on a certain service you offer or is asking for a donation to charity. In all of these cases an experienced member of staff is more likely to be able to cope better than one who is new or relatively inexperienced.

However, this does not mean that you should be unduly worried about ever asking anyone what they want! It is quite possible to give positive and courteous assistance to visitors *without* being able to give them the information they require. Indeed, you are better to give no facts at all than the wrong facts! Use the chart in Figure 3.2 to help you to work through the process you should follow, no matter how little you know or how inexperienced you are.

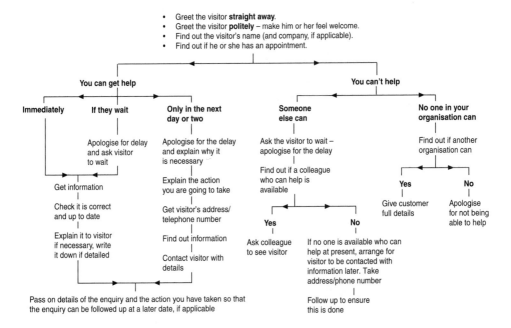

Figure 3.2 Dealing with visitors

Once a visitor has arrived and his or her destination identified, you will need to know the organisational policy on whether the visitor must be accompanied whilst in the building or can be given directions. Usually, high security organisations and production facilities opt for the first. In this case you must only escort the visitor yourself if there is someone to cover for you in the reception area. This must obviously never be left unattended. Usually, there is a clear directive on this and reception staff will notify security to provide an escort or arrange for the visitor to be collected from reception. If you work in a large organisation which allows visitors to roam freely, do be sure that you give clear, specific directions as to which room to go to. No one is likely to thank you if the visitor goes missing for half an hour trying to find his or her way there!

People skills questionnaire

Answer the questions below *honestly* and then decide what your major strengths and weaknesses are when dealing with other people.

1 I enjoy meeting new people.
  a Yes   **b** Sometimes   **c** No

2 I speak clearly.
  a Yes   **b** Sometimes   **c** No

3 I think before I speak.
  a Yes   **b** Sometimes   **c** No

4 I am very patient.
  a Yes   **b** Sometimes   **c** No

5 I cope well under pressure.
  a Yes   **b** Sometimes   **c** No

6 I find it easy to talk to strangers.
  a Yes   **b** Sometimes   **c** No

7 People think I have a very friendly manner.
  a Yes   **b** Sometimes   **c** No

8 I make decisions easily.
  a Yes   **b** Sometimes   **c** No

9 I find it difficult to deal with someone who has a disability.
  a Yes   **b** Sometimes   **c** No

10 People think I am moody.
  a Yes   **b** Sometimes   **c** No

Discuss your answers to the people skills questionnaire with your tutor (in confidence if you prefer!). Then think about how you could overcome your weaknesses if you regularly had to deal with visitors to an organisation.

Administrative issues

As an administrator you will be expected to set an example to junior staff in the way in which you deal with *all* visitors. Ideally, this means that you are diplomatic, can smooth ruffled feathers and yet be firm when the need arises. Do not worry if you have not achieved all these skills yet – most people take several years to develop them and some never succeed at all!

As an administrator you may not actually work in reception but be expected to keep a 'weather eye' on the staff who work there. In this case, you are likely to take responsibility for

- ensuring the area is kept tidy, that wilting flowers are removed, plants are watered, magazines and notices are up to date and organisational literature is replenished regularly

- overseeing the general appearance, behaviour and manner of reception staff

- greeting anyone you see 'hanging around' – both to prevent visitors being neglected and to monitor security (simply by asking them politely if they are being attended to)

- dealing with unexpected visitors, appointment clashes and other problems and emergencies.

A high-level skill which is nowadays expected of all staff is that of additional sales person. This means always promoting your organisation positively and never losing a potential customer. Indeed, you should actively look for opportunities when you can give visitors the type of information which will persuade them to buy one of your products or services. Such a skill is usually quickly noted by your line manager who will be delighted at your initiative and enterprise.

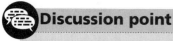

Discussion point

1   Discuss as a group and with your tutor how you would deal with each of the following problems.

a   A new member of the reception staff has a very obvious personal hygiene problem.

b   There is a foreign visitor who can hardly speak any English.

c   A visitor faints in the reception area.

d   A representative calls unexpectedly and will not accept the receptionist's response that callers to see the purchasing manager will only be seen by appointment.

e   A visitor unwittingly leaves his wallet in reception and later leaves the building. It contains £45 in cash and several credit cards. There is no address.

f   Three visitors arrive simultaneously to see the same person. One is late, another on time and the third is early.

g   A visitor starts to threaten a member of the reception staff.

h   A visitor who has an appointment arrives, but the relevant member of staff is nowhere to be found.

i   A blind visitor enters the reception area.

j   A visitor has her car vandalised in the company car park.

k   An important visitor arrives when you are in the middle of writing down a complicated telephone message from the sales director, an executive not noted for his patience or understanding!

2   You work for a firm of insurance brokers and are the only one in the office one lunch time. A woman calls in, obviously in a hurry, and asks whether you could insure her son, who is 21 next month, to drive the second-hand car she has bought him as a present. How would you respond

a   if you wanted to get rid of her?

b   if you simply wanted to keep her happy – but get rid of her for now?

c   if you wanted to gain her business?

Compare your answers and discuss the best responses with your tutor. Discuss, too, how you could gain her business if you are newly employed at the firm and know little or nothing about the insurance business!

● Secretarial/PA issues

In this role you are more likely to be dealing with visitors who have an agreed appointment to see your boss – or know him or her well enough to call in without an appointment. It is important that you quickly get to know those people whom your boss loves to see and those whom he or she does not!

You should also bear in mind the following.

- Greet regular visitors by name – the personal touch is always appreciated.

- If a visitor arrives 'in transit' between the airport and hotel with luggage, a briefcase and an umbrella, store the items safely and make sure the visitor and your boss know where they are.

- Give your boss adequate warning if a visitor arrives (or is due). Advance notification is welcomed if your boss always operates 'at the last minute' or is apt to get distracted or absent-minded when involved with a difficult job.

- Develop a code to rescue your boss from visitors who never know when to leave. This can be done easily by simply knocking on the door and saying 'I'm sorry, but I thought I should mention that your next visitor has arrived'.

- You should be able to announce the visitor politely to your boss and, if necessary, make introductions if the visitor is a stranger. Simply bear in mind it is usual to say the name of the more important person *first*. Therefore, if the managing director, Samantha Wilcox, looks questioningly at your new junior, you could say, 'Mrs Wilcox, this is our new recruit, John Brown'. Do not mumble the names so that neither knows who is who, or say them in such a rush everyone is breathless afterwards.

- Be able to make polite conversation with a visitor who is kept waiting and obviously wants to talk. The best gambit is to think of general, uncontroversial topics – such as the weather or holidays. Do not get drawn into a conversation about your organisation or your boss in case the visitor is 'fishing' for information.

- Serve light refreshments (ie tea, coffee and biscuits) to your boss and important visitors. If you regularly have important visitors, then you need to have reasonable quality cups and saucers, spoons and a dish for sugar or sweeteners. Check how the visitors would like their drinks, eg with/without milk, and put all the items on a tray. Leaving this on the desk is often safer than handing out the cups yourself!

Discussion point

1 As a group, discuss how you would cope if

  a your boss is due to meet an important visitor at the airport, but her car is off the road on the day the visitor is due, and she asks you to go in her place

  b a reporter calls into your office during your boss's absence, trying to find out if a dispute in the Production section is likely to lead to a mass walkout by staff

  c you spill hot coffee into the lap of an important guest

  d your boss is ill on the day he has three important visitors coming to see him

  e as you look out of the window you see a traffic warden in the street where your boss's wife's car is parked on double yellow lines (you know she is only calling in for a couple of minutes)

  f the managing director is entertaining important visitors and rings your office to ask your boss to join them immediately. She is nowhere to be found.

2 Your boss asks you to take an important visitor to lunch because she is held up at a meeting. She promises to join you later. At the restaurant you discover that the visitor is not only extremely sexist but keeps trying to find out some intimate details of your personal life. What would you do?

Purchasing goods and services

4

● Introduction

All organisations have systems to regulate the purchasing of goods and services. If they did not, then staff would be able to order what they wanted when they wanted – and the costs would be astronomical!

All organisations, no matter how small, will have a budget to control the amount spent on both consumables (eg stationery) and fixed assets (eg machinery, furniture and equipment). Usually, there are two separate budgets for these and the procedure to follow in both cases is likely to be different.

Consumable items, particularly those relating to the running of an office, are often the responsibility of an administrator or secretary. Generally, these include stationery and related items of small equipment, such as staplers, floppy disks, scissors, disk boxes, hole punches, etc. Other consumables used by the organisation, eg paper towels, food and drink and first-aid supplies, would normally not be part of your remit, unless you work for a very small firm.

Fixed assets are more expensive items and, for that reason, the purchasing decision usually rests with a senior manager. The title for this executive can vary from resource manager to purchasing manager, from chief buyer to facilities manager. In a large organisation this individual will be a specialist, able to evaluate the different methods by which expensive goods can be acquired, ie by renting, buying or leasing, and to suggest the best, most cost-effective option for the organisation.

The difference between renting and leasing is quite technical and beyond the scope of this book. However, most organisations prefer these options to buying the goods for three reasons.

- The item (eg a computer or car) can be upgraded at regular intervals.

- There are fewer problems if a breakdown occurs.

- Less capital is tied up, therefore more money is still available as working capital (ie the day-to-day expenses of running the business).

This latter concept is very important – particularly for small firms. It is no good buying the equivalent of a Rolls Royce if you have no money left to pay for the petrol! An organisation which spends all its money on equipment will have less left over for wages, rent, electricity, etc. In addition, the executive concerned with arranging the lease or rental will have a good knowledge of the law of contract and will have the authority to sign major contracts with suppliers on behalf of the company. This does not mean that you will have no part in influencing the process – it does mean that you will probably have little say in the final decision – and would not be expected to put your name to any formal legal agreement.

It is worth noting that even a senior executive may not be able to authorise very large amounts of expenditure. This may be a decision which can only be made by the managing director or the board of directors. The same applies to any policy which would involve a considerable amount of expenditure, such as the upgrading of all computers every two years or the building or refurbishment of a complete office block.

You must appreciate from the outset that all organisations are concerned with controlling costs and only spending what they can afford. They also want the maximum benefits for the money they spend. This not only means value for money in terms of the item purchased but, if possible, a tangible benefit which can be translated into monetary terms. For instance, if purchasing another computer would increase profits, then this would influence the decision more favourably than if it was simply a 'good buy'.

Controlling costs is partly achieved through a good stock control system, which ensures that

- no more goods are stored than are necessary (ie money is not tied up unnecessarily in stock)

- goods are used in rotation (ie the oldest first)

- essential items are never out of stock (eg letter-headed paper and envelopes)

- goods are safely stored and so less likely to be pilfered or damaged.

● Basic issues

All organisations purchase a range of goods and services. These include

- consumable items

- capital items or fixed assets

- raw materials (production firms only)

- services such as cleaning, security and window cleaning.

The system used to control purchasing will vary considerably from one organisation to another. A large company is likely to have a centralised Purchasing Department which monitors and controls a list of recommended suppliers. Your job, in ordering consumables, would be to make out an *internal* order form (sometimes called a **requisition**) to the Purchasing Department. The Purchasing Department would place all orders externally, on behalf of the organisation, to benefit from the discounts that bulk orders usually attract.

Some organisations only centralise the buying of expensive equipment. Consumables can be purchased departmentally against a predetermined budget. All expenditure is logged and monitored. In this case you would be expected to 'shop around' to find a competitive but reliable supplier.

In a small firm you may be able to buy items yourself and, indeed, it may be your responsibility alone to make sure nothing ever runs out or wears out! You must be careful, though, not to go on a spending spree with money the

---

MARKHAM ELECTRONICS PLC

Purchasing Procedure

The following procedures must be followed for all purchases.

Capital equipment/office services
1 A minimum of three quotations must be obtained from different companies. The quotations must include information on
   · specification of goods/service
   · price and discounts (including VAT)
   · delivery times and charges
   · warranties or guarantees (if equipment)
   · servicing or maintenance (if applicable).
   It should be noted that estimates are not acceptable.

2 The quotations must be submitted to a director of the company with a written recommendation for purchase from the potential user. This should be an objective report which includes an evaluation of the suppliers, their reputations for service, their location and credit terms offered.

3 Only after agreement from a director may an item be ordered. All goods and services must be ordered on an official order form. The form must give a clear description of the goods and state the unit price and catalogue number (if applicable). A copy must be sent to the Accounts Department.

4 The buyer is responsible for
   · checking that the delivered item/service is in accordance with that specified in the order
   · checking that the item is not damaged
   · passing the invoice for payment.

Consumable goods
1 This company has a policy of ordering consumable goods from local suppliers unless there is good reason to do otherwise.

2 Supplies should be replenished in line with the following guidelines.
   · No stock should exceed the maximum level indicated for each item.
   · Adequate time must be allowed for delivery time and availability, particularly for critical items such as letter-headed paper.

3 Prices must be checked when goods are reordered. An increase in price above 3 per cent must be reported to a director before the order is completed.

Figure 4.1 A company's procedure for purchasing goods and services

firm can ill-afford. A discussion on estimated usage and expenditure is vital in this situation. Usually, it is sensible, even in the smallest firm, for specified purchasing procedures to be defined – if only so that no one gets into trouble for not doing what they should! An example is given in Figure 4.1.

The provision of services is likely to be organised centrally in a large organisation. In a small firm these will usually be the remit of the administrator. However, if you work in a suite of offices which are part of a large office block, you will usually find that several services are organised and provided through the building or estates manager. These will include everything related to building maintenance, eg cleaning services, electrician, plumber, central heating, window cleaning, etc. Additional services, eg for equipment maintenance, you would have to organise yourself.

● Other considerations

If you are ordering goods yourself, then you will have to complete an official order form and have this countersigned by your manager. Suppliers may be willing to provide goods immediately if you order by telephone, but only if you quote them your official order number and then send the order to them as confirmation. In this case a fax machine is worth its weight in gold!

Whereas you might have been allowed to order a dozen boxes of paper clips by picking up the telephone, it is unlikely you would be permitted to replace your computer or photocopier by the same method! However, you may be asked to obtain details of suitable equipment to replace or supplement existing resources. You would then have to work out which would be the best buy for the company or department bearing in mind features and cost (similar to the exercise on the franking machine you undertook on page 49). You would need the ability to present your arguments clearly yet succinctly in a short report or memo. You would usually be expected to give information on

- comparative makes and features

- prices and discounts

- delivery times and charges

- length of warranty or guarantee

- servicing or maintenance agreements.

In some instances you may be better to obtain a written quotation from several suppliers and attach these to your report. Other factors which may influence your organisation's choice of supplier include

- the supplier's reputation – how well-established is the supplier, what reports have been received about the service it gives

- the supplier's location – a local firm may be better for consumables (which are required quickly) whereas an expensive item may be better purchased through a national supplier with a local service depot

- the supplier's sales terms, which relate to discounts and payment terms or simply the range of options available (eg leasing, buying and renting).

Once the purchase has been agreed, you will make out an order on behalf of your company. This should give an exact description of the goods, any reference number, the price and any terms of sale that you have agreed. If the purchase relates to a sales agreement, then you will able to check that the agreement matches the order you placed. Similarly, if the next step is the arrival of the goods followed by an invoice, this document will also need checking for accuracy.

Purchasing services also means you need to 'shop around' to find the best supplier at the most reasonable price. Bear in mind that you will often find that machine maintenance can be provided by the equipment supplier. However, be careful not to commit your organisation to a complex contract from which it cannot escape! Some photocopier agreements, for instance, are for a minimum period of five years and, even if you find a better deal 12 months later, there is nothing you can do about it.

Additional service providers, eg travel agent, insurance broker, employment agency (for temporary staff), etc. can often be found through recommendations from other people. Otherwise, write a short letter to about four local companies, asking them to detail the range of services they offer and their charges. Then compare their replies (including the length of time it took them to respond!). Overall, you want service providers that can meet your needs, are conveniently placed (particularly if you will need to visit them), will respond quickly and positively to any urgent or unusual requests – and not charge you the earth for doing so!

● Administrative issues

A good administrator will keep a list of key suppliers and catalogues and current price lists of the goods and equipment each supplies. In a small organisation he or she will also be responsible for checking that goods which arrive are those which were expected – and notifying the supplier if there is anything wrong, eg

- missing items

- damaged items

- items included which were not ordered.

Bear in mind that whilst, under the Sale of Goods Act, suppliers are legally bound to replace any items which were received damaged, they are *not* legally obliged to accept the return of any items which were ordered by mistake. If, therefore, your latest recruit has completed an order form incorrectly and inserted the wrong catalogue number, you are reliant on the supplier's goodwill – nothing else – if you want to return the goods!

In some cases the delivery note which accompanies the goods may state that goods are out of stock and will follow later. It will be your job to check that they do – and if they do not, remind the supplier and also check that the goods have not been inadvertently included on the invoice!

Once the goods have been received, then it is important that they are stored away as soon as possible to prevent damage and pilfering.

The way in which payment is made will vary. In a large organisation you would simply signify on an invoice that it must be paid. In a small organisation you may be responsible for paying the supplier yourself, and even keeping records of expenditure on consumables against budget.

As administrator you will also be responsible for ensuring that all equipment is functioning correctly and all services are being provided as agreed. If the photocopier service engineer has not put in an appearance for months then you should notice it (without being told!) and find out why. If there is the opportunity of buying new equipment, then your staff will be lobbying you with suggestions and ideas and – particularly if money is in short supply – you may have to control some of their more exotic suggestions! Whatever you do, do not feel guilty if you have to make a sensible economic judgement. Whilst everyone loves fancy equipment which take the slog out of work, no one wants the firm to go out of business because of it!

Finally, if you are responsible for buying stationery then you will need to know the following.

- The quantities in which you should purchase items (eg reams, quires, gross, dozens, etc.).

- The different types of products available and their purpose. For instance, floppy disks can be high density, double density or low density. Paper is graded by weight (thickness) – usually shown as grams per square metre (gsm). The higher the figure the thicker (more expensive) the paper. Some paper is specially treated, eg that for photocopiers. Paper less than 80 gsm is usually unsuitable for laser printers. However, the more uses for a particular type of paper the better, as discounts can usually be negotiated for bulk orders.

- Paper sizes range from A1 to A5, envelopes from C1 to C6/7 plus DL size which fits A4 paper folded in three. Envelopes are available in brown or white, in a range of qualities, some have windows, others are ready to seal and so on.

Knowing what to order saves costly mistakes!

Professional purchasing

Although it has no doubt never been your intention to become a professional buyer, there are certain key facts you need to know if you are regularly involved in buying goods for a company.

At the outset you may have the option of asking for a **quotation** (a detailed statement of cost) or an **estimate** (an overall figure). The latter is usually unacceptable because it is a general figure to which the supplier cannot be held. A **tender** is when suppliers are asked to bid to provide goods or a service. Tenders are sent in writing and all opened on a specified date (to prevent collusion or cheating). Usually the cheapest tender is accepted, but not always.

Note: Because many of the issues relating to purchasing relate equally to administrators and secretaries (depending upon the company), several of the points given below are equally relevant to administrators.

● Secretarial/PA issues

Unless you work in a very small firm, where you are responsible for doing virtually everything, your boss will expect that

- you can immediately lay your hands on anything he or she wants – no matter how unexpected the request!

- every item of equipment he or she needs to use is in perfect working order

- everything which is purchased for which he or she is responsible is recorded accurately and constantly monitored

- a request for a new service is met promptly, after a careful investigation of alternative providers has been made.

This may seem like a tall order, but, for the well-organised secretary, it will be little more than routine!

In the first case, over time, you will get used to knowing what your boss needs to use – and keep an emergency supply to hand if necessary. Most executives are not interested in elaborate control systems (apart from when they are checking costs). They simply expect you to make sure that everything which is needed is always available. Telling your boss, on a frantically busy day, that you cannot post his or her last-minute important letter because you have run out of stamps is unlikely to meet with a favourable reaction!

So far as equipment is concerned, you should keep a check on the amount of 'downtime' (machine breakdown time) on any piece of equipment that is essential to the efficient functioning of the office. If a piece of equipment is constantly malfunctioning, it may be nearing the end of its useful life and have to be replaced. If your boss instructs you to contact representatives to get some quotations, be aware that if you make several enquiries you may be constantly pestered by suppliers wanting to demonstrate their wares. A useful tactic, at the outset, is to specify on your enquiry that you want a written quotation only and that you will not consider any organisation which 'pesters' you for business.

If new equipment is being installed, then you will usually find your boss falls into one of two categories. He or she will either want to play with it and learn all the features or totally ignore it and expect you to learn what it can do. In either case it is worth learning how to use the equipment straight away – the fastest method is to be available when it is installed so that you can watch a demonstration and make notes on what to do. Then practise before you forget!

Knowing how to cope when a new request for a service is put to you is also important. If you work for a small firm, and are expected to sort out the problem yourself, then your local *Yellow Pages* can prove invaluable. You can quickly and easily find a locksmith, courier or carpet-fitter, simply by looking through the book and ringing round. An alternative is 'Talking Pages', a BT phone service available on 0800 600 900, that will help put you in touch with someone who can provide an emergency service in your area. Once you have used particular trades people or service providers and found them to be reasonably priced and reliable, make a note of their names and telephone numbers for the future. Most top secretaries have a list of useful names, addresses and phone numbers of local preferred organisations – from a florist to a printer.

If your boss is responsible for expenditure in a particular area, you can expect to be asked for regular reports. Often a verbal update will suffice with written details more infrequently. Work out with your boss whether you are supposed to give a full report or only report problems and difficulties. This is often known as **management by exception**, ie 'Don't bother me unless there's a problem – then tell me'. However, you need to define carefully what is meant by 'a problem'. If you see a problem as an occasion when you overspend by £100 and your boss sees it as one where you overspend by £5, you are likely to have a misunderstanding at the outset.

Finally, remember that a good secretary or PA is diplomatic! Do not choose the worst possible day in the year to create a fuss about a breakdown; do not announce an overspend when a visitor has just arrived. If, above all, you have the kind of boss who reacts very strongly indeed to any problems, then put them in writing – and place your memo at the bottom of the mail so that you are well clear when it is being read!

Check it yourself

There are some helpful hints and tips about how to buy goods and services at the front of your local *Yellow Pages*. These were compiled with the help of *Which?*, the consumer organisation, and the Institute of Trading Standards Administration. Read these yourself and note the key points which are made.

Discussion point

1   Obtain a set of office supply catalogues and note the way in which key items (eg paper, envelopes, pens, etc.) are described. Discuss with your tutor how you would complete an order for such items.

2   Despite having a fortnightly agreement with a local window-cleaning firm, no one has appeared to do the windows for at least six weeks. Every time you telephone, you are promised that someone will be round 'tomorrow'. So far your boss has not noticed, but you know it will not be long before she does. In the meantime, what do you do?

3   You regularly use a local taxi firm for collecting visitors from your office and taking them to the airport or station. Recently you have noticed a considerable increase in the bill. Discuss as a group
    a   how much of an increase you should tolerate before warning your boss
    b   what other information for him or her you could attach to your memo.

4   Your boss wants a new laptop computer for home use. Use a selection of catalogues to obtain information and write a brief report which gives **three** recommendations for purchase and lists suitable features of each, together with the price and any other relevant information.

5 Stock control

● Introduction

It is no use purchasing office supplies if there is no control over their storage or use. A small organisation may start with no official system or procedure but very soon may find that this leads to over spending and abuse – particularly if everybody simply helps themselves every time they need something.

Even if the managers of the organisation are not too bothered about this (which is unlikely), their accountants will not take the same view. Stock is an item of expenditure and as such must be recorded in the company accounts. Expenditure on capital equipment is also carefully recorded because an allowance can be made for wear and tear each year (known as **depreciation**). Because of the close links with the company accounting system, it is usual for there to be some checks on the usage of stock, if only to make sure that nothing essential runs out when everyone needs it!

● Basic issues

Stock control only relates to consumable items. A good stock control system

- checks the total usage of items – so that items no longer required are no longer ordered

- checks individual usage of items – to guard against waste and abuse

- ensures no more money than necessary is tied up in stock

- makes sure nothing runs out.

The first stage is to designate a lockable area for consumables and other items. This may be anything from a small cupboard to a large storeroom. Goods should be stored sensibly, with the heaviest items at the bottom, loose items (eg pens) kept in boxes, and shelves clearly labelled. Packet labels should also be outward facing so that it is easy to identify different items. Goods are better kept on slatted shelves because the flow of air increases their 'shelf life'. Stock must be used in rotation so that the oldest stock is always used first. It is tempting to put new stock on top of older items (because it is easier!), but this will eventually result in a great batch of yellowing paper stuck at the bottom of the shelf which is of no use to anyone! You may like to know that putting new stock *alongside* existing stock is usually more successful – because it is easier. You can then tell staff always to issue stock from, say, the left-hand side.

Special storage areas may need to be available for hazardous items (eg some cleaning fluids) and valuable items (eg camcorders or audio machines). Very dangerous substances need to be stored in a chemical safe or bonded store to conform with Control of Substances Hazardous to Health (COSHH)

Regulations (see page 107). Other safety considerations include keeping large and bulky items low down, so that there is minimal lifting for staff, and providing a safety stool for access to high shelves. It is also useful if fast moving items are readily accessible. Finally, there should be a strict no-smoking policy in operation in any stationery store.

The second stage is to design a system to prevent people taking stock without permission and to ensure that you always know how much stock you are carrying at any one time. This is dealt with below.

Other considerations

Before you design a control system, however, you need to make several decisions, ie

- which items you are going to keep in stock and which you will only buy when required

- what maximum and minimum quantities should be specified in relation to your budgeted allowance for stock, the storage space available, projected usage and 'lead times' for supply (see below)

- what method of stock control would be appropriate – manual or computerised

- how often staff will be allowed to order stationery – and what procedure they will follow

- how often you will check the system to
  - replenish stock
  - destroy obsolete or spoiled stock
  - calculate expenditure
  - **audit** the stock, ie to check pilferage, damage, usage, etc.

The first stage in setting up a system is usually to assess each item of stock to decide whether it is **highly active** (frequently used), **less active** (infrequently used), or **non-active** (rarely used). At this point you should take into account factors such as seasonal demand, proposed projects and so on which could affect demand for different types of items.

You then need to consider how long it takes to deliver different items. Remember that the fewer goods you keep in stock, the more you will help to reduce costs for your organisation! Therefore, if a local supplier can deliver photocopying paper within 24 hours, you only need to keep a small amount in stock. This is known as a **just-in-time** (**JIT**) system and is usually favoured by most organisations, again because it keeps down costs. The time lag between ordering goods and their delivery is often known as **lead time**.

Alongside each item you now need to decide the **minimum stock** and the **maximum stock** you should hold. You should note that you will actually reorder items before the minimum stock figure is reached, to allow for delays in the new stock reaching you and the fact that whilst the stock is still on its way people will continue to need supplies.

It is now a simple matter to calculate just how much you will need for your stationery budget by calculating the full value of all stock if all items were at maximum level. Bear in mind, however, that you should always plan to operate slightly below your budget allowance in case you suddenly have an emergency on your hands. At this point you would need to agree figures with your boss before doing any ordering!

Stock issuing procedures

Assuming everything has gone according to plan, and you now have a cupboard full of stock, you would be more than foolhardy if you just left the door open for people to help themselves! For obvious reasons, there needs to be some control on the issuing of stock.

Stock can be recorded manually (on record cards) or on computer. The latter system is more frequently used these days. Quite simply, a stock-control system is a customised database on which items are recorded on computerised record cards. The advantage is that you can then print out various reports on expenditure or usage without having to wade through dozens of cards or covering pages in calculations.

A stock record – whether manual or on computer – usually has similar headings. An example is shown in Figure 5.1. You should note from this that all internal items are only issued against internal orders or requisitions. This is a key part of your control system and stops people ordering items whenever they feel like it – particularly if they need the requisition to be countersigned by their line manager. It also covers you against claims that you let your favourite people have whatever they want, whenever they want!

STOCK RECORD

Item	A4 Bond paper (white)		Max	100 reams
Supplier	Office Supplies Ltd		Min	20 reams
			Reorder level	35 reams

Date	Rec'd	Issued	Dept	Order	Balance

Figure 5.1 A stock record card

By recording each item which is outgoing you keep a **running balance** which should, of course, be identical to the actual number of items in stock. As this approaches your minimum level, you will reorder the items, and so on.

 Discussion point

As a trainee administrator you have set up a simple stock-control system and are very satisfied with the work you have done. You have agreed to accept orders twice weekly (on Mondays and Thursdays) and deliver stock on the following day in each case. However, within three weeks of it coming into operation a barrage of complaints is received about the lack of a system for dealing with emergency requests. The situation took a distinct turn for the worst last week when the mailroom forgot to request a large number of envelopes for a mail-shot. Not only were you unable to supply them in time, but you did not have enough to cope – and the supplier cannot deliver any more for at least a week.

Discuss as a group

1   a procedure you could instigate to deal with genuine emergencies

2   what could be done to prevent a repeat occurrence with the mailroom

3   what you should do now about your envelope crisis.

Administrative issues

Even with the best stock-control system, it is usual not to leave it to chance that it is still operating smoothly in six months' time! Apart from anything else, as an administrator you will be expected to give regular reports to your boss – if only as to how much is being spent, where there are differences in demand, which items are now obsolete, and so on. If your boss is not interested, then your accountants will most certainly be keen to know – especially when they are doing the year-end accounts! For that reason, if no other, you can expect to have to carry out a periodic **stock audit.** This is a check on what you actually have – as compared with what your system says you have! Do not be surprised if the two figures are slightly different, but do be surprised if you are not asked to supply an explanation as to how this has occurred!

The procedure is normally as follows.

- A manual stock check is taken. This means counting every item and checking off the total against the printed or written total for that item.

- If the counts match, then the item can be ticked off.

- If the counts show a discrepancy, it is usual to double check and then note the discrepancy. *All* discrepancies must be reported to your line manager.

Obviously, there is some importance attached to the size of the discrepancy. Three pens and two small boxes of paperclips are likely to be overlooked. Five camcorders, 23 boxes of disks and seven reams of paper are more likely to be the subject of a full investigation!

At the same time, you will be expected to make a note of any stock which is damaged, obsolete or surplus to requirements. This is all classified as wastage – not only does it represent wasted items but also represents wasted money, so you should try to keep all wastage as low as possible. Stock which is damaged may have to be thrown away unless it is reusable in any way. However, you should obviously note the cause of the damage and try to prevent it in future. Obsolete stock is that which is no longer useful, eg business cards of a representative who has left the company. Again, such stock may have to be written off unless there is some other use for it. Audio tapes, for instance, which no longer fit company machines may be sold at a discount to staff.

Surplus stock is that which has been ordered and is no longer needed. Ironically, this often refers to expensive items which everyone 'saved for a special occasion'. One never occurred, and you now have half a shelf full of coloured, glossy, printed folders that no one wants! If the items are still in excellent condition and are not specialised items, then you may be able to find someone else in the organisation who can use them or, if you have a *superb* relationship with your suppliers, you may be able to talk them into taking them back. However, remember that they have no legal obligation to do so.

Computerised reports

If you operate a computerised stock system, then you will be able to run a variety of reports, whenever you wish, to help you to control the system. These include

- a print-out of all stock currently held at cost price – this will give you an instant stock valuation

- a list of all stock which needs to be reordered because it is nearing its reorder level

- a list of all items and the number currently in stock – this is helpful when you undertake a physical valuation as there is usually a blank column for you to record the actual number of items on the shelves

- an audit trail – this lists every entry, in or out, which has been logged on the computer since the last audit trail was printed. This is very useful for solving mysteries! If your shelves only hold five reams of paper and your system is saying you should have 5 000, the audit trail may reveal that rather than someone surreptitiously trying to steal 4 500 reams of paper one night, the problem has simply been caused because a junior member of staff added rather too many zeros the last time he recorded a delivery!

Secretarial/PA issues

If you are a secretary or PA, then you may use a centralised system to obtain stocks of consumables. However, you may still have to store valuable items for your boss – such as a laptop computer or video tapes – where he or she can gain access to them quickly and where they will be secure from theft.

You may also be involved in securely storing 'confidential' or valuable items which have been purchased. An example of the first might be gifts for important clients at Christmas, or leather-bound diaries for senior executives. Valuable items include travellers' cheques and foreign currency, which may have been purchased for trips abroad. Your safest option in this instance is to store them in a company safe – if you are in doubt, ask the advice of the company cashier or someone who handles cash on the premises. Or talk your boss into buying a small safe for the office (or even a filing cabinet with a dial safe lock on the top drawer).

Finally, if you are storing items for your boss in a place to which both of you have access, make sure your boss tells you if he or she removes a quantity of stock. Otherwise you may get a shock if the first time you find out is when you go to the cupboard yourself and find two empty shelves.

Outsourcing office supplies

As you saw on page 37, outsourcing refers to giving the responsibility of supplying a business service to an outside provider. Some companies outsource – or contract out – their requirements for catering, cleaning and security. Others outsource their office supplies purchasing.

Stationery suppliers will be invited to tender to supply the service – and provide anything from IT supplies to paper and scissors. Because the goods can be ordered (sometimes electronically) and delivered within 24 or 48 hours, there is no need for the company to hold comprehensive stationery stocks nor to spend time comparing prices of different suppliers or completing complicated order forms. There is much less chance of wasted or damaged stock and the supplier will also advise office staff of new products and 'best buys'. In addition, there is a major saving of storage space and staff costs in running an internal stationery system. Because of these factors, the trend towards contracting out stationery supplies is increasing every year.

Discussion point

1 There have been two accidents in the stock room recently and several 'near misses'. Yesterday a member of staff tripped over a box behind the door and two days later hurt herself when a box of heavy paper fell from a top shelf. Today you were horrified to find a delivery man lighting a cigarette near the stock of flammable liquids.

As a group, devise a set of safety procedures to minimise the possibility of such incidents recurring.

2 You have started work for a small organisation with no recognisable stock-control system. You want to propose one to your boss, John Evans.

As a group, discuss the types of problem John Evans will face if no system is introduced as the company grows in size. Consider also the likely financial implications.

3 Your boss is livid, having read in the press that, despite one relatively recent change to telephone codes, there is about to be another for your district in 12 months' time.

   a As a group, brainstorm to decide how many items of company stationery may be obsolete once the phone codes change.

   b As an administrator, what could you do to minimise the financial cost to the company of replacing all these items?

Financial matters

● Introduction

The degree to which you are involved in financial matters will depend greatly on the size of the organisation which employs you. A large organisation will have its own Finance Department and, unless you are directly employed in this area, you may deal only with specific areas of finance which relate to your department or your boss, such as monitoring the ordering of goods and the expenditure of your own section or department against the agreed budget for these items. If you work in a small organisation, then you may be involved with a wide range of financial matters.

A financial matter is anything which involves **money.** This can be cash, cheques or anything else which relates to money. Because the control of money flowing in and out of the company is so vital, and because of risks of theft and fraud, there are likely to be specified procedures governing the way it is handled, the checks that are made and the actions that must be taken by staff.

Overall, financial matters in an office are likely to be those involving

- receiving payments from customers
- checking invoices and paying suppliers
- banking cash and cheques
- monitoring petty cash expenditure
- monitoring orders and expenditure against budget
- checking and recording expense claims
- recording information for entry into the books of account.

In addition, in some organisations, there may be some involvement with wages and salaries.

When not to pay!

A new administrator, employed by a small firm of computer consultants, appeared very knowledgeable and efficient. Shortly before the financial director was due to travel abroad on business, he therefore made arrangements for her to sign cheques on behalf of the business. Unfortunately, he did not introduce any procedures to control this process!

Soon after he had left, the administrator had cleared her desk of outstanding jobs. She then moved into her boss's office to tidy it up before his return. In his pending tray she noticed six invoices which had not yet been paid – to some were attached red reminders which worried her. Being conscientious, she duly made out cheques for each invoice and sent them off by first class post.

When her boss returned the following week he was hórrified to receive a phone call from the bank. The company account was in the red – to a considerable extent. When he investigated he soon found out why. The paid invoices had unfortunately not been matched by money received from the firm's customers. Being a patient man, he sat down and gave his administrator a lesson on cash flow.

Discussion point

The news item above is true! If you are also taking the Business Administration module, then you will learn about cash flow. In the meantime, discuss with your tutor why the executive was so concerned and where the administrator went wrong.

● Payments inwards

Basic issues

In any given period a company will receive payments and make payments. Inward payments may be made by cash, cheque, debit card or credit card – depending upon whether the company is dealing face to face with customers or receiving all payments through the post. There obviously needs to be some system for recording payments received – especially if these are in cash – to prevent fraud and theft. Large retail chains not only have electronic tills but also empty the tills at regular intervals for security reasons. Even if you are in a small office, and receive all your payments through the post, you need to record these carefully and make sure that payments are banked as soon as possible – both for security and to improve the bank balance (cash flow)!

All staff need to know how to check that cheques have been completed correctly. If debit or credit card payments are acceptable, then it is likely your organisation has a link to one of the major automated processing services such as Streamline (NatWest) and PDQ (Barclays). These enable cards to be 'swiped' through an electronic reader and the card balance and transaction to be logged by the bank computer. However, all staff must know how to check cards to ensure they are valid, check the signature on any documentation and what to do if a 'not acceptable' message is received *without* upsetting the customer (in case it is the bank which is at fault!).

Other considerations

Whilst a small shop may receive payments in cash for everything it sells, it is doubtful if your employer will be the same. Most businesses allow other businesses credit when they buy goods – literally, they buy now and pay later. **Credit control** procedures obviously need to be in place to check payments which are overdue, chase these and make sure customers are not offered additional credit until they have paid the amount owing. The usual procedure is for customers to be reminded if they have not settled an account for some time. The first stage is to issue a friendly reminder, but eventually this may even turn into a solicitor's letter or be handed over to a credit collection agency.

Companies normally record late payments on an **aged debtors' report.** This does not mean that the debtors (organisations or individuals that owe money) are old, but that the account is an old one. The report usually shows how long (in months) the account is outstanding. Those customers whose accounts are long overdue may be blacklisted and no further transactions are allowed with these organisations until the debt has been paid. Needless to say, you will not be the most popular person if you forget to check the blacklist and allow a customer who already owes a fortune to buy more goods on credit!

● Payments outwards

Basic issues

In cases where payments are being made, then it is usual for the cheques to be made out centrally. If you write cheques on behalf of your company, it is doubtful that you will also be given the authority to sign them. However, you must know how to write a cheque so that it conforms to standard bank policy and prevents any opportunity for fraud. The standard procedure in business is for more than one signature to be required on each and every cheque. This protects the signatories as well as the company. For very large payments the managing director's signature may also be required.

Large companies may have an automated system controlled by computer, which records the payments in the accounts system at the same time as printing the cheque and a remittance form. The latter tells the payee the reason for the payment. Automation means that the signatures of the executives are stored electronically and then reproduced on each cheque. Such machines are closely guarded and kept locked when not in use.

You must never make any payment unless you are authorised to do so. Invoices received from suppliers are usually carefully checked to make sure they are correct – and that the goods have been delivered intact – before they are verified for payment. Very large organisations do not usually employ staff to check every invoice, particularly those for very small amounts. In this case invoices over a certain amount, eg £200, would be checked individually and the remainder would be batch checked, ie certain invoices would be checked at random. It is standard practice for any errors or discrepancies to be referred to a supervisor or manager.

Other considerations

As with payments inwards, a close watch must also be kept on payments outwards. Generally, goods will have been supplied to your organisation on credit and the invoice will arrive shortly after delivery followed by a statement of account at the end of the month. The time taken to pay bills often varies depending upon the size of the organisation. Although a small firm may find it difficult to pay all its bills on time (because its customers have not paid *their* accounts), some large firms may deliberately withhold payment for two or three months. The reason is simple. A supplier may refuse to allow a small business any more goods unless it pays on time. A large and important customer is more difficult to refuse because of the potential loss of earnings and profit. A large company may take advantage of this to keep the money in its own account earning interest for as long as possible. It is important that you know the payment policy in your organisation, if you are involved in settling accounts.

● Banking transactions

Basic issues

All organisations have at least one bank account, and possibly several. There will also be a company cheque book and a paying-in book. Anyone dealing with financial matters needs to understand standard bank services and documentation, eg

- standing orders and direct debits

- paying-in slips

- bank statements.

In a small company you may be the recipient of standing order or direct debit payments, as well as arranging these to cover the firm's standard overheads such as electricity and gas usage.

Even if some private individuals are quite casual about income and expenditure, a company is unlikely to take the same approach! There are likely to be several additional requirements.

- All cheque counterfoils must include the relevant invoice number as well as the payee.

- All paying-in slip counterfoils must clearly document the reason for the payment and details of the invoice issued (ie date and number).

  These enable the accountants to check the reason for any payments into or out of the account.

- All items on the bank statement must be checked carefully against the counterfoils and must agree with entries made in the company's accounts. This actually saves money as the accountant would otherwise have to be paid to track any payments or revenue not recorded in the company accounts. Doing it 'in house' is therefore cheaper. In addition, a **bank reconciliation statement** may be prepared which shows how much is actually in the bank (which is recorded in the Cash Book), rather than how much the statement shows. This is important because, since the statement was printed, other transactions may have occurred which affect the balance (see Figure 6.1). In a small company, as you saw above, day-to-day information concerning the bank balance may be critical!

Markham Electronics PLC
Bank Reconciliation Statement
as at 31 October 199–

Balance as per Cash Book	£11 975
Add cheques issued, yet to be debited	£425
	£12 400
Deduct cheques deposited, yet to be credited	£950
Balance as per bank statement	£11 450

Figure 6.1 A company's bank reconciliation statement

Other considerations

Nowadays all organisations can choose the methods by which they carry out their banking transactions. Telephone banking and computerised banking are quite common. Used with a range of software packages, these help companies to manage both the cash flow (the money in and out of the company) and the accounts. The only time, therefore, that anyone needs to visit the bank is to deposit or withdraw cash. The requirement for cash has also fallen, given that most bills are paid by cheque or direct debit and most employees receive their salary directly into their bank account (see page 88). In the future the banks are predicting that even cash machines will not be necessary through the introduction of **virtual cash.** Using this system the customer holds a smart card (such as the new Mondex card), where money can be downloaded into the card down the telephone line.

For security reasons, an organisation which still needs to pay in or withdraw large sums of cash (eg a large retail store) can arrange to have the money collected or delivered through a specialised service such as Securicor.

The range of bank services available for businesses is greater than those available for private individuals. There is a range of different accounts. Surplus funds, for instance, should always be deposited in an interest-bearing account. The type of account will vary depending upon the degree of access required and the amount being put on deposit. Businesses may also wish to invest surplus foreign funds rather than converting them into sterling and paying the transaction costs. Special services exist to transfer money nationwide or worldwide if required. Organisations can set up special payment systems so that creditors and employees receive payment automatically. Banks can also provide economic information and give credit references on other companies. Banks, of course, also give loans and provide overdraft facilities to business organisations.

The scale of charges on any business account is higher than on any personal account. Therefore mistakes can prove expensive. Obtaining a copy bank statement or stopping a cheque – or even receiving a bank letter – are all charged to your account.

In their own interest!

Imagine your parents give you a cheque on Monday and, being short of money, you put it into your account. Do you ever wonder why it may take until Friday to 'clear' so that you can use the money? Or, if your parents paid you a weekly allowance by standing order, the money may disappear out of their account on Tuesday and not arrive in yours until Thursday – despite the fact you may both have accounts at the same branch? You would be well within your rights to think that, in these days of electronic transactions and computerised banking, the money should be transferred on the same day.

The reason for the delay is simply because, by holding it back for their own use, the banks can use that money on the money markets to earn interest (additional profit) themselves. And you can do nothing about it.

Even worse, small businesses suffer because of these policies. A small business with under 200 staff cannot pay wages through BACS (Bankers Automated Credit System) (see page 90) which transfers the money on the same day. Instead, individual banks offer their own smaller-scale financial transfer systems. However, in this case the money takes two days to go from one account to another – thereby penalising small businesses, which can least afford it. If cash flow is a problem, then every single day is important.

● Petty cash

Basic issues

'Petty cash' is the term used for the float of cash kept in an office for small items of expenditure. Your boss would be very surprised if you demanded a company cheque to pay for two Jiffy bags at the post office or to buy some milk! For that reason every office keeps a small amount of cash available.

Again, a procedure is in place to control expenditure by petty cash, otherwise it is doubtful if the money would last for very long! The usual method is known as the **imprest system.** This means that you are issued with a basic amount (the imprest) at the start of a period (say each month). You then record expenditure and at the end of the month add up how much you have spent. You then request that your petty cash is 'topped up' by this amount – known as 'restoring the imprest'. This means that you should always have a regular sum of cash at your disposal.

There is normally a special slip (called a **petty cash voucher**) which must be completed when money is required. These are not specially printed – they can be purchased at most stationers. Each voucher has a number and gives details of the expenditure (how much and the item purchased). The voucher must be countersigned by a manager before the money is paid out. The recipient must obtain a receipt for the money which is then clipped to the voucher to authenticate the purchase.

All the details are kept in a petty cash book. Analysis columns can be used so that you can record expenditure under different headings, eg travel, stationery, postage, sundry items, etc. This enables you to see how much is being spent in each area over each accounting period. An example of a typical analysis page is given in Figure 6.2.

Receipts £	Date	Details	Vchr No	Total payment £	VAT £	Travel £	Stat'ry £	Postage £	Office sundries £
300.00	4 Oct	Balance b/d							
	6 Oct	Phone cleaning	620	12.50	1.86				10.64
	8 Oct	Newsagent	621	18.00					18.00
	11 Oct	Jug kettle	622	13.50	2.01				15.51
	12 Oct	Taxi	623	18.00		18.00			
	14 Oct	Stamps	624	20.00				20.00	
	18 Oct	Tea and coffee	625	7.20					7.20
	20 Oct	Advance to BT	262	80.00		80.00			
	21 Oct	Milkman	627	15.00					15.00
	22 Oct	Print cartridges	628	75.00	11.17		63.83		
	25 Oct	Datapost fee	629	16.80				16.80	
	28 Oct	Flip charts	670	19.00	2.83		16.17		
		TOTAL		295.00	17.87	98.00	80.00	36.80	64.35
	1 Nov	Balance c/d		5.00					
300.00				300.00					

Figure 6.2 Extract from a petty cash book

Other considerations

If one of your jobs is operating the petty cash system, then you need to be aware of the procedures which are likely to operate in this area to prevent misuse or abuse of the system. You already know that vouchers must be countersigned by managers before a payment is made and that a receipt must be attached to verify the expenditure. However, it is important that you also know

- which payments are acceptable and which are not

- what to do if your money suddenly runs out

- how to balance the books at the end of the period.

Areas of expenditure to be covered by petty cash vary enormously from one organisation to another. So, too, do the amounts of imprest allowed and the size of payments remitted. In one company you may find the petty cashier in charge of a float of £500 with the authority to pay any amount up to £100 as long as it falls within specified categories. In another, the float may be only £50 with allowable transactions of up to £20. The key point is that you need to know the system you are operating and the degree of responsibility and authority you have.

If the money suddenly runs out, then this could be because expenditure this month (or week) is unusual and you need permission to renew the float immediately. If this happens frequently, it indicates either that the total amount of the float is too small, or that too many items are being processed through the system. Either way, you need to inform someone in authority immediately. You may then be asked to monitor the system and produce recommendations as to how much is now required as a float for the system to work satisfactorily.

You can easily check expenditure if you look back at your petty cash records over the previous periods. You will also be able to see the balance you have calculated each month, ie the amount of money you have had left over. It is significant if this has been progressively getting smaller – as this indicates that there has been a steady increase in expenditure. If, generally, there has been a healthy balance but just on the odd occasion there has been an emergency, then this is a different situation entirely (see also discussion point on page 85).

● Estimating costs and monitoring expenditure

Basic issues

Expenditure in most organisations is predicted and controlled by means of a budgeting system. In this case the organisation will have prepared detailed budgets to cover expenditure in a wide range of areas – from staffing to consumables. The budget is a financial plan which is drawn up from information about the prediction of sales and future revenue and the prediction of expenses, costs and future expenditure. The accountants can then work out predicted profits. These are only likely to become a reality if the actual income and spending match those forecast in the budgets. If the Sales Department fails to obtain planned orders and everybody ignores their budgets for expenditure and spends freely, then it is very likely that any predictions of profit will rapidly turn into a loss!

The importance of working to budgets cannot be overestimated in today's business world. For that reason you can expect your boss to place monitoring of expenditure high on his or her list of priorities – mainly because it is a key area where your boss is also accountable upwards for his or her performance. In order that people take responsibility for budgets, specific members of staff are usually designated as 'budget holders' for a particular area. If the degree of budget devolution is very high in your particular organisation, you could find that you are the budget holder for a specific area, such as office stationery or petty cash. In this case it is your responsibility to make sure there is no overspend in either area. More frequently, you will find that your boss is a budget holder and expects you to monitor expenditure across all the areas for which he or she has responsibility.

Monitoring expenditure can be carried out in a variety of ways but today is nearly always undertaken with the help of a computer. You can then record expenditure under different headings such as planned, committed and actual.

The other point of budgets is, of course, the fact that expenditure for any job must be planned and agreed. Therefore, within your own area you may be required to estimate the costs of implementing any suggestions you have made or buying certain items or undertaking certain jobs. It is then possible to check whether you could go ahead given the total budget allocation. You would normally have to submit your estimates for expenditure to your boss, who may ask you to revise these before they are acceptable. Once your estimates have been agreed you will, of course, be expected to 'deliver' what you have promised within the predicted amount.

Other considerations

At a junior level, office staff are often charged with the task of simply entering figures into the budget so that comparisons of planned and actual spending can be made. As an administrator or secretary you would be expected to take a more proactive role. For instance, your role may include

- identifying where there is a difference between planned and actual expenditure

- finding out the reason for the difference

- analysing the implications on the total budget

- giving regular feedback to your boss or producing regular management reports which summarise the financial situation

- costing planned changes in the office and then monitoring expenditure on these.

A difference between planned and actual expenditure is known as a **variance** – and variances can either be **adverse** (an overspend) or **favourable** (an underspend). In either case you need to investigate why this has occurred – and certainly your boss will want to be informed of any possible adverse variances. Even an underspend may have serious implications, some orders or claims for payment may be outstanding. Allowance must then be made for these if they will be paid in subsequent weeks or months. If you simply assume that an underspend means there is more money to go round – and promptly spend the surplus – you are likely to find yourself in serious difficulties later in the year!

Budgets are usually prepared and monitored by the company **management accountant.** This individual prepares management reports based on actual expenditure for senior management and will highlight significant variances in any area. Your manager will be expected to give an explanation for these, often in front of his or her peers or superiors. For that reason, never think that you can quietly forget a budget or costing problem – before long it is likely to be highlighted by someone important!

Discussion point

1   You are in charge of recording orders for office supplies and monitoring expenditure against budget. Your computer system records these under three headings – planned, committed and actual. Under which heading would you enter each of the following?
    a   The payment of an invoice for £850.
    b   The estimated cost of photocopying in December.
    c   An order for £600 for reference books. As yet the invoice has neither been received nor paid.

2   Your boss is annoyed about an overspend on the staffing budget in August and September, caused by the hiring of a temporary office worker from a local agency. You explain this was necessary because there were several large mail-shots and you needed additional help to stuff and seal the envelopes in time.

    As a group, decide
    a   what alternatives are possible in these circumstances
    b   what the difference in cost would be, if you implemented these alteratives, assuming you would save the temporary worker's wages for about 12 weeks each year.

3   All casual staff in your section are paid when they submit their time sheets at the end of the month. It is your job to monitor receipt of these, check the hours claimed against budgeted hours and monitor spending on these wages against the budget for casual staff wages. Recently, you have encountered several problems, particularly with
    •   members of the casual staff 'saving up' their time sheets and submitting them every 3 months
    •   casual staff being employed for extra hours by a manager without consulting anyone.

As a group, discuss
a the effect of such actions on the monthly budget
b the procedures which should be introduced to prevent this
  happening.

Expenses

Basic issues

Whilst petty cash is useful for small items of expenditure, your boss is
unlikely to pay any expenses he or she incurs in the line of business by this
method. Imagine you are on a three-day business trip which involves hotel
bookings, meals with customers, petrol, parking charges and so on. Given
that a petty cash float is usually only small, you would have no money left if
you financed a business trip by this method. Instead, most organisations
operate an expense claims system. Your boss will write up his or her
expenses every month – to which relevant receipts should be attached – and
be reimbursed with the amount spent. An alternative is for executives to be
issued with company credit cards which are used to pay all items of
company expenditure. One advantage of this method is that the bill from the
credit company can detail how much has been spent by each person and is a
useful check on individual and total spending. An alternative for expensive
trips is for a cash advance to be given to the executive concerned.

Other considerations

Just as you analyse general office expenditure, so, in a different way, you are
usually expected to analyse expenditure on expenses. Not all expenses
incurred by employees can be reclaimed. The Inland Revenue states that
these must have been incurred 'wholly, exclusively and necessarily' in the
performance of the duties of employment in order to be allowable against
tax. This means that the company can claim the expense justifiably to
reduce its final tax bill. Allowable expenses would include

* company car repairs and expenses

* hotel expenses

* protective clothing and uniforms

* training fees for a work-related course

* travel on business trips.

Non-allowable expenses would include

* expenses on ordinary clothes

* travel between home and business

- interest on credit cards

- ordinary meals (eg at or near the workplace).

However, some organisations have negotiated additional allowable expenses with the Inland Revenue. This is known as a **dispensation.**

All allowable expenses are normally allocated an expense code – and a code column is included on company expense forms. The code enables an analysis of expenditure across different areas to be carried out – similar to the analysis carried out for petty cash. It also links the expenses system to the overall organisational budget.

Anyone checking expense claims needs to check that

- all receipts are attached

- all relevant columns are completed and the calculations are correct

- only expenses allowable by the company have been claimed

- any advance payments which have been made to the executive have been recorded and deducted from the total

- any mileage claims are accurate (most offices keep their own charts for checking these).

Mistakes and omissions must be referred back to the author of the form with a query. Persistent mistakes or claims for excessive amounts should be referred to your manager.

Books of account

Basic issues

At some stage all the income received by the company and all the bills paid and expenses incurred by the company need transferring to the books of account. In the same way that the management accountant is responsible for budgets and actual performance, the accounts are used by the financial accountants to prepare the key financial accounts for the company, ie the profit and loss account and the balance sheet. On a more frequent basis, the figures are also used by the management accountants to check that income and expenditure are in line with any financial forecasts and the budgets for each department.

Other considerations

All financial transactions are reflected in the account books of the company, which are often kept using a computerised accounts system. These usually include the following.

- A **cash book,** which records the transactions into and out of the bank account.

- A **sales day book** and/or **sales ledger,** which records all the sales that have been made on credit and who has paid and who has not. Individuals or companies that owe money to the business are known as **debtors** and it is important that debtors with outstanding bills are promptly reminded that payment is still due.

- A **purchases day book** and/or **purchases ledger,** which records all the purchases made by the company. These are items for resale not capital goods or consumables. These books therefore contain information on the company's **creditors** – those individuals or organisations to whom the company owes money. They must be paid regularly or they may be less likely to allow you to buy goods on credit in the future.

- A **general ledger,** which records company expenses and purchases on fixed assets.

Without going too deeply into the theory of book-keeping, you should appreciate that it is someone's job to balance all the accounts at regular intervals. From these balances are calculated the profit and loss account of the organisation and the balance sheet. Incorrect or unclear entries are unacceptable – and cannot simply be crossed through or the auditors will query them. Even with the latest computer software any adjustments are noted in the audit trail which logs all entries. This is obviously to protect against fraud. You must therefore be careful to ensure that any figures you record on any documents are accurate and notify your boss immediately if you note any discrepancies. It is better to check immediately, than to find out later there is a serious problem which it is now very difficult to rectify!

● Wages and salaries

Basic issues

Finally, you may have some involvement with wages and salaries, particularly if you work in a small firm. However, in most organisations this has been simplified by the introduction of computer payroll systems which do all the calculations. In addition, many organisations have nowadays contracted out this work to an external agency to save employing specialist payroll staff.

Today it is unusual to find office staff involved in the calculation and payment of wages and salaries. Unless you work for a very small organisation, it is unlikely you will undertake such a specialist task – and even then there are computer packages to help you. However, a broad appreciation of the processes which are followed and the services which can help an organisation is important.

The term 'wages' used to be confined to hourly paid employees, and 'salaries' to weekly or monthly paid employees. Today most people are paid monthly (even some Saturday workers) and the term used is nearly always 'salaries'. However, for those whose salaries are calculated on hours worked, there needs to be some recording system. This may be automatic, through a clocking-in device, or manual, such as a time sheet. The hours of work are added up and multiplied by the hourly rate to find the gross pay. Employees on an annual salary will be paid every month (ie 12 times a year) or every four weeks (ie 13 times a year). Their monthly gross pay will be the

appropriate fraction of the annual salary, assuming no overtime has been worked.

From the gross pay are taken statutory deductions and voluntary deductions. Statutory deductions are income tax and National Insurance (NI). Voluntary deductions may include pension deductions, union subscriptions and Save-As-You-Earn (SAYE) or charitable payments. The amount remaining is the net pay.

Other considerations

Those involved in calculating wages need to know

- the procedures to follow to notify the Inland Revenue about new employees and changes to individual circumstances (eg sickness, maternity pay, leaving the company, etc.)

- the correct Inland Revenue forms to complete in each case and the relevant calculations which must be made

- how to read tax tables and National Insurance tables and calculate tax and NI due

- the payroll system in use and how to ensure all employees receive payments on time

- the month-end and year-end procedures to follow to ensure payments are made to the Collector of Taxes on time and all the relevant forms are completed.

Anyone who undertakes salary administration using a computer will find much of the hard work is done for them. The computer stores all the 'constant' (unchanging) data about each employee such as name, address, employee number and pay rate. Variable data are then entered each week relating to hours worked, sickness and so on. The computer does the rest. The payroll print-out can then be handed to a bank which will make arrangements to pay employees automatically into their bank account – a system usually referred to as credit transfer. Large organisations may use BACS – Bankers Automated Credit System – through which thousands of salaries in Britain are paid automatically (see also page 81).

Discussion point

1   As a group, discuss the types of banking procedure you carry out as a private individual. Talk to your tutor about how these may vary in a business organisation. If you do *not* have a bank account and have never made out a cheque or paying-in slip, then obtain some leaflets from a bank branch and talk about how these documents should be completed in order to be acceptable.

2   Your brother has recently started up his own business as well as working part time during the week. He only has one bank account and has not bothered to open a separate one for his business transactions.
    a   His accountants are concerned that he is putting into one account money which he receives from different sources, ie his job and his business. Why would this concern them? (As a clue, think about the tax he would have to pay on the business.)
    b   His accountants have warned him that if he continues to run one account his bill from them will be very high at the end of the year. Why would it be less if he separated the accounts?

3   Ask your tutor to show you an expense claim form which is used by staff at your college. Discuss the various headings, why they are used and how such a form should be completed.

● Financial matters

Administrative issues

Apart from understanding a considerable amount of the detail of any financial matters dealt with in the office, your job as administrator is esentially to ensure that all the procedures to **control** finance operate effectively.

Payments inwards

If you are employed in a company which receives cash regularly, then you may have to supervise staff and make sure that adequate procedures for cash handling are in place and are being followed. You should also make sure that your staff are aware of the correct procedures to follow when

- receiving payments by cheque, credit or debit cards

- giving information to customers on methods of payment they can use and the relevant forms to complete if necessary

- money must be cashed up and taken to the bank.

In addition, you will have to check that security and confidentiality procedures are in force (see Chapter 7, page 96) and monitor the work of your staff to ensure there are no errors or discrepancies.

Payments outwards

You will have to ensure that payments are made at the right time and that any queries are referred to your manager. You may also have to write cheques yourself – particularly in a small firm – even if you are not allowed to sign them. As an administrator, however, you certainly need to know who can sign cheques in an emergency, particularly if you work for an executive who is frequently away on business.

Banking transactions

You also need to know the full range of banking services available and be able to recommend a change when required to help your company. For instance, most organisations today try to persuade regular customers to pay their bills by direct debit or standing order. This reduces the need to monitor payments received and issue reminders. Not all organisations, however, can obtain permission to offer a direct debit facility for customers. Several safeguards are in operation to protect the general public from unscrupulous operators. Less protection is needed for the standing order system since, in this case, the order to pay comes from the customer and not from the company. However, operating such a system does not mean that bills do not need to be sent. All customers must be notified if there are any changes to their payments – otherwise the bank has the right to refund the money to the customer. If you regularly make mistakes in this area, the bank may withdraw the direct debit facility.

Petty cash

It is likely to be your job to ensure that the system works properly, that the accounts are kept neatly and that no unauthorised payments are made. You will also need to check the balance is correct at the end of the period and obtain the money to replenish the float. If there are any queries, they are likely to be referred to you!

Costings and budgets

The most basic task of an administrator is to ensure that all expenditure is being recorded accurately and that a check is kept on total amounts. You will need to negotiate the level of variance which may be permissible (eg plus or minus 2 per cent), the level at which your boss should be notified (eg variance between 2 per cent and 5 per cent) and the level at which emergency action must be taken (eg variance above 5 per cent).

You will also have the problem of being lobbied by your staff for new equipment and other items, and often have to present their case to your boss. This is when you may be asked to undertake a cost-benefit analysis which will identify the potential costs or savings resulting from the change (see Chapter 18 pages 413–414).

If there have been problems keeping to budget in a particular year or money for resources is scarce, then you may even be involved in a cost-savings exercise to try to reduce expenditure from the forecast levels.

Expenses

You are likely to be the one who answers queries, refuses to accept expenses which are not allowable against tax – and even the one who shows new employees how to follow the system. If you are notified of updates (such as additional Inland Revenue dispensations), then it will be your job to ensure that all staff know about them.

Books of account

As an administrator you are less likely to deal with the financial accountant than the management accountant. It is the latter who watches the company finances on a day-to-day basis and monitors actual income and expenditure against planned income and expenditure. You are likely to be told, very quickly, if you are going over budget, ie spending more than you should. This may mean that cutbacks are made to bring spending back into line. You may even have the unenviable job of having to refuse staff requests because of lack of funds.

Wages and salaries

It is said that a sensible company makes sure that there are no problems in this area. Nothing irritates staff more than a mistake or delay with their pay. Even the most reasonable individuals can suddenly turn quite nasty if they receive much less than they expected at the end of the month. This is understandable if they have financial commitments to meet.

Your job is to sort out the problem, to the best of your ability, as quickly as possible. It may mean referring it to a specialist wages section or even to an external agency to see what can be done – or contacting the tax office yourself. Whatever you do, be *seen* to be taking some action – and report back on progress regularly. If you are totally desperate, you could always pass on the telephone number of the external agency/tax office to the employee concerned so that the problem can be sorted out directly between those concerned.

As an administrator you may be responsible for checking that new staff are included on the payroll system. This will usually mean handing them the appropriate forms to complete with their own details and their bank details. You will also be responsible for removing from the system staff who leave. Finally, you may be the person who receives time sheets for checking and authorisation. These should always take top priority, particularly if there is a set date by which all pay claims must be submitted for payment each month.

Secretarial/PA issues

Unless you work for a very small organisation, where you might be doing all the tasks above plus keeping the accounts, as a secretary/PA you will mainly be involved in financial matters relating to your own boss. These are likely to include

- obtaining UK and foreign currency for trips plus travellers' cheques – preferably paying the lowest possible commission charges

- completing expense claims on behalf of your boss

- making sure your boss's company credit cards are current and finding out the countries in which these can be used

- ensuring your boss's company charge card (eg American Express and Diner's cards) accounts are settled promptly

- arranging for money to be transmitted to other parts of the UK or overseas, sometimes in an emergency

- dealing with any problems, such as an important customer complaining his or her bill is incorrect or a supplier pressing you for payment.

You are unlikely to deal with salary issues relating to your boss, who is likely to prefer not to divulge what he or she is paid.

However, if your boss is concerned with budgets and targets for the department, then you may be given the job of investigating any variances in these areas. This means methodically checking records and accounts to make sure no omissions, errors or duplications have been made, and notifying the relevant people (including your boss) if you find any mistakes. If the variance is adverse, it also means identifying areas where overspending has occurred and then finding the reason for this. In some cases it may be unavoidable (eg a price rise); in others it may be because the costs on individual items have not been monitored closely enough. At senior level you may be expected not only to report on this situation but also to make suggestions as to what remedial action should now be taken.

The key points you must bear in mind at all times are

- the importance of accurate financial forecasting and accounting for company profitability

- the financial (business) needs of your boss.

All bosses have a healthy respect for profit and try to monitor costs and expenditure to keep them as low as possible. The more you can help them in achieving this, the more popular and successful you are likely to be!

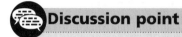

Discussion point

1   As a group, obtain from a variety of local bank branches some leaflets and booklets detailing services to business. (If you are also taking the Business Administration examination, then you will study bank services as part of this module.)

    Note down the services which are likely to be used by

    *   a small firm which has recently started in business
    *   a shop with town-centre premises
    *   a large organisation with over 400 employees which trades on an international basis.

2   Find out if any members of your group have worked on a part-time or temporary basis and what types of financial transactions they have been involved in. In particular, discuss the type of training they have received for dealing with cash and receiving cheques, credit and debit cards and the security measures which were in force.

3   Figure 6.3 shows a petty cash book, with analysis columns, which has been balanced at the end of the month. Go through each entry with your tutor, checking that you understand what has been written.

Receipts	Date	Details	Vchr No	Total payment	Expenditure headings				
					VAT	Travel	Stat'ry	Enter-taining	Office sundries
£				£	£	£	£	£	£
200.00	3 May	Balance b/d							
	3 May	Coffee	223	3.50					3.50
	7 May	Art paper	224	11.75	1.75		10.00		
	10 May	Buffet lunch	225	42.00				42.00	
	11 May	Taxi fare	226	5.00		5.00			
	14 May	Flowers	227	15.00					15.00
	17 May	Poster adhesive	228	8.05	1.05		7.00		
	17 May	Milk	229	23.00					23.00
	21 May	Window cleaner	230	8.00					8.00
	22 May	Petrol	231	16.45	2.45	14.00			
	25 May	Sandwiches	232	8.50				8.50	
	26 May	Marker pens	223	2.35	0.35		2.00		
		TOTAL		143.60	5.60	19.00	19.00	50.50	49.50
	1 June	Balance c/d		56.40					
200.00				200.00					
56.40	1 June	Balance b/d							
143.60	1 June	Cash received							

Figure 6.3 Balancing the petty cash book

4 Discuss as a group how you would deal with the following problems both immediately and, where appropriate, to prevent their recurrence.

a There is a £50 discrepancy between the record of cash takings for the day and the actual amount in the till.

b Your boss sees nothing wrong in sending a junior employee alone to pay large sums of money into the bank.

c A new representative has put in an unreadable expense claim, with no receipts attached, for the third month in succession.

d A student is employed over the summer. He is upset to find that tax has been deducted from his first month's salary.

e Your junior has lost the last two months' bank statements.

f The Finance Department sends a memo to inform you that your photocopying costs for last month are twice the budgeted amount.

g A very important customer rings you with an urgent order. She has not paid her account for the past three months.

h One member of the hourly paid staff has not submitted his time sheet for last month. You know he has personal problems as his wife is seriously ill in hospital. Unless it is checked and authorised by noon tomorrow, it will miss the agency deadline for payment this month.

7 Security and confidentiality

Introduction

In the last chapter the word 'security' was mentioned several times, particularly when referring to cash. However, cash is not the only valuable item on company premises. Equipment needs to be secure, as does important information and documents. Organisations are often more concerned, for instance, about the information stored on computer than the value of the machine itself. The computer can be insured, but the information which is stored may be irreplaceable. It is for this reason that back-up copies should be made and stored in a separate secure area. In addition, the organisation has legal responsibilities for the security of computer-based information under the requirements of the Data Protection Act (see page 220).

Information can only be secure, however, if there are security systems in force *and* if people treat confidential matters with respect. It is plainly useless to store important and confidential documents under lock and key if someone in the office is telling everybody what they contain!

For that reason there is usually a range of systems in place to try, as far as possible, to minimise both security and confidentiality risks.

Basic issues

A security system was once described as 'a system for keeping intruders out and valuable equipment in'! This is not far from the truth. However, as an employee you may consider that simply protecting equipment is not good enough – what about you, for instance, and your personal possessions?

All organisations have a range of security measures in place. Installations which deal with highly secretive work will obviously be more security conscious than others. However, today security guards, video cameras and strengthened glass are a familiar sight. So, too, are bollards and grass mounds to prevent ram-raiding, and burglar alarms to warn of break-ins.

Generally, there are three main objectives in installing security systems. These are

- to prevent buildings from being entered or vandalised by unauthorised persons

- to protect employees from personal attack or assault

- to minimise burglaries and theft. This includes theft and misuse of information, as well as theft from employees.

It is usual, therefore, for basic security measures to include the following five areas of control and protection.

1 Control over entrances and exits

Usually, visitors are only allowed to use one entrance and the number of entrances and exits is kept to a minimum. However, given that employees will need to leave the building quickly in an emergency, there may be emergency exit doors which can only be opened from the inside or which open automatically if the alarms sound. These must never be left open or wedged open, otherwise the security purpose is completely defeated!

Entrances to company car parks are usually protected by barriers which will only open when a special identification card is inserted. So that security officials can check the car park, only authorised vehicles may be parked – staff are usually issued with vehicle passes which must be displayed on the windscreen.

Entrance to highly secure buildings or areas is by key code, palm print or voice recognition. Electronic badges which trigger doors to open automatically can also be worn by nominated holders. However, there are obvious dangers here as these can be lost or stolen.

2 Control over visitors

Visitors are issued with passes which must be returned when they leave. Areas that are restricted should be clearly marked, so visitors know not to enter. Staff should be trained to challenge visitors who appear to be unauthorised or who are found in unlikely places. It is possible to do this without causing offence, simply by making a polite enquiry if you can help. If the reaction is strange or suspicious, do not press the matter, leave and contact security or your manager.

3 Control over buildings

All buildings are usually illuminated during the hours of darkness so that a person trying to enter can be seen easily. In addition, burglar alarms and anti-scaling devices such as spikes on roofs and walls help to deter intruders. Closed-circuit television (CCTV) may be used to flash from one area to another at constant intervals, or to provide continuous film which can be studied in the event of an incident.

Keys are restricted to nominated holders and a list of these is kept in a secure place. All windows and doors are checked each night and rooms (and toilets) checked to ensure they are empty.

4 Protection for staff

Walkways and car parks should be illuminated at night and security cameras installed. Those working in vulnerable (public) areas should have panic buttons behind their desks and be protected by toughened glass screens. All staff who may have to deal regularly with members of the public should receive special training in how to reduce tension if a potentially violent situation threatens. Those working in isolated areas (eg patrolling the perimeter of the building at night) should be protected by two-way radio.

Special security arrangements should be made for the handling or transportation of cash. This does not only mean visiting the bank. Staff responsible for emptying vending machines or cash registers are also vulnerable. Special goggles should be worn to protect against acid attacks and the cashier must always be accompanied by at least one security person. Cashiers are less vulnerable if they 'post' high denomination notes into a security box as they are received, and/or if their cash registers are emptied regularly (the latter should always be emptied and left with the drawer open at night). Pay phones should be converted to card phones to reduce vandalism.

5 Protection for equipment

All valuable items should be tagged or security marked for identification. Alarms should be fitted to computers. In some cases special security frames are used to lock a PC into position. These also prevent unauthorised access to the equipment, given that today many thefts are for the computer chips rather than the equipment itself.

If a piece of equipment is highly valuable, it can be anchored by means of a special security chain. It should be against company policy for valuable items to be stored near public areas, and the delivery and collection of goods must be closely controlled to ensure that

- goods being received are put away as quickly as possible

- items being collected are only handed to the authorised person(s).

Small items of equipment are more likely to go missing – as they are less noticeable in transit! For that reason such items must be stored in a lockable store room or cupboard.

A final word

All members of staff must be aware that there is little point in having security systems in operation if employees gossip outside the office about everything that is happening – or are prone to chatter to every caller – no matter who they are! Imagine the situation where a visitor quickly discovers that the receptionist is very talkative and obviously bored. It is a simple matter for a skilled person to find out all sorts of information about the organisation and its personnel – and to take advantage of this. Although it now seems very old-fashioned, during the Second World War there was a slogan 'Careless talk costs lives'. Although this related to confidential information about army manoeuvres and attack plans, if you tell a complete stranger that your friend is never around at 10 am because she takes the previous day's takings to the bank at that time, it may be tantamount to the same thing!

● Other considerations

Most of the aspects of security discussed so far refer to physical items. However, there are other important areas of security which relate to less tangible aspects of resources.

Security of information

There is a considerable overlap between the security of information and confidentiality – as you saw above. For information to be secure, then it has to be protected both from theft and from unauthorised dissemination! The Data Protection Act (see page 220) means that all organisations have a legal responsibility for data stored on computer. Soon this will cover paper documents as well, so it is better to have the same healthy respect for all information – no matter how it is held (see page 221).

There are various reasons why information may be confidential.

- It could be personal details about staff which they would not wish other people to know.

- It could be about new product developments, which would be of interest to competitors.

- It could concern sensitive financial details or employee negotiations which, if made available to the local media, could result in unwelcome publicity for the company.

- It could refer to possible internal plans which have not yet been agreed.

- It could relate to activities or habits a thief would like to know about – as you saw above.

It could even be a combination of these. For instance, if sensitive talks on possible redundancies because of a downturn in trade were leaked, this would frighten staff (possibly without just cause) and cause banner headlines. The last thing anyone needs is to find out by reading the local paper that he or she may be made redundant!

For these reasons a variety of security measures are used to protect important or confidential information, including the following.

- All confidential documents are put into an envelope before being despatched, even those for internal distribution.

- The number of recipients of confidential documents is closely checked and monitored – and kept to a minimum.

- Files containing sensitive information are locked in special filing cabinets and distribution/photocopying is restricted.

- A series of passwords on the computer system restricts the level of access to different users. Access can also be designated to certain users at different levels of authority on many software packages and by the network administrator on a networked (linked) system. Only those with a high-level authority code can access sensitive information.

- Encryption (coded information) is used in conjunction with other computer security measures (including special programs and files) to protect highly sensitive information from computer hackers who try to access the system illegally.

- Strict security measures control the use of floppy disks to prevent the introduction of a virus into the computer system. A virus is a rogue program which can wipe out large amounts of information or even disable the whole system. For that reason staff are likely to be forbidden to use any external disks and a virus detection system will be installed in the computer system.

- Confidential documents should never be taken into public areas (let alone left there!) nor typed on computers where visitors could see the screen.

- Sensitive documents are destroyed in a shredder, not simply torn once and placed in a wastepaper bin.

Security of personal possessions

Another key area where staff are prone to be complacent is in looking after their personal possessions. Even in the smallest and friendliest of offices thefts do occur. Don't become a victim yourself. You would be amazed at the amount of cash some people bring into work – often because they have withdrawn money from the bank at lunchtime and left it in their purse or wallet. They then leave their handbag or jacket by their desk and go out of the room. The problem is compounded if they also leave their car or house keys in the same place!

There are several important items which should never be taken into the workplace unless it is essential. These include credit and debit cards, cheque books, and passports. A cash card is normally quite sufficient, but telling everyone that you have just withdrawn £200 for your holiday is obviously foolish.

Staff must also know the procedures to follow if anything goes missing. The last thing you want is a mad panic with wild accusations being hurled around which will take months to forgive. If, after careful searching, the item is nowhere to be found, then an accurate description must be compiled for security purposes, the incident must be reported to the police and the company lost-property office must be notified immediately – in case the item is handed in.

Discussion point

Read the conversation below between a bored receptionist and a visitor. Then answer the questions that follow.

RECEPTIONIST (*yawning*): Yes, can I help you?

VISITOR (stranger – male): I was hoping to see the personnel manager. I'm looking for a job.

RECEPTIONIST: I doubt we've any vacancies here. We've been told there may be redundancies soon.

VISITOR (*curiously*): I'm surprised about that, I always thought this company did very well.

RECEPTIONIST: Huh! Managers here are a load of rubbish, that's what I say. Apparently we've lost lots of business to that new firm down the road.

VISITOR (*interested*): Never! Anyway, I'm sure someone as talented as you would find a job anywhere.

RECEPTIONIST (*warming to her theme*): Do you think so? I'm certainly not appreciated here, you know. Look at all this work I've to get through today – I'm expected to talk to people, type loads of documents, balance the petty cash and answer the phone as well. (*Points to petty cash box on counter and letter-headed paper near her.*)

VISITOR: It must be hard work. Do you have to work very late?

RECEPTIONIST: Not really. Everyone gets out on the dot of 5 round here. They've had enough by then.

VISITOR: I used to work for an organisation where everyone always left on time. I once left an important document on my desk and rushed back from the car park. By that time, everything was locked up for the night!

RECEPTIONIST: Good heavens, you wouldn't find that happening around here. Last week I left my keys on the desk and came back half an hour later. There wasn't a soul around and all the offices were unlocked. I don't think security lock up until about 6.30 – they're all busy having a cup of tea and a chat between 5 and 6.

VISITOR: Security sounds a good job to have! Are there any vacancies?

RECEPTIONIST: No. They're not employed by us anyway – we hire them in I think. We've some new lads on this week and they haven't a clue what they're doing. Most of them seem to be about 16!

VISITOR: So I can forget getting a job here, then?

RECEPTIONIST: Well, you might stand a chance if you're good with computers. We all use them now. Everything's stored on them – but half the time they don't work properly.

VISITOR: What would I need to know? They look very hard to me.

RECEPTIONIST: Oh, no – they're easy. Let me show you. Look, I simply put my staff identification number in – 420 – and then my password. That's supposed to be secret – it doesn't show on screen when I type it.

VISITOR: Do you never forget it? I'm sure I would.

RECEPTIONIST: I used to – and got into trouble. At the moment I'm using the name of my dog – I'm not likely to forget that, am I?

VISITOR: I had a lovely dog until recently – then he died. I was really upset.

RECEPTION: Oh, I couldn't stand that. I've had Sadie since she was a puppy.

(*Phone rings – rear of office*)

RECEPTIONIST: It's been really nice talking to you – but I'm sorry I can't help you. I'd better answer that though. Call in again, won't you?

VISITOR: Oh, don't worry, I will.

1 Identify as many lapses in security as you can. Then decide what you should do, as an administrator, to improve security, confidentiality (and loyalty!) in your organisation.

2 What would be the likely consequences if the visitor was
   a a journalist
   b a computer hacker
   c a thief or burglar
   d a fraudster.

3 Discuss as a group the *techniques* the visitor used to obtain the information he wanted. Beware of the same techniques being used on you!

Don't turn your head ...

The more casual staff you have, the more vigilant you will need to be about security. Imagine the problems for a large hotel, which not only has a large number of temporary staff, such as those who do seasonal work, but which also hosts important events – such as party political conferences – where the police check all visitors and staff beforehand.

The manager at a well-known hotel in the UK once gave a lecture to trainee secretaries and administrators on his security problems. He had experienced several shocks, he said, when he first took over the job. He noticed that huge quantities of food went missing from the kitchens each Friday (to save shopping time and expense!). He had also visited the cellar to replenish the drink stock one day and found only the top carton of whisky contained full bottles – all the rest were empty, but neatly stacked underneath. His worst shock, however, came the day that 12 new vacuum cleaners were delivered. They were left in the corridor for 10 minutes whilst the janitor was found to move them. In that time, they all disappeared!

● Administrative issues

As an administrator you have two main objectives.

- To make sure – a far as you can – that staff are vigilant about security and confidentiality. Generally, they will become quite complacent, especially if nothing has happened to make them think about it for months.

- To identify possible breaches of security which will affect your area. For instance, if a new piece of equipment is installed or a new system is set up, then you need to think about the security implications in each case.

You can increase staff vigilance by being alert yourself. If you see a member of staff putting her handbag by her desk, then leaving the office, remind her that she needs to be careful. If you notice a new member of staff being casual when cashing up money, then have a quiet word. This is kinder than taking the action resorted to by one administrator, who became so tired of seeing high denomination notes left on the desk of one employee that she removed some when he wasn't looking and then watched him panic for 15 minutes before telling him what she had done!

Equipment can be a security risk if there is no procedure for dealing with confidential documents. Security measures may include the following.

- More sophisticated fax machines have security features, such as passwords or pass codes. Incoming confidential messages can be stored in memory and only printed out when the correct password has been entered.

- Computer users should not be allowed to leave their PC switched on and go out of the room. If they are using e-mail, this gives anyone entering the office the opportunity to read their messages and send messages in the user's name, unless there is a separate e-mail password system in operation.

- There should be a separate area if high-level confidential work is carried out or if large sums of money are handled. This should be well away from reception, and users should have their own keys.

- Anyone using a photocopier to produce copies of confidential documents should be trained to check the glass afterwards. Many people forget to remove the original!

Needless to say, all administrators should be the epitome of discretion! No matter what you know or what you hear, you are paid to keep your mouth firmly closed. Be aware that the tactics used by the visitor on pages 101–2 can easily be employed by the office gossip from another department to find out what is happening in your area! Don't be deceived by flattery, shared confidences or sympathy into disclosing information in a way you will later regret.

● Secretarial/PA issues

You are more likely to deal with confidential information if you rise through the ranks to PA level, than you will as an administrator. This is particularly true if you work for a high-flying executive. Unless your boss can trust you implicitly, then neither of you can function properly. He or she can hardly do the job properly if half the time you cannot be told what is going on!

In this type of job you are more likely to be producing confidential documents and to be privy to confidential information. The type of procedures you need to follow are outlined below.

- Position your PC screen so that it cannot be seen by casual callers. If someone moves around the desk, turn down the brightness or simply switch off the VDU. If you need to leave the room, close down the system first or switch off your screen and lock the door.

- Make sure you lock away all computer disks and documents at the end of each day.

- Keep a folder on your desk so that you can always put sensitive documents inside if you have an unexpected visitor.

- Never leave tapes containing confidential dictation on an audio machine – lock these away or wipe them after transcription is complete.

- Keep a personal (small) shredder next to your desk.

- Never take more copies than you need. Use your printer, if possible, rather than the photocopier.

- If you find anyone in your office unexpectedly, tell your boss – particularly if the individual is acting suspiciously.

- Be wary of being 'pumped' for information. If in doubt, always feign ignorance. If you convince someone you do not know the answer, he or she will see there is little point in continuing to ask you!

Discussion point

1 You are administrator in an office with five staff. Your manager has recently appointed a new part-time member of staff who is a mature woman with several years' experience. The paperwork was handled by your staff.

At the end of the second day she asks to see you. She is upset that the staff seem to know everything about her – from her date of birth to why she left her last job. She is also extremely annoyed that her salary seems to be public knowledge.
   a Discuss how these lapses could have occurred.
   b What, as administrator, would you do to prevent a recurrence?

2 Your boss has a leaflet regarding a series of security seminars on her desk. As a group, discuss the type of organisations which will be interested in attending each one.
   - Mailroom safety and security – X-ray screeners and letter-bomb detectors.
   - Counter industrial espionage – secure communications equipment and encryption devices.
   - Dealing with workplace violence.
   - CCTV – its use and applications, including covert (hidden) cameras.
   - Computer security – protecting hardware and chips.
   - Computer security – protecting data and information.
   - Security for buildings with public access requirements.
   - The threat of terrorism – assessing the risks.

8

Health and safety

● Introduction

The key issues relating to health and safety legislation – and the responsibilities of employers and employees – are covered fully in the companion book to this, *Business for Advanced Secretarial Students.* For that reason, this book only contains an overview of the main aspects of legislation which need to be known by administrators and secretaries. Instead, the focus is on the practical application of health and safety procedures to ensure that the requirements of the relevant Acts are met. This includes procedures for emergencies, such as accidents and first aid, risk assessment, office equipment in general, work stations and VDUs in particular, plus other considerations, such as good housekeeping and workflow.

● Basic issues

Health and safety in Britain is covered by one main Act of Parliament – the Health and Safety at Work Act 1974 (HSWA). The HSWA is an 'enabling' or 'umbrella' Act, which means that Regulations can be introduced to update or modify it.

Since 1974 a series of Regulations has been introduced, some by the British government and others through the European Union. A list of all these Regulations is given in Figure 8.1 – and more detailed information on each one is contained in *Business for Advanced Secretarial Students.*

Health and safety in the workplace is monitored in Britain by the Health and Safety Executive (HSE), which employs inspectors who visit industrial premises to check safety standards and question employees. Offices and shops are visited by environmental health officers who are employed by the local authority. Any inspector can take enforcement measures to ensure that dangerous practices are stopped immediately.

Health and safety legislation requires *both* employers and employees to comply with certain minimum requirements. Both can be held responsible in law if they fail to do so. For that reason there will be company policies and procedures in operation to make sure that the law is complied with, as well as codes of practice so that employees know what to do in any given situation.

In many large organisations there is a safety committee with designated safety representatives. This committee monitors health and safety systems and procedures as well as bringing to the attention of management any working conditions which are in breach of the legislation – or changes which must be considered in order to comply with new legislation.

Health and Safety at Work Act 1974

This Act applies to all work premises and requires all **employers** 'as far as is reasonably practicable' to ensure the health, safety and welfare at work of their employees; prepare and continuously update a written statement on the health and safety policy of the company; and allow for the appointment of safety representatives selected by a recognised trade union. In addition, it requires all **employees** to take reasonable care of their own health and safety and that of others who could be affected by their activities and to cooperate with their employer on health and safety matters.

Health and Safety (First Aid) Regulations 1981

These cover the provision of first-aiders and their training (see page 110).

Control of Substances Hazardous to Health (COSHH) 1988, Control of Substances Hazardous to Health (Amendment) Regulations 1991/2

These Regulations cover the storage and use of hazardous substances and related protective clothing.

Electricity at Work Regulations 1989

These cover the design, construction, use and maintenance of electrical systems and installations.

Noise at Work Regulations 1989

These are concerned with noise hazards in the workplace and relevant protective clothing and equipment.

Fire Precautions Act 1971, Fire Precautions (Places of Work) Regulations 1995

These specify the actions which must be taken by owners of designated premises, eg offices, shops and factories, to reduce the risk of injury by fire and give the fire authority the power to prosecute companies which do not comply with the Regulations (see page 111).

Workplace (Health, Safety and Welfare) Regulations 1992

These cover specific areas of health, safety and welfare to supplement the provisions of the Health and Safety at Work Act. They relate to the working environment, general safety, facilities for employees and housekeeping (see page 119).

Management of Health and Safety at Work Regulations 1992

These introduced risk assessments and specify how risks must be assessed, recorded and minimised (see page 113).

Display Screen Equipment Regulations 1992

These were designed to protect employees who regularly use VDUs and cover both workstations and working conditions (see page 115).

Provision and Use of Work Equipment Regulations 1992

These regulations cover the maintenance of equipment and the training given to staff who operate equipment (see page 114).

Personal Protective Equipment at Work Regulations 1992

These cover the provision of protective clothing and equipment and its storage (see pages 118–119).

Manual Handling Operations Regulations 1992

These cover the manual handling (eg lifting and transportation) of goods (see page 118).

Health and Safety (Safety Signs and Signals) Regulations 1996

These determine the shape and colour of safety signs. They also include instructions applying to red fire-fighting equipment signs (see page 112).

Reporting of Injuries, Diseases and Dangerous Occurrences Regulations (RIDDOR) 1995

This is an updating of the 1985 Act which compels organisations to notify the Health and Safety Executive (HSE) of serious accidents or prolonged periods off work. The new legislation now includes as 'accidents' acts of violence done to people at work, and also requires organisations to notify the HSE of serious incidents affecting visitors to the workplace as well as employees.

Figure 8.1 Health and safety legislation, 1974–95

The Safety Representatives and Safety Committees Regulations 1978 give trade unions the legal right to appoint safety representatives provided that the union is recognised by the employer for negotiations. The union members, not the management, elect the safety representatives. The number of representatives varies depending upon the size of the organisation, the type of work carried out and the potential hazards. If you work in your local town hall, therefore, you can expect considerably fewer safety representatives than if you work in a large chemical or nuclear-processing plant.

Whether or not you are appointed as a safety representative, as an administrator or secretary you can expect to be involved in several aspects of health and safety. You will need to be a role model for junior staff in your own working practices and should monitor your own area(s) for possible risks and suggest improvements – as well as being able to cope with a range of emergencies which may occur. You will also have to monitor the procedures which exist and make suggestions for changes as and when required.

 Discussion point

1　Read the code of practice for dealing with accidents in Figure 8.2. Discuss with your tutor how this differs in any way from the procedures for dealing with an accident, either in your college or at any premises where you or your colleagues are employed part time.

2　Fire procedures were probably part of your college induction procedures.

 a　Check that you know what to do in the event of an emergency evacuation.

 b　Consider other precautions which can be taken to lessen the risk of fire. Think of fire exits, fire doors, fire equipment, smoking/non-smoking policies, disposal and storage of hazardous materials, and so on. As a group devise your own code of practice for fire precautions and check this with your tutor.

3　Can you think why, in an evacuation because of fire, you should leave your personal belongings behind, whereas if there was a bomb scare you should take them with you?

MARKHAM ELECTRONICS PLC
CODE OF PRACTICE

Accident Reporting

1 By law, all accidents must be recorded. A yellow Accident Report
Form must be completed giving full details of
- the person(s) involved – name and address
- the date and time the accident occurred
- the place it occurred
- the cause and nature of the injury
- the name, address and occupation of any witness or third person
reporting the accident.

This report must be sent to the Safety Officer within 24 hours of
the accident occurring. Staff should note that if they are injured
in an accident which is not reported, they may lose any DSS benefits
to which they would otherwise have been entitled.

2 'Near miss' accidents must be recorded on blue Accident Report Forms
and forwarded to the Safety Officer. This enables Safety
Representatives to check and monitor potential hazards and recommend
improvements.

3 If an accident results in injury, the nearest first-aider must be
contacted immediately. A list of first-aiders is kept in all
administrative offices. If there are any difficulties summoning a
first-aider, telephone the company emergency extension, 2020.

4 First-aid boxes are kept in all administrative offices and it is the
responsibility of the departmental first-aider to ensure that these
are kept fully stocked.

5 No drugs must be issued to an injured person in case of harmful
consequences or an allergic reaction.

6 In the case of a serious injury, the first-aider will recommend
whether a doctor or ambulance should be called. In the case of a
less severe injury which needs hospital attention, the first-aider
may order a taxi, at the company's expense, to take the injured
person to hospital.

7 In the case of a serious accident, the Safety Officer must be
contacted immediately. Nothing in the vicinity must be moved until
his or her arrival unless there is a substantial risk of another
accident occurring. The Safety Officer will be responsible for
notifying the relevant authorities and carrying out a detailed
accident inspection, in conjunction with a nominated Safety
Representative.

8 Frequency and type of accidents will be constantly monitored by the
Safety Committee. Accident procedures will be reviewed annually. The
Safety Committee is responsible for reviewing accident frequency in
its annual report.

Figure 8.2 A code of practice should explain procedures to follow in the case of an accident

Other considerations

The main areas of health and safety in which you can expect some involvement include

- dealing with emergencies, including illness, accidents and evacuations
- risk assessment in the workplace including
  - identifying hazards
  - monitoring layout and workflow
- ensuring that requirements relating to the positioning and use of office equipment are complied with and that staff are trained to use such items correctly
- checking that VDUs, workstations and conditions for those involved in IT work conform to the Display Screen Equipment Regulations 1992.

Illness, accidents and emergencies

Emergencies can happen in many ways. A visitor may be taken ill in reception, or there may be a serious accident on the road outside your office. Keeping calm, and knowing what to do in a crisis are both vital. However, this means recognising your limitations – as well as your capabilities.

Unless you are a qualified first-aider, never attempt to treat someone who has been taken ill. If the individual is in fact having a heart attack while you think he or she has indigestion, the consequences could be disastrous. In a large organisation you may have access to a medical unit staffed by either a doctor or a nurse. In smaller organisations there is likely to be at least one trained first-aider. The Health and Safety (First Aid) Regulations 1981 require a number of staff to be trained, depending upon the size of organisation, the type of industry, where the employees work and the location of the organisation. For example, if you work for a firm of accountants with five staff in an office next door to a health centre, you may not need a first-aider at all. As you might expect, a far larger number of trained first-aiders will be found on an off-shore oil rig.

'Trained' first-aiders are those who have been on an approved training course and been awarded a certificate of competence. A refresher course must be taken at least every three years. 'Occupational' first-aiders are those who have received additional training to cover particular hazards which may occur in a specific workplace, eg electrocution or poisoning. First-aiders should be notified of any employees with specific health problems which may lead to an emergency or complicate a situation, for instance diabetes or epilepsy.

Guidance notes to the Regulations give details of the contents of first-aid boxes and the quantities required. Drugs must never be issued by any employee or first-aider – if an employee suffered an allergic reaction as a result, he or she could take legal action. Many organisations equip a centrally located first-aid room (preferably on the ground floor, near an exit, in case of emergencies) with a medical couch and blankets. Stretchers can also be stored in this room. The aim is to provide suitable facilities for anyone who is not well, but who needs only to lie down quietly for a time, and an appropriate location for any medical health checks which the company organises for staff.

All accidents must be recorded, and those which cause serious or fatal injuries or lead to a considerable time off work must be notified to the HSE under the Reporting of Injuries, Diseases and Dangerous Occurrences Regulations 1995. All companies will therefore have an accident report form and employees should receive a code of practice (such as that illustrated in Figure 8.2) during their induction. Near-miss accidents are also usually recorded – often on a separate form – so that their type and frequency can be monitored. An example of an accident report form is shown in Figure 8.3.

Serious accidents will be investigated by either the safety officer, a safety representative or both. They will record details of the accident, take photographs, draw appropriate sketches and interview witnesses. They will also make notes on the working environment (eg the lighting, noise, positioning of equipment, etc.), the time of the accident, the name and job role of the person involved, the level of supervision, and the type of equipment the injured person was using. It is the job of the safety representative to advise any injured staff on their legal rights.

Employees should be aware that any refusal to cooperate with their employer, or any designated member of staff, may mean that they are in breach of the Health and Safety at Work Act. This refusal to cooperate can range from disregarding safety signs to refusing to wear protective clothing or failing to follow a specified procedure in an emergency. Although ignorance of the law is no excuse, to make sure that all staff are fully aware of their responsibilities, training courses are usually held which cover a wide range of situations and emergencies such as fire evacuations.

The company safety officer will be well aware that under the Fire Precautions (Places of Work) Regulations 1995, the fire authority has similar powers to the HSE and requires companies to comply with fire regulations. Designated premises, such as offices, shops and factories, each require a fire certificate showing a plan of the premises with the position of all fire-resistant doors and also the position of all fire extinguishers and break-glass alarms. There must be a proper fire-alarm system and also a protected means of escape. Fire drills should take place regularly with fire marshals appointed to monitor the evacuation. These are trained staff who make sure everyone leaves by the nearest exit, and then check the building to ensure it is empty. They are also responsible for the evacuation of any disabled people – particularly those stranded on upper floors.

MARKHAM ELECTRONICS PLC
Accident Report Form

Report of an accident or injury to a person at work or on duty
This form must be completed in all cases of accident, injury or dangerous occurrence and submitted to the Safety Officer.

Name of injured person ....

Date of birth..

Position held in organisation ....

Date and time of accident...

Particulars of injury/accident

Activity at time of injury/accident

Place of injury/accident

Details of injury/accident

First-aid treatment (if any) given

Was the injured person taken to hospital? If so, where?

Name(s) and position(s) of person(s) present when the accident occurred

Signature of person reporting incident ....

Date...

Figure 8.3 An accident report form

The safety officer (or safety representative) is responsible for ensuring that all fire-fighting equipment is regularly checked and serviced and that the location is clearly identified by the positioning of red fire-fighting equipment signs. He or she is also responsible for making sure that other safety signs are in place which conform to the Health and Safety (Safety Signs and Signals) Regulations 1996, and that fire assembly points are clearly designated and marked.

Safety signs are important because they minimise the likelihood of an accident.

- They may forbid dangerous behaviour or restrict access to a particular area. These signs always have a red edge and a diagonal red line and are **prohibition** or **must not do** signs.

- They may require employees to take a certain action, eg wear protective clothing. These signs have a circular blue background and are **mandatory** or **must do** signs.

- They may alert staff to a particular hazard or danger. These signs are triangular yellow signs and are **warning** signs.

- They may give details of first-aid points or emergency escapes. These signs are rectangular or square with a green background and are **informational** signs which indicate a safe condition.

Risk assessment

This relates to identifying possible risks and hazards in the workplace and reporting them. The Management of Health and Safety at Work Regulations 1992 require that potential risks or hazards are recorded in a certain way and that the risks attached to activities are also identified and assessed. You may therefore be asked to

- analyse which work activities in your area *could* entail a risk

- make an assessment of each in relation to
  - the activity itself
  - the possible hazard
  - the control measures which are in place (eg protective clothing or equipment)
  - the degree of risk (ie insignificant, low, medium or high) to both employees and others
  - possible remedial actions.

The higher the degree of risk, the more likely it is that protective equipment or clothing will be required and that only trained staff are allowed to undertake the activity.

Normal working procedures should not constitute a risk. You do not expect to have to wear a hard hat to be able to walk from your desk to the photocopier! However, unless there are procedures for monitoring standard working practices, good housekeeping (see page 118) and the correct positioning of furniture and equipment, then the area could start to resemble an obstacle course for users – and be just as hazardous. 'Safety' measures range from making sure that people have a reasonable amount of working space and that all walkways and 'traffic areas' are kept free, to having to insist that a desk or filing cabinet is repositioned because it constitutes a hazard or that staff move boxes or shopping they have placed on the floor. (You should note that workflow and office organisation are covered in more detail in the companion book, *Business for Advanced Secretarial Students*.)

Equipment

The Provision and Use of Work Equipment Regulations 1992 relate to the maintenance and upkeep of equipment in the workplace. Equipment can constitute a higher degree of risk than furniture – particularly electrical equipment. However, it is not unknown for people to have accidents with staplers and paper knives, simply because they were not concentrating. There are three aspects you need to consider about equipment:

- positioning
- usage
- maintenance.

Firstly, large items of electrical equipment need positioning where they will not be continually knocked or banged, and to be installed in accordance with any requirements stated by the manufacturer. Such items should not be moved, unless it is essential, and even then you may have to ask the supplier to do this for you. A large photocopier, for instance, needs checking to ensure that it is on a level surface and that there is sufficient air flow around it. There also needs to be room for the operator to work safely.

Manuals can be written to instruct people how to use a machine, or special training sessions can be given. Again, using a photocopier as an example, it is usually the case that only nominated *trained* staff can clear paper jams or remedy other faults. An untrained member of staff who puts his or her hand inside – without proper training – could receive a nasty burn from the fuser unit. In addition, he or she is quite likely to make the problem worse by inadvertently causing internal damage to the machine at the same time. Other useful instructions for staff include a directive to close the lid during the operation of the machine (and *never* to look at the bright light).

Electrical equipment needs checking to ensure that wires are not left hanging or trailing, that no wires or plugs are damaged, and that there are sufficient sockets so that adaptors do not need to be used. Many types of office furniture are now advertised as incorporating **wire management.** This simply means that there are special channels for the positioning of wires, such as those leading from a computer or a VDU.

Equipment maintenance should be carried out regularly. However, the Act recognises that the type of checks and maintenance will vary considerably depending upon the types and complexity of the equipment and the degree of risk. A check can therefore range from a basic inspection of a hand-held device, such as a stapler, to a substantial maintenance programme for complex machinery and equipment.

VDUs and workstations

The Display Screen Equipment (DSE) Regulations 1992 introduced minimum standards for the use of VDUs and the design of workstations. All equipment, both new and old, had to comply with these Regulations from 1 January 1997.

VDU users are protected in that the employer must

- analyse and assess display screen workstations to assess and reduce risk

- ensure that all workstations meet the minimum requirements of the display screen equipment, any related furniture, the working environment and software used

- plan activities to ensure users receive regular breaks or changes in activity – it is illegal for them to work continuously at a computer all day

- arrange an eye examination, on request, for those who use a VDU for more than one hour a day, and provide special spectacles if the test shows that these are required

- provide users with adequate health and safety training relating to their equipment.

The Regulations also require the following.

- **Display screens** must have well-defined characters of adequate size, a stable image, easily adjustable brightness and contrast, be able to tilt and swivel easily, and there must be no reflective glare.

- **Keyboards** must be tiltable and separate from the screen with sufficient space in front of the keyboard to provide a 'rest' space. They should have a matt surface, be easy to use with clearly contrasted symbols on the keys.

- **Work surfaces** must be sufficiently large and be of a low reflective finish. There must be a flexible arrangement of equipment so that it can be changed to suit the needs of the user.

- **Work chairs** must be stable and allow the user easy movement and a comfortable position. The seat height must be adjustable and the seat back must be tiltable to give good back support. Foot rests must be provided on request.

- The **working environment** must provide satisfactory lighting but with as little glare as possible. Windows should have blinds and/or workstations should be positioned to avoid reflections. Noise and heat levels should be such that they do not cause distraction or discomfort. Radiation levels must be negligible and humidity must be controlled and maintained at a satisfactory level.

- **Software and systems** must be suitable for the task, user friendly and appropriate to the level of knowledge of the user.

Many of the Regulations have been the result of concerns expressed about repetitive strain injury (RSI) – an injury caused by continually making awkward or repetitive movements and, in particular, tenosynovitis, which is the inflammation of the tendon sheaths in the hand, wrist and arms. The latter is an officially recognised industrial disease and sufferers can claim DSS benefits if they have medical support for their case as well as evidence of negligence on the part of their employer.

There have also been concerns about the stress levels of VDU workers, particularly those who have been required to input a high number of characters a day. Staring at the screen without a break for hours (particularly one with indistinct or flickering characters) can cause headaches and migraine attacks and there have been concerns that this can also trigger epileptic fits (although it cannot create an epileptic condition where one does not already exist). Concerns have also been expressed about the radiation hazards for pregnant women using VDUs. However, the Display Screen Equipment Regulations specifically state that in the light of scientific evidence, pregnant women need not stop working with computers. They do, however, recommend that female VDU operators who are pregnant or planning children should be given the opportunity to discuss any concerns they may have with an appropriate specialist.

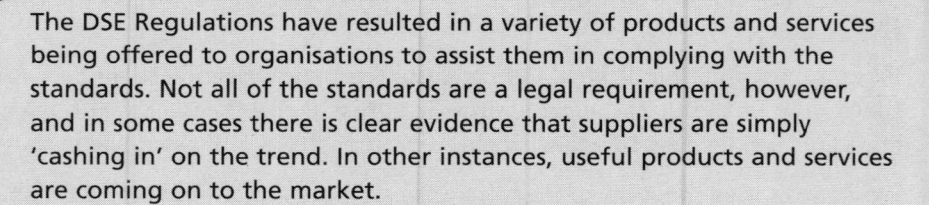

Discussion point

The DSE Regulations have resulted in a variety of products and services being offered to organisations to assist them in complying with the standards. Not all of the standards are a legal requirement, however, and in some cases there is clear evidence that suppliers are simply 'cashing in' on the trend. In other instances, useful products and services are coming on to the market.

As a group, decide which of the following you would consider the most and the least beneficial. Discuss your views with your tutor.

a   Specialised computer-cleaning products including screen wipes and keyboard sprays.

b   Wrist rests for computer users to reduce discomfort, fatigue and pressure points and to provide a neutral 'resting' wrist position.

c   A software package which contains a stretch and exercise program for VDU/keyboard users to help prevent RSI and relieve shoulders, neck, hands and back.

d   Fully adjustable seating which allows the user to adjust the back and seat to his or her own needs, is fully and *easily* height adjustable, has a swivel seat and castors as well as footrests.

Check it yourself

1 You can obtain a copy of the booklet *Working with VDUs* from HSE Books by phoning them on 01787 881165. This offers basic advice for all VDU users.

2 Check if your college library has the following HSE book in stock – *VDUs: An Easy Guide to the Regulations.* If not, ask if your tutor can arrange for the library to obtain it, especially as it only costs £5.

Unearthed – and unsafe

Because offices are statistically quite safe places to work, employers may be less vigilant than in other, higher risk areas. The result is often the flouting of health and safety regulations, particularly for office equipment.

In 1996, a Job Centre worker in Barnsbury north London received a severe electric shock at her computer terminal. The employee was rushed to hospital with suspected heart failure and later recovered. Investigations revealed that her desk, which contained metal, was not earthed. When the cabling from her computer frayed, the metal frame of the desk and the metal socket box below it became live. The management is now facing a bill of £6 million – the cost of earthing all 35,000 desks at Job Centres and other employment service offices around the country.

The London Hazards Centre, which advises organisations on workplace health and safety, has reported on other equipment hazards. Photocopiers and laser printers are often badly positioned, poorly maintained and overused. The result for office staff can be eye, nose and throat irritations, dermatitis, headaches and even cancer hazards.

However, the highest degree of risk for office workers is apparently on the stairwell. In winter, rain and snow brought into the building make the stairs slippery – a frequent occurrence is someone slipping and breaking a leg. The moral appears to be: watch where you sit, what you touch and how you walk!

● Administrative issues

The key roles for an administrator in the area of health and safety are likely to include

- checking that recommended safe working practices are being followed by staff – including good housekeeping and compliance with company procedures

- maintaining ongoing risk assessment, plus bringing hazards, complaints or incidents to the attention of the line manager or the company safety officer

- liaising with the safety officer over issues relating to the office.

Safe working practices

In the same way that staff can become complacent about security procedures, they are apt to show the same tendencies about safety. You may like to note that the word 'accident' has actually been defined as 'an unplanned event, which results in injury to a person or damage to property'. Therefore, no one plans to have an accident! However, after months and years of nothing going wrong, people get careless. They may not look where they are going and fall over something; they may put files, books and papers on top of a cupboard, which eventually fall off and hit someone; they run down corridors or up or down stairs; they leave cupboards and drawers open, and so on.

Keeping the working area clean and tidy is known as **good housekeeping** – often this alone can prevent many accidents. Making sure that any broken glass is wrapped in paper before throwing it away or storing items safely and cleaning spillages immediately are simple actions, but essential if mishaps are to be avoided.

A second area which must be monitored is ensuring that staff use the right tools for the job *and* use them in the correct way, eg standing on a safety stool (never a swivel chair!) to reach things on a high shelf, and lifting and moving equipment only in accordance with specified procedures. Under the Manual Handling Operations Regulations 1992, the provision of trolleys and trucks to lift heavy loads is essential. In addition, staff should know how to lift items safely. This includes knowing that they must

- disconnect electrical equipment before trying to move it

- never try to lift a load which is too heavy

- take the weight in their legs, not their back (by bending the knees first), if they *do* have to lift anything.

A third area is to ensure that staff who should use protective clothing or equipment do so. The Personal Protective Equipment (PPE) at Work

Regulations cover special clothing and equipment which must be worn when a risk cannot be eliminated. There are four main types of protective equipment, including

- head protection, eg industrial safety helmets, scalp protectors, caps, hairnets

- eye protection, eg safety spectacles, eyeshields, safety goggles, faceshields

- foot protection, eg safety boots or shoes with reinforced toe caps, slip-resistant soles, foundry boots which are heat resistant, wellington boots for protection against water, anti-static footwear to prevent the build-up of static electricity and to give some protection against electric shock

- hand protection, eg gloves designed to protect from cuts and abrasions, extremes of temperature, skin irritation and dermatitis, contact with toxic or corrosive liquids.

In some circumstances, protective clothing for the body is also necessary, eg overalls and aprons to protect against chemicals and other hazardous substances, clothing to protect against extremes of cold, heat and bad weather, and high-visibility clothing (such as that worn by motorway contractors).

Staff should not only be made aware of their requirements to wear PPE, but also where it is stored and their rights of access to it.

Ongoing risk assessment

Whilst this subject has already been covered on page 113, it is important to note here that the risks in an area can change over time and in different circumstances. An office area may be well equipped and furnished but, unless it is carefully maintained, some things will become shabby, other things may break and need to be replaced. These are then **potential hazards** – sometimes called 'accidents waiting to happen'. If you see that the carpet is lifting in one area, your job is to notify the person who usually carries out the maintenance work to see what can be done – or tell your manager. *Don't* ignore it until someone trips over it. If a pane of glass breaks in a door or window, then it is a safety hazard until it is repaired. Other typical examples are a drawer which will not close properly or a shelf which is working loose. At present they merely constitute a risk, but if you ignore them, you do so at your peril!

The design of buildings and the safety features which should be incorporated into them are covered in the Workplace (Health, Safety and Welfare) Regulations 1992. These cover minimum legal standards for the working environment (eg ventilation, temperature, lighting), safety in relation to floors, windows, doors, escalators, etc.; facilities, such as toilets, seating, rest and eating areas; and good housekeeping in general.

New buildings are usually less problematic than old, converted buildings. In a 'safe' building you may find wide doors, anti-slip floors, non-flicker uplighting and emergency lights to show the route to exits if the power fails. Some workers in older buildings have complained of suffering from 'sick building syndrome'. This is where workers suffer from a range of problems, including headaches, dizziness, nausea, skin problems or eye irritation caused by a problem with the building itself. It may be because of inadequate ventilation, too much fluorescent lighting, chemical emissions from equipment, dust or static build-up from synthetic carpets. If you notice a particular pattern of complaints or problems occurring with your own staff – and particularly if you work in an older building – you should bring this to the attention of your safety officer, who can then make further investigations.

Discussion point

1   Obtain at least one book from a safety signs/equipment supplier and note the type of products which are available to companies. One such supplier – which your tutor could contact on your behalf to obtain a catalogue – is Seton Limited, Banbury (Tel 01295 226600).

    As a group, discuss the items you would order if you had been asked to help set up a safety training room where staff would attend short courses on health and safety.

2   As a group, design a risk assessment form which will enable you to assess your own work area. In particular you should examine
    • the buildings and workplace conditions
    • equipment and wire management
    • VDUs and workstations
    • good housekeeping practices (in your own classroom and other rooms).

    Undertake an investigation, draft a group report and discuss your findings with your tutor.

3   Although your organisation has carefully designed procedures to ensure health and safety, several problems have arisen recently in your area. Discuss as a group how you would cope in each of the following situations.
    a   During a recent fire drill a senior member of staff refused to leave her desk, saying she had far too much work to do.
    b   During the same drill, a visitor in a wheelchair was left to his own devices and was found trying to use the lift to leave the building.

c Despite people ringing the maintenance staff on several occasions to report minor hazards, nothing has yet been done.

d You receive a telephone call from the site engineer who is responsible for the current roof repairs. He reports that twice in the past week he has seen one member of your staff walk underneath the scaffolding despite warning signs not to enter the area.

e A new, temporary VDU operator comes into your office in tears saying she has just spilled coffee all over her keyboard.

Watch for the colour change!

From 1 January 1997 the introduction of a new European Standard changed the colour of many British fire extinguishers. All new fire extinguishers must have red bodies, not just those containing water. However, because of the confusion this could cause as existing green, black, blue and cream change to red, the British Standards Institute has produced a British Standard to allow manufacturers to attach small colour-coded panels on to the new bodies to give users guidance as to the contents.

Old extinguishers can still be used until they are no longer capable of being operated safely and must be renewed. In the meantime, organisations are being encouraged to check their extinguishers weekly to make sure they have not been moved (accidentally or deliberately) nor tampered with. They also have to arrange training for staff to bring them up to date with the look of the new models.

● Secretarial/PA issues

Any involvement you have with health and safety, above and beyond the procedures mentioned earlier, will be mainly concerned with the role of your boss. If he or she has a key safety role in the organisation or chairs the safety committee, for instance, then you can expect to be highly involved. It may be your job to file accident forms safely, to monitor these at regular intervals and to deal with all the paperwork relating to the safety committee.

Even if your boss is not directly involved in health and safety, he or she will undoubtedly need to keep a file of the correct company procedures and you should be able to locate this quickly whenever it is needed. You should know enough to give sensible advice on any issue to junior staff and to be a model 'good housekeeper' yourself.

However, you may be concerned with one particular type of health and safety hazard – that of stress. If you work in a highly pressurised environment or suffer from an unreasonable or moody boss – or have two or more bosses who often give you conflicting instructions – this can create a stressful situation. You may find that you start to suffer from headaches or tiredness, you are unable to sleep well or relax when you leave work, you are irritable or depressed. At the furthest extreme, stress can result in high blood pressure, skin rashes, aches and pains, migraine, ulcers and arthritis.

How do you cope?

The first thing to note is that we all need some 'stress' to make us function, otherwise life would be very boring indeed. However, people vary in the amount of stress they can cope with. Some people get extremely upset even if the smallest things go wrong, eg if the bus is late or they are asked to do an extra job. Someone else would take these things in their stride and never give them a moment's thought. Therefore, you must first learn your own tolerance level – and discover the type of situations *you*, personally, find stressful. For instance, you may find that you get stressed or upset when

- you are asked to do a lot of work in a very short time

- you are asked to do work you do not understand

- you find people (either your boss or your colleagues) difficult to deal with

- you are asked to do something new or unexpected

- you have an argument with someone

- you have personal problems and are unable to 'switch off' from them when you get to work.

At this stage of your career you should try to find a mentor in the office to whom you can talk in confidence. This may be someone of your own age, but it is often better if you find someone slightly older, who has worked in the organisation for some time. Talk through your problems and difficulties and listen to their advice. If your work is the problem, then your mentor may help you to find a way to approach your boss to talk things through. Often saying what you feel – in a non-aggressive and calm way – will help you feel better. Bear in mind also that your boss cannot help if he or she does not know how you feel! If you are a genuine hard worker who is trying his or her best, then your boss is very likely to want to improve the situation – if only to keep you!

At the same time, review your personal life and your hobbies and interests. Try to develop an area of your life where you can work off any *angst* you might be feeling – whether this is an aerobics class, a night at the pictures or just a long lazy bath and a good book! It is important that you learn to balance work and play so that you keep any problems in perspective and do not magnify them into the impossible.

Finally, if you ever find yourself in an intolerable work situation, then *leave*. If necessary, do temporary work for a while to keep yourself solvent. If you are well-qualified as an administrator or secretary, then you will always be able to 'temp' and it will not be long before you find another job. It really is not worth making yourself ill by trying to cope if your work is making your life unbearable. There are so many good employers around that you should not let one bad one ruin your life!

 ## Discussion point

1   On your own, write down two examples of occasions which you think would cause you stress at work or create a situation where you would find it difficult to cope.

Then, as a group, pool your ideas to see if there are any common areas of concern. Suggest how to cope with such problems. Finally, include your tutor in your discussions – after all, for the time being he or she is your mentor, and may be able to give you a considerable amount of very helpful advice!

2   Your boss is Christine Oguma, computer services manager in your organisation. She is concerned that several VDU operators are very casual about their posture and the way in which they treat their equipment. As a group, design a basic checklist of good practice for all VDU users, which can be printed on a poster and placed in all the offices.

 ## Revision practice

Short answer questions
1   What is risk assessment and why is it necessary?

2   State three strategies you would employ for keeping down mail costs.

3   Identify four health and safety requirements when storing stock.

4   State three reasons why you should obtain more than one quotation for a new item of equipment.

5   Identify five security considerations when handling money in an office.

6 State four requirements of the Display Screen Equipment Regulations.

7 Identify four ways in which expense claims can be monitored. Why is this important in an office?

8 State the different types of safety signs which are in force. Which legislation requires their use?

9 State six safety considerations which should be borne in mind when siting or using a piece of electrical equipment.

10 Identify five ways in which an organisation could improve security for staff and visitors.

Essay questions
1 Explain how you would deal with the following items in your incoming mail. They arrive while your boss, Robina Moore, is away in the United States for two weeks.
  a a letter marked both Personal and Urgent
  b an invitation for her to speak at the annual dinner of Women into Industry in one month's time
  c a letter of complaint from a customer saying she will take legal action if she does not receive compensation from your organisation within the next seven days
  d an urgent memo from the managing director asking for a copy of last month's sales report together with an evaluation of the difference in sales between this year and last – these are required for the board meeting next Tuesday
  e a quotation for a new fax machine at a discount price – the offer is only valid for the next 10 days
  f the written resignation of a key member of the departmental staff.

2 You have recently taken over the responsibility for administering the petty cash in your office. The previous employee who undertook this work has left the organisation. You find that the analysis is incomplete and does not balance with the cash.
  a What are the main objectives of a petty cash system which must be observed?
  b How would you cope with the current problem?

3 **a** Explain the advantages of recording stationery stock on a computerised system
  b What procedures would you introduce to ensure
    i there is always sufficient stock
    ii costs are kept as low as possible?

4 As part of your work, you handle a considerable amount of confidential information. Identify systems of work you would use to ensure the security and safety of both the paper documents and the electronic storage media you use.

5 To comply with current legislation, both employers and employees have a joint responsibility for health and safety.

    a Give examples of the actions an employer will take to ensure the health and safety of staff.

    b Identify the main responsibilities of staff and give examples of the type of precautions which they can take to protect themselves and others against needless accidents.

Case study

You have been employed as administrator for Petersen Consultants, which recently opened an office in your locality. There will be 14 consultants and six office staff working on the premises. As one of the senior members of the office staff, you have been asked to help prepare a staff handbook. In particular, your boss, John Mayer, has asked you to prepare

a a brief procedures sheet for the opening and distribution of incoming mail which could be used by all office staff when they take their turn at this duty

b an information sheet containing the *main* Royal Mail services and when these should be used (it has been suggested that you group these into four sections – valuable items, fast delivery, overseas mail and parcel post)

c a guidelines sheet for dealing with visitors for the new receptionist

d a suggested system for the purchase and control of stationery items

e an information sheet headed 'Security is everyone's business' which can be used to remind staff of important security considerations

f a suggested procedure for reporting and dealing with accidents which occur on the premises.

Discuss with your tutor whether these tasks will be undertaken collectively by your group or on an individual basis.

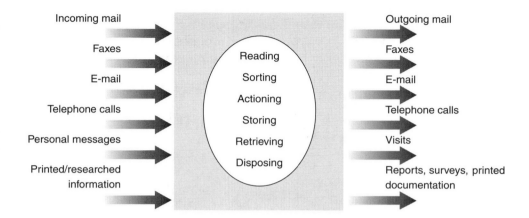

Incoming mail		Outgoing mail
Faxes	Reading	Faxes
E-mail	Sorting	E-mail
	Actioning	
Telephone calls	Storing	Telephone calls
Personal messages	Retrieving	Visits
Printed/researched information	Disposing	Reports, surveys, printed documentation

The information process

● Processing information

Information is the life-blood of organisations, because without it they would be unable to function. A huge amount of information is received every day by organisations – through the external and internal mail, by fax, by e-mail, by telephone. Information is generated by managers and office staff who are busy analysing, interpreting and commenting on information they already have and new information they have researched. All this information is used to make or inform decisions about what to do next. Some of these will be simple decisions, others will be complex. However, for the best possible decisions and responses to be made, the information available must be

* accurate and up to date

* relevant and valid

* complete.

The job of administrators and secretaries is to recognise the importance of accurate, timely, relevant and complete information to the managers of the organisation. Unless the information they provide meets all these criteria, wrong decisions can easily be made, which may have serious consequences.

The role of most administrators and secretaries is likely to encompass all aspects of **processing** information. This means you need the ability to

* research and select appropriate information as required

* produce and reproduce information in an appropriate format

* store information safely, using a variety of systems

- retrieve information promptly when it is required

- transmit information to other people using the most appropriate method.

With the exception of producing and reproducing information (which is covered in Section 4), this section concentrates on the skills required by both administrators and secretaries to process information promptly and effectively.

Information overload!

The quantity of information which can be collected, processed and analysed by organisations has increased to an incredible extent over the past 30 years. The length of time needed to process one electronic operation by computer has fallen by a factor of over 80 million since 1960! One expert compared this with what a similar advance would mean to the motor industry – saying that the equivalent would be to buy a car which was capable of doing 15 million miles to one gallon of petrol!

However, computers can be both a blessing and a menace when they are used to process information. The biggest danger is that so *much* information can now be made available that no one knows how to use it. This is known as **information overload.** Pages and pages of data can be produced which are not all relevant but which some unfortunate manager or administrator has to try to read and understand. When there is too much information and much of it is irrelevant, this makes decision-making more difficult. So many details are hitting everyone's desk that no one can cope with all the information they are receiving, let alone act upon it promptly. In other words, too much information is as bad as too little information. It will lead to delays, errors and problems as managers – and administrative staff – struggle to cope with it, and to a new, stress-related condition known as **information overload syndrome.**

Researching and selecting information

9

● Introduction

Researching information is common practice in many organisations. You will undertake research when the basic facts which are known are not detailed enough for an accurate decision to be made or an action to be taken. However, what you are asked to research can vary enormously – from finding out a telephone number to investigating the views of your customers on a new product or service! However, there is likely to be some sort of pattern to the type of research you will be asked to undertake, depending upon the organisation which employs you and the department in which you work. A secretary or PA working for a human resources director may be asked to find out the details of the Disability Discrimination Act, whereas a finance director may ask his or her administrator to compile a report on the number of outstanding debts at the end of last month. Whereas one would set off to the library, the other is more likely to turn on her computer. Therefore, how you undertake the research – and your sources of information – will be different depending upon what you have been asked to find out.

● Types of information

When you hear the word 'information', it is not surprising if you think of pages of text. However, in the course of the average day you receive a variety of different types of information – from several different sources – including the following.

- **Verbal information** – from friends, colleagues and members of your family. We all regularly exchange information with other people on a variety of topics. Verbal information may also be received if you listen to the radio or play audio tapes or listen to messages left on an answering machine.

- **Printed information** – such as that contained in newspapers, journals, magazines, books, leaflets, catalogues, etc. This is standard information which is received by many people. However, the type of magazine or newspaper you buy will affect the type, style and slant of the information.

- **Written information** – found in letters, postcards, printed course notes, reports and other documents. In this case the information is likely to relate to a particular issue and be more specific to you as an individual.

- **Financial information** – this arrives in a variety of different ways. You receive financial information if you are given a bill or a receipt, if the bank sends you a statement or if you update your building society pass book.

- **Graphical information** – found in illustrations, pictures, cartoons, line drawings, graphs and photographs. These are usually used where they would make something clearer than words. A car maintenance handbook or a video instruction manual are likely to contain illustrations and sketches to show different procedures because these make them more easily understandable than pages of text.

- **Electronic (visual) information** – now common everywhere – whether you 'read' a visual display on a microwave or watch a television programme or video, play computer games or surf the Internet, you will be reading information on a screen, rather than on a printed page.

All this information influences decisions you make every day. For instance, if you receive a telephone call to say a friend is in hospital, you may make a decision to buy a get-well card or visit her. If you receive a bank statement saying you are overdrawn by £20, you would be foolhardy to make a decision to buy a new outfit. If you watch a holiday programme on television which appeals to you, then you may want to know more about a destination shown. In this case you may see what details are given on Teletext, visit your travel agent or telephone the tour operator for a brochure. In this case you are carrying out research to find out more details about the general information you received in the first place. Only then will you be able to make an informed decision whether to book the holiday.

 **Discussion point**

1   All the types of information mentioned above are also commonly found in business. As a group, think of as many types of information as you can under each heading that you would find in an organisation. See how many ideas you can come up with yourselves – and then ask your tutor to add any important ones you may have missed.

2   As a group, can you think of one occasion when an administrator may be asked to find out further details of something, ie to research information?

The skill of researching

There are five main stages before you start to research any information. You need to

1   define what is needed

2   clarify your objectives

3   identify possible sources

4   decide which techniques are the most appropriate

5   think through the implications.

As an example, think back to the idea of watching a holiday programme and then deciding whether one of the holidays shown appeals to you. In this case you would need to do the following.

1   **Define what you need to know.** This is always easier if you have made the decision about what you need yourself. Here you want to find out more about a particular holiday shown on the programme – let's say it was in Italy. However, if your boss is giving you instructions, then you have to make sure that you *clearly understand* what it is you are being asked to do. This is crucial if you are not to waste time and effort going down the wrong path – or spend days worrying about what is really required.

2   **Clarify your objectives.** This is the way in which you 'narrow down' your search to make it more manageable. For instance, finding out about every single type of holiday you could have in Italy would take you so long that you would never get there! So you need to be more specific. Do you want information on just one type of holiday (eg hotel or self-catering) or just one resort? Do you have a spending limit? Are you restricted as to the dates you could go?

    In a working environment you would discuss your boss's objectives – and maybe suggest some of your own. In this way your 'brief' would become clearer and you would know exactly what it is you have to achieve.

3   **Identify your sources.** There are a wide range of sources you can use to obtain information (see pages 468–70). For the holiday in Italy, you may decide to visit a travel agent, or read advertisements for Italian holidays in a Sunday newspaper, or scan Teletext for last-minute cheap breaks. You might decide to contact the Italian Tourist Office for their advice. However, your sources may be restricted by your objectives. For instance, it is no use scanning Teletext for last-minute holidays if you do not plan to go until next year.

    This is the first stage of planning your investigation. At work, you could suggest sources to your boss or he or she may suggest a useful starting point to you.

4 **Decide which techniques to use.** There are many techniques you can use to find out information. Much will depend on the type of research you have been asked to carry out, the time available, the level of detail you require and the sources you have listed. For your holiday in Italy, are you going to visit everyone on your list or ring up one or two? If you are still collecting basic information, it may be easier to ring people and ask for a brochure you can look through at your leisure. However, if you want to discuss your needs in detail it would be more appropriate to visit a travel specialist and obtain professional advice face to face.

5 **Think through the implications.** The information you obtain may mean you have to rethink some of your objectives. For instance, if you had planned to rent an apartment but cannot afford to do this unless there are at least four of you, you would have to decide whether to change your holiday or ask your friends if they are interested. If you can only afford to go during May or June, but not in the peak season, then you would have to find out if you can get time off work then – and also work out if you could last until Christmas before your next break – and so on.

Being able to think through the implications is a skill which separates the barely average researcher and the true professional.

You may find, that after obtaining all the details, you cannot manage to visit Italy for quite some time. In which case you would be foolish to throw all your hard work away – if you store it somewhere sensible, then you can always go back to it in the future, without having to start all over again. However, you would need to update it as, at the very least, all your estimated prices would need to be revised to allow for any increases. In the same way, sensible administrators and secretaries always keep a copy of information they have researched – together with the date on which the information was current. This can save many hours of work in the future, if they are asked to make another search on the subject. If nothing else, at least they have their list of sources to hand from where they can obtain updates.

Primary or secondary?

Many people do not realise that there are two different ways to research information. One is known as **primary research,** the other is called **secondary research.**

Primary research is concerned with finding out new information. It involves undertaking research on something for the first time. If you wanted the views of staff on a new vending machine, the opinions of shoppers on whether stores should have crèche facilities, or to investigate how many women feel they cannot progress into management because of sex discrimination in their organisation, then you would not find the answer by rummaging in your filing cabinet! Instead, you would have to supplement any informal feedback or reading you have done by asking people directly. You may decide to carry out interviews, to design a survey or questionnaire or carry out observation yourself. Primary research is sometimes known as 'field' research.

Secondary research is sometimes called 'desk' research and involves accessing information which already exists – either inside or outside the organisation. If you want last year's sales figures, information on a large organisation, or personal details of a famous sporting personality, then you would look at existing information and select that which is relevant to your needs. Your sources may include your files, computer databases, CD-ROMs, reference books, journals and newspapers.

● Information sources

There are a considerable number of information sources which you can access when you are researching. These fall into the following broad categories.

- **People and organisations** – either locally or nationally.

- **Paper-based information** – from files to reference books and journals.

- **Computer-based information** – from company databases to library databanks, from CD-ROM to the Internet.

You also need to be aware of the difference between public and private information. Information which is **public** is available to anyone, free of charge. This is the type of information you will read about in books and newspapers. However, this does not mean that you can copy it all with impunity! The law of copyright exists to protect those who have created original works. This means that you cannot just visit the library and take 20 copies of two chapters in a book and three articles in a newspaper to distribute them to everyone. However, you *can* take a copy for your own research use. In addition, you can quote from an original work provided you acknowledge the source of your information and do not claim it as your own research. This is usually done by using footnotes at the bottom of a page or endnotes at the end of an article. (Further information on copyright law and presentation of documents is given in Chapters 13 and 14.)

Other information, however, is classed as **private.** In some cases this means you cannot have access to it at all, in other cases it means you will be charged for the privilege. Here are two examples. Your boss is the manager of a large computer centre. He has received an order from a new firm in the area but does not want to supply goods on credit unless he is certain the firm can pay. He asks you to find out whether the firm is credit worthy. He has also decided that he would like to undertake a marketing exercise whereby he writes to all young people in the area just before their eighteenth birthdays offering them a home computer at a reduced price. He asks you to get him a list of the names and addresses of those people in your town who will turn 18 this year.

 Test yourself

Before you read any further, can you identify the sources which could give you the information you need for these two tasks? Discuss your ideas as a group.

The restrictions on private information

You would have two sources of information to identify. The first would ascertain the credit worthiness of the local company. In this case you may decide to obtain a bank reference. You could ask the firm for the name and address of its bank and write for details. You will be sadly disappointed if you expect the bank to give you details of the firm's account balance, as this is private information. Instead, the bank will give a more general reference, based on its knowledge of the organisation as a whole.

For the second source you would contact the local town hall to see if you can obtain a list of the 'new' voters in your area this year – as all these people will turn 18 this year. The woman to whom you speak agrees that the information can be provided, but says there will be a charge of £20 for the database. You now have to check with your boss whether he is willing to pay for this or not.

Therefore, you need to be aware that not all information is accessible, and not all information is free. However, providing that you do not do anything unlawful, much information may be available if you are fairly ingenious. To test your own ingenuity, try the discussion point below!

Discussion point

You work for the manager of an employment agency in a large town. Your agency is involved in providing staff to fill permanent and temporary secretarial and administrative vacancies of local companies. Two other agencies have recently opened in the area and your boss is concerned that you may lose business if they give a better service, offer a better hourly rate to temps or charge less to firms in the area.

As a group, discuss how you could try to find out about your competitors' service *without* doing anything illegal!

People and organisations as an information source

Quite often, you can save yourself a lot of time and energy simply by asking someone else for information. For instance, if you work for a large company you could ask

- your safety officer for information on health and safety

- your staffing officer or wages clerk for information on National Insurance and PAYE

- your credit controller for information on existing customers and their credit ratings

- your computer services manager for information on computer software and CD-ROMs.

These are all people who work in the organisation and who specialise in different areas. Sometimes, however, you may need to contact someone outside the organisation for information. You may contact

- existing suppliers (or potential suppliers) for details of different products

- the Public Relations or Marketing Departments of large organisations for details of their products or services

- your service providers for information relevant to their own area, eg the accountant, bank, company solicitor, insurance broker or travel agency

- local organisations which can help you with a particular enquiry relating to their own area, eg government offices such as the Department of Social Security, Inland Revenue, local Customs and Excise office and Job Centre, the Post Office, the police, your local reference library, town hall, newspaper, Citizen's Advice Bureau, Chamber of Commerce and Trading Standards Office/Environment Health Office

- national organisations such as the AA, RAC or National Breakdown, foreign embassies and tourist information offices, airline and shipping offices, British Rail, the English Tourist Board, passport offices, consumer reference agencies, hotel booking agencies, the Health and Safety Executive, Equal Opportunities Commission, Race Relations Commission, the Consumers' Association and consumer watchdogs, eg OFTEL, OFLOT and OFGAS

• organisations which specialise in providing information on or for business, eg the London Chamber of Commerce and Industry, the Institute of Management, the British Standards Institute, the Office of Fair Trading, the Department of Trade and Industry. In addition, your organisation may be a member of a trade association or a professional body which can give you expert advice on issues relevant to your own industry.

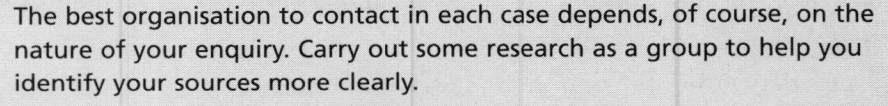

Discussion point and research activity

The best organisation to contact in each case depends, of course, on the nature of your enquiry. Carry out some research as a group to help you identify your sources more clearly.

1   Divide up the names of all the organisations and types of organisations given above between you. Then, for your own individual list, write a brief paragraph on the type of enquiries they could handle. If you do not know, then find out – by using the college library as your information source. Then exchange your list for those prepared by other people so that everyone has a complete set.

2   Find out the names of *at least* six trade associations and four professional bodies, and identify the industries and professions to which they relate.

3   In your spare time you help out at a local centre for the disabled. Last year the centre was awarded a grant through the National Lottery fund. However, despite several promises no money has yet been received. Which of the above organisations should you contact to complain about the delay?

Paper-based information

Despite the modern advances in computers, by far the greatest mass of information is still held on paper. You only have to visit your local library or a large bookshop to see this for yourself! In a business organisation you can expect to find relevant information in

- your personal files and notes
- the main office files
- leaflets, brochures and catalogues
- newspapers, journals and periodicals
- specialist papers and reports
- reference books.

Personal files and notes

Any professional administrator or secretary is well aware of the importance of personal reference documents and will gradually build up a customised set of files which contain key information for his or her job. Its contents will depend upon the exact area of work and the needs of any executive to whom the administrator reports. However, a general guide would be the inclusion of

- names, titles and telephone extensions of all personnel in the organisation
- name, title, address, telephone number and fax number of all important customers and contacts (plus the name of his or her secretary or administrator as appropriate)
- name, address, telephone number (and contact name) of any previously used and reliable agencies and external organisations – from a good courier to a translation bureau or interpreter
- a list of approved suppliers for both office stationery and office services, including an electrician, plumber, locksmith and central-heating engineer (unless such services are provided by the organisation itself)
- a list of personal contacts which relate to his or her boss, eg doctor, dentist, garage, vet, local airport enquiry number, preferred car-hire firm, florist, dry cleaners.

Some administrators and secretaries may also keep a 'cuttings file' of publicity stories on the organisation for their boss and/or regularly scan the local or national papers for information on their competitors which may be of interest.

In addition, notes on any previous research tasks will be filed safely – and dated – for future reference if required.

The main office files

The main office files are likely to contain information on

- customers – including correspondence and sales documentation
- suppliers – including quotations, orders, invoices and current agreements in force

- specific topics related to the company or departmental business. As an example, if you worked in Marketing, you would be likely to have files for advertising, publicity, mail-shots, advertising agencies, sales seminars and exhibitions. If you worked in Human Resources, you may have files for the Inland Revenue, Department of Social Security, sick pay regulations, maternity pay regulations, National Insurance and holiday entitlement.

However, you may not have open access to all the office files. Personnel files, for example, are usually confidential because they contain personal information on staff as well as current salary levels. They may also include information on job performance or any grievance or disciplinary procedures which have been instigated. They are therefore another example of **private** information. You may have to refer an enquiry about a member of staff to a member of the Personnel or Human Resources section who has the authority to access the file and may then be able to give you the specific information you need.

Leaflets, brochures and catalogues

Many organisations issue leaflets about their current services. The Post Office, Inland Revenue, Office of Fair Trading and the banks are typical examples. Obtaining a range of leaflets on the relevant services you need is useful – providing you remember to keep them up to date. Leaflets are helpful because, providing they are current, they usually give you easy-to-read information at a glance.

Another information source is brochures and catalogues. These are usually produced by suppliers to give illustrations of goods they can provide. However, they may only be published infrequently because of their cost – so it is important that you make sure that your price list is current, or your final estimate of expenditure is likely to be very much on the optimistic side!

Newspapers, journals and periodicals

Generally, these are extremely useful sources of information because they are issued frequently – even daily – and therefore the latest issues contain up-to-date information. Many organisations – and certainly most managers – purchase at least one of the more 'serious' newspapers everyday because of the wide range of useful information which is included. Not only are business news and financial information (eg share prices) included, but also most papers give details of national roadworks, weather forecasts and currency exchange rates.

The types of journal and periodical which are purchased can vary considerably. Just as there are magazines to cover a myriad of hobbies and interests, so too there are journals to cover different areas of work. You may have seen this when you have visited your doctor, for instance, and found dozens of magazines on staying fit and healthy! In business very many areas are covered – from accounting to computing and from human resources to management or marketing.

Specialist papers and reports

These are produced by a variety of specialist organisations on topics which they have researched or are keenly interested in. The following are some examples.

- The London Hazard Centre (there are other hazard centres around the country) undertakes research and keeps relevant papers on health and safety.

- The Trades Union Congress (TUC) carries out research on working conditions, employment and employment legislation.

- The Office of National Statistics (ONS) undertakes research for the government on topical issues and produces related statistical reports.

- The Advisory, Conciliation and Arbitration Service (ACAS) has a Work Research Unit which gives details of published articles on all aspects of employment.

- The Commission of the European Union publishes background report sheets on a wide range of topics relating to the EU.

Some of these reports will be available as abstracts in your library, others you can obtain through the library or direct from the supplier on request. In some cases you will have to pay a small fee to obtain the information.

Reference books

No organisation will keep a full set of reference books on every possible subject. Many are very expensive and would be used only occasionally, if at all. For that reason, only very general reference books are likely to be kept in an office plus reference books specific to the nature of the organisation. Generally, you can expect to have available.

- telephone and fax directories (including *Yellow Pages* and *Business Pages*)

- a good dictionary and a thesaurus (which gives alternative words)

- road maps and street plans for major cities regularly visited and at least one guide to hotels and restaurants (eg *AA* and *RAC Handbooks, The Good Food Guide*, a *Michelin Guide* or *Hotels and Restaurants in Great Britain*).

Thereafter your organisation may have books which purely relate to professional needs or none at all! In that case you would have to visit your local library to find out more detailed information. However, you must remember some key points before you make your visit.

- Books in a library are not scattered around at random. They are usually classified according to subject and recorded in a **library catalogue,** which is a list of all the books held. The catalogue may be in a card index or accessed through a computer terminal. Even if a book is not in the catalogue, it does not mean that staff could not obtain it for you.

- Staff in the library are trained to help you – but can only do so if they know exactly what you want. Giving them a general request will normally get you a general response – they will be better able to give you specific guidance if they know exactly what you want to find out.

- Many books in a library cannot be taken out on loan – you can only read them whilst you are there. This means taking a notebook with you and some money for making photocopies of the key pages or article you need.

Test yourself

You were no doubt introduced to your college library during your induction, but how well do you *really* know it?

1 Visit the library with the list of journals and periodicals given in Figure 9.1. Check which are kept by your library and add any others *which are kept which would be relevant to general business* but are not on the list.

Computer Services – *Computer Bulletin/Computer Weekly*
Financial – *Accountancy, Management Accounting*
Health and Safety – *Premises and Facilities Management, Practical Office*
Human Resources – *Human Resource Management, People Management, Industrial Relations Journal, Training*
Management – *European Management Journal, Journal of General Management, Management Today, Modern Management, Executive Travel, Business Traveller*
Marketing – *Journal of Marketing*
Purchasing – *The Buyer, Business Equipment Digest, Office Equipment News, Mind Your Own Business*

Figure 9.1 Business periodicals and journals

2 Look at the eight lists of reference books classified under different headings in the Appendix on pages 468–70. As a group, divide up the lists between you. Visit your college library and check how many are kept there. For *at least* six different books on your list make a note of the contents. Then exchange your lists.

3 Investigate the classification system used in your library. Assume you have been asked to write a brief user's guide for new students by your tutor. From the information you have obtained, prepare the guide, keeping it as simple and user friendly as possible.

Computer-based information

If your college has an up-to-date library, you will have noticed that in addition to books and journals you could also have accessed a variety of information on computer. In fact, today many libraries are equipped with a range of computer terminals for users. These usually give access to information held on CD-ROM, in library databanks and public databanks.

CD-ROMs

CD-ROMs are an invaluable resource aid for researchers. A CD-ROM is a small optical disk which contains a huge amount of information and can also incorporate graphics. On multimedia machines there may be sound and animation as well, depending upon the software you are using. Today, several encyclopaedias and reference books are being converted to CD-ROM format because it is much easier to search for the topic of your choice using this method. You are also less likely to be distracted by irrelevant information – given that the system will immediately go to the subject you have specified.

One very useful application for CD-ROM researchers has been the transfer of national newspapers to disk format. Many newspapers are now available on disk – you simply buy the one you want and then purchase the updates every six months. Given the immense difficulties of searching through hundreds of newspapers to find articles on a particular topic, this method enables readers to have immediate access to current articles simply by entering in key words on which the search should take place. Selected articles then appear on screen as headlines and you can browse through these and read or print out those you need.

Library databanks

A databank is a large database which is usually held by an external organisation. A library databank contains details of books available on various topics. In addition, some will also provide summaries of book contents or journal articles.

To use an external databank, you need to have a computer which is equipped with a modem and is connected to a telephone line. When you select to use the databank, you will be linked with the outside world through special communications software installed on the machine. You are charged for the links you make, including the telephone call and, in many cases, the ability to access the databank. For that reason you are unlikely to find that your college library allows you free access to any external databank of your choice for as long as you want! In some libraries – particularly public libraries – you may have to ask the librarian to institute a search for you, rather than do it yourself. In addition, because of the costs of access, you may be charged a small fee.

Examples of library databanks include:

- MARC (Machine Readable Cataloguing), which gives details of books and journals published worldwide

- DIALOG, which gives information on publications from a variety of general sources

- IRS (Information Retrieval Service), which gives information on a wide variety of topics

- TOXLINE/MEDLINE, which gives information on medical matters

- LEXIS, which gives information on legal matters and cases.

In addition, BLAISE (the British Library Automated Information Service) provides computer access to a British Library database which endeavours to keep a copy of every book published in Britain.

Public and private databanks

If your college has a computer network, then you may be able to access specified databanks or CD-ROMs without even visiting the library! This is because a networked system enables all the software to be available centrally and for all specified users to have access from any terminal. You may even be able to access the Internet, the fastest growing public databank of them all.

The Internet contains a huge variety of information – from news and travel, to the complete works of Shakespeare, to commercial information from hundreds of organisations all of which have 'user sites'. Research papers are often available on the Internet and there are user groups who use the Internet to send electronic mail to each other on a particular topic. An additional piece of software gives access to the World Wide Web – a network which includes multimedia libraries, newspapers, magazine publishers and others.

An advantage of the Internet is that it is an **interactive** system. This means that users can respond to each other over the system, rather than just reading information. One of the disadvantages of the Internet is the expense, which includes the cost of telephone calls you make to link you to the outside world, plus the fee to any service provider you use. Service providers charge a registration fee and monthly fees as well as charging for the time you spend linked to their computer. A further disadvantage is that the information is not stored in any organised way. That, plus the fact that access can be quite slow at times (unless you dispense with the graphics), can mean that it may take you a considerable amount of time to find what you want. 'Surfing the Net' is not something you want to try to do in a hurry! Finally, as you may know already, there are no legal controls over what can be published on the Internet, so you might find some of the information contains very personal views or is even offensive material. (The

Internet is discussed again in connection with e-mail on page 177 and with hardware and software in Chapter 14).

Finally, you should to be aware of the other main public databanks which are available through Teletext. In the UK, Teletext is available as Ceefax (the BBC service) and Oracle (the ITV version). A wide range of current information is available on Teletext from news headlines to travel, sports, weather and financial information.

Business organisations are unlikely to use Teletext, as the information is mainly general and it is not interactive (which means you can only read the information, you cannot respond to it). In addition the information is shown on a television screen, rather than a computer.

Prior to the development of the Internet, a popular choice for some organisations was New Prestel, a viewdata system and electronic mail service provided by BT. This is an interactive system, available through a computer (again, provided it is equipped with a modem and there is access to a telephone line). An index of all the information held is displayed on screen and there is also a directory which gives further details. A basic subscription entitles the user to access general information which is available to all users. However, by paying additional fees the user can obtain access to a variety of private viewdata systems *in addition* to the public system.

Private viewdata systems are operated by private organisations which charge a fee for access. They may restrict access to organisational staff and clients. An example is the system you can view in any travel agent when you make a holiday booking. The agent will have access to the databases of all the major tour operators – so he or she can find out what vacancies exist with all the major holiday companies simply by scanning through the different databases or searching on specific criteria. In addition, because the system is interactive, once you have decided upon the holiday you want, the travel agent can make the booking on computer and print out an immediate confirmation. Note that this is an example of a private system – so access is strictly controlled for fairly obvious reasons!

💬 Discussion point and research activity

Reading about electronic sources of information is one thing – using them is quite another! Some people get 'hooked' on using a computer to find information – as the growth of Internet cafés and Internet users up and down the country proves!

Discuss with your tutor the facilities available in your college for accessing electronic information. Then use them to find out information on one topic in which you are personally interested. Bring the information back to your group and discuss how much you found and where and how you found it.

● Research techniques

There are many techniques you can use to find out information. A good way to begin to consider this is to look through a few pages of a daily newspaper and to think about how the journalists acquired their stories.

- Some will have been sent in by press agencies, businesses, the police, the general public and other sources (eg the Meteorological Office produces weather forecasts).

- Some articles (particularly features) will have been researched by journalists looking at old press files, referring to computer files or looking at reference books and documents.

- Some people will have been interviewed to obtain their comments on a story.

- Journalists will have visited the locations of newsworthy events all around the world – from a party political conference in Britain to a war zone – and made their own observations. They may also have interviewed people 'on the spot'.

- Some stories will be comments on the results of questionnaires and surveys undertaken either by the paper itself or by other agencies.

- Some journalists may have arranged to experience a particular event so that they can write about it – from bungee jumping to taking the theory part of the driving test.

You should note that whenever a paper carries a story where it has obtained information from an outside source, it acknowledges the source – just as you must do!

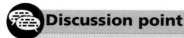

Discussion point

As a group, look through two or three different daily papers. In each case try to identify which of the above research techniques were used to produce at least ten different stories in the paper. Try to find at least one example of each technique, if you can.

When researching is above par!

To improve coverage of the 1996 Open Championship at Royal Lytham Golf Course, the *Blackpool Evening Gazette* set two young reporters the task of finding a wide range of interesting stories to complement the traditional sports coverage. The idea was to bring the event to life by going behind the scenes to find out the truth about staging one of the world's largest sporting events.

The first step was to decide which stories would make the most interesting reading. Ideas were gathered and divided into topics – backstage, technology, people, local.

Backstage ideas were formulated into stories by speaking to the people who were responsible for getting the event off the ground. BT provided a perfect starting point. By speaking to the coordinator who was responsible for the event, a staggering amount of interesting information was collected. It took around 60 engineers three months to set up a mobile exchange capable of handling the massive number of communication systems which were necessary, ie the equivalent of providing phones for a small village for just one week.

Local angles on technology were also easy to find. One engineer who normally fixed domestic phones suddenly found himself connecting satellite links capable of carrying pictures half-way around the world in seconds.

The catering company Town and Country was another organisation approached in the course of research. Setting up enough watering holes and eating establishments to feed 200,000 hungry spectators during the course of the tournament, not to mention 500 thirsty journalists from around the world, was no easy task and provided a very interesting feature.

To put together 'people' stories of local interest, the first step was to talk to the headteachers of local schools who supplied hordes of enthusiastic teenagers to work as litter pickers, ball collectors and message runners. Another local story involved Lytham's own professional golfer, Paul Eales, who was taking part in the competition. Instead of speaking to him, however, the research went a little further and a story was written from the angle of Mrs Eales on what life is like for the wife of an international golfer.

A key point for the journalists was to check that all their facts were correct before they put together their information in the form of a story. After all, how would a famous golfer react to having his comments misquoted or some inaccurate rumours about him printed on the front page? One response could be a swift libel action against the paper concerned (see also page 153)!

Choosing the best technique

The technique to use depends upon what you have been requested to do. If you have been asked to carry out secondary research, then you will be expected to obtain a wide variety of books, leaflets and papers related to the subject and to go through these to extract relevant information (see page 149 for how to do this). (If you have forgotten the difference between primary and secondary research, turn back to page 133 and refresh your memory!)

If you are expected to undertake primary research, then you have to work out how you are going to obtain new information yourself. Usually, whenever you are involved in primary research, you will be involved with **people**. At this stage you have several choices of method, depending upon what you have been asked to do.

You might decide to ask for an **interview** or an informal discussion where you could talk about the topic in more detail. This obviously means preparing *thoroughly* in advance so that you have a set of questions to ask. Interviewing is a skill, particularly if you have a talkative person who is apt to veer off the topic! The art is to keep the interviewee talking about relevant points whilst managing to write at the same time! However, be warned that some interviewees can give you useful information unasked, so by controlling the interview too much you could lose out on some valuable material. You may find it helpful, if your interviewee has no objections, to tape the interview so that at least you can stop worrying about writing legible notes at the same time!

Bear in mind that if you are interviewing people about a particular issue, then you may need to find out the views of a few people to obtain a representative sample. This may mean that a small meeting would be a good idea (providing everyone has the opportunity to give their opinion); alternatively a questionnaire or survey (see below) would be more appropriate than a series of interviews.

Another method is to **observe** what is happening yourself and to write about it. In this case you need to plan what you are going to see and when – and keep your eyes open! You will also need to make clear notes so that you can refer to them later. Taking a video camera with you is usually not a viable proposition and will probably inhibit anyone to whom you want to talk from expressing their opinions!

Finally, you could draw up a **questionnaire** or **survey** for a selected group of people to complete. A questionnaire is a short version of a survey – and easier to write and analyse. The main thing is to give people clear options to each question, so that you do not have to try to evaluate 25 different opinions when you obtain the results! Writing a proper survey – such as the type issued by market research agencies – is a skilled job and difficult to do properly. It is very easy to miss out a few key questions, with the result that your findings are unclear, ambiguous or just plain useless!

If you are asking staff in your organisation for their views, then the simplest method is to send a brief memo with a simple form or questionnaire attached (an example is given in Chapter 12).

Discussion point

1   As a group, decide which technique, or combination of techniques, would be the most appropriate if you were given each of the following primary research tasks.

   a   Deciding whether a training course on your organisation's new telephone system is required.

   b   Finding out how many cars park on your company's car park each day without permission.

   c   Finding out what improvements your group would like to see made to this year's course so that next year's students will benefit.

   d   Finding out how it feels to be a National Lottery jackpot winner.

   e   Discovering how many people use the company canteen (or college refectory) each day and what they like and dislike most about it.

   f   Finding out whether staff are clear about
      i   what they should do if the fire alarm sounds
      ii   their responsibilities under the Health and Safety at Work Act
      iii their rights if they are VDU operators.

2   As a group, design a short questionnaire to check your group's opinion on the college library, its hours of opening, resources and the attitude of the library staff. In addition, leave a small space for 'suggested improvements'. Check your form with your tutor.

   Photocopy the best form and circulate it around the class, and then analyse the replies. Give a brief verbal summary of the final analysis to your tutor.

Interpreting your findings

One problem for researchers is often the amount of information which they have collected on a topic. Usually, there either seems to be very little or too much! Having obtained the information, you then have to make sure that you can understand it and that it is appropriate for your research topic before you start to write about it! Assume you have been given a project to do on advertising agencies. You are asked to find out all you can about them.

This is a fairly 'woolly' brief, because you have not been asked to find out specific information. However, you begin by carrying out the following.

- You find out the names and addresses of the top ten agencies in your library.

- You write to them to ask for information on the services they offer.

- Whilst you are in the library you notice that the Advertising Association oversees the work of advertising agencies, so you write to it as well. You also write to a few 'controlling bodies' for advertising, such as the Advertising Standards Authority.

- You search a CD-ROM containing a popular newspaper over the past 12 months and print out 25 articles on advertising agencies – all on different topics (from advertising awards to new contracts, and even the merger of two agencies).

- You borrow two books on advertising from the library and two journals about current issues in marketing and advertising. One of the magazines contains a lot of up-to-date information on the cost of advertising projects and the popularity of different advertisements.

- You also manage to arrange to interview two people in your area who work for advertising agencies. One has a fairly senior job and the other is a new recruit.

Assume that the majority of people to whom you wrote reply with brochures and leaflets. You are now looking at a desk full of information – plus your own notes and two interview tapes. Where do you start?

Your first task (if you have not already done so) is to obtain a clearer brief on what it is you are expected to find out. There is a huge difference between being asked for a one-page summary on the work of advertising agencies, brief notes on the job roles of advertising agency staff, a two-page document on the legal and voluntary controls on advertising and a 25-page project on advertising and its role in the modern world. For that reason, the clearer the brief you have before you start researching, the better!

In the case of the first three briefs above, much of the information you have obtained will not be relevant to your investigation. Only in the fourth case will you need most of the material you have acquired.

Organising your material

Before you can decide to discard any information, you will need to organise your research material. This may consist of books, journals, leaflets, notes you have made in the library, computer print-outs, tapes and even responses to questionnaires or surveys. Keeping your exact task clearly in mind, proceed as follows.

- Go through the books, checking the indexes to make sure there is information which clearly relates to your topic. Discard any books which do not cover what you are trying to research, or books which you cannot understand.

- Place paper markers between pages which are relevant in both books and journals. (Do not mark any pages in a publication which does not belong to you!)

- Check your leaflets, highlighting any useful information. Do the same with your computer print-outs.

- Check your own notes carefully. If they are pages of indecipherable scribble, then type them out neatly. This will not only make them easier to read but refresh your memory about the information you found!

- Check the questionnaires and summarise the answers. This is easy if you have asked 'tick box' questions, as then you can simply count the answers to each one.

Put any surplus information and material to one side. Now go through the information you have identified, checking it against the 'key rules for selection' given below.

Key rules for selection

For any information to be useful it must meet several criteria. It must be

- up to date
- accurate
- relevant
- valid
- complete
- legally acceptable.

Checking the date

Always discard old information in preference to the latest version you can get your hands on. This means that the later the edition of the book, newspaper or magazine, the more likely it is to contain up-to-date information. Therefore, the first thing you should do is to check the date on any source material you are using. This is particularly important in the business world, as so much changes so quickly. Legislation is updated; governments change their policies; businesses open, close, merge with other companies, are taken over by other organisations or simply change their name; ideas and strategies change and go out of date; new machines and pieces of equipment are invented – and so on. You only have to look at an old textbook on office procedures to see how much things have changed in the past ten years in the way office work and administration is carried out, or at an old atlas which shows countries which do not even exist today or which have changed their names.

Do remember to check the date *first* before you start marking any material or preparing any notes. It is very frustrating to find out after you have written two pages that at least half the information which you have included is now out of date!

Checking accuracy

Your boss *must* be able to rely upon you to give him or her accurate information. If you once let someone down on this, that person is unlikely to trust you easily again – and may suspect everything else you produce! For that reason, never be tempted to invent something if you cannot find the answer!

The *degree* of accuracy that is expected will depend upon your topic and the reason for your research. If you were giving the size of the population of the UK, an estimate would be acceptable, but if you were stating how many employees left the company last year, you would be expected to give a precise figure. Equally, if you were describing the comparative size of office machinery, you may give an estimated size of the photocopier. If you were calculating whether it would fit in a particular space in a new office, then you would need to give a precise measurement.

If ever you are in doubt about the accuracy of your information, then do cross-check it, so that you have verified (checked) it is true from more than one source. You can do this by

- asking for the opinion of *at least* one expert who can help you

- checking one or more sources of reference.

The biggest problem you may encounter is to read two sets of conflicting information on the same subject in two different source books. Some people assume that everything they hear on television or read on a printed page is correct in every detail! Unfortunately, this just is not true. Quite apart from the fact that people make mistakes and information goes out of date, in some cases there is also the *slant* of the information to consider. Several newspapers (and some television programmes) are past masters at telling you only the parts of a story which suit their purpose! This is the case, too, if you ever contact a company which has a vested interest in a particular issue. You need to make sure you obtain the other side of the story before you put pen to paper (or fingers to keyboard), and make sure that you give both sides of the argument clearly and objectively. This means sticking to the facts and keeping your personal opinions to yourself, unless you have been specifically asked for them!

Discussion point

All the following issues would involve, or did involve, two points of view – depending upon who you interview! Can you identify

a what the opposing views are (or were)

b which group of people or type of organisation would give you which view

c what you would have to do to ensure you had a balanced story at the end of the day?

(*Note*: If you are unsure what any of the following were about discuss them with your tutor.)

    i The Royal Mail strikes in 1996.
    ii Smoking in the workplace.
    iii The proposal to introduce a minimum wage for all employees.
    iv The building of the Newbury by-pass in Berkshire.

Checking relevance

Relevant information is that which is specifically concerned with your query. Anything else is irrelevant. If your boss has asked you to find out information on mobile phones, he or she wants some examples of the best-selling makes, their features and prices. What your boss does not want is

- the history of how they developed

- the advantages and disadvantages of using a mobile phone

- three paragraphs on different types of telephones

- useful alternatives to a mobile phone

- anything at all about fax machines or other methods of communication!

Being selective about what you include can be difficult. If you have worked for days to obtain a considerable amount of information, then there is always the temptation to prove how hard you have worked by putting everything in! Try to resist this. Most busy people skim read a document for information – you will lose their attention if they have to wade through half a page to find the bit they want. Remember, you can always indicate that you have further information available if they wish to know more.

One further point – books published for overseas markets (and CD-ROMs produced in the USA) often include a considerable amount of information which is either not relevant to your search, too detailed or contains words and phrases which you may not understand. Always favour 'home-produced' material unless you are absolutely stuck for information.

Checking validity

Whereas accuracy relates to facts, validity relates to assumptions. If you are only asked to give the facts, then you will not have to worry too much about validity. The time to be concerned is when you are asked to draw some conclusions from your research or make recommendations.

An 'invalid' statement is easy to identify if you think of the writer as having made 2 + 2 = 5! This is when two or more different facts have been linked together to draw the wrong conclusion. Unfortunately, we are all apt to do this in our personal lives. You see two friends talking to each other, they then glance at you, they then move closer and continue to talk. What is the conclusion you reach? Most people would start to think that they were the subject of the conversation and were being discussed 'behind their backs'! In other words, they jump to conclusions that may, or may not, be true. Do not do this when you are presenting your case in writing.

The temptation to make invalid assumptions becomes even greater if the people you talked to have a personal involvement or opinion in the matter. Read the following sentences and see if you can identify the flaw in the conclusion.

The car park has just been repainted and new spaces defined. Two staff have very large cars which won't fit into the spaces. Therefore all the spaces are too small and should be repainted.

In this case, the writer has let the people who have large cars (which may be the only large cars owned by staff!) influence his or her judgement about the car park. There is also the assumption that all the spaces are the same size, which they may not be.

Frequently, you will see basic facts and invalid assumptions used to support an argument. As an example, try the discussion point on page 154.

Checking the information is complete

There is nothing more annoying for a recipient than to be told half a tale! For example, someone takes a telephone message for you but forgets to include the telephone number. This is a minor irritation if the number is listed in the phone book, but a major problem if the caller is ex-directory and you therefore cannot return the call.

The more complex the document you are writing, the more important it is that you prepare carefully. Given that you now have a set of information which is up-to-date, accurate, relevant and valid, you need to make sure that everything you need is included. If there is an obvious gap, then do not be tempted to gloss over something because you could not find enough information. If you cannot find the answer to something, then you would do better to admit this at the outset – perhaps your boss can come up with some useful ideas as to where you can find the additional information you need.

Checking legality

You must make certain that you are not breaking copyright law by reproducing anything which is not general or public information without permission. Nor must you ever claim that work which is someone else's is your own! This is known as 'plagiarism' and is unacceptable.

A key area which particularly concerns journalists (see page 145) is that of defamation. If a paper prints something which is untrue about someone, then it may find itself in the middle of an expensive libel action. (Remember, slander relates to the spoken word, libel to the written word.) The biggest danger is repeating hearsay or including speculative comments (ie gossip!) made by other people. Bear in mind that you could also be guilty if you do not check all your facts thoroughly before you repeat them – especially if they concern other people!

Discussion point

1   You work for a Safety Group and are undertaking research on road accidents. You find the following item in a newspaper. As a group, discuss whether the writer has drawn a logical conclusion from the numerical facts (which are true) or whether the conclusion is invalid. Can you say why?

> Cars can kill. In the past 100 years 500,000 people have been killed in road accidents in Britain. This is greater than the number of people who are murdered or die through disease. Cars are the greatest killers of the modern age so cars should be banned.

(Turn to page 156 for some clues if you are completely stuck!)

2   You work for the human resource manager and have been asked to compile some facts and figures for a study on absenteeism. Because the systems for reporting absence and booking holiday leave are not very good in your organisation, you are struggling to find data on individual employees. However, in several offices staff have given you their views of their colleagues' absences. Given that you are short of material you are tempted to include this information.

As a group, discuss the dangers of this approach.

Organising your research notes

By now, all your information should be clearly marked. File anything you do not need for this investigation. (To throw it away may be a bit hasty at this stage, unless it is clearly out-of-date. You may be asked at a later date to expand on something you have written.)

Now decide the order in which you should present the information. If you have been given a simple list of tasks to undertake, then use this list as your basis for a reply. If there is more than one major topic on the list, then you could write a covering memo (see Chapter 12) and then attach individual sheets for each topic behind the memo. This makes life easier for your boss, who might want to file the papers under different headings. If you have several queries to answer, use clear headings so that the answers to each are easy to identify.

It may be that you have been asked to prepare a report on your findings. In this case you will need a logical format for the report and to make sure it has a beginning, a middle and an end! Information on report writing is given in Chapter 12.

Inaccurate, exaggerated or just misleading?

In October 1995 the media were full of stories about a new generation of contraceptive pills which *doubled* the risk of blood clots. The research received very wide coverage on television, the radio and in the press.

The result? Hundreds of thousands of women stopped taking the pill – many of whom later became pregnant. What they didn't know was that the risk of blood clots from pregnancy was twice as high as the risk from the pills they had stopped taking!

The true measure of risk from taking the pill was very low indeed (1.5 per 10,000 women). Even when the risk doubled it was still extremely low (3 per 10,000 women). However, the media chose to ignore this aspect – because alarmist stories sell papers, and simple warnings do not.

The result was that the Chief Medical Officer is now trying to prevent this problem recurring by defining 'risk' and 'risk levels'. Whether this will stop the media distorting such issues in the future is another matter.

At this stage, it is useful if you make a list of the areas you were asked to investigate and then make sure you have the answers to each one. Tick these off methodically and then put your information into the order in which you will refer to it when you are writing.

A key tip! If you are going to insert any quotations and have to identify the source of your material, then *do this as you go*! Many is the writer (or student) who has written a project, only to have to spend a couple of days looking back for references he or she should have included! At the very least, make a note of the source at the time, even if you insert the footnote later.

Write clear sentences which summarise what you have found. Do not include anything you do not understand and avoid writing about anything which would be clearer to represent as a table or graph (see page 279). In the early stages of your career it is useful to write a draft first, then to check this with your boss to make sure you are on the right lines. As you progress, you will become more used to the types of presentations required in your organisation and the preferences of your own boss – and will be able to research and present your information with confidence!

Discussion point

Start to practise your research skills. Choose one topic which is either in the news or which is connected with a hobby or an interest of yours. Check your topic with your tutor.

1 Research the information and prepare a short (five-minute) talk which will interest the rest of the group.

2 Prepare a summary sheet which lists the key points of your talk and give this to each member of your group.

3 Attach to the summary sheet for your tutor a list of references and sources you have used.

Clues to the discussion point on page 154

Think about the following issues.

- Has the number of road deaths been constant over the past 100 years, rising or falling? (Think about drink-driving, seat belts, air bags, etc.)

- Are all road deaths caused by 'cars'? (What is the role of the driver in this? What about the responsibilities of pedestrians?)

- Even if there are more deaths on the road than by other methods, is the answer to ban cars? What would be the result? What other options are available?

These suggestions should trigger other ideas!

Transmitting information

10

● Introduction

If you undertook the discussion point at the end of Chapter 9, then you have been involved in transmitting the information you researched to your group using a combination of verbal and written methods of communication!

All information passes through four stages.

1   It is received and passed to the correct person(s). This may be the incoming mail or verbal information given at a meeting.

2   It is processed by
    - actioning it (eg letters, memos, faxes and e-mails are answered; researched information becomes part of a report; meetings are minuted)
    - throwing it away (eg unwanted mail)
    - marking it for filing (eg documents which are for information only).

3   The actioned or processed documents are transmitted to other interested parties.

4   Used documents which will be required for future reference are stored for later retrieval.

In reality, virtually all documents which are initiated or processed in an organisation are then transmitted to someone – otherwise there is not much point in preparing them! Usually, someone else needs the information which the document or message will provide. Sometimes the information is required urgently and must be provided by a specific deadline. In other cases there is more flexibility in this respect.

This chapter considers the different methods of communication which are used to transmit information in different circumstances and the types of equipment, facilities and services you can use to help you make sure that you choose the best and most appropriate method available to you at the time.

● Methods of communication

There are essentially three ways in which you can communicate with someone. This can be

- verbally,

- in writing, or

- electronically.

Each of these methods has benefits and drawbacks.

Verbal communication

If you talk to someone face to face or over the telephone, then you are using verbal communication. However, 'face to face' can signify anything from an individual interview to a group meeting to a large gathering. Today, we are used to communicating with people on the telephone and leaving messages on an answering machine. A variation of this is voice mail, where messages can be left for internal extension users in an organisation – in just the same way as you would leave a message on an answering machine connected to a private telephone.

Advantages

- It is a fast method of communicating.

- It is relatively cheap (unless you are making an international phone call or spend ages talking about something on the telephone).

- It enables you to use your voice to emphasise important points and the tone of your voice to imply your feelings.

- It enables you to obtain instant feedback from the recipient.

- It enables you to check that you have the listener's attention.

- Face-to-face communication also allows you to use gestures, facial expressions and other forms of body language to emphasise your meaning and attitude.

Disadvantages

- You need to be able to say what you mean clearly and unambiguously.

- You need to speak clearly – and have the confidence to speak to strangers.

- If someone cannot hear you clearly, then that person may not be able to receive your message correctly. This can be for a variety of reasons – from a bad connection on a telephone line, to several people speaking at once in a meeting, to a person having a hearing disability.

- People have short memories! If the message is long or complicated, it may be easily forgotten.

- If someone asks you a difficult question then you may find it hard to answer them.

- People can be distracted or biased in a face-to-face meeting, eg if one person fidgets, is not conventionally dressed or has a speech disability.

Written communication

There are many types of written communication used in business – letters, memos, reports, notices, questionnaires, forms, advertising literature and even handwritten notes, which may be used to pass on urgent telephone messages.

Advantages

- Documents can be filed and kept for future reference – or studied again and again before a reply is made.

- Documents can easily be copied by the sender so that they are received by many people – or copied by the recipient if he or she wishes to convey the information to other people for comment

- Long, complicated, complex or important information can be read and studied carefully. You would not want to use a sachet of dye on a favourite pair of jeans if you had only brief verbal instructions on what you must and must not do!

- The communication can be such that it has formal authority – which can be useful in certain circumstances. Solicitors, for instance, put everything in writing!

- It provides a permanent record of what was said and agreed. This may be vital in the case of any misunderstanding or dispute (yet another reason why solicitors put things in writing).

- It 'distances' the sender from the recipient. This can be useful if the information is 'sensitive' or of a contentious nature. If your organisation decided to reduce staff holidays next year, you would no doubt be informed in writing – no manager would want to face the reaction of staff by telling them in an open meeting!

- Information which is better conveyed in a table, graph or through an illustration can only be sent by this means.

- Colour can be used to good effect – and even used for mass communication using a colour photocopier (see Chapter 14).

Disadvantages

- Anyone composing written correspondence must be able to write clearly and must possess good grammatical skills. A good command of spelling and vocabulary is also important.

- Handwriting can be variable – from very clear to almost illegible!

- Documents which need to be produced in typescript need to be keyed in to a computer. If a manager does not possess these skills, then the cost of a secretary's or administrator's time must be added to the cost of stationery and postage.

- A complicated document can take several hours to write and produce.

- This method may be slow. Unless a courier or express delivery service is used (which may be expensive), several days may elapse between the composition of the document and receipt – particularly if the recipient is abroad.

- The fact that there is a permanent record can be a disadvantage if
  - the writer later regrets sending it
  - there are several factual or other errors in the document
  - the situation is changing rapidly and by the time the document is received, the contents are out of date.

Electronic methods of communication

Today communications can be sent by fax and by computer. Most people are familiar with fax machines (see also page 173), but you may be less certain how a communication can be sent by computer. There are two ways in which this can be done. One is by direct computer-to-computer communication, either by a direct link between two branches or organisations which communicate regularly, or through the ISDN (Integrated Services Digital Network) system (see pages 163–4). Using this method, whole files can be sent from one computer to another without any difficulty.

The more usual method of electronic communication, however, is electronic mail – e-mail for short. This is quite common, particularly in larger organisations. There are many different e-mail packages on the market. If one of these is installed on a networked system (see Chapter 14) all computer users can then send e-mail messages to other computer users in the organisation. They can also attach to their message other electronic documents, eg a copy of a report prepared on a word processing package or a copy of a spreadsheet. If the company also subscribes to the Internet, then messages and documents can be sent all over the world, to any other Internet subscriber. (Further details of e-mail are given on page 176.) Many organisations use fax and e-mail in preference to traditional methods because they combine many of the advantages of both verbal and written communication systems.

Advantages

- They are incredibly rapid. Digital impulses are transmitted at the speed of light so it is virtually as quick to send a fax to Australia as it is to a nearby town!

- Graphics and text can be sent electronically. Pages of print and drawings can easily be transmitted by fax. Modern computer software programs enable documents to be created on a variety of packages – from word processing to spreadsheets – and then attached as 'files' to an e-mail message.

- The whereabouts of the recipient is immaterial provided there is a communications link. Travelling executives can receive faxes at their hotels, those with a laptop computer and modem can receive e-mail messages from their workplaces, those with an Internet link can receive messages anywhere in the world.

- They are relatively cheap, given that there is only the transmission time to be taken into consideration. This is usually less than the time that would be taken up with a telephone call because the message is short and to the point.

- There is a permanent written record. It is easy to print out e-mail messages – or to save them to the computer hard disk drive.

- It is easy to respond – fax messages can be returned at any time of the day or night (providing the fax machine is left switched on). E-mail has an in-built facility for the recipient to reply, forward to another person or even send to a group of people (see page 178).

- On an internal e-mail system it is possible for senders to see when recipients opened and read their message.

Disadvantages

The drawbacks are relatively few but include some possible technical problems.

- Transmission breakdown. This may happen when a long fax is being sent, and will interrupt the transmission. The operator will have to identify when the problem occurred and resend the missing pages.

- Equipment breakdown. It is no use having an e-mail facility if the computer system is down, or owning a fax if it is not working properly.

- Address difficulties. You need to know someone's fax number or e-mail address before you can send a message. Internet address lines can be very long and one mistake (even entering a space where there should not be one) will mean the e-mail will not reach the recipient.

- Receipt unknown! It is not possible to check that you have sent a fax to the correct organisation unless you talk to the recipient on the telephone or he or she responds to your fax. This is because nobody 'answers' on a fax and there is nothing printed on your fax to indicate who received it. Equally, if you send an e-mail via the Internet, you cannot tell when or if the recipient received or opened the message.

- Document size and quality. Fax machines will only accept A4 documents, and those of variable quality must be photocopied first.

● Equipment, facilities and services

Although you may be able to identify some occasions when one communication method might be more appropriate to use than another, you will certainly find this easier if you know more about the range of equipment, facilities and services that are available. You should not only know about different items of equipment but also exactly how to use each one. Otherwise you could easily ignore a very convenient feature without even knowing about it! A typical example is the facility on many phones to arrange to have them ring you back if the extension you want is engaged. If you do not know about this, then you can waste valuable time trying to get through to a very busy extension when the system could do it for you!

A useful test is your home video recorder! If you are equipment-minded, then you will be well aware of all its features, how to pre-set it to record – even when you are on holiday – how to adjust the tracking to improve the quality of the picture and so on. In this case you are likely to get the best out of any equipment you use and enjoy learning about all the facilities which are available. If you are not equipment-minded, then it might be all you can do to rewind a tape! In this case you will have to be a little more self-disciplined when you start to use telecommunications equipment and make notes, if necessary, to prompt you on the key features.

Telephone systems

Today there is a wide range of telephone systems for business users and additional facilities and services which link to these. The different types of equipment you should know about include

- switchboards and handsets
- voice mail and answering machines
- mobile phones and pagers.

The telephone is a major link between every organisation and the outside world – and many customers judge an organisation on its ability to answer their calls quickly, efficiently and courteously. In addition, the telephone system is an important method of communication within an organisation, enabling staff at every level to be able to obtain and exchange information.

Rapid technological development has virtually revolutionised the facilities available through a telephone system over the past ten years. You will probably have noticed this yourself. If your home telephone is connected to a digital line (you can find out by checking if you can use the 1471 service to learn who called you last), then you will also have the choice of a wide range of other Select Services (see page 180). For example, if you wanted to telephone your local multiplex cinema, not long ago you would have to keep trying if it was engaged. Today you may be connected immediately and have the choice of keys you can press (according to instructions you are given) to obtain either current information, make a booking or find out about forthcoming releases. Only if you select the relevant option will you actually speak to an operator – other information will be pre–recorded. This enables one operator to cope efficiently with up to three times as many callers.

The digital revolution

One major innovation in the past few years has been the introduction of ISDN (Integrated Services Digital Network), a system now used by more than 20 per cent of UK companies and predicted to double in size by 1998.

ISDN is a digital phone line which allows users to send and receive various types of information – such as voice, graphics, data, text, fax and video – to other organisations with an ISDN line. The lines are digital and are therefore fast – information is communicated rapidly, which reduces the cost of the connection. In addition, some switchboard and telephone systems have the ability to be connected to both ISDN and ordinary lines. Having access to ISDN means that a much wider variety of sophisticated services is available through the telephone system – even for smaller organisations.

A summary of the applications of ISDN and the telephone services available through ISDN is given in Figure 10.1.

Switchboards and handsets
Equipment

The technical name for a telephone switchboard is a **PBX – a Private Branch Exchange.** These require a dedicated operator to answer incoming callers and connect them to the correct extension. However, this is only suitable for a large organisation which can afford a full-time switchboard operator. A small company may instead have a **key system** in use. This comprises 'feature' phones so that anyone can answer incoming calls. A popular choice for many medium-sized and small companies where the volume of calls may vary at different times of the day or year is a hybrid system. This system comprises one or two feature phones with everyone else having standard **handsets.** The system can then operate in one of two ways. The feature phones can be used as a PBX with all calls being received through them or the system can be used as a key system during quieter periods.

You may be a little confused about the term 'handset' and the difference between a handset and a telephone. In business, both PBXs and key systems can be grouped together under telephone systems. The term 'handset' is used for an individual extension telephone which has its own features, such as programmable keys, message-waiting indicator light, personal abbreviated dialling, automatic extension transfer and frequently a display panel which can give prompts or show the current status to the user. If you have a modern telephone at home, then this is more likely, today, to be termed a handset. All these features are described in more detail below.

Applications
- UK and international phone calls
- Transfer of PC data files and databases from one computer to another
- Voice/computer link so that sender/receiver can 'share' a screen of information for discussion
- Transfer of photographs, graphics and artwork to a remote computer
- Desktop video conferencing between PC users in remote locations
- Transmission of fax messages from PCs

Telephone services

ACD **Automatic Call Distribution** is used by many large organisations which regularly handle multiple calls or have help desks for customers. The ACD system automatically places calls to the next available extension – if none is free, the calls enter a queueing system where the caller hears messages or music.

CTI **Computer Telephony Integration** links the computer and phone system so that multiple calls – both incoming and outgoing – can be handled as efficiently as possible. An extension of this is **CLI (Calling Line Identity).** With this system, the computer record of the incoming caller automatically appears on screen whilst the phone is still ringing. This is useful for Accounts Departments, which may be discussing the details of a client's account, or Sales Departments, which can immediately access details of the customer and his or her usual requirements. Many companies use CLI for teleselling. The phones of telesales staff are linked to a database of telephone numbers. Calls are made either automatically by computer or by clicking on the number shown on the PC.

DDI **Direct Dialling In** to extension users – even on small phone systems. Extension users have their own direct line number that they can give customers to reduce the volume of calls handled by the switchboard operator.

If individual handsets have a display screen, then an additional feature is the identification of incoming callers (their number or even their name!), which appears on the display so that important customers can be greeted individually.

IVR **Interactive Voice Response** systems play a recorded message followed by information to which the caller can respond by either saying 'yes' or 'no' or pressing appropriate numbers on their handsets. Depression of the required key can then route callers automatically to a predetermined extension.

Figure 10.1 ISDN applications and services

Features and facilities

At one time there was a tremendous difference between the facilities available on digital PBXs and those available on smaller key systems. Modern technology is changing this so that even the smallest systems now have an additional array of features. Handsets, too, often offer a range of facilities, and more are being developed all the time.

All telephone system providers pride themselves on offering a specific range of features and facilities. Therefore, you may find that the choice offered on any system you use varies a little from those listed in Figure 10.2. Your first task as a new telephone user in an organisation should always be to obtain a copy of the user's handbook which will show the facilities available, both through the main system and on your own handset. If you are going to be responsible for answering a switchboard or a main console in a key system, then you will usually need specific training.

Abbreviated dialling Enables regularly used numbers to be saved in abbreviated form. Particularly useful for long DDI numbers. Also used for suppliers, associated companies, branch offices and key customers. *See also* **personal abbreviated dialling**.

Account codes System which automatically allocates specific calls to nominated accounts. Makes it easier for clients to be billed with the cost, where appropriate.

Call barring Enables the operator to prevent certain extensions making certain types of calls, eg international calls or to find out the cricket score!

Call forwarding Routes incoming calls to another extension whilst the extension user is away from his or her desk.

Call logging System of telephone management where the origin, destination and duration of all calls is recorded for accounting purposes.

Camp on busy If an internal extension is engaged, the call can be 'booked' so that the telephone will ring automatically when the busy extension is free.

Conference calls Enables one external caller and several internal line users to talk to each other simultaneously. *See also* **trunk conferencing**.

Cordless telephones Can now be used as part of a PBX with a cordless facility. Enable users to take their handsets around with them without being physically connected to the system.

Digital voice announcement System which automatically answers calls, plays a personalised message and then routes calls to their extensions or department. Provides a useful 'back-up' for the switchboard operator during busy periods.

Display message Enables one extension user to key in a message which will be displayed on the LCD (liquid crystal display) of another extension user. For instance, a caller who is away from the office may set up his or her extension so that those who ring are given his or her whereabouts, eg 'in a meeting'. A caller to a busy extension may key in a message to ask the other person to ring when free.

Discriminating ringing Difference in ringing tones between internal and external calls.

Distinctive ringing Nearby handsets or phones can be programmed to ring differently so that users can identify which one is ringing.

Do not disturb Temporarily blocks incoming calls to an extension.

Door intercom/opening Enables the operator of a key system to speak to visitors on an intercom and then release the door lock. Excellent for security if the reception is far away from the entrance.

Exchange line status indicator Shows the status of exchange lines, ie whether they are busy or available.

Exclusive hold Gives an extension user the ability to put a caller on hold without anyone else being able to access the call.

Extension lock Allows users to key in a lock code to their phone or handset to prevent unauthorised use (usually excluding 999).

External/internal line distinction Enables certain buttons to be programmed to show whether an incoming call is external or internal.

Group hunting Calls which can be dealt with by several people can be placed into a 'group hunt' which will find the first free extension. Groups should be kept small to prevent callers having to wait for ages whilst a free extension is found.

Hands-free speech Enables a handset to be used without picking up the receiver.

Hearing aid compatible No feedback is received from the handset when the user is wearing a hearing aid.

Hot line Selected phones can be programmed to dial a pre-set number automatically as soon as the handset is picked up.

Interrupt Bleeps the line to notify the user of a phone that another call is waiting.

Last number redial Automatically redials the last number called.

Least cost routing Provided there is access to different telephone services (eg BT, Mercury and cable operators), the system will always access the cheapest line at any given time. *See also* page 179.

Listen on hold If extension users are asked to 'hold', gives them the ability to replace the handset, monitor the call on hands-free and pick up the call when the other person comes back on to the line.

Manager/secretary operation Enables a manager's calls to be diverted to the secretary who can then announce them.

Memory protection In case of a power cut or system shutdown, all programmed features in the system are automatically saved into memory.

Message waiting indicator Either a sound or a flashing light on a handset which indicates that a message has been received and stored.

Messaging Facility for leaving messages on the display of handsets. *See also* **display message.**

Music on hold Intended to console callers while they wait but may be more of an irritant. Proves the connection is still intact and callers have not been cut off by mistake. *See also* **user-defined music on hold.**

Networking facility Allows the phone system to be linked to other offices or branches on a private circuit. Enables a large organisation to operate the whole network with virtually the same range of phone facilities available, eg extension dialling, paging, camp on busy, etc.

Night service Routes incoming calls to specific extensions after hours.

Paging Ability to access selected extensions with a paging message through the speaker.

Personal abbreviated dialling Enables the user of a handset to store his or her own most frequently used numbers as codes in the handset.

Reminder call holding Reminder that a caller is still waiting to be connected.

Trunk conferencing Enables a conference to be held between one extension and two outside lines.

Trunk-to-trunk transfer Automatically diverts an incoming call from an internal extension to another phone, either mobile or fixed, outside the office. Enables busy executives to transfer all their calls to a mobile or home telephone after hours.

User-defined music on hold Gives the operator the ability to choose which music to play to external callers who are waiting to be connected.

Voice mail Add-on or integral feature of many phone systems today which enables voice messages to be left in a mail box and for messages to be redirected to other members of staff (see below).

Figure 10.2 Telephone system facilities

Voice mail

The era of voice processing

You may often have heard the phrase 'information processing', but did you know that voices can also be processed these days?

Voice processing is the name given to add–on systems which allow organisations to record, send and retrieve messages all day, every day on a global basis. In addition, they also help to handle calls to reduce the number being processed by the switchboard operator.

Most systems can be programmed and managed from a personal computer which will provide management reports on usage on request. A sophisticated system includes the following.

*   A **voice mail service** means each extension has a personal answering machine or mail box which answers calls with a personal or pre-recorded message. Stored messages are retrieved by keying in a user identity (ID) code. This not only improves customer service but also means that all telephones in the company can always be answered, even when the user is absent.
*   An **automated attendant service** automatically answers incoming calls both in and out of normal working hours and directs the caller to the required extension.
*   A **bulletin board** gives pre-recorded information to all incoming callers. It is useful for giving general information about company products and services (eg multiplex cinemas).

*   An **interview service** automatically obtains specific information from callers by asking them a number of pre-recorded questions (usually no more than ten). This means, for instance, that requests for brochures or orders received can be handled automatically. The information gathered can also be used to create a customer database.
*   **Internal/external messaging** means voice mail messages can be programmed to be accessed from a remote location by the user.
*   **Group delivery service** sends a voice mail message simultaneously to a number of individuals.

The disadvantage with voice processing is the fact that some people may switch over to voice mail every time they do not want to be disturbed, which can be annoying for customers if they continually have to leave messages. Some people also have a dislike of a disembodied recorded voice giving them information or, even worse, asking them questions – and elderly people in particular may struggle to cope. Business-to-business applications for this are therefore more likely to be successful than private individual to business. What are your views?

Answering machines

An alternative to voice mail for smaller businesses is, of course, an answering machine. These are now a common feature in households too – not only to take messages when individuals are out but also to allow people to 'screen' calls – and only pick to up the receiver if they want to speak to the caller.

Answering machines can be integrated with a telephone or may be stand-alone and are of two types. Older models use micro-cassettes to store the recorded messages whereas the newer, digital models store all the messages electronically. The total message storage time can vary considerably – from as little as 5 minutes to 20 minutes. However, the new models do record calls more quickly and give better speech quality.

Features

Some features are common to virtually all answering machines, such as volume control for listening to messages and a light or digital display to indicate a message has been received. Most machines now give the user the facility to access messages from a remote location simply by phoning the number and entering a code number on the keypad of the handset. Additional features are shown in Figure 10.3.

Call forwarding After a message has been received, or at a pre-determined time, the machine rings the user at a pre-programmed phone number (either fixed or mobile) and informs him or her that there is a message.

Dial back and record Machine identifies the telephone number of callers who leave no message.

Interrupt from extension Enables the user to interrupt the pre-recorded message which stops playing if the handset is picked up.

Mailbox Allows multiple users to have their own code so that callers are prompted to key in a number relating to the person for whom they wish to leave a message. Messages are then stored separately. Avoids everyone having to listen to each other's messages to find their own.

Power failure protection Enables the machine to operate even during a power cut.

Remote announcement change Enables the user to change the pre-recorded message from a remote location.

Toll saver Prevents the machine responding to a call by the user to retrieve messages if none has been left. Means the call will not be charged.

Variable messaging Enables different messages to be played at different times of the day, eg a formal message during business hours and an informal one during the evening or at weekends.

Voice messaging Machine automatically sends a message to several locations.

Figure 10.3 Answering machine facilities

BT Call Minder

The BT alternative to an answering machine is its Call Minder service which stores telephone messages on a computer. Each message is recorded digitally by BT in the subscriber's personal mailbox. Users can then tell if there are calls waiting because they will hear a distinctive tone when they next pick up the handset. To listen to the messages users dial 1571 (free of charge) and follow the pre-recorded voice prompts. Messages can also be accessed when users are away from home by phoning their own number and keying in a personal four-digit number. In this case they pay for the cost of the call.

The service has two advantages over standard answering machines. It operates if the telephone is engaged, and then calls users to say a message has been left. In addition, if the mailbox is getting full, the service rings users to warn them. However, incoming calls cannot be screened by Call Minder and neither can it be used in conjunction with the 1471 facility – so the number of the last caller is not obtainable. However, for small businesses which are not too interested in call screening, the service is an extremely economical alternative to buying an answering machine.

You should note that Call Minder is only one of BT's Select Services – and that other telecommunication service providers also offer similar services (see page 180).

Mobile phones

Most people today are familiar with mobile phones – even if they do not own one themselves. However, if your boss is thinking about buying one – or is continually walking into the office, throwing it on your desk and saying how useless it is, would you know enough to advise him or her?

The biggest mistake most people make when buying a mobile phone is to think only about the purchase price. However, the main charge depends upon the tariff for the particular system being used, which can vary considerably. In addition the coverage of the network is important, plus the terms of any contract which has been agreed. All of these facts are considered below.

There are two types of mobile phone – analogue and digital. Both use radio signals to transmit calls, but digital signals are computer-coded for security. It is therefore impossible for people to eavesdrop on calls or to 'clone' the number to make calls at the user's expense. This is not the case with analogue phones.

Four companies run the mobile networks. Vodafone and Cellnet operate both an analogue and a digital network, whilst Mercury and Orange only run a digital network.

With any mobile it is only possible to make and receive calls in the areas covered by the network you have joined – and none of these covers all the UK. Rural areas, in particular, are less likely to be covered. Each network issues a map which shows the areas it covers. However, it is possible to subscribe to more than one network if this would improve coverage. If your boss wants to use his or her mobile elsewhere in Europe, this can only be done by using the digital services provided by Vodafone or Cellnet.

The user is normally billed monthly and there are several charges to consider. All new users are charged a connection fee and then there is the purchase price of the phone and the rental fee to the network. Anyone choosing a Mercury or Orange service will pay the rental direct to the company. Those using Vodafone or Cellnet will pay a service provider. Finally, there are call costs to consider. It is worth noting that it is expensive to call some mobiles – even if you are talking on a fixed phone. Calls to Vodafone and Cellnet average about £1.70 for a five-minute call, whilst those to Mercury and Orange average about 65p!

Users can choose from a range of tariffs which are priced depending upon usage and the time of day at which calls are most likely to be made.

However, the biggest problem for mobile phone users is getting 'locked into' a contract and later discovering that it can cost several hundred pounds to get out of the agreement – or that the minimum term of the agreement is one year or longer. The terms of mobile phone contracts are currently being investigated by the Office of Fair Trading in that some could contravene the Unfair Contracts Terms Act, but as yet no case has been taken to court.

Features
Mobile phones are now small and light, and most easily fit into a pocket or handbag. Most have a rechargeable battery and charging unit. All have a digital display, a memory for storing frequently used numbers, a backlit keypad and last number redial. Some offer functions not usually connected to phones, such as a voice memo, calculator, calendar and clock! Useful features are shown in Figure 10.4.

Alphanumeric store   Each number is stored in the memory against the person's name. The name can be used to recall the number.

Call timer   Displays the time of an individual call. Some phones bleep each minute and others enable the user to enter a maximum call time into the phone. Useful if the network allows a free air-time limit.

Car kits   Enables the phone to be used safely in a car by placing it in a hands-free holder. An aerial is also fitted to improve reception, given that mobile phones do not work well inside a building or car. If your boss is tempted to drive with one hand and hold the phone with the other, you may try saying tactfully that he or she could be prosecuted for driving without due care and attention!

Mailbox   Similar to the service available on answering machines. Unconnected calls made to the phone are diverted to a central mailbox on the network where the caller can leave a message. Not offered by Orange.

Message facility   Records and stores text messages and the time and date of the call.

Personal assistant service   Service offered by Cellnet which allocates the user a personal contact number on which the service can answer, screen and divert calls, take messages and store or divert faxes. If users provide the service with a schedule of locations and times (worldwide) then the 'find-me' facility will locate the user by following the schedule and trying the most probable number first.

Unanswered call store   Indicates that someone called whilst the phone was switched off. As yet it is not possible for UK phones to store a number and automatically redial it, but Vodafone plans to introduce this on its digital network shortly.

Figure 10.4 Mobile phone facilities

An alternative mobile – with no call charges

Because of the high costs of mobile phones, many organisations are turning to private mobile radio (PMR) which has many of the benefits of a mobile and no charges for call time.

PMRs allow two-way voice communication over increasingly large distances. The system works by transmitting on a frequency allocated by the Radio-communications Agency and connection is instant. For this reason, it is commonly used by security staff and the emergency services. Now it is used by organisations such as service companies which have engineers working in the field. The group call facility means that a central operator can relay the same message to a team simultaneously.

Wider access is obtainable by subscribing to a Public Access Mobile Radio (PAMR) network such as National Band III, which offers radio communications throughout the UK. There is a monthly subscription fee but again no charge for call time. The latest development, however, is Short Range Business Range (SRBR) which covers distances of around 400 metres. This was announced by the government in January 1996 with the aim of making radio technology more accessible to businesses.

Pagers

Pagers are small, hand-held, pocket-sized devices on which people can be signalled quickly and easily. There are three types of pagers – those that call the user with a bleep tone, those with a numeric or alphanumeric display and those which allow two-way speech.

Tone–only pagers are the cheapest – the holder knows to call a certain number when the bleep sounds. Those who expect to be bleeped by different people either need a numeric pager (on which callers leave a contact number) or an alphanumeric pager (on which callers can leave a text message as well as their number). The type which allow two-way voice communication from either pager to pager or pager to telephone are linked through a PBX, with the operator making the link between the two units.

The coverage of pagers is again dependent upon the zones covered by the network to which the user subscribes. However, there is a choice of coverage areas and more than one may be selected.

Pager features are shown in Figure 10.5.

Alarm clock function Can be set to remind the user when to make a call or undertake a task.

Answering machine link Pager and answering machine are compatible so that the latter can inform the paging unit when a message is waiting.

Back-lit display Useful for reading messages in the dark.

Call transfer Enables calls to be transferred from an office telephone extension to a paging unit.

Message store Messages are stored for later access, sometimes with a time and date stamp.

Mode selection Enables the user to choose a variety of 'modes' in which to receive the signal, eg tone, vibrate, music or silent. Vibrate is useful in a noisy area or in a meeting when people would not take too kindly to a loud bleep interrupting the proceedings.

Figure 10.5 Pager facilities

Discussion point

As a group, discuss the different types of telephone equipment and features which would be most suitable for each of the following. Be prepared to justify your own decisions!

1 The college you attend. (Try to think of all the different types of employees and what they might need, as well as the obvious answers!)

2 A small business with two travelling executives, one secretary/PA and two other office workers.

3 The service centre of a large firm of household appliance manufacturers (eg freezers, microwaves, washing machines, fridges, etc.) which receives constant calls and enquiries from customers and has a team of engineers visiting homes to make repairs.

Fax machines

Fax machines are in common use today. Traditionally, an added extra for medium- and large-sized businesses, they rapidly became an essential. Today the biggest growth in demand is from small businesses which are taking advantage of the falling prices of fax machines and the introduction of combined phone/faxes and other multifunction devices (see page 176). The benefits of being able to transmit text, graphics, photographs and anything else which can fit on to a sheet of paper quickly, easily and cheaply to almost anywhere in the world are too good to miss.

A fax machine works by scanning a black and white document and converting what it sees into a signal which is then transmitted down a telephone line. Faxes are known by CCITT (the Consultative Committee for International Telephone and Telegraphy) international groupings and the majority now in use conform to Group 3. A few state-of-the-art Group 4 machines exist. When two machines connect there is a brief 'handshake' period in which each machine identifies the grouping of the other. The transmission speed is governed by two factors – the speed of the slowest machine and the speed at which the modem will operate. This is a device through which the digital impulses pass to the outside world (see also Chapter 14). High-speed transmission saves money as the connection time is less and is particularly beneficial for companies which send many long-distance or international faxes.

Fax machines are also popular because they are extremely easy to operate. In most cases it is simply a matter of putting the fax in the document feeder, dialling the number of the recipient's fax and pressing the relevant keys. After transmission the document is ejected from the fax with a mark which shows it has been processed. A transmission report is then printed to confirm the length and time of the connection and whether transmission took place satisfactorily. If the transmission was interrupted, for instance, this would show on the report and the sender would have to obtain a reconnection for the missing pages. Whilst this describes the basic operation of a fax machine, most machines have a variety of additional features which are given in Figure 10.6. Obviously, the more features that are required, the higher the price of the fax.

Faxes also come in four different types, depending upon the printing method and type of paper used.

- The paper can be thermal paper (which has a special coating) or plain paper. Plain paper is normally preferred because it is cheaper and does not curl. Thermal paper is wound on a roll – as the roll is used, incoming faxes are likely to be ejected tightly rolled and take some time to flatten out. In addition, the image fades in time and rolls regularly need replenishing.

- On plain paper machines there is a choice of three different types of printing.
    - Inkjet (called Bubblejet by Canon). This is relatively slow but good quality. The cartridges need replacing after about 700 pages and cost between £12 and £40 depending upon the type of machine/cartridge being used.
    - Thermal ink transfer. This is slightly quicker with very good quality print-out. The ribbon cartridge needs replacing after about 750 pages and costs about £17.
    - Laser (or LED). This gives high-speed, top-quality print-outs. The toner cartridge needs replacing every 2000 to 6000 pages and costs from £5 to £140 depending upon the type of machine being used. In addition, the drum unit also needs replacing after about 50 000 pages and would cost about £150.

The type of machine purchased will depend upon the frequency of use and the expected volume of incoming faxes.

Abbreviated dialling Same facility as found on modern telephone systems.

Activity log Machine prints out a report on all faxes sent/received since the last report.

Anti-junk feature Enables the user to block calls from such senders.

Automatic dialling/redialling Machine automatically starts transmission once the connection is made and/or continues to redial the number if it is engaged.

Automatic timer/deferred dialling Machine can be programmed to send faxes during cheap-rate and off-peak transmission times.

Broadcast facility Sends a specified number of pages to several different numbers automatically.

Cost savers Features built in to the machine to help reduce the costs of operation. In addition to deferred dialling, other features include an inksaver mode to double the life of a cartridge, an energy-save mode and a Mercury key so that documents can be sent by the cheapest route.

Cover sheets Machine automatically precedes each fax message with a specially printed cover sheet giving the name of the organisation and sender.

Dual access Facility to send faxes at the same time as machine is receiving them.

Fax header Automatically prints the name and number of the sender on the top of all outgoing faxes.

Fax on demand Produces a printed copy of any information stored in the machine's memory. Enables the operator to load information into the memory against specific dial codes. The information can be accessed by callers who are given voice prompts to key the correct number. They then press their 'send' button to have pages of information sent to them automatically. This feature is becoming increasingly popular. For instance, potential visitors can be asked to access a location map; suppliers and distributors can access price lists and product information.

Fax routing Only possible if there is ISDN access. Using the DDI, users have their own individual fax numbers. The incoming fax is then routed directly to the recipient's PC. The ideal system if confidentiality of faxes is required.

FIFO filing Incoming and outgoing faxes are stored in a file on a hard disk so that users can check on messages or re-send them if required.

Half-tone mode Enables the fax to recognise shades of grey – the more shades of grey it recognises, the more clearly will photographs or fine-detailed drawings be transmitted or received. However, both sending and receiving machines need to support this function for it to be successful.

Memory Used to support various functions such as **abbreviated dialling,** the **broadcast facility,** error correction (eg evening out jagged lines on incoming faxes) and **half-tone mode.** However, the main use is to store incoming faxes if paper or toner runs out. Generally, the more memory the better.

Network capability Machine can be linked to receive fax messages from any PC on the computer network and transmit them as instructed. A special fax server can also route incoming faxes (similar to **fax routing**).

Number search Enables the operator to search quickly for a stored number.

Paper out warning Signals when paper is running low.

Polling Ability to call another machine and 'collect' messages left for it. Now often called 'fax on demand'.

Resolution mode Controls the quality of incoming faxes. The finer the mode, the better the quality, but the slower the speed. Standard mode is suitable for most transmissions.

Signature storage Enables a previously stored signature to be reproduced at a specified point.

Transmission reservation Enables the user to programme the machine to send a fax as soon as it is free, rather than waiting.

Turnaround polling Enables the machine to send a fax and poll the called machine in the same call.

Figure 10.6 Fax machine facilities

Note: You may see some faxes advertised as having colour printers. This does not yet allow faxes to be sent or received in colour – although this is an obvious next development.

Multifunction devices

All fax machines are multifunctional in that they can do more than one operation. At the simplest level, there are fax machines with a telephone handset and a built-in answering machine, which will also copy ordinary pages one by one. Compare this with a sophisticated (and obviously more expensive) multifunction device which can operate as a computer printer, a fax, a full-scale copier (with colour as an option) and will also scan images for transfer to a PC.

Quite obviously, there are several benefits, particularly for small businesses. The cost of buying a multifunction device is cheaper than buying a single-function printer, copier, scanner and fax machine. In addition, one device takes up a lot less space than four. Critics, however, argue that high dependency on one machine can mean disaster if there is a breakdown and that there are fewer features available for each operation.

One alternative for a small business could be to expand its administrator's PC with software which will make it a combined fax, phone and answering machine. The system enables voice calls to be made through a speakerphone and the modem gives access to the Internet and a voice mail system. The system can even be used to take messages and signal a pager that one has been received.

Electronic mail

E-mail is a method of sending messages directly from one PC to another through a 'mailbox' system. The mailbox stores messages until the user is ready to access them. The user can reply, save or delete messages, print them out, forward them to other people with a comment and even check if the messages sent have been opened by the recipient.

E-mail is a common feature in organisations which operate a computer network. A wide range of e-mail software is available for networks – some of which is compatible with both DOS and Windows environments (see Chapter 14). If the e-mail system is compatible with other software packages, then users can prepare documents by using a word-processing, spreadsheet or graphics package and then attach this file to their message. This saves keying in the document twice. Using e-mail dramatically relieves the load on the mailroom as far fewer internal memos are sent. If the network also includes other branch offices and frequently used suppliers, this will also reduce postage costs. Access to the Internet means that messages can be sent to any other Internet subscriber, all over the world.

Advantages

- It provides a written record for future reference if required. For this reason it is often preferred to the telephone.

- Unlike voice mail, where you can only ask the absent person to call you, with e-mail you can actually leave a full message. This gives the recipient time to think about his or her reply before responding.

- All types of data can be transmitted.

- There is complete confidentiality, as only the user can access the mail through using a personal password and user ID.

- Messages can be sent to several users simultaneously.

- Travelling executives can access their mailbox via a laptop computer from most places in the world.

Features

The features available will depend upon the e-mail package used by the organisation. Windows-based packages contain more graphics (Figure 10.7), and often more features, than DOS-based packages. However, on all e-mail software you should find that the options listed in Figure 10.8 are available.

The latest form of junk mail – junk e-mail!

A radio station in the USA caused havoc when it bombarded dozens of media organisations across the western world with a junk e-mail. As if one e-mail was not bad enough, a computer problem meant that the messages were sent continuously, clogging up all the recipients' computer systems.

The latest problem, it would appear, with cyberspace communications is the growth of junk e-mails. Commercial companies are cashing in on the increasing popularity of the Internet by compiling selling lists of users' addresses – a practice known as 'spamming' in the USA. The users are then bombarded with information from retailers, suppliers and anyone else who has something to sell.

Perhaps the next feature on e-mail and Internet software could be a facility to keep out junk messages. If spamming increases, this could be a major selling point in the future.

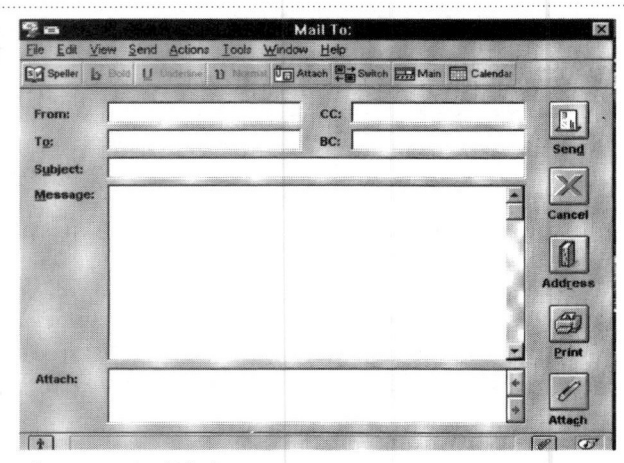

Figure 10.7 E-mail screen using Windows

Address Lists all individual users and their IDs as well as all the user groups (see below) on the system.

Blind copy Enables the user to send a copy of a message to other users without the main recipient(s) knowing that this has been done.

Cancel Enables users to change their minds about sending a message.

Copy Sends a copy to other users. The distribution list is printed at the foot of the message.

Delete Enables clearance of mailbox (which would otherwise become so full that the user would hardly be able to find anything). Allows deletion of message sent to someone *providing the recipient has not yet opened it.*

Forward Enables the user to send on a message already received to another user or group of users for their comments or as information.

In mailbox Mailbox in which incoming mail is stored. Mail is displayed in 'envelopes' on the screen. Unread mail is differentiated either by highlighting, a different colour or a different graphic alongside.

New message (or a similar command) Gives access to the screen for creating a message. The user's name or ID and the date and time are automatically entered on the top of each new message.

Note On some systems this enables different types of messages to be sent, eg for speech to be included.

Out mailbox Mailbox in which outgoing mail is stored. Again the user may be able to tell by the colour of the message summary or the graphic whether or not each message has been opened.

Phone message Optional screen available on some packages with a pre-printed phone message form for easy completion.

Print Enables the user to print the contents of messages.

Reply Used to send a reply to a message the user has received. Because this is a reply the recipient's name is also included automatically in the heading.

Save Ability to save a partially written message for later completion.

Send Command which transmits the message.

User groups Can be set up centrally by a network administrator so that when the name of the group is entered, all members receive the message simultaneously. In addition, users are usually able to create their own 'personal groups'.

Figure 10.8 E-mail facilities

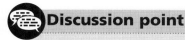
Discussion point

You can read page upon page about telephone systems, answering machines, pagers, mobile phones, faxes and e-mail, but you will never really understand them unless you see them in operation. It is even better if you can use them yourself.

As a group, undertake the following.

1 Find out if any of your colleagues have a sophisticated phone system, an answering machine, mobile phone or fax machine at home. Ask what they think about them.

2 Try to arrange with your tutor to see most of these in operation. In a large college there will certainly be a central switchboard, the security staff or caretakers will have pagers or radios, there will be at least one fax machine. If there is a networked computer system, then e-mail will be available, if only for staff use.

Comparing telecommunications services

In the UK there are a number of companies which operate as telecommunications providers, especially to businesses. As well as BT and Mercury, there are now cable companies in many local areas. In addition, there are specialist business suppliers such as Energis, Norweb and Ionica.

The two main considerations which need to be borne in mind when selecting any supplier are

• the range of comparable service(s) on offer

• the tariffs or charges of different suppliers.

BT is, of course, the historic provider of telephone lines in Britain. Today, it is facing considerable competition from the cable companies and, more recently, from the launch of Ionica's line, which started in the Cambridge area and is now planned to expand across the country. Mercury, the other most well-known name, does not install lines. This means that the subscriber must still have a BT line installed for local calls. Mercury offers subscribers the opportunity to use their network as a cheaper alternative to BT – particularly for long-distance and international calls.

The providers mainly compete on costs. Cable companies claim that their subscribers can save up to 25 per cent of all their telephone bill compared with paying BT rates. Mercury Communications claims that its charges represent a saving of about 20 per cent on long-distance and international calls – particularly for calls which last a long time. It also offers savings to mobile phone users. Ionica is aiming to set its rates at about 20 per cent lower than BT for line rentals and 15 per cent lower for local, national and international calls.

Competing companies offer different packages, depending upon whether the user is a residential (private) customer, or has a small, medium-sized or large business. Note that Mercury does not offer a service to residential customers and its business customers use BT for local calls. However, using the Mercury network is beneficial when linked to fax or telephone equipment which automatically selects the lowest-cost route. Customers who choose to subscribe to suppliers other than BT can often still use BT services, or the provider will offer a comparable service. As an example, subscribers to Mercury or Energis still have access to the BT network (Select) services such as **caller display, call return** and **call barring.** Virtually all cable companies offer similar services, some at a reduced charge. Ionica plans to offer some of these services free of charge (eg call barring) and other new services, such as distinctive ringing tones for each member of the family!

For businesses there is a range of services available from different companies, such as the 0800 freefone number, 0345/0645 low-charge call number (both allow customers to contact the organisation cheaply or free of charge), ISDN links, voice mail, international operator service and so on. The cable companies are offering even small businesses the ability to access services normally only available to larger companies by linking them to the local digital cable switchboard and exchange. This means that a company with relatively basic telephone equipment can enjoy all the facilities it would normally obtain only if it purchased a large digital PBX (see pages 165–6).

The task of assessing which provider could provide the best package of services and most competitive tariff would normally be given to a senior executive such as the facilities manager. Quite apart from obtaining up-to-date information on all the different providers in the area, meetings would be arranged to discuss the proposal in more detail and to obtain sufficient information to project different cost-savings. It is likely that the company would choose the supplier which could provide the best package at the most reasonable rate. This incentive is likely to result in even greater improvements to services and more competitive pricing strategies over the next few years.

Discussion point

Nominate one person to undertake each of the following tasks and then analyse your information as a group.

1   Find out which cable company operates in your area by phoning 0800 300750. Then contact the cable company and ask for information on its services.

2   Contact Mercury Communications on 0800 424 194 and ask for information on its services for small businesses and an up-to-date tariff of charges.

3   Contact Mercury Paging on 0500 505 505 and obtain information on its paging products and services.

4   Contact BT on 0800 800 855 and obtain a copy of its latest business catalogue.

5   Find out details of the range of services to which you would have access if you installed a BT Feature Line.

Decide as a group which provider you would recommend to your college's facilities manager, and give reasons for your choice.

£6bn to take on BT

In October 1996 Cable and Wireless announced a merger between itself and three rival cable television companies at a cost of £6 billion. Cable and Wireless now owns Mercury Communications, Nynex Cablecomms, Bell Cablemedia and Videotron. The resulting line-up means that Cable and Wireless now poses the biggest threat to BT's near monopoly of phone lines into most homes and offices.

Cable and Wireless Communications (CWC), as the new organisation will be known, has pledged to slash the cost of telephone charges and provide on-line viewers with a combination of services including telecommunications, data transmission, video shopping and Internet access. The aim is a 'revolution for consumers', as the strength of the Mercury all-digital national network is combined with the power of the cable networks in a concerted move to capture 35 per cent of the market.

● Telecommunications versus postal services

You learned about Royal Mail postal services and courier services in Chapter 2. If you carried out the activity on page 47 (and saved the information as instructed!), then you are now in a position to compare the types of delivery services offered by Royal Mail and couriers with those available by using telecommunications equipment.

 **Discussion point**

> Given the growth and popularity of telecommunications equipment, why do you think so many items are still sent by traditional postal services?

Choosing the best method

When choosing a method of transmission, you will have several aspects to consider. These include

- the general advantages and disadvantages of different methods (turn back to pages 158–61 if you have forgotten about these!)

- the urgency of the situation – both in terms of transmitting the information and in terms of feedback or response from the recipient

- the comparative costs of different methods

- the distance involved or the location of the recipient

- whether the information is simple and straightforward or complex and involved

- whether you know the person well and he or she is at roughly the same 'level' as you in the organisation or whether the person is more senior than yourself or someone unknown to you

- whether, for any reason, you need a permanent record of the fact that you passed on the information

- the degree to which the information must be passed on precisely and exactly to the recipient

- whether the information is confidential or relates to a 'sensitive' or contentious issue

- the format and length of the information – whether it is in text or graphics, black and white or colour, one page or 1000 pages

- the facilities you have available

- the number of people who must receive the information – and whether their views and responses are required

- the most sensible and convenient method, under the circumstances, which meets your most important needs.

Discussion point

As a group, identify the best method of sending the following items of information. In some cases, you may come to different conclusions – and you must be prepared to defend your choice! Assume that in each situation you have the options of

a a face-to-face discussion
b using the telephone
c sending a fax
d sending an e-mail
e writing a memo
f sending the document(s) by first or second class post
g sending the document(s) by a Royal Mail special service (be prepared to identify which would be the most appropriate service to use)
h sending the document(s) by courier.

1 An A4 wiring diagram to an engineer who works from home – you need his immediate confirmation that it is correct.

2 A short, but important message, to the manager of one of your branch offices asking for comments on a two-page report you have prepared for your own boss which must be submitted urgently to the managing director.

3 A request to your boss for leave to attend the wedding of a relative.

4 The signed copy of an important legal document.

5 An urgent message to all staff informing them that the canteen will be closed tomorrow because of repairs to the water main.

6 An advertisement to appear in the local paper which must be received before 12 noon tomorrow.

7 The artwork for a new brochure which must be received by the printers (in the next town) in its original form by 5 pm today.

8 A confidential request for a reference for a job applicant.

9 An urgent order for envelopes to your stationery supplier.

10 Completed security forms and your boss's passport, which will give him clearance to a local defence establishment which he visits regularly.

● The art of telecommunicating

The most sophisticated equipment in the world is useless unless staff can use and maintain it properly. In addition, they need to be polite and courteous to customers and to be *efficient* in the way that they deal with calls and enquiries. Ignoring the telephone because you are busy or burying an e-mail at the bottom of the in–tray because you do not understand it, are hardly the actions of a professional administrator or secretary!

Composing messages and correspondence is dealt with in Section 4. The remainder of this chapter concentrates on the additional skills you need to be able to use telecommunications equipment effectively, both to increase your own professionalism and to assist any junior staff who may be struggling. In some cases this takes you back to examining the procedures you may introduce to support these operations.

Telephone skills

As a business professional you must be able to cope with making and receiving calls to and from a wide variety of people on a range of different matters.

Making calls

It is important that you prepare well before making a call, particularly one which relates to a complicated or complex matter.

- Make sure you know the name of the person you are calling, his or her telephone number and extension number.

- Jot down headings so that you will not forget the items you have to cover. Put these in a logical order.

- *Always* make a call with a pen in one hand and a notebook on the desk.

- When your call is answered, clearly ask for the person or extension you require. Do not be distracted if you are asked 'Who's calling?'. Simply give your name and that of your organisation.

- If the person you require is unavailable, then find out when he or she will be back. It is better to arrange to call back later rather than ask for the person to ring you. This saves you hanging on for hours waiting for a call which may never be made, and you keep the initiative.

- Be prepared to leave a short message on an answering machine. In this case, do not forget to leave your name and number.

- When you are connected, give your name and say why you are calling.

- Make notes on any information you have been asked to obtain. Check any names, dates and figures carefully. Do not worry about asking the other person to repeat anything you do not hear clearly.

- Remember that the person who makes the call should conclude it. A useful way is to review the information you have received, thank the person for his or her help and then say goodbye.

- If you have taken a message for your boss, write or type it out whilst it is still fresh in your mind.

Many staff dread making international calls as they are concerned that they will not be able to cope. The key points to remember are that the ringing/engaged tones you hear might be different and the person you call may not be able to speak English! You also need to consider the time difference – especially if you are making a transatlantic call or one to the Far East.

Most foreign commercial organisations nowadays employ at least one English-speaking staff member – although this may not be the case if you are contacting somewhere completely off the beaten track. In this case you might be wiser to use BT's interpreter service or arrange for a local translation bureau to 'conference call' the other person with you.

Even if the person receiving the call can speak English, remember basic courtesies and avoid slang, colloquial or regional expressions, or long and complicated words. Remember too that American English differs from the English spoken in the UK and identical words can have different meanings. If you were phoning an American car company, for instance, you may have to think carefully before you start, bearing in mind that 'bonnet', 'boot', 'petrol' and 'puncture' will all be unfamiliar terms!

Finally, make sure you have a good connection – do not struggle on if you can hardly hear each other or have a pronounced echo on the line. Today a good international call is very clear. However, do allow for a slight delay on the line if the caller is very far away – otherwise you will both speak at the same time! If you have problems making a connection, remember that both BT and Mercury can help you if you dial the international operator.

Receiving calls

This is often a nerve-wracking task for junior staff, especially as it could be almost anyone on the line asking about almost anything! Knowing what to do, or following a standard procedure, therefore helps to instil confidence in inexperienced staff. They know that if they follow the procedure, then they cannot go far wrong! The main points of good telephone technique procedure are as follows.

- Answer promptly with your name and department (or organisation if you are answering a switchboard or key system console). In some organisations staff are trained to answer with a specific response which always includes their name.

- Always have a notepad and pen at the ready.

- Sound pleasant! Many people confuse being abrupt with appearing efficient.

- *Always* find out
  - who is calling
  - to whom the person wishes to speak
  - what the call is about.

  There is nothing more annoying for your boss than to receive a message that a complete stranger has phoned and must be called back *without* knowing what it is about. This gives your boss no opportunity to prepare for the call.

- Make sure you know who should deal with the different types of calls you may receive – in case the caller does not know who to ask for.

- If the correct person is not available, either take a message or arrange to call back. In this case check when the caller will be available to receive a return call.

- If a message is taken, make sure you include *all* the key facts. A pre-printed message form is ideal as it 'prompts' you to collect the essential information, ie
  - name of caller, organisation and telephone/extension number
  - subject of the message
  - time and date the call was received plus who took the call
  - whether the person will call back or is expecting your boss to return the call.

  If the message is complex, then read it back at the end of the call to check that all the important details (especially figures!) are correct.

- Check that urgent messages are not only dealt with but read by the recipient. Simply leaving them on a desk is not good enough! If the recipient is away on business for three days, this could be a recipe for disaster!

A final point: do make it the exception rather than the rule that staff use the company telephone system for personal calls – either incoming or outgoing. Most organisations these days provide payphones or cardphones for staff, in order to keep their phone bills down. In addition, staff are paid to work whilst they are on the premises, not put their feet up and chat to their friends!

Health and safety – and telephones

There are various products on the market which link health and safety issues to the use of the telephone. Firstly, there are headsets for those who use a telephone constantly (especially staff who use a PC at the same time) since the repeated lifting and replacing of a handset has been linked to RSI. Modern headsets can be used to adjust the tone of the caller's voice, reduce external noises and provide amplification where required.

Both headsets and other telephone handsets must be kept scrupulously clean – and a range of products can be bought specifically for this purpose.

Some organisations can be subcontracted to provide a telephone cleaning service throughout an organisation.

A more recent innovation is a telephone rest which positions the telephone *above* an office desk. This is said to have two advantages. It gives employees exercise as they have to stand up to answer the phone. It also keeps calls short – as staff are less inclined to prolong the conversation. Whether it would be welcomed by busy office workers is quite another matter!

Discussion point

Discuss as a group, and with your tutor, how you would deal with the following problems.

1   A junior member of staff is incapable of taking a coherent message. He regularly leaves out important information or mishears the telephone number, thereby creating considerable inconvenience for other staff.

2   Your boss refuses to speak to anyone when he is busy and regularly 'forgets' to return calls so that you have to deal with irate callers ringing again and again.

3 A junior secretary always repeats her boss's remarks verbatim when he is commenting to her on the internal line about a call. Yesterday she upset a member of staff when she told her 'It's no use ringing again. He's just said that he'll swing for you if you disturb him again'.

4 An urgent call received from
 a an important customer when your boss is away on business for the week
 b the managing director when your boss is out having a hair cut
 c a caller pressing for confidential information
 d someone inviting your boss to do a presentation. She is out until tomorrow, the caller needs an urgent response and you do not have a clue whether your boss will want to do it or not.

Fax skills

You may think that if fax machines are so simple to use, no skills are required. You would be wrong! Everyone needs some basic guidance the first time they use one – if nothing else to prevent silly mistakes such as putting in the original upside down and sending blank pages. Knowing how to get the best out of your fax machine means that it will last longer and the total cost of faxes will be kept down.

Again, you can help new or junior staff by devising a list of instructions or procedures to follow and keeping this next to the fax machine.

Sending faxes

Your instructions will differ depending upon the type of fax machine. In particular, whether it takes the document into the machine or has a flat-bed platen (similar to a photocopier) on which documents can be placed. If there is a document feeder, then this again will affect your instructions. The key points all staff must remember are as follows.

- Faxes only recognise black and white – coloured originals result in poor definition for the recipient so they should be photocopied first. So should important or flimsy documents – particularly if they would be 'fed into' the machine.

- The header or cover page must state the name of the person sending the fax, the organisation and the number of pages being transmitted. A fancy (or long) header increases transmission time so should be avoided if possible.

- Each page of a fax should be numbered, eg page 1 of 4, page 2 of 4 and so on – so that the recipient can check easily that all the pages have been received.

- Make sure the pages in a multiple-page fax are in the correct order!

- Make sure the fax is placed in the document feeder the right way up for the machine to read it. Some faxes will read two-sided documents, many will not.

- Fax numbers can be stored in most machines and automatically dialled. The UK Fax Book gives a list of subscribers, and international fax numbers can be found by phoning 153.

- All staff must know how to cancel a transmission if anything goes wrong, eg the wrong number is dialled or the original jams.

- Fax machines are perfectly capable of feeding pages and ejecting pages themselves – without any help from the operator!

- After transmission the document should be returned to the originator for his or her records.

- If your fax has other facilities, make sure that staff know how these operate before letting them have free run of the machine. It is useful for you, for instance, to be able to delegate the job of accessing faxes stored in memory without having to do it yourself all the time.

Receiving faxes
The biggest single problem with incoming faxes is delayed distribution. The main reason for using a fax machine is to send relatively urgent information. This objective is defeated if a fax received at 10 am is only delivered at 5.30 pm when the recipient has gone home!

You need a clear system whereby the fax machine is regularly checked for incoming messages and these are distributed immediately.

Fax maintenance and economies
There is an old saying, 'Old soldiers never die, they simply fade away'. According to research, much the same happens to fax machines. As companies upgrade their main machine, they do not throw away their old one(s) – these are progressively moved around the organisation, finding their way into different departments and on to different desks. The problem is that nothing lasts forever, even an old and trusty fax.

The basic aspects of fax maintenance which you may be asked to help to solve are

- day-to-day operational difficulties

- simple faults

- basic maintenance

- what to do when something goes seriously wrong.

In addition, you may be asked to suggest ideas for saving money.

Day-to-day difficulties and simple faults are usually covered by the user manual – which you must read! Often there is a trouble-shooting guide to help you. It will remind you, for instance, to check that the machine is actually plugged in and switched on. There will then be guidance on how to rectify basic faults such as a paper jam or misfeed. Some machines display error messages on an LCD and give you instructions on what to do next. Some self-diagnostic machines even contact their own base when they know they have a problem!

Basic maintenance includes operations such as filling the paper tray, changing the ribbon or cartridge, changing the battery (which often controls the time/date function) and keeping the equipment clean. If your organisation has entered into a service or maintenance agreement with the supplier, then regular cleaning will be a feature of this and is worth having if you have anything more sophisticated than a basic fax. If you do not have a contract and want to clean the machine yourself, remember that water and electricity *do not* mix – there is a range of alcohol-based cleaning products for all types of electrical equipment available.

Some organisations subscribe to a service organisation which not only advises about purchases, supplies basic machines, cleans machines and offers training but also has a telephone helpline in case there is a fault or problem. The helpdesk will check through basic issues such as connections and consumables and if required, transfer the call to an engineer who can often give advice on how to rectify the problem over the telephone.

Finally, your boss may ask you for advice about reducing the cost of running the fax machine. A Gallup Poll survey on cost and wastage identified that an average large UK company has a total annual telephone bill of as much as £25 million and half of this is for fax traffic. Forty per cent of the bill is for long-distance calls. However, given that a second report found that a company which sends just 150 documents a week by fax instead of post could save £1200 per year, it is not sensible to throw out the fax machine to save money! Instead, using it wisely can reduce costs and wastage.

Several points have been made above about costs. In summary, the main considerations should be

- the suitability of the machine for the amount of fax traffic

- the speed of the modem, particularly for international calls (see page 173)

- the use of the memory for delayed send to reduce transmission costs

- a short header followed by concise fax messages

- using economy mode for transmission of standard documents.

The considerations above are, of course, in addition to adequate staff training to avoid expensive mistakes!

Discussion point

As a group, decide which type of fax machine and features would be suitable for the following.

1 A medium-sized company which has a parent company in the USA and exports machinery all over the world.

2 A local BBC radio station which receives far more faxes than it sends from news providers and main BBC studios.

3 A multinational oil company with offices and refineries all over the world, including off-shore oil rigs and specialist engineers, designers and trouble-shooters who work from home.

4 Your own college.

E-mail skills

There are very few skills you need to use e-mail – particularly if you use a software package which includes a spell check facility. Otherwise you will find that any spelling or grammatical skills you lack are quickly noticed by everyone else in the organisation! You also need suitable presentation skills (see Chapter 13) and to be able to embolden and underline text to differentiate headings and other key points. On e-mail you will normally find that this simply changes the colour of the text on the screen. This is sufficient, but in addition, good spacing, the use of numbered points or bullet points and proper paragraphs will make your e-mails easier to read quickly. Bear in mind that as an administrator or secretary everyone will expect you to produce top-quality e-mails!

In terms of e-mail courtesy, you should make sure that the people who are receiving your e-mail know who you are (eg add your title or department if they do not know you). You should also be aware that it is considered unprofessional to type e-mails in capitals. It is actually called shouting! It makes e-mails more difficult to read and will annoy everyone.

Providing all the networks (and your PC) are operating properly, you should have few problems. The worst thing is if the system 'locks out' when you are part-way through a message. This is easy to identify as everything 'freezes' on your screen. Do not be tempted to hammer every key in turn – this will not improve matters. All you can do is to accept defeat and report the fault to your network administrator. Do close down your machine, however. Depressing Control/Alt/Delete simultaneously often helps you to do this, even during a lock-out.

If there is a fault with an external transmission (eg through the Internet), your network administrator will often contact you to tell you. In some cases, where each PC has its own communications software, you must remember that simply switching off will not cancel your own call. You would have to reboot the machine and then instruct the phone to hang up. Otherwise you will retain your phone link for some considerable time and run up quite a bill for the organisation!

Storing information

11

Introduction

In the majority of offices, the bulk of information being received every day is stored rather than thrown away – mainly in case it is needed in the future. Conscientious administrators clear their files at least every year; conscientious secretaries clear both their files and those of their boss. If they did not, then over time the organisation would have to expand continually to store all the information it has retained.

Despite much talk of the 'paperless' office, a considerable amount of information is stored in hard copy (ie paper) form. This is mainly because people still prefer to see information on paper – if only because it is transportable and readily available. It can be taken to a meeting, back to the office, then home in a briefcase. As yet the laptop computer does not quite fulfil the same role! The holder can also add notes and comments which can be stored along with the original.

However, in addition to paper copies, there is also a considerable amount of information stored electronically – either in computer directories or, in some more advanced organisations, in electronic filing systems.

Whereas, once upon a time, 'filing' was seen as a job for the most junior member of the office staff, today it is a fundamental part of information processing and is usually known by the term **information storage and retrieval.** With the huge amount of information now required by organisations, a misplaced file or misfiled document can create havoc and, in certain circumstances, have potentially disastrous results.

As an administrator or secretary, you will not simply be involved in operating storage and retrieval systems, but also in establishing or extending these. You will need to be well informed on the type of equipment, methods of classifying and indexing information, retention periods for important documents and electronic options. You will also need to decide the best location for files, how to control the access and movement of files and the procedures which should be used to archive documents.

This chapter examines the different ways in which information of all types can be classified and stored, the equipment which is available and the procedures which can be introduced to ensure that all storage systems operate effectively.

The principles of efficient storage and retrieval

There are two main aims of any storage system, which are

- to retain documents in good condition

- to retain documents in a system where they are easily retrievable.

However, to achieve this in an organisation which deals with thousands of documents every day or week is not quite so simple! Before any procedures to establish or control the system are introduced, it is important to think about what you are trying to achieve and why.

The main features of a storage and retrieval system should be that it is

- **easy to use** – the system must be easy to follow, understand and operate so that there is never any confusion as to where a document might be stored or how it can be retrieved

- **cost-effective** – the system must operate as cost-effectively as possible both in relation to the cost of equipment and staff time

- **space-saving** – the equipment must store the greatest number of records in the minimum amount of space (this has been a major factor behind the introduction of electronic filing)

- **accessible** – files must be easily accessible and available to those people who use the system

- **flexible** – it must be possible to expand or adjust the system so that it can cater for the changing needs of the organisation.

In some organisations the majority of files are stored in a **centralised** system. A typical example would be the head office of a building society which may store thousands of property deeds. The advantages of storing these centrally are that the organisation benefits from the following.

- **Economies of scale** – more expensive equipment can be purchased. Most building societies have a completely automated filing system in their head offices which can automatically store and retrieve any document. The system is controlled by a bank of central consoles.

- **Standardisation** – the same type of system is used for all documents.

- **Specialist staff** – staff can be trained to operate automated systems and to use the specified procedures. This ensures greater control over the whole system as access is restricted.

- **Efficiency** – there can be no danger of filing accumulating if staff are specifically employed to do this task. There is also less chance of a backlog accumulating because someone is off sick or on holiday.

However, there are certain disadvantages with operating a centralised system. Firstly, quite apart from the fact that the job can become boring or monotonous, centralisation can lead to bureaucratic procedures which mean that it is difficult to obtain files quickly in an emergency, unless staff are very cooperative. In addition, if a file is mislaid, there may be a tendency for filing staff and departmental staff to blame each other. Moreover, there will still be a need to keep some documents within a department, for instance confidential records or a manager's personal files. For that reason, even a mainly centralised system is likely to coexist with some degree of departmental or individual office filing. However, if you are an administrator in charge of a highly decentralised filing system – so that you are responsible for all the storage of information in your section – it will be vitally important that you operate an effective system which can easily be monitored and controlled.

Forms of information

Although there are various types of documents you may have to store, there are basically two forms of information:

* hard copy

* electronic media.

Hard copy

This refers to paper documents, which are still numerous in business organisations. This form of information can include business letters, memos, reports, purchasing documents (estimates, quotations and orders), financial documents (invoices, statements, banking documents), leaflets, brochures, booklets and catalogues. Some information will relate to current transactions and events, others will be concerned with 'one-off' enquiries or sets of information received into the organisation. In many cases these can be more difficult to store for rapid retrieval as they may not directly relate to the existing system in use – or be too bulky for normal storage.

Electronic media

If you have ever created any type of document on computer and stored it in a directory on a hard or floppy disk, then you have used electronic media.

You have already read about CD-ROMs on page 141. These are electronic media which store large amounts of information, such as an encyclopaedia or a database. A different type of optical disk, a CD-WORM (Write Once Read Many times) disk is used with electronic filing systems. This disk enables users to write information to the disk but it cannot be erased.

Comprehensive electronic systems can be purchased which enable documents to be scanned into a computer system, stored on a CD–WORM disk and accessed by means of a search facility on a special computer program. Because of the cost, **total document management** – as it is called – has so far only been installed by a minority of companies, although as system prices fall it is predicted to become far more popular in the future. More details of this type of electronic media are given on page 199.

A point to note is the storage of electronic media itself. Video tapes and computer disks are two obvious items which may need careful labelling and storage in a specially designed lockable cabinet.

A waste of time?

According to a survey carried out by one filing organisation, Avery, the average office worker wastes over one and a half hours a week looking for documents which he or she cannot find! If you ever work in a disorganised office (or for a disorganised boss), you may put the figure far higher!

Other findings by the experts include the following.

- Companies that insist on a 'clear out' remove about one ton of paper for every 50 employees – not surprising when 85 per cent of people apparently file papers 'just in case'.

- Up to 50 per cent of papers on the average desk are completely unnecessary.

- 70 per cent of organisations consider they need a better filing system as they regularly lose documents and have to manage without them.

- 62 per cent of organisations consider they cannot locate a document quickly.

- Despite the growth in computers, up to 70 per cent of computer files are also filed as hard copies.

So if you work as an administrator or secretary, probably your first starting point should be to train your boss and the rest of the staff – as well as reorganising the filing system!

Methods of storage

Traditional paper-based storage systems

A wide range of storage systems is available in both wooden and metallic finishes. Although systems currently available are described below, you are advised to look in a current supplier's catalogue to identify them for yourself.

Vertical filing cabinets

These cabinets are still the most popular in many organisations. They comprise between two and six drawers – though four-drawer cabinets are the norm in most offices. The drawers can be fitted with suspension pockets into which document folders are placed. Tabs are attached to the suspension pockets so that the files are easy to identify.

Cabinets are available which are fire and impact resistant (in case they have to be thrown out of the window in a fire or flood). All are lockable and have a standard safety feature that only one drawer can be opened at once, to stop the cabinet tilting towards the user.

Advantages
- They are a familiar sight and most people know how to use them.

- They are quick and easy to use, especially if the files are clearly labelled.

- If the files inside are in a jumble, or the drawer only holds the teacups, nothing can be seen once the drawer is closed!

Disadvantages
- They are about the least space saving of all systems.

- There is a tendency to ignore the bottom drawer (this is the one which contains the teacups!) This results in an unbalanced cabinet as technically the *heaviest* items should be at the base, not the lightest.

- They are a hazard if someone leaves the bottom drawer open.

Horizontal filing cabinets
These are used for storing large documents, such as architects' drawings. The drawers are not normally deep and the cabinets are available in a wide range of sizes to fit up to A0 size paper.

Advantages
- Large documents are kept flat and protected from damage.

- They are easy to use if the drawers are clearly labelled.

Disadvantages
- Too many documents in one drawer can make a small document difficult to find.

Lateral filing cabinets
These are rather like a large (open) cupboard. Instead of normal shelving the cupboards contain suspended pockets in rows across the cabinet. Many are equipped with a sliding door or blind which can be pulled down at the end of the day to protect the files from dust and dirt, and can be locked.

A small business may find a multipurpose lateral cabinet more useful. This often allows for a combination of both lateral and vertical filing and includes shelves and storage space for consumable items and box files.

Advantages
- The system is space-saving as it is possible to store records from floor to ceiling.

- Several people can access the files simultaneously.

- Every file can be seen at once.

- Colour coding can be used to excellent effect to identify certain types of files.

- Purpose-built cabinets can be installed in alcoves, corridors and other wasted spaces.

- Modern lateral cabinets can *rotate* – often at the touch of a button. One type, produced by Railex, offers a Doublestore system with files stored both at the back and the front of each rotating cabinet – see Figure 11.1. The makers claim each unit holds more than five vertical cabinets yet only takes up 1.67 metres of floor space.

Railex Doublestore is a filing revolution. Now you can double your filing using no more floor space. Or use Doublestore imaginatively to gain extra benefits for your organisation.

Two, eight tier lateral filing systems are contained in each compact Doublestore steel cabinet. That's the same capacity as up to five, traditional four-drawer filing cabinets. Rotating the central core provides easy access to both sets of files and both sides of Doublestore's massive filing capacity. Despite the weight of files, Doublestore is always finger light and moves easily when a hand height button is depressed. There are no handles or protrusions to catch clothes or trap fingers. When closed, Doublestore units form an attractive wall. Choose either goosewing grey lightly embossed with a hide grain or light oak Metalwood finish to complement your decor. And if you choose Doublestore, nothing could be simpler. Our consultant will check the space you have available and produce a computerised plan if necessary. Each Railex Doublestore unit is delivered and installed, just where you want it. All this is included as part of the Railex service.

Figure 11.1 Doublestore filing system

Disadvantages

- Safety stools must be provided to allow staff to access high shelves safely.

- Manufacturers' catalogues all show such systems beautifully neat and orderly! Many working systems are not quite so immaculate and yet are on full view to staff (and visitors).

Automated filing

These systems are usually only installed by large organisations with thousands of bulky documents to store – as in the example of the building society head office described on page 194. In some cases an entire new building may be constructed around a 'well' in the centre in which the automated filing system is situated. All the racks and tiers are designed to rotate by commands issued through the operators' console – with each operator controlling an entire tier of files which can rotate vertically. The row of files on which the required folder is to be found also rotates so that the correct file is adjacent to the operator's access window and can then be extracted.

The system is only suitable when filing is centralised and is extremely efficient. However, there is usually a maintenance agreement to cover the equipment in case of mechanical breakdown as a systems breakdown would obviously create a serious problem.

Electronic storage systems

Why bother buying three vertical filing cabinets when you can put the contents on one optical disk? Why make staff visit and revisit the filing area to look for paper documents when they could access anything from their own desktop? Given that it is estimated that the average office worker creates about 2000 sheets of paper a year and 4000 sheets of photocopying, and spends 60 per cent of the time sorting through this paper mountain, why make life worse by asking him or her to index it and file it as well? Especially when most office workers are sitting and looking at their own PC most of the day!

These are the basic arguments in favour of electronic storage systems. Despite talk of the paperless office, the number of documents has actually increased by 600 per cent in the past 25 years. Yet the importance of obtaining accurate data quickly in this 'information age' has never been greater.

For a moment, imagine the office of the future, somewhere you might work – but not for another ten or 20 years. Now read the article on page 204 and see how close you were!

PC storage

Everyone who uses a PC saves and stores information electronically. Even the homeworker who uses a basic computer for standard word-processing applications will save documents to either floppy disks or a hard disk. Hard disks are more common these days as the main storage media, with floppy disks simply being used as back-up files.

It is, of course, possible that when you are creating documents on a word processor you also print them out. However, keeping a copy in both hard copy format and on disk is wasteful once the document is no longer active. It is possible to argue that at this point you should opt *either* to keep your piece of paper (and file it!) *or* to put your document into long-term storage on disk, but not both.

Generally speaking, it is arguable that there are very few documents you need to keep for years on end. Therefore, not only should you sort out your paper files but also your disk files. This is easier if you have stored your documents on disk methodically!

The usual system of storage is to set up **directories** on a disk in which you keep specific documents. You could have directories for the topics you deal with, the customers you deal with or for the types of documents you produce. Each should be labelled clearly. Providing you are working in the correct directory, then any documents can be stored in this disk area automatically. Directories should be checked at regular intervals so that unwanted documents are deleted and – if the whole directory becomes obsolete – the directory should also be deleted. These operations are often termed **file management** and are essential if you are going to be able to find documents quickly over a long period.

Bear in mind that administrators and secretaries operate other packages in addition to word-processing software! They may create and store spreadsheets, devise graphics for a presentation and keep databases of customers (actual and potential) including their names, addresses and telephone numbers. A database can be 'home produced' for existing customers or purchased from a commercial company. For instance, extracts can be purchased from the Business Database from *Yellow Pages,* which contain the names, addresses and telephone numbers of selected companies in a designated areas.

Using a PC to store documents electronically is ideal when a small amount of information is being created and saved by a user. But what about information which takes up a lot of disk space or is needed by several people?

Imported graphics or a large database could take up literally dozens of floppy disks. Imagine loading all these on a computer, one by one, to find a picture or to print out address labels! One option would be to buy an optical disk and reader. As an example, a 230-megabyte optical disk will hold the contents of 160 floppy disks. This could be kept by one user or held in a central store for several computer users to borrow.

A preferable alternative would be to hold this type of data on a computer network. Computers which are linked in a network have access to the same information. There is usually a **network administrator** who is in charge of the network and who 'manages' it. One key task is to make sure that suitable software is installed on the system for all users. The system can store information which can be accessed by *all* users – such as a large commercial database. It also enables easy access by *all* users – although the network administrator can limit access to any area if required.

The network can easily be configured to give users access to CD-ROMs holding a wide variety of information – including electronic databases (see also Chapter 14).

Electronic document management systems

Figure 11.2 An electronic filing system

Electronic document management systems (EDMS) is the new term for electronic filing (Figure 11.2). In this type of system the organisation has gone one stage further. Instead of holding the majority of its information on paper, documents are scanned into the system or imported from other computers to be stored on CD-WORM or laser disks. In a large system these may be kept in a **jukebox** which is a device to hold several disks simultaneously. When a document is accessed, the system identifies the correct disk and loads this on-line for reading.

EDMS is predicted to become the fastest growing new business activity as the millennium approaches. Initially, many organisations liked the idea, although some were nervous about throwing away their paper documents. However, there were two major drawbacks.

- The high cost of the equipment made it unaffordable for small businesses.

- There was concern that electronic documents would not be admissible in a court of law.

Today, however, the price of electronic filing packages and equipment is falling dramatically. A small company can now buy a complete system for under £13 000. In addition, a Code of Practice was published by the British Standards Institute for Legal Admissibility of Information Stored on EDMS in February 1996. This was developed to give guidelines on 'best practice', ie on how electronic filing should be carried out for documents to have the same degree of authority as an original document.

An organisation which wants to implement an electronic filing system needs to consider various aspects.

Document capture

This involves scanning paper documents into a computer system. A scanner digitises the image through the use of Document Image Processing (DIP) software. The scanner is attached to a computer terminal and operates from special software which transfers images into the computer.

The scanning software undertakes three functions.

- It creates the file record.
- It allows the operator to adjust or change the image (or clean it up if necessary).
- It then indexes the document so that it can be retrieved rapidly.

Document indexing

The more effective the indexing, the easier the later retrieval of any document – whether it is in paper form or electronic. EDMS allows for dozens of ways of indexing – using keywords, customer numbers, dates, postcodes, geographic areas or any other form of recognition. Some indexing systems are 'intelligent' in that they can recognise repeated documents and automatically store them in the correct file.

Document storage

The recommended 'best practice' as advocated by BSI is for electronic documents to be stored on WORM optical disks. The major benefit of this type of system is that copy disks can be stored off the premises. In the case of a disaster such as a fire or a bomb blast, the back-up information is readily accessible. It is notable that following the Docklands bombing, most companies in the area transferred to electronic storage as a safer way of keeping important documents than paper systems.

Document retrieval

The operator can search for a document using a variety of criteria, including keywords or the approximate date of inputting. This reduces the time taken to retrieve a document. The document can then be displayed on the PC (or any PC in a networked system), or printed out, or even faxed automatically to another organisation.

Retention policies

All organisations transferring to electronic filing need to decide

- which documents should be kept in paper form

- which should be put on to optical disk

- how often the system needs to be reviewed to delete or archive outdated documents.

There are legal requirements for the length of time many records must be kept. For instance, payroll records must be kept for seven years, accounts documents for between three and six years (depending upon the type of organisation) and employee attendance records for three years.

In addition, all the personal information stored must comply with the conditions of the Data Protection Act (see page 220).

COLD and computer-produced documents

The term 'COLD' is used to describe direct Computer Output to Laser Disk. In this case all the documents and print-outs produced on computer are sent direct to laser or optical disk rather than being stored on hard or floppy disk. There are two advantages.

- It reduces the need for bulky files containing print-outs.

- Because the data are still held digitally, they can be manipulated to produce calculations or graphs on command.

This obviously 'completes' an electronic filing system – as there is little point in scanning in ordinary documents if the bulk of computer-produced documents are held in paper form!

Outsourcing electronic filing

A final point you should note is that not all organisations manage their own electronic filing systems. Specialist companies exist which will undertake any of the operations relating to document scanning, indexing and storage on disk as a service to other organisations. They will also store back-up copies of the disks on their own premises in case of disaster. Some organisations provide an 'on-line' service so that the paper is scanned in at the point where it is received or created and downloaded to the service provider by computer.

Working in admin – around the year 2015

Eleanor had started working at Electronico plc six months ago. Today, as she arrived, she stopped to have a word with the mail-processing clerk who had loaded the document scanner with the incoming mail. The paper documents would be held for only 24 hours before being destroyed – apart from brochures and catalogues. Personal mail was individually barcoded with a special ID for the recipient's attention, and general items of interest were scanned into the company 'shareware' program on the network.

She went to her own office and accessed her boss's electronic diary to look through the day's appointments. She noticed he had a video conference booked for 10 am and that he needed several documents to be retrieved from the electronic filing system before then. She accessed the documents quickly and wrote a brief e-mail message to her boss to which she attached the electronic files. Then she dealt with the messages waiting on her own electronic mail.

She settled down to completing the report she had started yesterday. On completion she e-mailed it to her boss for approval. At this point she brought her own post on to the screen. One letter was an answer to a customer's query, and she quickly faxed it to her with an accompanying electronic note. Approval for the report came through at 10.45 am with a request that she send electronic copies to all the directors and a hard copy to the customer. She duly sent off the report by e-mail and, through her PC, instructed the laser printer to produce one hard copy and an accompanying standard letter. She then e-mailed the reprographics controller to ask her to mail the report to the customer. Finally, she ordered some stationery through her electronic link with the supplier.

At this point, she decided, she had earned a cup of coffee. What a nuisance, she thought, that she would have to leave her desk to fill the kettle.

Discussion point

As a group, discuss the advantages and disadvantages of working in 'the office of the future'.

● Classification of information

As you have seen, for retrieval of documents in any form to be efficient, they have to be **indexed.** Indeed, the key to rapid retrieval is correct indexing. Indexing is the way in which documents are grouped for storage. Another term used for this is **classifying information,** ie dividing it into different groups or classes. There are various ways in which you can do this, depending upon the type of documents you are storing. Note that within one organisation *different* classification (or indexing) systems may operate – as you will see below.

There are two main types of classification system used in paper–based systems.

- **Direct access** – in this case if you know the name, you can go straight to the file. The system is quick and easy to use, but usually only suitable for low or medium volumes of files or folders.

- **Indirect access** – in this case you need to refer to an index before you can locate the file. Whilst the system is slightly more complex, it is far easier to expand and therefore more suitable for large volume use.

Direct access systems

Alphabetical

This system uses the **surname** of the person or the **name** of the organisation as the main item for classification. It is most commonly used for small numbers of documents or for name listings. A typical example is *The Phone Book* which gives the names of all subscribers in alphabetical order. In business organisations this is a popular choice for storing customer or personnel files (Figure 11.3).

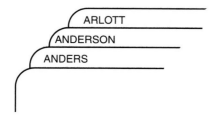

Figure 11.3 Alphabetical classification

Advantages
- It is easy to use providing you know the rules for alphabetical filing. A brief checklist is given in Figure 11.4.

People
- Surname first – short names before long (Clark; Clarke; Clarkson)
- Follow first name or initials if surname identical. Bear in mind that 'nothing' always comes before 'something' (Clark P; Clark P M; Clark Peter)
- Treat Mac and Mc as Mac – and file before Ma (McDonald; MacInnes; Mablett)
- Ignore apostrophes (Obertelli; O'Brien; O'Connell; Oldfield)

Organisations
- Ignore 'the' and change numbers to words (Fight for Fitness Action Group, The; Five Star Inn, The; Four Feathers Hotel, The)
- If names are duplicated, then follow street or town (Four Feathers Hotel, Bradford; Four Feathers Hotel, Bristol)
- File initials before full names and ignore the word 'and' (CB Motors Ltd; C & T Suppliers; CVA Employment Agency; Cabinets Galore)
- Treat Saint and St as Saint (Sainsbury J plc; St John Ambulance; Salisbury Associates)
- File public bodies under name or town if there is duplication (Sheffield City Council; Social Security, Dept of; Social Services Dept, Bradford North; Social Services Dept., Bradford South)

Figure 11.4 Checklist for alphabetical filing

- You can access every file directly – providing you know the name.

- Documents which are a 'one-off' from a person can easily be accommodated in a miscellaneous file. A miscellaneous file can be created for every letter of the alphabet.

Disadvantages
- It is inappropriate for large systems as confusion or congestion may arise with common names or frequently used letters.

- It is difficult to expand without rearranging the whole system.

- It is easy to confuse names, particularly where they are very similar, which can lead to misfiled documents.

Subject
In this case the **topic** is the main item of classification. The topics are then arranged in alphabetical order. Popular topics can have subdivisions within them. It is frequently used for files on products and services and a popular choice for secretaries who keep their boss's files – given that each executive normally has specific areas of responsibility which easily convert to 'subjects' (Figure 11.5).

Figure 11.5 Classification by subject

Advantages

- It is easy to add additional topics and subdivisions.

- It is simple to follow and operate.

- The papers on one topic are filed together – which is useful for taking to meetings, writing a report, etc.

Disadvantages

- There can be considerable overlap of topics, eg should a seminar on training go under 'seminars' or 'training' if both subjects are in the system? This may mean considerable cross–referencing is required.

- There can be a proliferation of files on a very popular topic and subdivisions can create even more overlaps.

- If there is more than one user of the system, each may file papers under a different topic and there may even be a duplication of a topic under different names, eg advertising and publicity!

- A file list may be essential if there are large numbers of files, several users or if a manager identifies the topic under which a document must be stored and later expects his or her secretary or PA to retrieve it!

Geographical

In this system the **place** is the key item for identification. The folders are placed in alphabetical order of location (Figure 11.6). This type of system is often used for sales territories or by mail order companies. Organisations which import or export may store customer files by country.

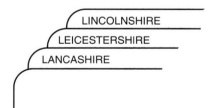

Figure 11.6 Geographical classification

Advantages

- Users do not need to know the names of individual organisations (useful for foreign names!).

- It is a simple and easy system to use if the location is known.

- Cross-references are unlikely to be required.

Disadvantages

- Expansion can be difficult without reorganising a substantial number of files (for instance, if business in one location increases substantially).

- It is a specialised system, not suitable for general use.

- There may be some confusion over identical place names, eg Richmond (in both Surrey and Yorkshire), Boston (in the USA and in Lincolnshire).

Indirect access systems

Numerical

In this case each grouping of documents (eg by customer, supplier or topic) is allocated a **number.** Usually this is a sequential system, ie the first folder is given number 1, the second number 2 and so on (Figure 11.7). A variation on this system is **alphanumeric** when each file is given a different (sequential) number *per letter of the alphabet* – again in the order in which the files are created, eg Alpha Trading = A1, Access Trading = A2; Barden Associates = B1, Blockleys Ltd = B2 and so on.

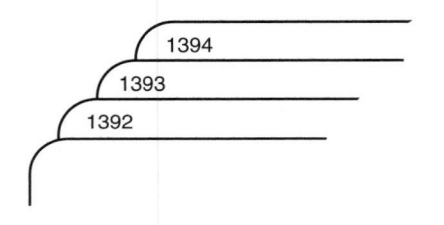

Figure 11.7 Numerical classification

Advantages

- Both systems are capable of unlimited expansion. No reorganisation at all is required for a basic numerical system as it increases in size.

- Each file folder has a unique number.

- The file number can be used in correspondence so that users can refer to this to file and refile quickly and easily.

- Individual departments can be allocated a block of numbers, eg Marketing = 1–999, Finance = 1000–1999 and so on.

Disadvantages

- An index is essential for the files to be found.

- Transposition of figures can cause problems.

- Miscellaneous documents can be difficult to store.

Terminal digit

In this system the file numbers are read in **groups** from right to left. Each set of two or three digits represents specific information. As an example, file 14 04 16 may be located only if you know that

- 16 is the folder number

- 04 is the drawer number
- 14 is the cabinet number.

As an alternative, imagine that you work in your college's administration office where central records are kept for all students. (In reality, these will probably be held on computer!) However, if this office used a system of terminal digit filing you may find that your ID number of 98 05 689 means that

- you were the 689th student to enrol
- in Administrative Studies – Department 5
- during the academic year 1998/9.

Advantages
- The system is very easy to expand.
- It is difficult to misplace a file, particularly if there is colour coding linked to the numerical system (eg for each department in the college).

Disadvantages
- The system is complex and difficult for inexperienced staff to follow.
- An index is essential.

Chronological
In this system the **date** is the most important item and it is this which is the key item of information (Figure 11.8). The applications of this system are therefore very limited.

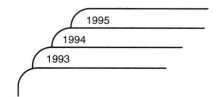

Figure 11.8 Classification by date

Advantages
- The system is useful when the date has a particular significance, eg for petty cash vouchers or birth certificates.
- The system is often used in conjunction with other systems. For instance, enrolment forms in your college may be stored in alphabetical order, but in general files under the year in which the enrolment took place.

Disadvantages
- On its own the system is useless without an index.
- The system is too specialised for general use.

Discussion point

As a group, decide the best method of classification to use in each case given below.

1   Personnel files in the Human Resources Department.

2   Holiday documents held per client by a travel agency.

3   Minutes of the safety committee.

4   The managing director's personal files

5   The supplier files of a large retail company.

6   Insurance policy documents which need to be indexed to cover both the type of policy and the year of issue.

7   The customer files of a freight forwarding company which operates on an international basis.

● Storage and retrieval procedures

In Section 2 you learned that it is important for staff to follow certain procedures for any office service to operate effectively and efficiently. This is just as important in the storage and retrieval of documents as it is in the mailroom, the reception of visitors, stock control and all the other aspects of office services.

Storage and retrieval and record-keeping systems

Basic issues

All staff should be aware of the basic procedures to follow when

- indexing documents

- storing documents

- cross-referencing documents

- allowing files to be borrowed

- opening new files.

Standard guidelines should be issued to all new staff along with adequate training to make sure that everyone involved with the system knows exactly what to do with standard documents – and how to cope with a problem. This saves staff from being tempted to throw away a document or 'hide' it in the first file they see because they do not know what to do with it!

Standard filing procedures

- Only file documents which have been released for filing. It is sensible for these to have a release mark (such as a tick, initials or a cross on them) to differentiate them from documents which are still being used.

- Know and understand the particular system in use, and how it works.

- Pre-sort documents *first* to save any unnecessary moving about from one cabinet to another or from one file to another.

- Undertake basic 'good housekeeping' tasks on documents. Remove paper clips (they hook other papers behind them), and staple related documents. Repair any torn pages.

- File documents in date order with the most recent document on the top.

- Punch documents squarely and place in the file folder neatly. In many organisations (but not all) they are fastened by a metal or plastic clip.

- **Cross-reference** any documents where there may be confusion as to the location of the original document. This means putting a copy, or a cross-reference card in the secondary file and putting the original document in the most obvious file.

- When files become bulky, start a second folder. Put the start and end date clearly on the first folder and the start date on the second folder.

- Never lend single documents – only complete files. In this case book out the file to the borrower (noting the file name/number, date of removal, name/department of borrower and date of agreed return) and replace it with an absent card or 'out' marker in the filing system.

- Follow up all loaned files if they have not been returned within the agreed period (usually three to seven days).

Other considerations

As an administrator or secretary you must be prepared to give guidance and introduce procedures to cover other aspects of storage and retrieval, ie

- what to do with 'problem' documents

- how to store confidential documents

- records retention policies

- how to cope in an emergency or crisis.

Problem documents

These may include

- 'one-off' documents or those which do not conform to the system

- those which could be placed in any one of several files

Barcoding and computerised 'follow-up' systems

There are some modern PC-based solutions to the problem of missing files – without introducing electronic filing.

One system is to utilise PCs to produce colour-coded files. A colour-coded label can be produced on demand for any file. According to the manufacturers, Cave Tab, files are 40 per cent quicker to find and refile using this system – because a misplaced file stands out so clearly.

An extension to this system is to use the company's File Tracker system. Each file is barcoded and the information on the name and location of the file is automatically entered into the PC system. The system can also be used to track files when they are borrowed and returned. An alternative system is offered by MasterTrak. A scanner is 'swiped' across the barcoded label to log the file in and out (Figure 11.9). The system then creates borrowing history reports for access by the operator.

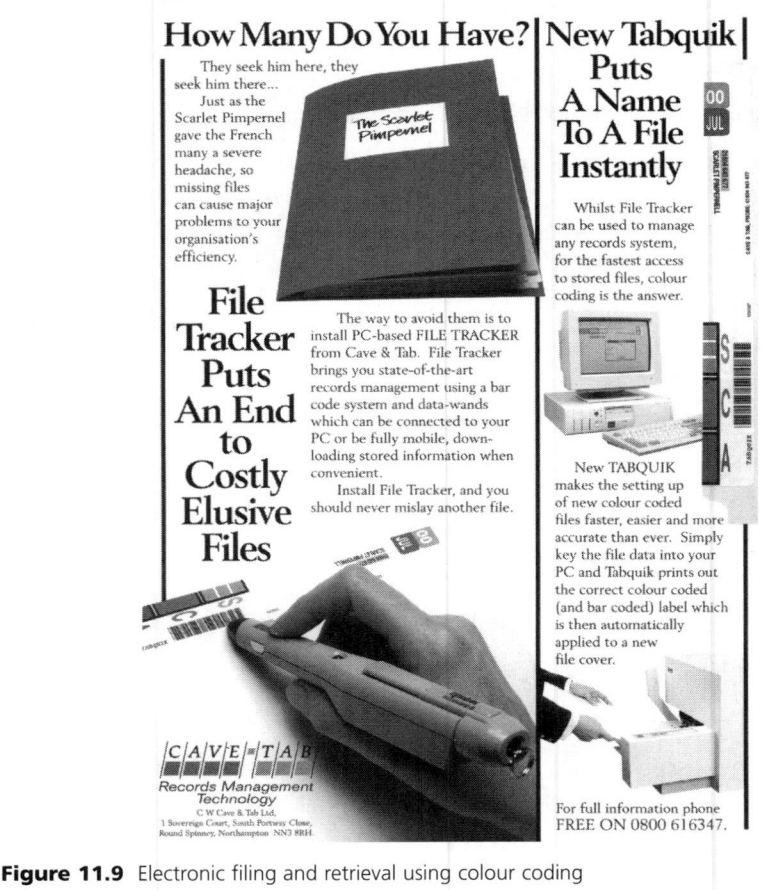

How Many Do You Have?

They seek him here, they seek him there... Just as the Scarlet Pimpernel gave the French many a severe headache, so missing files can cause major problems to your organisation's efficiency.

File Tracker Puts An End to Costly Elusive Files

The way to avoid them is to install PC-based FILE TRACKER from Cave & Tab. File Tracker brings you state-of-the-art records management using a bar code system and data-wands which can be connected to your PC or be fully mobile, downloading stored information when convenient.

Install File Tracker, and you should never mislay another file.

C|A|V|E|-|T|A|B
Records Management Technology
C W Cave & Tab Ltd,
1 Sovereign Court, South Portway Close,
Round Spinney, Northampton NN3 8RH.

New Tabquik Puts A Name To A File Instantly

Whilst File Tracker can be used to manage any records system, for the fastest access to stored files, colour coding is the answer.

New TABQUIK makes the setting up of new colour coded files faster, easier and more accurate than ever. Simply key the file data into your PC and Tabquik prints out the correct colour coded (and bar coded) label which is then automatically applied to a new file cover.

For full information phone FREE ON 0800 616347.

Figure 11.9 Electronic filing and retrieval using colour coding

- those which one person wants to keep out of the system to work on but which other people may need to refer to

- those which are too bulky for the normal filing system.

Whichever system you use, you need to have a procedure for miscellaneous documents. If you are really worried you will lose track of these, you could record them in a special book – or just have one file in which they are all stored to prevent problems.

If you receive a document which covers a range of issues, then you have three choices.

- If the contents are important, you have little option but to put a photocopy in each file.

- If some contents are important and others are not, then put photocopies where they are most relevant and a brief note in the other files to indicate where additional information can be found.

- If only one or two items are important, then you might decide to ignore the other files completely.

In the case where someone wishes to keep a document to work on it, try to persuade that person to use a photocopy instead and return the original to the file.

Finally, some documents are unsuitable for standard filing. They include legal documents, bulky contracts and project submissions, catalogues and brochures. You should remember that other types of files and filing equipment are available, such as

- box files (for documents which cannot or must not be punched)

- lever arch files (for related documents on a particular topic)

- envelope wallets (which are usually used for storing documents on a temporary basis)

- customised boxes for storing high-density cassettes or digital audio tapes

- customised units for storing videos and optical disks.

Confidential documents

These should not be on open display *at any stage* of the filing process. They are usually kept in separate files and only stored and accessed by those who have specific authority to read the contents. In some organisations they are stored in the executive's office, rather than the secretary's, and may even be in a cabinet which is controlled by a security code. Restrictions may be placed on access, photocopying and distribution and their disposal may have to be supervised, with all documents shredded.

As you will see on page 221, the EU Data Protection Draft Directive 1995 requires, as from late 1998, that organisations will have to ensure that personal data held on computer *and* in paper form are stored securely. It is therefore going to be essential that all organisations which hold personal information on their clients, eg financial institutions, healthcare providers and solicitors, make adequate arrangements about handling and storing this type of information securely.

Access to confidential documents is easier to control if they are stored on computer. User passwords and access levels controlled by a network administrator can be used to protect this type of information.

Records retention policies
Organisations cannot keep their files forever. Otherwise the office space would have to keep expanding purely to accommodate the amount of paper held! Given that the retention of some documents is regulated by legal requirements, then there should be a clear policy in force. Junior, new or inexperienced staff should never be given the responsibility of clearing out files, just because someone wants to make more room in their filing cabinet, as they will not know which documents are no longer required, which must be kept, or what to do with those which are no longer current but might be needed at some date in the future.

There is a variety of choices as to what should be stored, how it should be held and for how long.

- It is unwise to file everything that is received. The waste bin is a realistic alternative to the filing cabinet for junk mail!

- Documents which must be kept for a specific length of time include
  - sick pay records (three years)
  - accounts documents (three years for a private company, six years for a public company)
  - tax documents, pay records, customs documents and purchase orders (six years)
  - tax assessments, sales orders, quotations, dividend payments and contracts under seal (12 years)
  - accident reports (30 years)
  - Certificate and Articles of Incorporation (indefinitely).

- The time scale for holding general correspondence will vary depending upon the type of organisation you work for. Solicitors, probation officers, social services and accountants are likely to hold client documents for many years – though not in active storage. A commercial company which deals with business organisations is likely to keep its documents active for less time than this. Retail organisations or those offering a 'one-off' service may not hold records for very long, given that previous correspondence is redundant quite quickly. All they will retain is their customers' names and addresses on their database so that they can inform them about future offers and promotions.

- When documents are cleared they may be
  - thrown away
  - archived.

Archiving means putting into permanent storage (often in the basement!). In some cases, where many documents are involved, they may be microfiched by an agency because microfiche takes less room to store than paper. Another option is to pay a particular service supplier to store the documents in archives in its warehouse.

Crises and emergencies

The most common crisis is that relating to the 'lost' important document required by your boss in a hurry. Murphy's Law nearly always applies to filing in that

- the file your boss wants urgently is the only one which is not in the system

- the file you give him or her is complete apart from one piece of paper you have not yet filed – this is the one that is needed

- the file is complete apart from one missing document – this is the one which is critical to a forthcoming contract

and so on!

You will obviously have fewer crises and emergencies if you follow the procedure below.

- Documents should be filed **daily** – not left until the filing tray is a complete jumble and staggering under its own weight. As a halfway measure, if you are very busy, at least pre-sort the documents and put them into a concertina file.

- The indexing system should be clearly understood by all staff.

- Borrowed files should be booked out and then regularly chased up if they are not returned on time. This should be done by introducing a proper follow-up or 'tickler' system where people are regularly reminded about overdue files. As you have seen above, this can be done manually or by computer.

However, this does not mean that an emergency will never occur. In this case think and act methodically.

- Do not panic! This never helped anyone.

- Do not apportion blame. At this stage you do not know *who* is at fault!

- If you are searching, start with the obvious – the filing tray, the pre-sort concertina file, the file itself (the paper may have been overlooked). Then move on to the second stage – your boss's pending tray (and your own), your boss's desk (and yours), any files which are similar in name, any files which may contain the original which should have been cross-referenced in the incomplete file.

- Ask your colleagues – someone may have seen it or remember handling or filing it.

- Unless the document is a legal agreement, in which case you may have a problem, it is nearly always possible to obtain a copy. Was anyone else on the distribution list? Will you have to ask the sender for a copy? Do you *really* need the original?

- If you have no alternative, then own up, apologise and take the blame! If you are normally very efficient, then there is little likelihood that this will be a permanent blot on your copybook. Then investigate why the problem or crisis occurred and re-examine your procedures to try to prevent a recurrence.

Discussion point

1   As a group, discuss the average 'life' of a customer or client document in the files of each of the following organisations.
    a   an insurance company
    b   a travel agency
    c   a hotel
    d   a pension or investment fund
    e   a mail order company
    f   an estate agent
    g   an accountancy firm.

2   Again, as a group, decide how you would solve each of the following problems.
    a   A senior member of staff borrows files and does not return them even when reminded.
    b   A junior member of staff was seen looking through the contents of a confidential file.
    c   A boss regularly blames you for missing documents – which you later find in the muddle on his desk.
    d   A member of your team always find another job to do when some papers need filing.
    e   A junior tries hard but *frequently* misfiles documents.
    f   You have just found a pile of papers on a windowsill next to the filing cabinet.

Administrative issues

As an administrator you are likely to be involved in organising the storage and retrieval of documents within a section or department. How the files will be organised, and which systems and procedures will be used may be completely up to you. Whilst it may seem unfair, given the importance of efficient storage and retrieval, it is a fact that managers are likely to show little interest in this area until something goes wrong!

You should bear in mind that most staff do not like filing. Everyone will prefer to do something else. Therefore it is an obvious job for sharing out, but this implies everyone knows exactly how the system works. Some people will take to it more easily than others – if they are particularly self-disciplined or naturally neat and tidy. However, you have to ensure that these members of staff do not bear the brunt of what is, to most people, a very tedious job.

The golden rule is to keep your procedures as simple as possible, give training where necessary and make sure that people realise that leaving filing to build up simply creates a worse chore!

Finally, you may be asked to undertake a **filing audit.** This is carried out when the company has reached the stage where it really does need to stand back and assess its systems and procedures and review them. This may be because of increased growth or a change in the type of business undertaken. Whilst many specialists will undertake such an audit free of charge, you may be asked to make a start on reorganising the files yourself.

The way to do this is as follows.

- Obtain views and information on the main problems currently experienced by all the users and operators of the existing system.

- Discuss the main objectives of the new system with your boss.

- Decide what retention policies will be in force.

- Decide the format in which current and archived records will be kept.

- Identify the most appropriate type(s) of indexing for your needs.

- Consider how to process and store confidential documents – much will depend on the quantity you regularly handle.

- Identify the range of sizes of documents to be stored.

- Consider the projected growth in paper and documentation over the next few years.

- Determine which would be most appropriate for central storage/accessing, and which should be retained as decentralised information systems

- Obtain quotations for a range of solutions including electronic filing, automated systems, mobile shelving, rotating vertical units, filing cabinets and fire- and burglary-resistant file safes.

- Plan how the new system could be introduced – it is usually better to phase this in rather than expect everyone to work all weekend to convert the old system! Much of the work can be done in advance, such as preparing new folders, labelling and setting up the equipment. Only when this is completed should you take the final step of transferring documents. If this must be done in stages, then do it logically – either by letter, by area or by number – depending upon the indexing system which was in force.

- Make sure staff are trained in how the new system operates. You will find that staff who have been involved in the audit process and who have contributed towards the final decision will be far more motivated to make it work than those who have not. For that reason, you will ignore their views at your peril!

Secretarial/PA issues

If you work for one or two executives, then you will be more likely to be filing their documents rather than those applying to a whole section. If you are really lucky, you will have someone to file the main bulk of the documents for you – all you will have to do is to monitor and file the confidential documents. Bear in mind that it is no use being in charge of a cabinet containing confidential information if you do not remember to lock it whenever you are leaving the room!

You may find, however, that you are given little guidance on the system to use (you will be expected to devise one to meet your own needs) and no information about retention. How often you clear out the system, when and how will be up to you. All your boss will be interested in is the fact that you can lay your hands on any document which has been received, instantly, over the past few years! One trick to help you is to read documents quickly before you file them. If you can *remember* receiving them, then you can develop quite a formidable reputation! If you can do this, and lay your hands on the right document immediately 99 per cent of the time, then even your boss will hesitate to challenge you on the odd occasion when a document is missing and you say adamantly that you know you have never received it!

Discussion point

You work for a medium-sized business and control the files of four directors. The amount of paper received and created by the organisation has increased dramatically over the past two years and you think there would be definite advantages if you could install an electronic filing system.

Your boss is sympathetic to your needs but thinks there could be certain disadvantages.

As a group, discuss how you would argue your case for this type of system, taking into account your boss's concerns about the idea.

Information management systems

As you saw earlier in this section, the computer revolution has given organisations the ability to create vast amounts of information. Managing this information has become of critical importance, as has the need to control the use of these data and to protect the privacy of the individual in the 'information age'.

Some basic rules therefore need to be followed by all those involved in processing information.

- Systems need to be in place to enable people to share information quickly and easily. Whilst one option is to photocopy documents, modern computer systems, EDMS and e-mail offer other, faster, alternatives.

- All the hi-tech equipment in the world is of little use if there is not a consistent approach to managing information across the whole organisation. Otherwise, if there is a weak link in the chain, information systems can easily break down.

- In the future, there may even be a role for a specific information manager who has complete responsibility for the management of information throughout an organisation and the dissemination of data to those who need it.

- The key role of information is to support the main business function – which is often concerned with obtaining and fulfilling customer orders. Systems and procedures should be designed to provide information promptly to those who need it – and this must be the main objective – not the needs of administrators!

- All information must be accurate and up to date. There must therefore be a consistent approach to all aspects of information processing – from creation through to indexing, storage, retrieval, retention and disposal.

- The need for confidentiality, security and compliance with legal requirements should be a major consideration of all system designs. This is particularly important given the requirements of the Data Protection Act and the EU Data Protection Directive (see below).

Data protection

The Data Protection Act 1984

The Data Protection Act 1984 is concerned with protecting the collection, storage, processing and distribution of 'personal information and data' stored about people on computer. It protects individuals, who may investigate information which is held about them, challenge it and obtain compensation if the information has been obtained unlawfully, is incorrect or has been misused in some way. This means that organisations which keep information on their employees, customers and clients, for instance, must follow the requirements of the Act. Figure 11.10 gives more details of the Act and the information it covers.

The Data Protection Act 1984

The Act requires employers using a computerised data system to register as data users. They must state

- what information is being stored on computer
- why it is stored in such a way
- how and from where they have obtained it
- to whom it will be disclosed.

The Data Protection Registrar must then try to ensure that personal data

- is obtained and processed fairly and lawfully
- is held only for one or more specified and lawful purposes
- is adequate, relevant and not excessive
- is not kept for longer than necessary
- is stored in a way which prevents unauthorised access of accidental loss or destruction.

Additional safeguards are required in respect of personnel data covering

- racial orgin
- political opinions or religious or other beliefs
- physical or mental health or sexual life
- criminal convictions.

Note: Employees have a **right of access** to all computerised information held about them and may claim compensation for damage and distress if the information is inaccurate.

Exemptions

The provisions of the Act do not apply to data held for

- the purpose of national security
- the detection or prevention of crime
- calculating payroll or for keeping accounts
- household affairs or recreational purposes
- the subsequent preparation of text (such as documents held in a word processor)
- the purpose of recording the 'intention' of the data user.

Figure 11.10

The EU Data Protection Directive 1995

The EU Data Protection Directive was published in 1995, and Britain, in common with other member states, has until 24 October 1998 to pass legislation to implement the Directive. This may mean that the Data Protection Act will be updated or that new Regulations will be passed to extend its applications.

The Directive is concerned with several areas including paper records which contain personal data and which are not currently covered by legislation. It is also likely that from 1998 individuals will have to give their consent for personal data about them to be processed. There will also be more extensive grounds for compensation.

Discussion point

1   Research the type of filing systems available by looking through a business equipment magazine or a catalogue of business products from a local supplier. Identify all the types of systems discussed in this chapter.

2   Your brother is a talented motor mechanic. Five years ago he set up his own business doing basic repairs and vehicle services. Two years ago he brought in a partner who was qualified to carry out MOT tests. They have now expanded to incorporate hire cars and vans and to buying and selling used cars.

    When you visited his garage last weekend you were horrified by the paper mountain all over the office. He still has two four-drawer vertical cabinets but no organised system. Stung by your critical remarks about the mess, he has asked you to undertake a systems audit and to recommend what he should buy and how he should organise his filing. You have a budget of £5000.

    As a group, carry out the audit and make your recommendations, with your tutor taking the part of your brother.

3   An excellent report on data protection was published in *Which?* magazine in August 1995. Visit your college or local library and look up a copy of this report to check your own legal rights

    a   as a student, and
    b   as a consumer

    in relation to data held on you by your college, bank, GP and other organisations.

4   The government was quoted in autumn 1996 as saying that it 'intends to go no further in implementing the European Directive

than is absolutely necessary'. This is despite evidence that some employees have been unfairly discriminated against when asking for references or applying for promotion because of incorrect information held in their personnel (paper) files.

Discuss as a group what measures you think employees could take to check whether the data held in their personnel files are correct (eg punctuality, sick leave and work performance records) *without* upsetting the whole of the Personnel section!

Revision practice

Short answer questions

1   State four advantages of sending information in writing rather than giving it verbally.

2   Identify four techniques you could employ to carry out research.

3   Identify six common facilities available on modern telephone systems.

4   State clearly the difference between a mobile (cellular) phone and a pager.

5   State five facilities commonly available on fax machines.

6   State three advantages for an organisation of having an electronic mail system in operation.

7   Identify three main principles of storage and retrieval systems.

8   State two advantages and two disadvantages of operating an electronic filing system.

9   What is a records retention policy and why is it important?

10 Explain four common methods of classifying information and give an example of when each would be used.

Essay questions

1   Explain clearly how each of the following can assist business to function more effectively:
    a   fax
    b   electronic mail
    c   cellular telephones
    d   courier services
    e   telephone answering machine.

2   Your organisation is about to convert much of its routine paper-

based filing into electronic format. State the steps you would take to ensure the successful change from one system to the other.

3 **a** Identify why it is important that those who process information should be aware of the requirements of the Data Protection Act.

   b State the main provisions of the Act.

   c In what way will the introduction of the EU Data Protection Directive affect staff who work in this area?

4 You have been asked to carry out a research assignment relating to various aspects of the National Lottery.

   a State the preparations you would make before beginning your research to ensure you focused your enquiries accurately.

   b Identify some of the sources of information you would use.

   c How would you organise your material prior to producing your final report?

5 State how you would deal with each of the following telephone calls:

   a a request for a colleague's home address

   b a foreign caller who speaks limited English

   c an urgent call asking if your boss, who is currently in a board meeting, can attend an important meeting with a customer in two days' time – your boss has taken his diary with him

   d an irate customer who is annoyed about the non-delivery of an order

   e a journalist from the local paper, asking for comments on an ex-employee's letter alleging that your organisation does not comply with health and safety legislation.

Case study

You have recently been promoted to the position of secretary to Daryll Davies, the new human resources manager in your organisation. The Human Resources Department is soon to move to new office accommodation in another building and Daryll is keen to reorganise several of the systems which are used and update certain types of information. To help, Daryll has asked you to undertake each of the following tasks.

1 Research the requirements of the Disability Discrimination Act which came into force in 1996. Daryll has a broad knowledge of the requirements but needs more details for a presentation she will be making at the board meeting at the end of next week. She has asked you to provide one A4 page giving the main requirements of the Act.

2   Provide an information page for *each* of the following topics to go into the new staff handbook she is preparing:
   a   how to send faxes
   b   how to use the internal telephone system
   c   professional telephone techniques.

   (It is suggested that you base your information for these on any equipment with which you are familiar at your college.)

3   Daryll is reviewing the storage system for personnel records which has become untidy and unwieldy. A large amount of information is held in the area – from personnel files, to health and safety and accident records, to information on training and development. The system needs completely reorganising and new equipment will be purchased for siting in the new office area. Daryll has decided that a summary of the information should be held on a computer database cross-referenced to the paper filing system, which will include the main documentation. She has asked you to send her an e-mail which gives your views on:
   a   the items of information you would recommend for inclusion on the database
   b   the filing system(s) you recommend for the paper which will still be stored – together with your reasons
   c   the equipment you would recommend
   d   any requirements of the Data Protection Act which Daryll should bear in mind.

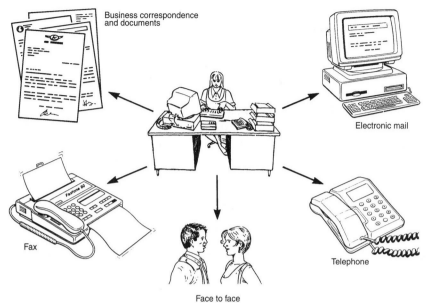

The communications function

● Processing communication

The ability to communicate promptly, precisely and courteously is the key element which separates the efficient and effective organisation from one which is slipshod, and the professional administrator or secretary from the amateur.

An essential requirement for producing effective communication is the mastery of English. A good command of vocabulary and grammatical conventions is a critical component of both written and verbal communications. Accurate spelling and punctuation is a basic requisite of written documents. You cannot expect to be taken seriously in business without such skills.

The skill of writing documents is, however, only one side of the picture. The ability to consider the needs and perceptions of the recipient is critical to successful communication. Equally, the presentation of the information and the production of the documents must be professional and impressive.

This section will help you to achieve all these objectives – overwhelming though they may seem at this stage. Chapter 12 considers the principles of effective communication and the composition of business correspondence and other documents. Chapter 13 identifies the various forms of presentation usually found in business. The type of equipment and processes used to produce and copy documents are discussed in chapter 14, and guidance is given to help you choose the most appropriate methods. The law on copyright is also considered.

Effective communication in business correspondence

12

● Introduction

All forms of communication are an attempt to make a link or connection with another person. The more precisely and unambiguously this link is made, the more effective the communication. The aim is to transmit thoughts and ideas from one person to another. The more accurately the 'message' is sent and received, the greater the likelihood of an appropriate response. This chapter looks at the principles of effective communication and the skills required to produce the different types of *written* communication that may be produced in business. There is also the opportunity to assess and improve your technical skills.

● The principles of effective communication

Every communication has two important aspects.

- It needs to be **technically correct** – this means that the spelling, grammar and vocabulary must be accurate. In one sense, this is the easiest skill to learn because you can practise constantly to improve any weak areas – although self-discipline is obviously required!

- It needs to be **appropriate for the recipient** – the needs of recipients have to be carefully considered, as well as the preferred action or response you wish to evoke. This is a more difficult skill to master as, to a degree, it involves empathising with recipients, ie 'getting inside their heads' and seeing the message from their point of view.

You cannot expect to be taken seriously in business – or to elicit the best response from the recipient – unless you possess *both* of these skills!

In addition, the most appropriate method for transmission must be used. (see chapter 10).

Discussion point

The possession of excellent technical skills is useless if you cannot identify the appropriate type of response for different people. A letter to an elderly person about a fault with a household appliance should obviously be phrased differently from a memo to the service engineer about the same matter!

Assume your boss has had to visit an important customer in France at the last minute and is therefore having to postpone a meeting with the managing director and a colleague. He has prepared three notes to send as e-mails. One is to his colleague, the second to the managing director and the third to you, his secretary. Each is reproduced in Figure 12.1.

Note 1

> I've had to postpone the meeting booked for room J202 next Thursday at 10 am. Please cancel the room booking and the order for tea and biscuits. I'll be in France until Friday – try not to ring unless it's desperate! Thanks

Note 2

> Sorry, but I'm going to have to postpone our meeting for next week – I've been called away to France to try to make some money for us for a change! I'm assuming that you won't want to go ahead alone. Will ring you on my return to fix another date – with a bit of luck most of the costing problems will have been solved by then!!

Note 3

> Unfortunately, I am having to postpone our meeting for next Thursday regarding the costing of the new project at J M Blythe. I have been asked to visit Technique et Cie in Lyons to discuss our latest proposal and I think it is fairly certain that we will gain the contract if the terms are agreeable.
>
> I will contact your secretary on my return to arrange an alternative date for the meeting.

Figure 12.1 Three notes in different styles

1   As a group, decide which message should be sent to each person.

2   What differences in 'tone' can you identify?

3   Now discuss the consequences of sending each message to the wrong person!

The communication cycle

This consists of five separate stages. At each stage something can go wrong. Being aware of where problems can occur means that you can be more vigilant to prevent them!

Stage 1

This is the stage where you decide to send a message – either because you have had an idea or received information you need to pass on to another person.

Possible problems
- You do not understand the information you have received.

- You do not take the time to prepare properly before starting to communicate.

- Your information or idea is vague and woolly – or full of irrelevant detail or not detailed enough.

- Part of the information you were given has been lost or forgotten.

Stage 2

At this stage you have to 'encode' your message. This means putting it into an appropriate language *bearing in mind the needs of the recipient and the action / response you desire.*

Possible problems
- Your symbols are unknown to the receiver (eg a foreign language, technical jargon).

- Your symbols are ambiguous, confused, vague or incomplete.

- The overall 'tone' of your symbols is inappropriate for the person or situation.

Bear in mind that at this stage you may consider that a graphic or a verbal message is more appropriate than written words. In another situation, non-verbal communication may be more suitable, eg if you were acknowledging someone from a distance, it may be more appropriate to wave than to shout!

Stage 3

You transmit your message using the most appropriate medium. If you are writing your communication, then you may produce an e-mail message, a memo, a letter or a report.

Possible problems
- You choose the wrong medium for transmission.

- Your transmission is distorted or interrupted.

- You transmit at the wrong time, in the wrong place or send the symbols in the wrong order.

- It is impossible to transmit at this time.

Stage 4

Your receiver decodes the language. Unless it is completely understood, then it is likely that any actions taken are not those intended by the sender.

Possible problems

- The receiver does not understand the language used.

- The receiver stops decoding part-way through the message (the message is too long, too complex, the receiver was not listening).

- The overall 'tone' of the language is considered insulting or inappropriate by the receiver and these 'feelings' take precedence over the content of the message itself.

Stage 5

The receiver gives feedback to check understanding. This is important because it confirms to the sender that the message has been received and understood.

Possible problems

- No feedback is sent/received.

- Feedback is sent too late to be received in time.

- There is no time for feedback.

In summary

Problems in communication mainly arise because of

- the wrong choice of vocabulary

- the use of jargon or technical words

- the inability of the receiver to listen

- the inability of the receiver to understand the message (this may not be his or her fault!)

- the inability of the sender to communicate appropriately

- a lack of a proper system of communication.

🗨 Discussion point

Discuss as a group the most likely stage(s) of the cycle at which communication has broken down in each of the following situations.

1   You ask your boss if you can leave early just as she is leaving for a meeting. She agrees. The following day she accuses you of not having asked for permission.

2   You have problems explaining why you like a particular type of music to your parents.

3   You fail to contact a friend to tell her a night out is cancelled. She doesn't have a telephone and lives several miles from you.

4   You go abroad on holiday and cannot make yourself understood.

5   Your grandfather talks for hours, usually reminiscing about his youth. He is upset when, in the middle of his tale, you fail to react to the news that he slipped and fell yesterday afternoon.

6   You take down the telephone number of a caller wrongly, so it is impossible for your boss to return the call.

7   A representative rings you from overseas. You cannot understand half of his message because of interference on the line.

8   You receive a garbled message over the telephone but do not have the confidence to ask the caller to repeat it. You pretend you have understood it and ring off.

Communication flows

Within any business organisation communication is a continuous process. Almost by the minute, messages flow downwards to staff from management, upwards from employees to their boss, and horizontally from one member of staff to another. If you add to this the amount of gossip and speculation which is passed on through the grapevine, you can start to envisage the whole organisation as a continual hive of communications activity! (*Note*: Lines of communication are covered in more detail in the companion book, *Business for Advanced Secretarial Students*.)

For this amount of communication to be received, interpreted, encoded, transmitted over and over again, so that the minimum amount is lost, distorted or misunderstood, the whole system has to be **managed** in some way. Generally, this means that systems are put in place to *minimise* communication problems as much as possible, eg

• There is suitable accommodation for face-to-face verbal communication (such as interviews and meetings) to minimise interruptions.

- There are quiet areas where people can compose complex communications in peace.

- There is a clear structure to the organisation so staff know to whom they can communicate without exceeding their authority.

- There are clear guidelines (such as a common house style) so that staff can give a consistent corporate image when communicating externally.

- Staff are given training in the aspects of communication which are relevant to their own job role.

- Staff are encouraged to form positive working relationships, to assist each other where possible and to cooperate rather than compete with each other.

Summarising the principles

From the main points which have been discussed so far, it is possible to identify the basic principles of effective communication. These should not only be known by all staff but also systematically and rigorously applied throughout the whole organisation.

- All incoming correspondence and messages must receive prompt attention and action.

- All documents must be written clearly and simply in plain English.

- The needs of the recipient(s) must be considered at all times.

- The required response from the recipient should be considered *before* the communication is drafted.

- Facts should be accurate and presented objectively and unemotionally.

- The communication must be courteous and keep to the point.

- The presentational style of the document must be such that it is easy to follow and understand (eg the use of headings and numbered points).

- Wherever possible, feedback must be obtained to ensure that the message has been understood. If required, clarification should be given immediately.

Use plain English!

Organisations which produce information materials for the general public have often been criticised for lengthy, complex and jargon-ridden leaflets and pamphlets which confuse everyone. In some cases they even appear to have been written so as to dissuade people from reading them in-depth!

In an attempt to tackle this problem the Plain English Campaign launched its Crystal Mark (Fig. 12.2). This is a special mark which can be placed on all literature if its clarity has been approved by the Campaign. The text must be easy to follow and understand and any jargon or specialist words must be clearly explained and essential to the content.

Crystal Mark

Clarity
approved by
Plain English Campaign

Figure 12.2 Only leaflets written in easy-to-follow English are approved to carry the Crystal Mark

It is worth looking at the back of the next booklet or brochure you obtain to see if it has 'passed the test' and been approved to carry the Crystal Mark.

● Composition of business documents

Although it may seem unlikely at the start of your career, before too long you will certainly be expected to compose basic documents yourself. You are likely to have to write telephone messages, compose your own e-mail messages and even memos fairly shortly after starting work. Straightforward letters then follow. As you continue in your career, you will be expected to compose replies to a variety of correspondence, write brief reports, summarise articles and produce a précis, draft notices and advertisements, initiate correspondence according to instructions and so on!

Assessing and developing technical skills

You have already seen that **technical skills** are needed to compose documents which are grammatically correct, punctuated properly, with every word correctly used and spelt accurately. If this seems a tall order, then the technical skills assessment on pages 257–74 should help you. It comprises

- five self-assessment tests – in vocabulary, spelling, punctuation, grammar and sentence construction

- a key to each test – so that you can assess yourself

- guidance notes on each area.

Don't follow the experts

If you think the experts never make mistakes, then you are wrong! Mistakes often occur in newspaper and television reports.

A TV reporter was covering an attempt by Railtrack to try to reduce the number of low bridges damaged through bus drivers failing to read the 'low bridge' sign and running into them. Railtrack hired the services of a stunt man to crash a bus into a low

bridge in front of the cameras. The reporter then announced 'Drivers say Railtrack must be more careful'.

Try inserting some commas and moving them about in this sentence to obtain two interesting versions. You may like to note that from the way in which the sentence was spoken, it is doubtful if most listeners realised what the reporter actually meant!

 Test yourself

Turn now to pages 257–74 and work through the five self-assessment tests. Then mark them using the key provided. If you obtain 100 per cent marks (ie 160 in total), then you have no need to worry about your written English skills. If you obtain marks of 130 or more, then you will have only one or two areas to improve – and the guidance notes will help you. If you have an average score of around 100, then you have some work to do – and should discuss with your tutor how best to improve your skills. If you have a very low score, then it is important that you find out about any help or assistance which is available to bring your skills up to scratch before you start looking for a job!

Developing composition skills

If technical skills are the 'tools' you need to work with, then composition skills are the ability to use these tools effectively. For each type of document you need to compose, you should have a good understanding of

- the degree of formality required and how this affects the tone, style and presentation of the communication

- the structure and sequence of the information which would be most appropriate

- the best layout to use on each occasion so that the information is presented in a way which is pleasing to the eye and easy to follow.

Tone, style and presentation

At the beginning of this chapter, you were introduced to the issue of tone and style when you studied the three messages regarding your boss's visit to France (see page 227). In business, written documents can vary from being extremely formal to being informal – with a range of options in between! The **degree of formality** will be affected by the person to whom you are writing and the type of document and its content.

The recipient

Considerations include

- his or her status

- whether the recipient is a member of the organisation or someone outside the company

- the writer's own relationship with the recipient (long-term/short-term, distant/familiar, whether colleague/superior/subordinate)

- the 'power' of the recipient.

It is usual for communications addressed to high-ranking officials or important people to be written in a formal style. If the document is being sent outside the organisation, then it will be written in a more formal style than if it is internal. Therefore a letter sent by your boss to the managing director of another company will generally be more formal than a memo to the managing director of your own organisation. However, much depends upon who is writing the document! Communications which are 'upwards' (ie to a person of higher status) are more formal than those which are 'horizontal' (to someone at the same level) or 'downwards' (to a subordinate). Communications between long-standing colleagues or friends are likely to be more informal than those to new acquaintances.

Power is the final issue to be considered. People can be powerful in two ways. They may have the ability to cause serious problems for you and/or the organisation or they may have direct power over you! A customer who is annoyed at your casual reply could complain to your boss or a senior executive in the organisation, or might even contact the local press; either way, this could mean problems for you and/or bad publicity for your organisation. Your own boss could take offence at a casual, impolite or discourteous note and make your life very difficult. For this reason it is usual to be more careful and use more discretion when drafting a communication to anyone who could take offence at the contents and then take action against you.

The document

Factors affecting the tone and style include

* the type of document being produced

* the topic of the communication

* the reason for the communication

* the response required.

For instance, legal contracts and agreements, which must be precisely worded to avoid ambiguity or misunderstandings, are drafted by specialists. Public documents, such as brochures and leaflets, are usually carefully checked by organisations to make sure that the information is accurate, clear and in house style.

More general types of documents, such as business letters, may be formal or informal. They will be formal if they deal with important matters such as a legal claim or serious complaint.

The reason for communicating will influence both the tone and style of the document. A letter to an employee containing a written warning will be formal, whilst a memo agreeing that an employee can take an extra day's leave will be much more informal.

There are many reasons for communicating in business. You may wish to

* inform the recipient about certain facts

* complain about an issue

* acknowledge you have received information

* praise or congratulate someone

* explain why something occurred

* apologise for an error

* persuade someone to do something.

Bear in mind that there may be a mixture of reasons for sending a document. For instance, you may want to apologise for an error, explain why it occurred and then try to persuade the recipient to disregard it!

For that reason, the next stage should be to consider the *response* you are trying to obtain. For example, if the aim is to pacify the recipient, then the tone will be conciliatory and helpful, even apologetic. If, however, the document is being sent to reprimand someone, then the tone may be critical or accusatory. Whilst you are unlikely to be sending the latter type of document yourself, you may wish to

- receive an acknowledgement

- obtain compensation

- impress someone with your efficiency

- accept an apology

- persuade a person to drop a complaint

- agree you will follow instructions.

All these factors will influence the content and tone of your communications.

Discussion point

1   Score each of the following types of documents from 1–5 in terms of formality, where 1 = very informal and 5 = very formal. Then compare your answers as a group.

    a   The Chairman's annual report.
    b   A letter giving a reference about a previous employee.
    c   A memo to all staff informing them about the (poor) results of a fire drill.
    d   A letter responding to a customer's complaint.
    e   A telephone message to your colleague at the next desk.
    f   A memo confirming arrangements for an appraisal interview.
    g   A report on security to be presented to the board of directors.
    h   A report you have written to your boss reviewing the current office layout.
    i   A telephone message to your boss.
    j   A sales letter to your customers.

2   The staff in the Sales section are demotivated at present. Business is poor and there have been rumours of redundancies. To add to the problems some staff are absent through illness so the rest are working twice as hard. Your boss decides to write them a memo.

    Figure 12.3 shows several options. As a group, critically evaluate each of these and then decide which one (if any) he should send. It will help if you first consider what the response of the staff is likely to be to each one.

Version 1

I refer to the latest sales figures which are again disappointing. I am aware that you are under pressure at present but this is unlikely to ease over the next few weeks. Whilst the management is hoping that no redundancies will be necessary, unless the situation improves there may be few other options.

I trust you will all do your best at this very difficult time.

Version 2

At the last staff meeting I told you all how important it was that everyone worked hard at this very difficult time. Imagine my disappointment, therefore, when I found that three more staff were absent this week. This simply puts more pressure on everyone else.

The absence/attendance situation is critical to our success. At the moment work is piling up with no one to do it. Unless the situation improves I will have no option but to introduce Saturday morning working for everyone.

Version 3

I know that many of you are concerned about the current situation and the fact that orders are low at present. I also know that many of you are working extremely hard, under tremendous pressure, to try to improve this situation.

Our past history proves that the ability of our sales staff to work as an effective team is second to none. For that reason I have every confidence that, if we continue to operate in this way, we will overcome our present difficulties.

I will obviously keep you informed about our sales situation on a weekly basis. In the meantime, if anyone has any particular worries or concerns, do not hesitate to see me.

Version 4

I heard about your concerns the other day and would like to reassure you about the present situation. Unfortunately this is difficult because I am still not sure how it will all turn out. I do think that if we all pull together it will help, but I'm obviously as worried as everyone else.

All I can do is to assure you that if I hear anything definite from the senior management, I'll let you know immediately.

Figure 12.3 Four versions of a memo to staff

Structure and sequence

You probably remember that when you first started writing essays at school, you were told that each should have a beginning, a middle and an end! In this respect, business communications are the same. The aim is to 'lead' the reader through the document by making sure that all the relevant facts are included in the most logical order.

The most usual structure and sequence of specific business documents are discussed below and exercises are included to help you develop these skills. However, a useful starting point is to note some general rules which apply to all documents.

The beginning

A good technique is to move from the known to the unknown. Therefore, if your recipient already knows certain facts, you can start with these. This is why so many documents start with phrases such as

'As you may be aware, the Sales office is being repainted next week.'

'Further to our telephone conversation of last week ...'

'With reference to your letter of ... '

'Thank you for your letter of ...'

'I refer to the investigation you asked me to undertake ...'

The middle

This is where you present the facts and information you need to communicate in a logical order. If there are only a few basic facts, then you may be able to cover everything adequately in one paragraph. If there are several facts, you may need two or more paragraphs – where there are many facts, numbered points may be the best way to present them.

The end

The final paragraph or concluding part of the document may be used to review what has already been said. However, its more usual purpose is to emphasise to the recipient the response you wish to achieve or now expect. For this reason there are a range of final statements often found in business, eg

'We look forward to hearing from you.'

'If you require any further information, please do not hesitate to contact us.'

'I will contact you again within the next few days to discuss the matter.'

Discussion point

Below are notes made by an office junior when she took a telephone message. From the notes made, discuss as a group the most appropriate and logical order for the information to be written out for your boss, Cathryn Barnes, a senior partner in a firm of solicitors.

Then write out the message, disregarding any unnecessary information and using suitable words and phrases for your boss, who you know to be a stickler for accurate and precise communication!

- Has appointment for 3 pm today.

- Caller can't make it because he's had to cancel his half day off because of pressure of work. He'll be in his office until 6 pm on 582727 and then at home after that on 209093.

- Received Miss Barnes' letter on Monday and must see her urgently because he doesn't agree with a couple of things she wrote in the draft tenancy agreement. Wants to talk to her about these as soon as he can.

- Wanted another appointment this week – but from the diary it looks as if Miss Barnes is in court for the rest of the week.

- I said Miss Barnes would ring him back later today and either make a new appointment or discuss the parts of the letter he's bothered about.

- Caller's name is Martin Wilmott.

- He rang while you were at lunch – about 12.30 pm.

- He's worried if he doesn't speak to her quickly and get the tenancy agreement sorted before next Tuesday, his clients will go elsewhere.

Composing memos

Memos, or memoranda, are used for internal communication only. They are relatively informal and are often sent to give information.

The main points to remember are as follows.

- The layout of memos varies little between organisations. Most have a standard memo heading, ie To/From/Date/Subject. This may be stored on computer. You simply complete the space opposite each line of the heading.

- There is no salutation (eg Dear Bill) or complimentary close (eg Yours sincerely). However, some organisations prefer you to include both name and job title after 'To', whilst in others only the name is required. Much depends on whether there could be any confusion between recipients of the same name.

- Memos may be initialled but are rarely signed.
- They are usually fairly short – but not always. A long memo will usually have an opening paragraph and then the main section as a series of numbered points. This makes it easier to read.
- A memo is usually written on one topic only. Otherwise filing them would become very difficult.
- They are transmitted through the internal mail network.
- Multiple circulation requires the inclusion of a distribution list. If too many people need to receive the memo to enter all their names in the heading, then you can enter 'see below' in this part and add the distribution list at the bottom. It is usual to put this in alphabetical order and tick off each person's name on his or her individual copy.
- Confidential memos must *always* be marked as such and placed in a sealed envelope.
- Sometimes you may send a memo where you need a specific reply. In this case it may be useful to design a brief tear-off slip for people to complete and return.

Discussion point

1   Figure 12.4 is a first attempt at a memo by a junior employee, who was told to write to all staff to try to persuade them to have a free flu vaccination. As a group, comment on her attempt and then rewrite it appropriately yourself.

2   As a group, decide on the wording of a memo to give information to all the class on a proposed day or evening out. (You can invent all the details yourself!) Then discuss with your tutor how you could design and word a tear-off slip for people to complete so that you can check who has responded, who wants to come, the type of food they prefer and whether or not they have paid a deposit.

3   Memos should always be straightforward and to the point – though you may have to balance this with tact and diplomacy.

Write a memo to cover each of the following situations. If you wish, discuss the content and wording as a group before you begin.

On this occasion, you work for John Heynes, the marketing director of Markham Electronics plc.

a   A memo from your boss to Alan Pierce, the technical director, informing him that there will be a meeting with Ketesh Thiru of

Patterson Products plc about a components fault at 2 pm next Thursday (give the date). Since it appears to be a technical problem it would be useful if Alan Pierce (or one of his staff) could attend. The meeting will be held in John Heynes' office.

b A memo from your boss to the advertising manager, Judith Baynes, asking why the advertisement in this month's issue of *Electronics Monthly* was half the requested size.

c A memo from you to your boss, requesting a day off, two weeks on Friday, to attend a friend's wedding. You feel awkward about this because you have only just returned to work after being absent for two weeks with flu.

MEMO

TO   All staff

FROM   Jane Dyer, Human Resources Department

DATE   (today)

INFLUENZA VACINNATION

We all hate to have colds and flue in the winter. Plus if we are absent then the work piles up. For that reason the company is offering free vacinnations to avoid an epidemic – but I need to know if you want one by a week next Wednesday.

The vacinnations will be carried out in the medical room on C floor by Dr Jenkins on various dates next month. Simply let us have your name and we will include you on my list.

If you are worried weather you might have an allerjic reaction then this can be checked with a simple test beforehand.

Figure 12.4 A first attempt at a memo

Composing business letters

There are various types of business letters, including those which

- make or answer an enquiry
- make or answer a complaint
- ask for settlement of an account
- invite someone to an event
- give someone basic information
- sell a product or service
- outline interview arrangements
- offer or refuse employment
- provide a reference.

All letters must be carefully planned – simply because they are a written advertisement for your organisation. In addition, if you give incorrect information or rashly promise something you cannot do, then there may be repercussions which could create considerable difficulties. As always, the basic rules before you begin should include

- thinking about the recipient (and the response you are trying to obtain)

- checking your facts

- writing the contents in a logical order.

- considering the 'tone' you are going to use, given the facts you know about the recipient and the contents of and reason for the document.

The main points to remember are as follows.

- Business letters are *always* written on headed paper.

- The layout of business letters may vary slightly from one organisation to another but all have certain common components. These are shown in the example on page 255.

- All letters are dated. It is also usual to include a reference (often the initials of the writer and the typist).

- The name of the recipient is given in full, followed by his or her official designation and organisation's address. A modern trend is to omit the title and just put the name, eg James Blunt or Josie Blunt, not Mr James Blunt or Mrs Josie Blunt.

- The salutation and complimentary close must match, ie Dear Sir/Yours faithfully; Dear Mr Blunt/Yours sincerely. The 'Dear Sir/Madam' approach is less often used today as it is so formal.

- The name of the organisation is sometimes included immediately below the complimentary close – to indicate the writer is sending the letter on behalf of the company.

- Enclosures should be indicated, usually by inserting the word 'Enc' or 'Encs' at the foot of the letter.

- If the letter takes more than one page, organisations vary on how they mark continuation pages. Some simply put the page number at the top, others include the name of the recipient and date as well.

- Abbreviations are not included in business letters (eg 'isn't' or 'don't') – and neither are slang phrases or colloquial expressions.

- Confidential or personal letters are always marked as such and placed in an envelope which is similarly marked.

- The rules for signing letters vary from one organisation to another. In one company you may be allowed to sign any letter you write, in another only senior members of staff may be allowed to sign. If you sign a letter in your boss's absence, it is usual to put his or her name, your signature and the letters 'pp' before it. This indicates you have signed *per pro* or *on behalf of* your boss.

On guard with a reference

Never be persuaded to write a glowing reference for someone you hardly know or for someone whose whereabouts have been completely unknown for several years. Unless you are careful about how you phrase your reference, you could find that you are liable in law if you give false and inaccurate information. If an acquaintance of yours is given a job on the basis of your testimony about his or her honest character, and later disappears with Saturday's takings, you could find yourself in court!

To guard against this, many organisations insist that references must give factual information about the position held, dates of employment, competency, honesty and reason for leaving. In addition, a written disclaimer may be added to say that the reference has been prepared in good faith but that the organisation cannot accept liability for any errors or omissions in the information or for problems or loss resulting from any subsequent appointment.

A word of advice for your own referees – always ask *in advance* if you can use a person's name as a referee and, if that person has not seen you for some time, take the opportunity to bring them up to date with your achievements!

 Discussion point

As a group, decide which of the following openings
a   would *never* be suitable to start a business letter
b   would be appropriate for a sales letter
c   would be appropriate for a letter of complaint
d   would be appropriate as a response to a letter of complaint
e   would be appropriate as an acknowledgement letter to a potential customer.

1   Have you ever thought how much money you could save if your central heating system was efficient?

2   Thanks for getting in touch with us.

3   Thank you for your enquiry about our family holidays in the Caribbean.

4 We refer to the photocopying machine you installed recently in our sales office. Unfortunately, although it has only been in operation for three weeks, it has already broken down on three occasions.

5 I refer to your letter regarding your recent order. I was concerned to read that several of the items were received in a damaged condition because the packaging was flimsy and had broken open whilst in transit.

✓ Test yourself

1 For each of the openings given above, draft a *second and/or third* paragraph which continues the theme. Use your imagination to supply the details! Then check your paragraph(s) with your tutor.

2 Now select a suitable ending from the suggestions given below *or* amend one of these suitably to 'customise' your own final paragraph.

   a Please let me know if you require any further information.
   b I would be grateful if you could give this matter your immediate attention and let me know as soon as possible the action you intend to take.
   c Take advantage of this special offer immediately by completing the enclosed pre-paid reply card.
   d I hope that this will now solve the problem, and apologise for the inconvenience you have been caused. If you have any further problems please do not hesitate to contact me.

Developing your letter-writing skills

The best way to improve your skills is to practise by writing a variety of letters on different subjects and of varying length and complexity. If you begin with simple letters on topics you know about, then you should find this relatively easy. You are likely to find that you receive clear guidance or instructions from your boss for the first letters you write or draft on his or her behalf. This will mean putting your information into a logical order and preparing a draft for approval. Now that word processors are in common use, this is a simple matter, as any amendments or corrections made by your boss can easily be made on the final document.

Later you will start to write letters yourself and may be able to send them out in your own name. However, if ever you have any worries do ask someone in authority to check your document for you – this is much better than sending out a letter which contains factual inaccuracies or upsets an important customer.

Test yourself

1   Draft out each of the following letters and check them with your
     tutor. Again assume you work for John Heynes, Marketing Director
     of Markham Electronics plc.
     a   A letter to the Devonshire Hotel, Staveley Road, Oxford
          OX2 7EK confirming a single room with bath for two nights –
          next Wednesday and Thursday. Approximate arrival time will be
          8 pm. (It is normal practice for the executives at Markham
          Electronics to settle their own bill by credit card.)
     b   A letter to Mr Whiteside, manager of Jefferson Carpets Ltd,
          Water Street, Hightown HG2 3MP. Respond to his letter asking
          for a convenient date to fit the new reception area carpet by
          reminding him that it was agreed this would be fitted over a
          weekend and that any Saturday and Sunday would be
          convenient but that you wish the work to be completed within
          the next four weeks. Ask him to confirm which date the fitting
          will take place.

2   John Heynes is overseas this week. Whilst he is away, you receive a
     letter from an important customer, Mrs Petra Jacobson, production
     director of Abbinger Associates Ltd, Brinscoll Hill, Hightown
     HG2 3MP. The letter complains about the non-delivery of part of her
     order 20394. The components are required urgently.
     a   When you mention this to John Heynes over the phone he asks
          you to
          i   send an urgent memo to Paul Tabiner, the production
               manager of your own organisation, asking for an
               explanation. Apparently, John Heynes thought the
               components would all be delivered last week.
          ii   write to Petra Jacobson acknowledging her letter and
               saying the matter is being investigated as a matter of
               urgency.
     b   Two days later Paul Tabiner telephones you to say that the
          delay was caused by a machine fault which resulted in two
          defective batches of components being produced. The problem
          has now been rectified and the components will be sent by
          express delivery tomorrow. Write to Mrs Jacobson giving her
          this information. Bear in mind that by the time she receives the
          letter, the components should be arriving!

Composing a report

There are various types of reports and report forms which may be used in different situations. One example is an accident report, which is usually written on a standard form.

Reports are concerned with giving information about a situation in a clear, concise and logical order. You may be asked to investigate a situation and produce a report. Alternatively, you may be asked to report on something which already happens or to expand on a suggestion you have made or an event you have attended.

Written reports in business are usually produced in one of two ways.

- **The informal report** is often produced in memo form and is simply a summary comprising an introduction, an analysis of the situation and a conclusion. The style and tone is usually informal.

- **The formal report** has standard headings and layout. This type of report is produced when the report will be sent outside the organisation or is for consideration by senior management (eg for discussion by the board of directors). The wording, style and tone are more formal in this type of report.

The main points to remember are as follows.

- A report should be an objective statement of facts. Do not give your own personal opinions unless you have been asked to do so.

- You may be asked simply to give the results of your investigations without suggesting a solution. If you are asked to make suggestions, list these as 'recommendations' – they should be brief and to the point.

- Reports should be set out in a logical order, but the amount of background information you include will depend upon how much previous knowledge the recipient possesses on the topic.

- Think carefully about any sensitive areas of the report – for instance, if they relate to confidential issues or legal/financial matters. If there are any particularly contentious issues, then check what may be included, who is on the circulation list and whether the report should be classed as 'confidential'.

- Reports should be easy to read. This may mean attaching explanatory information on separate pages (known as appendices) or including charts and graphs. Complex data are usually clearer if they are presented in graphical form (see page 280).

- Remember to acknowledge any sources if you have obtained professional assistance or undertaken any research (see Figure 12.6, page 251 and Figure 13.1, page 281).

Writing an informal report

All reports give information, usually in a standard order. In an informal report you are normally expected to

- start by referring to the subject of the report, ie what it is about

- summarise how you obtained your information – this may have been by asking people, experiencing something or researching information

- summarise the information you have obtained

- state the conclusion you have reached

- you may be asked to conclude by giving your recommendations.

Discussion point

1 At Markham Electronics there have been substantial delays recently in mailroom deliveries. Katy Roberts, the senior administrator, was asked to investigate the situation by Sarah Knowles, the administration manager and produce a report. She was also asked to give her recommendations for any changes in procedure which would be useful.

Her completed report is shown in Figure 12.5.

As a group, study the report linking it to the main requirements of report writing given previously. Katy has used headings to make the report easier to read and you should be able to see how these relate to the sections of a report outlined above.

2 You have recently attended an external training course on using the Internet. The course was expensive – £300 for the day. Your boss, John Heynes, has asked for a report on the course and for your recommendations on whether it would be useful for other members of staff.

Below are the notes you made after you had attended.

- Organisation good – greeted promptly and by name and given log-in ID.

- Large spacious room, 18 Pentium computers. Hardware/communications good – gave fast access to system (though two machines not working).

- Tutor rather disorganised at the start – later proved helpful and well informed.

- Started with explanation about Internet and Net jargon. Went on too long – everyone wanted to get on with it!

- Good information on service providers and how to access different types of information. We also used on-line and printed directories and the World Wide Web was explained. Some good tips for quickly finding way around. Then left to use it (for too long?). Many sites American and after an hour it was a bit boring.

- After lunch – review of necessary equipment/software and advantages and disadvantages of Internet. We then went on to access public services and download software and other information.

- From 2 pm involved in creating Internet pages and learned a little bit about HTML – the world standard language for writing Web pages. This was the best part but was compressed into about an hour.

- Overall course useful as an introduction, but not for those who already know about Internet. Advanced course is now planned to concentrate on HTML and other aspects of Web authoring.

- Better if only specialist staff attend advanced course – and only if we intend to create our own Web page. We can pass on the basic information in-house through our own system.

Prepare the report he has requested.

MEMO

TO   Sarah Knowles

FROM   Katy Roberts

DATE   (today)

REPORT ON INCOMING MAIL DISTRIBUTION

I refer to your request that I investigate the reason for the recent delays with the distribution of incoming mail.

Investigation procedure

I investigated the reason for the delays by visiting the mailroom on two occasions and interviewing mailroom staff and departmental staff. I also checked the responses of staff with the standard procedure laid down to ensure that this was being followed.

Findings

As a result of my investigations I discovered the following.

1   On one occasion last week the mail was received later than normal because of a delay at the sorting office. The Royal Mail service

confirms this information and does not think such delays are likely to recur.

2   Two members of the mailroom staff were absent last week through illness. Under these circumstances they can call upon assistance from other departments but were repeatedly told that no one could be made available to assist them because of pressure of work.

3   The normal collection time by departments means that mailroom staff are under considerable pressure to process all the mail for prompt collection. When there is a large delivery this exacerbates the problem.

4   Although departmental staff were notified that the mail would be available later than normal for collection and distribution, no specific time was given. Instead, on the first three days a telephone call was made to each department when the mail had been processed. However, some departments failed to send staff to collect the mail until an hour later.

5   Departmental heads told me that it was more difficult to send staff later in the morning because they were, by then, involved in other duties or on their breaks.

Conclusions

My conclusions are that

1   There seems to be no enforceable system in operation to cover for absenteeism in the mailroom.

2   The current time for collection puts extreme pressure on staff given the continual increase in volume of incoming mail.

3   Delays with processing the mail on arrival were compounded by late collection of mail by departments.

Recommendations for improvement

To prevent these problems recurring I recommend that

1   A rota for mailroom cover in case of absenteeism is prepared which 'spreads' the cover between each department on a daily basis. This is agreed with departmental heads who must supply cover staff on their allocated days, if requested to do so. Any refusal to do so should be reported to yourself.

2   The collection time by departments is changed from 9.30 am to 10 am. Departmental staff must be available to collect mail promptly at 10 am.

3   Any emergency which means that a change in collection time is required must be agreed by the mailroom supervisor who will inform you immediately. She will also need the authority to communicate this direct to departmental heads, rather than their staff.

Figure 12.5 A report on mailroom problems

Writing a formal report

Some organisations have a set house style for formal reports which everyone must use. This may even be stored as a format in the computer system so that the 'blank' document can be brought on to screen and completed by the writer.

Generally, the layout provides for the same type of content as an informal report. However, given that this is produced as an individual document, rather than as a memo, there are certain differences.

- **Heading** – this usually states the title of the report.

- **Terms of reference** – this is not always necessary but, if so, will usually include the reason for the report and the name of the person who requested it.

- **Procedure** – states the sources of information.

- **Findings** – gives the results of the investigation.

- **Conclusion** – usually just a short summary

- **Recommendations** – usually more detailed than the conclusions.

- **Signature and date.**

The following items may also be included.

- Specific references to a source by using a footnote (see Figure 12.6, page 251).

- Appendices – to include more extensive information than could be included in a footnote.

- A bibliography – which includes the title of any publications you have used, the surname and initials of the author, the name of the publisher and the year of publication.

- A circulation list for the report. This is usually easier to include at the end of the report, rather than at the beginning.

Remember that just because a report is formal it does not mean it must be longer! However, if it is to be written for an outside organisation or for consideration by senior management, you may be expected to write it in the third person. This means that you do not write the word 'I'! Instead of writing 'I therefore recommend that ...', you would say 'It is recommended that ...'.

An example of a short formal report is given in Figure 12.6.

**REPORT ON CONDITIONS OF EMPLOYMENT FOR
DISPLAY SCREEN EQUIPMENT USERS**

1 Terms of reference

Following the introduction of legislation specifically relating to
workstations and equipment,[1] a review was carried out of the
workstations, equipment and software used specifically by DSE operators.
At the request of the systems manager, this report has been prepared
evaluating whether all the requirements of the current legislation are
now being met.

2 Procedure

The procedure which was adopted is outlined below.

2.1 A comprehensive list was compiled of the workstations installed
(see Appendix I).

2.2 The software and systems in use were listed and the features of
each were identified (see Appendix II).

2.3 A survey of all DSE users was carried out and the results
analysed (see Appendices III and IV).

3 Findings

3.1 All the workstations comply with the requirements of the
Regulations.

3.2 All software and systems are user friendly and comply with the
requirements of the Regulations.

3.3 Frequent DSE users are aware of their rights and obligations.
However, those who only use a computer for part of their working
day or on an occasional basis are less well informed.

4 Conclusions

4.1 All the requirements of the Act are being fulfilled in relation
to equipment, furniture and software.

4.2 Most DSE staff are well informed. Some problems exist with other
staff.

5 Recommendations

5.1 A training session is held for all existing staff who use
computers as part of their job.

5.2 A handbook is issued to all staff giving information on the
Regulations. This is issued to all existing staff and to new
staff during induction.

Petra Roberts
Health and Safety Manager

25 July 199-

[1] Display Screen Equipment Regulations 1992

Figure 12.6 A short formal report

🗨 Discussion point

You work for Jack Richards, the facilities manager at Markham Electronics. He is concerned that there are problems with the security procedures given the following recent events.

- Three visitors were found wandering around the premises, on separate occasions, without a visitor's badge or anyone to accompany them.

- There have been some thefts of staff personal property in and around the reception area.

- Security staff are regularly reporting that windows are left open and doors left unlocked at night.

You have been asked to investigate the matter and prepare a report which he can present to the managing director.

1 Review the information given on security on pages 96–105.

2 As a group, decide how you would investigate the problem and the type of findings which might result. This would make a good brainstorming activity with everyone giving their suggestions and ideas!

3 Write up the report so that it has a title plus a terms of reference, procedure and findings sections.

4 Individually, decide on your conclusions and recommendations and include these in your report.

5 Do not forget to add your name and the date!

Composing other types of document

Whiles memos, letters and reports are the most likely documents you will be asked to compose, there are other types of documents that you might be asked to prepare. Below is a brief summary of these, together with the main rules to follow in each case.

Notices

Today most notices are prepared on computer. If you have a desktop publishing package or can use graphics software you may be able to produce a professional-looking notice by 'importing' ready-made graphics (if appropriate) to make it eye-catching and interesting.

The main points to remember are as follows.

- Check where the notice is to be placed and the size of notice which would be most appropriate. Remember that if you are preparing it on computer, you may be restricted to A4 size because of the capability of your printer. However, if you have a colour printer and colour photocopier (see pages 315 and 324) then you can make it far more attractive.

- Check how long the notice is likely to be in place. Most notices are only temporary. Those which are more permanent should be laminated to preserve their condition.

- Write the notice using clear and simple language so that it is easily understood by everyone who reads it.

- Notices are usually informal, so you can use an arresting heading which catches people's attention.

- Keep it brief and to the point.

- Set the print size large enough so that at least the main points can be read from a distance.

- Date the notice – so that you can tell when it was prepared. This gives an indication when it is too old to be of further use and should be taken down.

- Some organisations insist that notices are signed. This prevents unauthorised notices being put up on company noticeboards.

 ## Discussion point

1   Some organisational issues are too sensitive to be public knowledge. Discuss as a group
   a   your reaction to finding that your most recent examination results had been posted on a college noticeboard
   b   the type of information which would not be suitable for announcing on a notice.

2   Check the notices displayed on noticeboards in your college and 'score them' for presentation, wording and design. Decide as a group the factors which make them attractive and eye-catching.

3   The college refectory will be closed for the rest of this week because of an equipment fault. A junior member of the administrative staff prepares the following notice to put outside the door.

   REFECTORY CLOSED. STUDENTS KEEP OUT.

   a   What would be your reaction to reading this notice?
   b   The refectory manager sees the notice, takes it down and asks you to write one which is more appropriate. She will then have it prepared on computer. Compare your version with those of other members of your group.

Invitations

There are two types of invitation.

- Those which are sent in letter form (Figure 12.7).

- Those which are pre-printed.

When you reply, it is usual to send the reply in the same format as the invitation you received.

Invitations can be formal or informal. You are probably aware of this from your personal life. A formal invitation to a wedding, for instance, is written in the third person (Mr and Mrs John Parker have pleasure in inviting ...) — and the reply should be written in the same way. An informal invitation is written in the first person (I would like to invite you to...) and again the response should be in the same terms.

If you are sending an invitation, you must make sure that you include

- the date, day and time of the event

- where it is being held

- the purpose.

People usually have little difficulty in writing a brief acceptance to an invitation – the difficulty arises when they want to refuse one! In business, you should note that it is normal to give a brief explanation of why someone cannot attend, rather than just say 'No'!

Test yourself

Your boss has received an invitation from the local council, which is shown in Figure 12.7.

a Draft a short letter in reply, assuming Louise Helm would be pleased to accept the invitation.

b Draft a short letter refusing the invitation because Louise Helm has a prior engagement to speak at a conference on that date.

Check your wording in both cases with your tutor.

Summaries

A summary is an abbreviated version of an article, a document or a series of correspondence. All explanatory material is removed and only the key facts are given. This enables the reader to grasp the main points quickly and easily.

UPLANDS BOROUGH COUNCIL

Town Hall
HIGHTOWN
HG1 2PM

GP/PA

10 February 199-

Ms Louise Helm
Human Resources Manager
Markham Electronics plc
Windham Way
HIGHTOWN
HG4 9DM

Dear Ms Helm

HIGHTOWN COMMUNITY ACCESS POINT

I am pleased to invite you to the official opening ceremony of the new Community Access Point which will take place on Wednesday, 3 March 199- at 1.30 pm.

The event will commence with an informal buffet followed by the official opening ceremony at 2.15 pm. Our local MP, Georgina Hayle, has agreed to unveil the official plaque.

Your organisation has been extremely supportive of our efforts to create an access point in Hightown and we would be delighted if you would be able to join us on this occasion. To help you to find your way there easily, I am pleased to enclose a simplified sketch of the area showing all main roads and the location of the Access Point.

I look forward to meeting you again.

Yours sincerely

Gerald Prescott

Gerald Prescott
Chief Executive

Enc

Figure 12.7 A letter of invitation

You will be asked to prepare a summary when your boss needs to use some information but does not have the time to go through the original documentation. You will also find summarising a useful technique when you are researching – as you refer to an article, note down the main points and then use these as your reference rather than the original document.

Sometimes a summary is required because a document prepared by a colleague is too long to be used in its original form. A typical example is an advertisement. The charge for advertising in the press is directly related to the size of the advertisement. In addition, too much text means that the advertisement loses impact.

Finally, you should consider the 'angle' required when you summarise a document. Are you seeking to extract information relating to advantages, disadvantages, key points or main features? Much of this will depend upon the reason for the summary.

Discussion point

1   A member of staff has been absent through illness on numerous occasions over the past 18 months. Your boss has now decided that some formal action should be taken. The human resources manager has asked for a one-page summary of events.

    As a group, discuss the key information that should be included in the summary.

2   When you start work, your boss is interested about the course you attended at college because his daughter is interested in a career in administration. He asks if you could write a brief summary of the subjects you studied, the topics you covered and any other information his daughter might find useful.

    Prepare the summary with a suitable heading. Add your name at the end and do not forget to date the document.

Tables, graphs and charts

It is often more appropriate to produce information in graphic or tabular format than in written form. This is particularly the case if figures or statistics are used – or if you wish the reader to see trends or patterns easily.

The creation of such documents is covered on pages 279–87.

Form design and composition

You have no doubt completed many forms in your life. You may have applied for a passport or driving licence; you will certainly have completed an enrolment form. Important forms which will be completed by many people are usually professionally designed – and this process and the factors which must be taken into consideration are covered in the companion book to this, *Business for Advanced Secretarial Students.*

Brief tear-off forms were covered on page 240.

● Technical skills assessment

Below are five sets of questions. Take your time in answering them. Then check your answers for each set of questions with the key on page 261 and record your score (out of 160).

Guidance notes on each area are given on pages 265–74.

Set 1: vocabulary

1   Insert the correct version of there/their/they're into the following sentences.

   a   Is it true that _____ going _____ on _____ holidays next year?
   b   _____ keen to give _____ views on the subject to _____ boss.
   c   How are you going to get _____ , given that _____ address has changed?

(8)

2   Clearly state the difference in meaning between each of the following pairs of words.

formally/formerly	summary/summery
discrete/discreet	practice/practise
principal/principle	confident/confidant
equable/equitable	deprecate/depreciate

3   Give one word for each of the following definitions.

   a   easily broken
   b   occurring once every two years
   c   a person who always looks on the black side
   d   a four-footed animal
   e   able to use both hands alike
   f   no longer in use
   g   full agreement of everyone
   h   a specialist or expert who is paid to give advice
   i   loss of memory
   j   a likeness which is exaggerated so it appears ridiculous
   k   a crime against the sovereign or state
   l   views and principles which are deliberately spread around to influence public opinion.

(12)

4 An adjective which refers to 'having to do with the nose' is nasal. Write the appropriate adjectives which link to the following words in the same way.

teeth   hand   intelligence   face

(4)

Set 2: punctuation

1 Punctuate each of the following sentences *in two ways* to show differences in meaning.

   a The tutor said the student was a liar.
   b Men who have not kept up to date or are blinded by prejudice know little about how much women have achieved.

(4)

2 Identify the incorrect apostrophes in the following paragraph.

The curse of the apostrophe is upon us! How many excessive apostrophe's do you meet every day? Wrong statement's by grocers and greengrocers add punctuation to potato's and even pea's. It's a shame! In this day and age it's still the case that the apostrophe is misunderstood – despite it's many uses!

(5)

3 Punctuate the following passage.

john left his hotel by car arrived at the airport about noon and checked in for the flight to new york the last time he had visited the city he mused he had arrived at kennedy in the middle of a snowstorm and had been driven to manhattan in a swirl of snowflakes exhausted and cold he had livened up considerably when he had passed maceys department store near fifth avenue christmas trees had been everywhere adding their brilliant lights to the glitz of times square todays arrival couldnt have been more different with temperatures in the 80s and tourists queuing for the boats to staten island and tours of the statue of liberty.

(31)

Set 3: spelling

In the following list of words, 40 are spelled incorrectly. Identify these and write the correct spelling for each one.

absence
acceptence
accessable
acceptable
accommodation
achieve
appalling
auspicious
auxilliary
benefitted
bereft
bulletin
calender
campaign
circuit
collegue
competant
consensus
connoiseur
conscientious
convertable
decieve
definate
despondent
disasterous
discernable
effervesce
elligible
exhorbitant
farenheit
fulfilling
feign
forego
grammer
harrassed
honorary
haemorrhage
independant
indispensible
justifiably

kaleidoscope
labrinth
liase
limosine
liquidator
maintainance
malingerer
manouvre
masquerade
nieve
negligence
objectionable
obsolesence
occurance
odity
oppression
peaceable
pertinant
priviledge
questionnaire
rememberance
reminisence
seperately
sojourn
subsistance
surriptitous
synthesis
tactician
tambourine
temporarily
unexceptionable
vaccinnation
vaunted
vengence
volunteer
warranty
wimsical
withhold
wooly

(40)

Set 4: grammar

Rewrite each of the following sentences, correcting the grammatical error.

1 Due to an error, the document could not be posted.

2 Can you divide the profits between the three partners?

3 There are less students on the course than last year.

4 You have the option of the red or blue one.

5 Referring to your letter of last week.

6 The committee are meeting next Thursday.

7 His collection of postcards were valued very highly.

8 This is one of the papers that is to be sent to him.

9 Either the salesman or his assistant are able to take the call.

10 Each of the girls is doing their job well.

11 I am sure that we will be able to help you.

12 Whose going to the party?

13 That is the man who the police officer said was guilty.

14 Please tell me which person I should write to.

15 I thought you would buy an outfit which was different to mine.

16 The best of the teams won the football match.

17 Does he want you and I to go to the meeting?

18 You and me need to complete it quickly.

19 She promised to quickly contact me.

20 She said she had failed to fully understand the implications.

(20)

Set 5: general sentence construction and miscellaneous errors

The following sentences all contain common errors or are badly written. Can you say why and, better still, correct them?

1 She sold a wide variety of vegetables, ie peas, beans and carrots.

2 I, too, have also been to Rome.

3 Waste paper is a safety hazard because it is highly inflammable and catches fire very easily.

4 Jill told Jackie that she was untidy.

5   My uncle saw a bear on his holidays.

6   They ate food in the pub which was very tasty.

7   They gave donations for their colleagues in the boxes.

8   He stopped at the newspaper kiosk which made him miss his bus.

9   It needs cleaning badly.

10   I only want to ring him.

11   Although we have our backs to the wall I still think we need to go with the flow.

12   At this moment in time – and far be it from me to ask you to do this – it stands to reason we should leave no stone unturned to find the truth.

13   I regret I was off recently but I picked up a nasty bug and it has taken me quite a bit to shake it off.

14   The integration of applications packages to facilitate document transferability is the norm even on DOS systems today.

15   The forms will be expedited immediately your request is received in writing.

16   I should have liked to have known him.

17   Could you make me a cup of coffee?

18   Should I tell him you will visit them?

19   He doesn't think like I do.

20   He doesn't say nothing.

(20)

● Key to technical skills assessment

Set 1: vocabulary

1   a   Is it true that **they're** going **there** on **their** holidays next year?

   b   **They're** keen to give **their** views on the subject to **their** boss.

   c   How are you going to get **there,** given that **their** address has changed?

2   formally – in a formal or stiff manner
formerly – before now

summary – a brief or shortened extract
summery – like, or suitable for, summer

discrete – separate, independent
discreet – able to keep a secret

practice – (noun) eg the choir practice
practise – (verb) eg to practise driving

principal – the main or chief one
principle – a basic truth

confident – sure or certain
confidant – a person who shares one's secrets

equable – calm, even tempered
equitable – fair, just

deprecate – to disapprove
depreciate – to fall in value through use

3 **a** fragile
   b biennial
   c pessimist
   d quadruped
   e ambidextrous
   f obsolete
   g unanimity
   h consultant
   i amnesia
   j caricature
   k treason
   l propaganda

4 **a** dental
   b manual
   c intellectual
   d facial

Set 2: punctuation

1 **a** The tutor, said the student, was a liar

       The tutor said, the student was a liar.

   b Men, who have not kept up to date or are blinded by prejudice, know
       little about how much women have achieved.

       Men who have not kept up to date, or are blinded by prejudice, know
       little about how much women have achieved.

2 The curse of the apostrophe is upon us! How many excessive
   apostrophes do you meet every day? Wrong **statements** by grocers and
   greengrocers add punctuation to **potatoes** and even **peas.** It's a shame!
   In this day and age it's still the case that the apostrophe is
   misunderstood – despite **its** many uses!

3 **John** left his hotel by car, arrived at the airport about noon, and checked in for the flight to **New York. The** last time he had visited the city, he mused, he had arrived at **Kennedy** in the middle of a snowstorm and had been driven to **Manhattan** in a swirl of snowflakes. **Exhausted** and cold, he had livened up considerably when he had passed **Macey's** department store near **Fifth Avenue. Christmas** trees had been everywhere, adding their brilliant lights to the glitz of **Times Square. Today's** arrival **couldn't** have been more different with temperatures in the 80s and tourists queuing for the boats to **Staten Island** and the **Statue** of **Liberty.**

Set 3: spelling

acceptance	labyrinth
accessible	liaise
auxiliary	limousine
benefited	maintenance
calendar	manoeuvre
colleague	naive
competent	obsolescence
connoisseur	occurrence
convertible	oddity
deceive	pertinent
definite	privilege
disastrous	remembrance
discernible	reminiscence
eligible	separately
exorbitant	subsistence
fahrenheit	surreptitious
grammar	vaccination
harassed	vengeance
independent	whimsical
indispensable	woolly

Set 4: grammar

1 Because of an error, the document could not be posted.

2 Can you share the profits between the three partners?

3 There are fewer students on the course than last year.

4 You have the choice of the red or blue one.

5 I refer to your letter of last week.

6 The committee is meeting next Thursday.

7 His collection of postcards was valued very highly.

8   This is one of the papers that are to be sent to him.

9   Either the salesman or his assistant is able to take the call.

10 Each of the girls is doing her job well.

11 I am sure that I will be able to help you *or* We are sure that we will be able to help you.

12 Who's going to the party?

13 That is the man whom the police officer said was guilty.

14 Please tell me to which person I should write.

15 I thought you would buy an outfit which was different from mine.

16 The better of the teams won the football match.

17 Does he want you and me to go to the meeting?

18 You and I need to complete it quickly.

19 She promised to contact him quickly.

20 She said she had failed to understand the implications fully.

Set 5: general sentence construction and miscellaneous errors

1   She sold a wide variety of vegetables, eg peas, beans and carrots.

2   I have also been to Rome.

3   Waste paper is a safety hazard because it is highly inflammable.

4   Jill told Jackie that she (Jackie) was untidy *or* Jill accused Jackie of being untidy *or* Jill admitted to Jackie that she was untidy.

5   While he was on his holidays, my uncle saw a bear.

6   The food they ate in the pub was very tasty *or* The pub food was very tasty.

7   The donations for their colleagues were placed in the boxes.

8   He stopped at the newspaper kiosk and the delay meant that he missed his bus.

9   It badly needs cleaning.

10 I want to ring only him *or* I want only to ring him.

11 Although times are difficult I think we need to let events take their course.

12 I think we need to do everything possible to find the truth.

13 I regret I was absent recently but I was ill with a virus and it has taken me longer than expected to recover.

14 Many computer software packages today link together so that documents created in one package can easily be transferred to another.

15 We will send the forms immediately we receive your written request.

16 I should have liked to know him.

17 Would you make me a cup of coffee?

18 Shall I tell him you will visit them?

19 He doesn't think as I do.

20 He doesn't say anything.

● Guidance notes

Vocabulary

A key skill for all administrators and secretaries is the ability to select the most appropriate word for the situation. This means continually expanding your vocabulary and always looking up the meaning of unfamiliar words. It also means knowing the difference between words which look and sound similar (homonyms). Having a broad vocabulary helps you to avoid repeating a word within a sentence because you can choose from various synonyms without always searching a thesaurus. For example, 'Please give generously – your donations are always welcome' is preferable to 'Please give generously, your gifts are always welcome'.

Homonym check

In addition to the words given in the test, check that you also know the difference between

accede/exceed
accept/except
affect/effect
aggravate/irritate
allusion/illusion
alternate/alternative
complement/compliment
comprehensive/comprehensible
continuous/continually
council/counsel
defer/differ
draft/draught
eminent/imminent
lose/loose
passed/past

persecute/prosecute
personal/personnel
respectfully/respectively
stationery/stationary
uninterested/disinterested.

You should also be aware of the difference between nouns which take the letter 'c' and verbs which take the letter 's', such as licence/license and advice/advise.

Punctuation

The normal usage of common punctuation marks is given below.

The full stop
• Use at the end of a sentence, *not* after a heading or (usually) in standard abbreviations, eg BA, MP.

The comma
• Use to separate words in a list (but do not use before the word 'and'), eg game, set and match.

• Use to separate phrases in a sentence, eg

The dog, a labrador, loved its daily walk.

• Use before a quotation, eg

Peter said, 'They'll never win the match.'

The use of open punctuation in virtually all business letters means that commas are *not* used at the end of lines of an internal address or after the salutation/complimentary close.

As you saw in question 1 on page 258, the position of a comma can change the meaning of a sentence. Look back to these examples (and the key on page 262) and discuss the sentences with your tutor if you are unsure about the alternative meanings. .

The apostrophe
• Use to indicate a missing letter or letters in a contracted word, eg you'll, shouldn't, he's.

Note that contracted words are not used in business correspondence. Note also the difference between it's (it is) and its (possessive), eg

When it's raining, the cat rushes in through its flap.

• Use to show possession, eg the student's books = the books of the student but the students' books = the books of the students.

Generally, insert an apostrophe, then add an 's' – unless the word already ends in 's', eg St Mark's church *but* St James' church (one 's' is sufficient here).

The same rules apply to plural words which do/do not end in 's', eg children's coats, boys' ties.

Make sure you check words which change from singular to plural, eg company's results (the results of the company), companies' results (the results of several companies).

Also use in phrases where time is possessive, eg one year's time (time of one year), three years' time (time of three years).

Hyphens and dashes

- Hyphens are used in compound words after certain prefixes, eg red-haired, semi-detached, pre-1960, anti-apartheid. However, their usage is declining in the printed form – you may therefore see occasions when hyphens have been omitted, eg in phrases such as up-to-date or part-time, unless they are used before a noun. For example, 'her hairstyle is up to date', but 'she has an up-to-date hairstyle'.

  However, hyphens are essential with the prefix re-, indicating that something will be done again, where the word would have a different meaning without the hyphen. Eg resound (re-sound), resign (re-sign), recover (re-cover).

- Dashes are used to denote a longer pause than a comma, or before a list, eg

  The boy stopped – waited a moment – then continued on his way.

  The test covered several areas – inputting, transcription, spelling and grammar.

Semi-colons and colons

- Semi-colons are less frequently used than commas. They indicate a longer pause than a comma, eg

  The jacket was available in two styles; straight and long or short and fitted styles were in stock.

- Colons are generally used to introduce a list (as a more formal alternative to the dash) or before a quotation, eg

  Please order the following items: ballpoint pens, rulers and staples.

  The Chairman said: 'This year has been excellent with record profits in all Divisions.'

Question marks and exclamation marks

- Use a question mark only after *direct* questions, eg 'Are you going?', not after indirect questions, eg 'I wondered whether you were going'.

- Use an exclamation mark to give additional emphasis (mainly in sales material) eg 'Free gifts!' or 'You'd never believe it!' In informal correspondence an exclamation mark may also be used to indicate humour or deliberate exaggeration, eg

That firm is hopeless, they promise to deliver in January and you're lucky to receive it in July!

Quotation marks

- Rarely used in business correspondence because their major function is to separate direct speech, eg

Jennifer said, 'That's the second time this week I've been asked to work late. John really should plan his work better.' Julie nodded in agreement.

- Use to show that you are quoting from someone else but only if you are repeating the actual words spoken. Otherwise use indirect speech and note the source, eg

'I never let schooling interfere with my education' (Mark Twain) *or*

Mark Twain said he never let schooling interfere with his education.

- Use to indicate slang words or terms which must not be taken literally, eg

One of John McEnroe's favourite comments was 'it's the pits'.

Brackets

Brackets, or parentheses, are not often used in formal correspondence. They are used to separate an explanatory phrase or clause, eg

Travel towards the town (on the A583) until you reach the roundabout *or*

(Use brackets sparingly in business correspondence.)

If the whole sentence is contained in brackets, then the full stop is placed within the closing bracket. If only the last part of the sentence appears in the brackets, then the full stop is placed outside the closing bracket, eg

Take the right turn and travel on to the crossroads (the Red Lion is on your right).

Capital letters

- Capital letters are used at the beginning of a sentence and to indicate the start of direct speech in the middle of a sentence, eg

He said, 'You win.'

- They are used for titles and proper names, eg

President Nelson Mandela visited London recently.

- They are *decreasingly* used for ordinary titles and in headings, eg

'Sales department report on recent sales conference' is more usual nowadays than 'Sales Department report on recent Sales Conference'.

Spelling

It is not good practice for aspiring administrators/secretaries to ignore spelling and totally rely on their PC's spell check facility! The spell check will not, for instance, be able to identify whether you have misspelled a word if your 'substitute' is also a recognisable word or is a homonym. Remember, too, if you use e-mail, then you are signalling your spelling abilities instantly around the organisation – probably every day.

The easiest and most painless way to improve your spelling is to read as much as you can. Misspelled words then start to 'look' wrong. Use a dictionary to check anything you are uncertain about – or check that particular word on your spell check facility.

Some rules you may find helpful are given below. However, if you find some of these confusing, an easier method is to identify those words you have trouble with and learn the correct version by heart! Another tip is to let your fingers 'see' the word! Expert typists and data inputters can 'feel' a spelling or keying-in error *as they type*. Sometimes they will even check a spelling by making the finger movements for the words. This is no doubt the modern alternative to writing it down to check the spelling!

Basic rules

- 'i' comes before 'e', except after 'c' and where the sound says 'a', eg

  achieve, piece;
  receive, deceive;
  reign.

- Words ending in 'our' usually drop the 'u' before adding a suffix, eg

  rigour but rigorous;
  vigour but invigorate.

- Most words ending in 'e', drop this before adding 'able', eg

  move, movable;
  love, lovable.

  The exception are words where the 'e' softens a 'c' or 'g', eg

  manageable or noticeable.

- In words of more than one syllable, a final consonant is not doubled before a suffix when there is no stress on the last syllable, eg

  benefit, benefiting *but*

  commit, committing.

Grammar

There are many books written on the niceties of grammatical construction. Luckily, today, people are more relaxed about grammar and unless you have a particularly pernickety boss, you should have few problems except if you drop an obvious clanger! The errors to avoid (and most common pitfalls) are given below – and most were highlighted in the sentences on page 260.

Word confusion

The following pairs of words are often used incorrectly – see sentences 1–4 on page 260.

Due to/owing to/because

Only use the words 'due to' after the verb to be (is/are), 'seem' or 'appear', eg

The fault is due to a radiator leak *but*

Owing to a line fault, the train was delayed by two hours.

In most cases it is better to use the word 'because', eg

The fault is because of a radiator leak *or*

Because of a line fault, the train was delayed by two hours.

Between/among

Use 'between' when only two people or items are involved but 'among' if there are more than two, eg

Divide the money between the two of you.

Divide the money among the three of you.

Less/fewer

Use 'less' for uncountable quantities, 'fewer' for countable ones, eg

There is less chance of winning the lottery than the pools *but*

There have been fewer fine days this week.

Alternative/option

'Alternative' means a choice of two, 'option' is a choice of more than two, eg

You have the alternative of making the appointment on Tuesday or Friday *but*

You have the option of visiting any day next week.

Note form

All sentences must be complete. Writing in note form means you are missing either the subject, the object or the verb. Starting a sentence with a word ending in 'ing' often has this effect, such as 'Hoping to see you soon'. Avoid this by writing 'I hope to see you soon'.

Matching the subject with the verb

Where the subject of a sentence is a singular (plural) word, the verb which relates to it must also be singular (plural) – see sentences 6–8 on page 260.

The *committee is* meeting next Thursday.

His *collection* of postcards *was* valued very highly. (The singular word 'collection' is the subject, which is matched by a singular verb.)

This is one of the *papers* that *are* to be sent to him. (Here the subject is the plural word 'papers' so the verb should also be plural, ie 'are'.)

Variations include sentences which start with 'either', 'neither', 'each', 'every', 'any' or 'none'. All these refer to a single person or entity, not a group – and so the verb which follows must also be singular, eg

Neither of the applicants *is* suitable for the job.

Each of the girls *is* doing her job well.

Matching pronouns

Wherever possible avoid mixing 'I' and 'we' (singular and plural) in a sentence. Therefore 'We think that we can help you' *or* 'I think that I can help you'. Many organisations insist on staff writing in the plural form to indicate they are not corresponding personally but on behalf of the company.

Whose/who's and who/whom

The difference between 'whose' and 'who's' is simple. 'Who's' stands for 'who is', whereas 'whose' indicates possession, eg

Whose coat is this? *or*

Who's going tomorrow?

However, 'who' and 'whom' are often confused. **When in doubt it is easier to rewrite the sentence.**

The rule is that 'who' is used for the subject of the sentence and 'whom' for the object, eg

Sandra (subject), *who* works in Sales, has been promoted to departmental administrator.

That is the man (object) *whom* the police officer said was guilty. (See sentence 13 on page 260.)

However, to avoid any difficulty the second sentence could easily be rewritten, ie 'The policeman stopped that man'.

The use of prepositions

A common fault is to end a sentence with a preposition, eg to, of, with, about.

Sentence 14 on page 260 (Please tell me which person I should write to) can be changed to avoid this by either writing

Please tell me to which person I should write *or*

Please tell me to whom I should write.

Note that some phrases end in certain prepositions, eg relevant to, dependent on, comparable with, similar to, different from. You should never write 'different to' (see sentence 15 on page 260).

Comparative and superlative

Remember that terms which compare two people or items end in 'er' and those which compare more than two end in 'est', eg 'the better of the two teams' *or* 'the best of the three runners'. For words which cannot be suffixed by 'er' or 'est', use 'more' or 'most' eg more difficult (out of two), most difficult (out of more than two).

I, me, you or us

Deciding whether you call yourself 'me' or 'I' can often present difficulties. There are two ways to solve the problem.

The first is to substitute 'we' or 'us' – and see which one fits. If 'we' fits, then you need to write 'I'; if 'us' fits, then you need to write 'me'. For example, in the sentence 'Would you make me a cup of coffee?', 'us' can be substituted for 'me'. Therefore, the use of 'me' is correct.

Another test is to leave out the mention of the other person. Look at the sentence below.

Do you think you and I should volunteer?

Leave out the other person (ie 'you') and the sentence reads well, ie

Do you think I should volunteer?' Therefore, the use of 'I' is correct.

Now consider the sentence 'Would he like you and I to volunteer?'. Omit the other person and you have 'Would he like I to volunteer?'! This is obviously wrong – therefore, the correct version is 'me'.

Split infinitive

Try to avoid inserting an adverb between the infinitive of a verb, eg to *quietly* say or to *seriously* consider.

Shall/will and should/would

Think of these in pairs – and do not mix them in a sentence eg

I *shall* go there if you *will* come with me.

Should Alex be unable to attend, we *would* like to invite Suresh.

Sentence construction

ie versus eg

A common error is to confuse 'ie' and 'eg'. The abbreviation 'ie' means 'that is' and is used for specific/discrete examples.

The Leader of the Labour Party, ie (that is) Tony Blair, took his seat in the House at 2 pm.

The term 'eg' means 'for example' and is used to give several examples out of many.

Redundancy/tautology

Sentences 2 and 3 in Set 5 on page 260 include repeated, unnecessary words. Other examples are 'final conclusion' and 'new innovation'.

Ambiguity

Pronouns can cause ambiguity unless you are careful. In sentence 4 (page 260) you cannot tell which person is untidy and in sentence 5 (page 261) the bear appears to have been on holiday! Read your sentences carefully to check you have avoided this problem, particularly if you have used the word 'it'!

Mixed metaphors, verbosity, slang and cliches

Try to avoid metaphorical phrases – and never mix them up as in sentence 11 on page 261! Some cliches simply make the writer appear to have a very poor grasp of words and phrases (eg 'far be it from me' or 'be that as it may'). Verbosity is the result of lengthy phrases which say very little. Also avoid overworked words such as 'nice', 'got', 'pretty'. Finally, do not use slang in a business context (see sentence 13 on page 261).

Jargon

Jargon is specialist vocabulary which relates to a job, profession or trade. It may be acceptable (and even necessary) between specialists, but should never be used when writing general communications simply because it is unlikely to be understood.

Some people think that by using long words, complex phrases and abbreviations they will impress their reader. This is rarely the case.

Could/would/and can/may

Make sure that you understand the difference between 'could' (able to) and 'would' (willing to). In sentence 17 on page 261, it is likely the listener is able to make a cup of coffee, it may be less likely that he or she is willing to make one!

'Can' and 'may' are similarly misused. Saying to a caller 'Can I help you?' is incorrect because it implies 'Am I able to help you?' – and only you know the answer to that! 'May I help you' indicates you are able and willing to help!

Only

The word 'only' is often misused or inserted in the wrong place in a sentence. In sentence 10 on page 261 (I only want to ring him) it is doubtful if the writer 'only' wishes to ring a certain man rather than another person!

Now look at the following examples of how the placement of the word 'only' alters the sense of the sentence.

Only I want an red umbrella. (Only me, no one else.)

I only want a red umbrella. (Don't try selling me anything else!)

I want only a red umbrella. (No other colour is suitable.)

Like/as

Do not be tempted to use the word 'like' when you are joining two parts of a sentence (for example, as a conjunction). In this case use 'as' or rephrase the sentence eg

He doesn't play the piano as Sarah does or

He doesn't play the piano as well as Sarah does.

You can, however, use 'like' as an adjective (He is like his father) or as an adverb (He ran like the wind).

Double negatives

You may have progressed a fair way beyond writing sentences such as 'He don't do nothing' but be careful that more complex double negatives do not find their way into your writing – because they always cancel each other out.

Misplaced adverbs

These cause ambiguity, eg

He needed his hair cutting badly.

If you are ever in doubt about ambiguity, ask someone else to read your sentence and see if he or she understands it in the same way as you!

Presentation of information

13

● Introduction

Presentation skills are considered only briefly in this chapter as these are covered in greater depth in your text-processing lessons.

Regardless of your technical ability or composition skills, no one will be impressed with the documents you produce if they are poorly presented. Trainee secretaries used to be told that they were artists with a sheet of paper as their canvas! The way they presented the work on the page was their opportunity to show their flair and creativity. You may think that there is little room for manoeuvre if you are simply producing an A4 letter and matching envelope. However, this really is not true. A balanced document will always look more pleasing, and the judicious use of enhancements such as capitalisation and emboldening, as well as justified margins, can add to its appeal. If you are asked to produce a more elaborate document, such as a newsletter, notice or bulletin, then you can really enjoy planning the presentation.

It is possible to produce professional-looking documents even if your artistic ability is close to zero! Most business documents have some standard conventions you can follow. If you use a computer, there is a wide range of text, font and enhancement features available. If you learn how to use a desktop publishing (DTP) package such as Pagemaker, then you will be guided in more sophisticated design techniques.

When considering presentation, you have the following three aspects to think about:

- the physical appearance of the document
- the layout of the text and/or graphics
- the type of graphics or tables to use.

● Physical appearance

When you are setting out a document remember

- it must be pleasing to the eye
- important information must take prominence.

The modern approach is to keep the style simple whilst following the standard conventions discussed below.

The range of features you have available to enhance the physical appearance of a document will be dependent upon the system you are using – and the presentation of documents using computer software and equipment is covered in more detail later in this chapter.

Standard conventions

Spacing
• Leavie a clear space before and after a heading and between paragraphs.

• Leave one or two spaces after the punctuation mark at the end of a sentence (but be consistent) and one space in other cases.

• Leave a clear space before and after separate items within a document.

• Check that all spacing is consistent within a document.

Document style
• Use *either* open *or* full punctuation within a document (open punctuation is more usual today) – do not mix the two styles.

• Use block paragraphs (unless house style or instructions state otherwise).

Headings
• Highlight headings in **bold** rather than underlining them.

• Keep headings simple (eg capitals and bold).

• Block headings unless centring would obviously be better (or you are following precise instructions).

• Make sure different types of headings in a long document are presented consistently (ie all main headings are in one style, subheadings in another, etc.).

Consistency
Make sure you are consistent in your use of the following.

• Capitalisation.

• Spelling (where alternatives are available).

• Measurements, weights, times, money and figures. Do not, for example, mix times between the 12-hour clock and the 24-hour clock in one document.

In addition, of course, it is expected that you would follow any specific instructions you are given on the general style of the document.

Additional features

Enhancements you may want to consider include the following.

• Emboldening important or key words.

• Using special text features, such as italics or underscore.

• Using different types and sizes of characters (see also page 321). This will depend upon the layout of your document and the size (see below).

- Using different paragraph layouts, such as numbered paragraphs, decimal numbering or bullet points. Bullet points are usually preferred when there is no particular order to the points, whereas numbering paragraphs is apt to make the reader consider that the first point mentioned is the most important.

Decimal numbering is often easier when there are many subsections, eg

1   Printers
    1.1   Ink jet
    1.2   Laser
        1.2.1   Postscript
        1.2.2   Non–postscript
    1.3   Dot matrix
2   Photocopiers

- Insetting text – either from the left side only, eg

    This is an example of inset text from the left side only.

or equally from both margins, eg

    This is an example of inset text from both left and right margins.

However, remember that too much variation makes the document seem messy and confusing. Simplicity is the key!

Layout

Imagine you have a plain piece of paper and have to position various articles and/or graphics on it. No doubt you would move them around quite a bit to obtain the best effect before attaching them to the paper. This, fortunately, is one of the benefits of modern software programs – you can virtually create all the components and then put them together on screen in different ways to see which looks best.

For a standard document you will again follow some basic conventions. This prevents you having to spend hours on each document deciding how to design the layout! Some organisations even have their own house style for documents (see below) which may be stored on computer so that you can access a template for, say, a memo. A template is simply a computerised version of a basic form with standard information already entered.

The main points to consider when deciding a layout yourself include

- thinking about the type of information the document contains, its complexity and its intended audience

- choosing the most appropriate paper size and then deciding whether this should be portrait or landscape

- deciding the size of the margins – left, right, top and bottom (the default is equal horizontally and then equal vertically for good effect)

- using the most appropriate line spacing (unless you have received specific instructions)

- deciding whether the text should be justified at the right-hand side (usually yes, although there is a move away from this now – see this book!)

- deciding whether the document should be paginated

- deciding whether headers and footers are required (see page 320)

- choosing the type or font and size of characters to use

- deciding how to display the information on the page.

Remember that there is a major difference between displaying text in a straightforward report and producing a newsletter which needs an eye for design and the careful use of white space for effect. You also need to consider carefully whether graphics and tables could usefully be employed to 'break up' the text and make complicated explanations easier to understand.

Designing your house style!

A corporate house style is laid down by organisations that prefer all their documents to look the same. Without a standard house style, a large organisation could find that each originator and typist produces completely different documents – which does little for the organisational image! House style may simply refer to the layout of the document or it may also define the style of headings, typeface, font and the fact that a logo must always be included at the top right-hand side! Modern software packages enable these features to be incorporated in a standard way – usually by setting them up as a template or master document on the system.

If you work for a large organisation, you will be expected to follow house style – usually easily identified by referring to the corporate style manual or by looking in the files and asking around! If you work for a small organisation or for a new business, then your ideas to introduce a corporate style may be appreciated by your boss. In this case it is useful to create a house-style manual containing examples of all the documents and the required formats. This way no one has any excuse not to keep to them!

If you decide to make recommendations in a large organisation, then you are advised to wait until you have settled into the job before you do so! You are also likely to have more success introducing new styles if you make them simpler rather than more complicated than the existing version.

Tables and graphics

So far you have only considered the production of documents which are in textual form, ie they contain text but nothing else. In business, however, you may be asked to produce other types of documents or to incorporate statistical information, tables or graphics into a textual document. In many cases modern software packages can help you (see pages 304–5). The basic facts you should know about each of these types of information are considered below.

Statistical information

Statistics are figures or calculations which are usually presented in tables with appropriate headings. If you think about it, you are surrounded by this type of information, eg the football league results printed in the Sunday papers or the weather temperatures around the world published in the daily papers.

Because you will probably be given statistical information in the required format, you will have fewer decisions to make about its style of presentation. However, there are some important points you need to remember.

- Because statistical information is numerical, it is much more difficult to check than narrative information – and spell check facilities are useless! Frequently, accuracy is essential – eg for sales statistics, budgets and accounts information – so this means one person reading the figures aloud whilst the other checks the information patiently. Note too that a computer spreadsheet will always add up the figures accurately, but this will be useless if the figures you have entered are incorrect!

- Sets of statistics are usually incorporated into a document when it is easier to reproduce the figures than to describe the information in words. Obviously, the statistics must be included at the most appropriate point in the text. If this is impossible because you are near the foot of the page, then you can refer to the table with a figure number (as in this book) and then include the actual table later.

- It is usual to provide a commentary to explain a set of statistics (or any other type of table) and why it has been included. Remember that if you are writing the document yourself, you will have to write the commentary!

🗨️Discussion point

1   See if you could write a simple commentary! The table below shows sales for three different products made by a play equipment manufacturer in different quarters of the year. What does it tell you?

Product	Jan–Mar	Apr–Jun	Jul–Sep	Oct–Dec
Large rocking horse	140	240	150	1210
Garden playframe	17	530	321	150
Playgroup bouncy castle	150	172	30	125

2   The following is a commentary for customers. Design the table which would illustrate the information much more simply and clearly than the text.

This organisation manufacturers three different models of shredder for the small business. These are known by the model numbers S1000, S2000 and S3000. The capacity of these shredders is as follows: the S1000 will take 5/6 sheets of paper at once; the S2000 will take 7/8 sheets; and the S3000 will accept 9/10 sheets. Both the S1000 and the S2000 shred documents to a width of 4 mm, the S3000 shreds them even more finely to 3 mm. The prices of these models are, respectively, £180, £250 and £400.

Graphical information

Graphical information can often be included in documents through the use of 'clip-art' which incorporates images that have been prepared professionally and stored on disk. However, in business you are more likely to find that you are expected to include charts and graphs as your graphics rather than illustrations. (If you are using a desktop publishing package (see page 305) the situation may be rather different.) Explore the WP and spreadsheet packages on your computer to find out how they can help you to do charts and graphs.

There are several different types of charts and graphs. However, each one is usually used for a specific purpose and is more appropriate in certain circumstances than others.

Pie charts
These show percentage divisions of a whole. For instance, you would use a pie chart if you wanted to illustrate

- the proportion of sales in each geographical region

- the proportion of sales going to different types of customer

- the proportion of different types of expenditure to the whole amount spent

- the proportion of time spent on different types of expenditure

- the proportion of time spent on different activities.

A pie chart is created by drawing a circle and then dividing it into proportional segments (Figure 13.1). Each segment can be shaded or coloured to represent different areas. If you use a computer to design your pie chart, you can enhance it by 'exploding' certain wedges (Figure 13.2) or even by creating a 3-D effect (Figure 13.3).

Pie charts are not suitable for very detailed information and often a clear key is required.

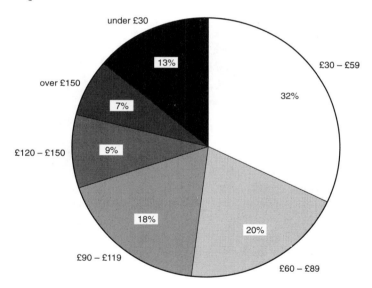

Spending on children's Christmas presents
(Source: *Right Start* magazine)

Figure 13.1 A simple pie chart

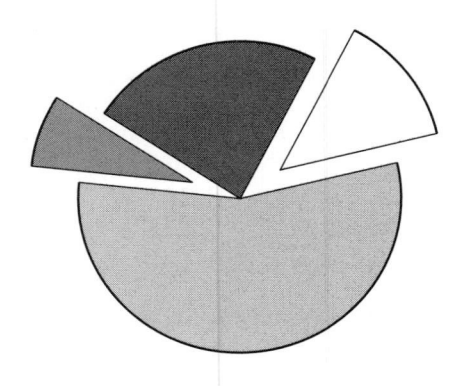

Figure 13.2 Pie chart with 'exploding' wedges

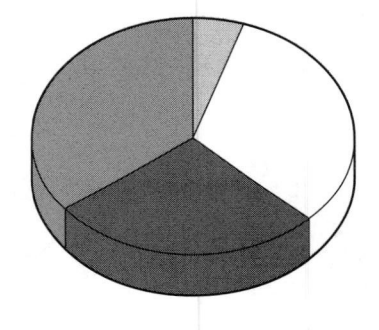

Figure 13.3 Pie chart using 3-D effect

Line graphs and multi-line graphs

A line graph may have one line (Figure 13.4), or several lines – in this case it is known as a multi-line graph (Figure 13.5). In a multi-line graph the different lines have to be distinguishable in some way and a key may be required.

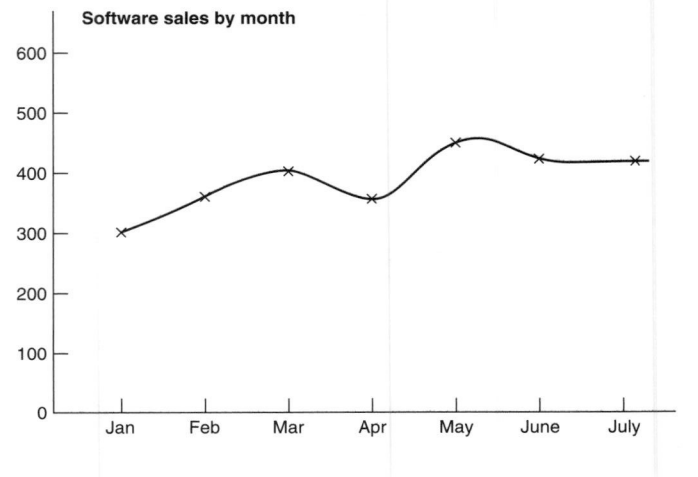

Figure 13.4 Line graph

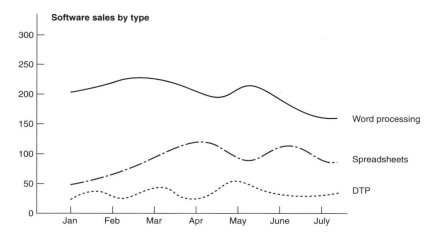

Figure 13.5 Multi-line graph

Line graphs usually show comparisons or indicate a trend such as

- comparison of sales of different products or in different areas over time
- income and expenditure over time
- usage of facilities or consumer demand at different times.

In *all* graphs and charts the vertical axis usually represents quantity and the horizontal axis represents time.

Z-chart

This is a type of line graph which is used in Sales or Production to indicate individual figures as well as cumulative figures for the whole period and a moving total. Its shape represents the letter 'Z', hence its name (Figure 13.6).

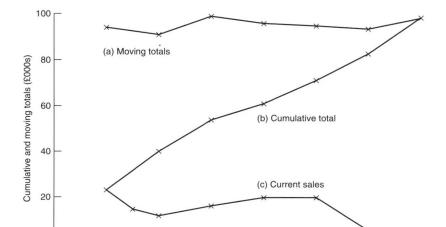

Figure 13.6 Z-chart

Bar charts

Bar charts are very popular because they are often eye-catching and very effective in indicating comparisons. They are more detailed than a pie chart, but precise contrasts are more difficult to work out than on a line graph.

There are several variations to the basic vertical bar chart.

• **A horizontal bar chart** – where the bars extend across the page (Figure 13.7). A specialist type of horizontal bar chart is known as a **Gantt chart** (Figure 13.8). This is used to show comparisons between work planned and work accomplished in relation to time schedules. It compares the actual performance against the planned, anticipated or target performance (see chapter 19).

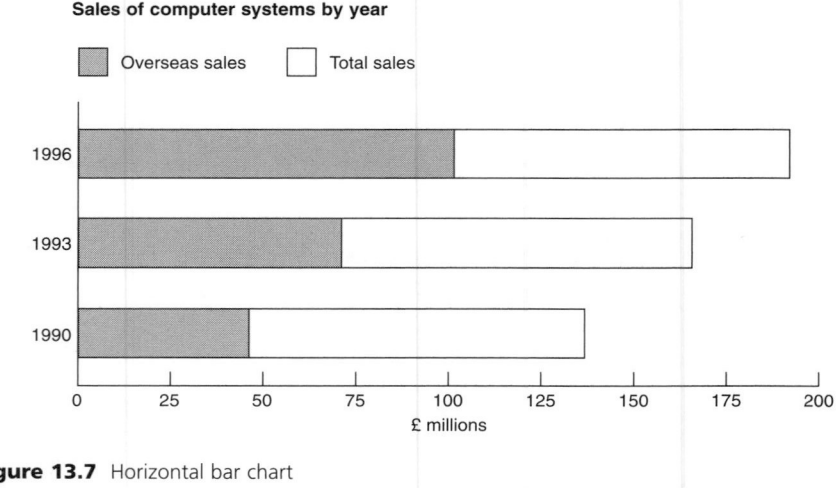

Figure 13.7 Horizontal bar chart

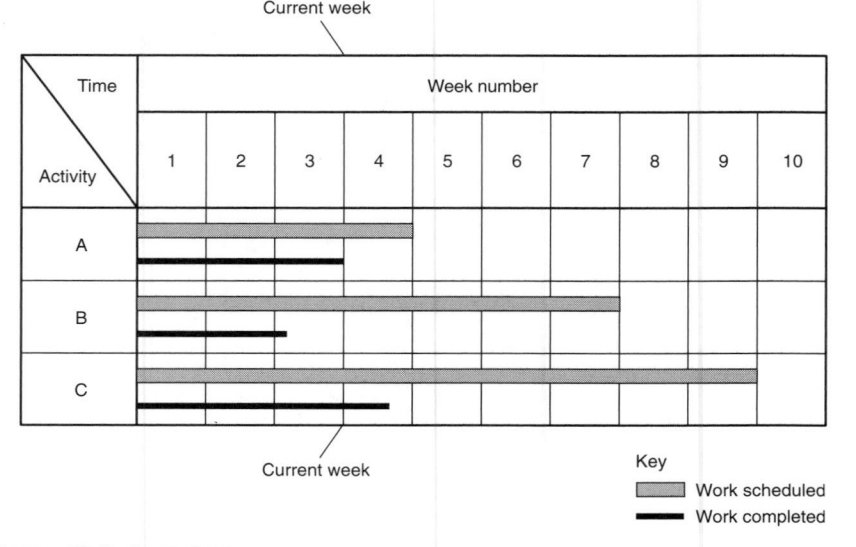

Figure 13.8 Gantt chart

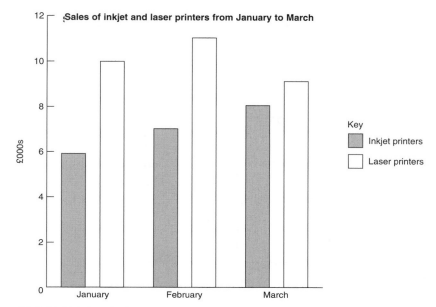

Figure 13.9 Multiple bar chart

- **A multiple bar chart** – where more than one bar is put against each time period – usually to indicate comparisons (Figure 13.9).

- **A compound bar chart** – where the bars themselves are divided into different sections (Figure 13.10). Each section shows the proportional parts which make up the bar.

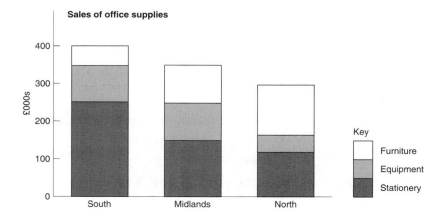

Figure 13.10 Compound bar chart

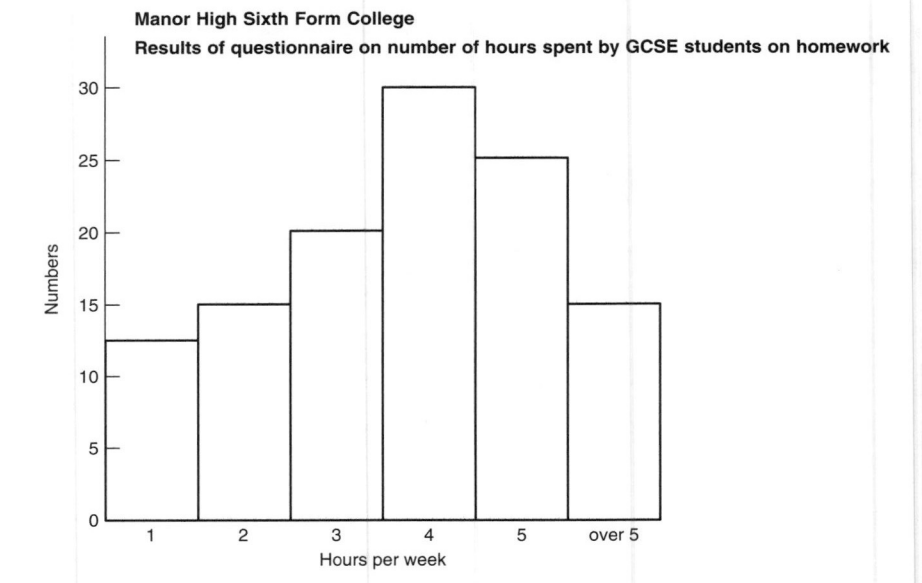

Figure 13.11 Histogram

*   **A histogram** – where the area of the bar, not just its height, is related to the information (Figure 13.11). The blocks are often drawn close together or joined up.

Bear in mind that a clear key is essential.

Virtually all these types of graphs and charts can be produced easily on a computer package. They are normally a feature of all spreadsheet packages so that tabular data can easily be converted into graphical format for illustrative purposes.

Pictograms

These can be extremely eye-catching and are ideal for an audience which does not require much detail and when you want to attract the reader's attention (Figure 13.12). In this case pictures, symbols or other graphics are used to represent a quantity. For greater quantities, the compiler has the choice of either increasing the size of the graphic or increasing the number

Increase in the number of laptop computers sold between 1990 and 1996

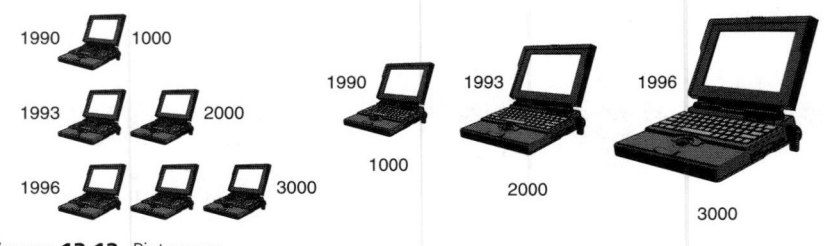

Figure 13.12 Pictogram

of pictures. It is normal to select a picture or symbol which is relevant to the information being displayed.

Other types of graphical representation include

- **flow charts** which show a series of steps either in a course of action to be taken or in the progress of a document – the aim is to break down a relatively complicated operation into a series of simple steps

- **algorithms** which are similar to a flow chart but which require a yes/no answer for every stage.

Discussion point

Your college is holding an open day for potential students and their parents in the spring and you have been asked to help create a short handbook describing administrative and secretarial courses. You are expected to keep the text to a minimum but to create a variety of graphics which people can 'skim' and still obtain the main information. Your tutor has informed you that these will be produced by one of the administrative staff, in colour, on a computer – after you have suggested the best graphics to use.

For each of the following, decide which type of graphical representation would be the most appropriate. Try to select a different option each time. Then do a brief sketch in each case to test if your idea would work!

a The number of student computers in the department – which has trebled over the past four years.

b The average proportion of time taken studying different subjects on full-time administrative courses.

c The fact that the number of student applications for administration courses has increased from 40 to 105 over the past three years.

d The outcomes of three different courses last year where students either obtained jobs, went on to higher-level courses within the college or left for university.

e The comparison between the number of students who obtain jobs after completing their administration course and the number who obtain jobs after leaving school – shown over the past three years.

14

Production processes and equipment

● Introduction

Within any organisation, information is composed and initiated in a variety of ways and by a variety of people. The previous chapter discussed the importance of making sure that it is presented effectively for visual impact and ease of reading.

The creation of all types of textual and graphical documents in business is made much easier if a range of modern equipment and computer software is available. This means that the most appropriate process can be selected for each particular task at each stage of the production process.

At the input stage, documents may be drafted by hand or on computer, recorded on audio equipment or dictated to be taken down in shorthand. Other alternatives include document scanners (as used in electronic filing systems – see pages 195 and 199) and voice recognition. As yet, there is no computer fast enough to recognise human speech patterns (or writing) accurately, though computer chip manufacturers are working on the problem!

At the processing stage, documents may be designed using a variety of computer equipment and software, depending upon whether a textual, graphical or statistical document is required.

At the output stage, documents may be produced on a variety of computer printers and reproduced on one of the many types of copiers available. You also need to know the types of finishing processes available so that the document is presented in the most appropriate way for its purpose.

In a large organisation you are likely to have a range of options from which to choose – and possibly the services of specialised staff. However, you obviously need to have some basic information on the different types of processes and equipment to make an informed choice yourself. In a small organisation you may be more restricted, but you should be aware that other options are available through local printshops. It may also be part of your remit, as administrator or secretary, to advise which processes and equipment *should* be available to produce professional documents – even if they are not yet installed.

This chapter looks at each stage of the process and examines the options available. It assumes that you have a basic knowledge of both IT and audio equipment and wish to consolidate and develop this in line with the additional knowledge and skills required by administrators and secretaries.

● The input stage

As an administrator, you are more likely to be handling documents produced by several authors than is a secretary. In addition, you may have the responsibility of ensuring these are processed by several people. The greater the number of people involved, the more important it is that some standard procedures exist to control the range of acceptable input and the requirements of the authors. In whatever job you have, you cannot cope with trying to turn round dozens of complex, professionally produced documents in very little time from illegible drafts. Any secretary who works for more than one boss will tell you that one key area of conflict can be prioritising the work of different bosses – all of whom think their work is the most important and all of whom have no idea of the workload being created by their colleagues!

ioritising work is dealt with on page 431. This chapter concentrates on sic standards and equipment for input documents.

Handwritten documents

The main factors you need to consider include

- length of document

- complexity/technical content of subject matter

- quality of handwriting of originator

- 'cleanliness' of copy (ie number of amendments, alterations and modifications)

- composition skills of originator

- freedom of action of inputter

- final quality required.

The longer and more complex (or technical) the document, the more time it will take to produce. If the originator's handwriting is difficult to read and there are additions, alterations and amendments to consider, this adds to the time. You may need to make minor corrections to grammar and spelling *but* some authors react more strongly than others to someone altering their wording. You will have to find out whether you are supposed to refer back any queries or whether you have the freedom to make alterations yourself – and to what extent. Finally, you will obviously be able to work more quickly if you are producing a rough draft which is going to be checked and amended after its creation. You will have different standards to meet where the document has to be produced in final format first time round.

Most secretaries become familiar with their boss's style, handwriting and idiosyncrasies when creating and amending documents – and become expert at persuading the boss to give adequate notice of difficult documents. They also become familiar with technical words and the preferred style of presentation. As an administrator, you may have to deal with a wider variety of work and, occasionally, protect any staff for whom you are responsible from unreasonable requests or incomprehensible drafts. As you will see in chapter 15, there are various strategies you can employ to persuade people that there are *mutual* benefits to be gained from following sensible guidelines on document creation. Junior executives who ignore these will have to be prepared to have their work returned with several queries attached or their draft documents produced in very 'rough' condition – although you might be well advised to warn your own boss of the action you intend to take to protect yourself first!

Computer drafts

Given that most executives today have their own PC, it is becoming more common for them to create documents themselves for you to edit and format later. This, at least, has the advantage that there are no handwriting problems to cope with! You may find that short documents are sent to you through the e-mail system, or are keyed in, printed out and handwritten amendments added. More and more executives are preparing documents at home and e-mailing them to their secretaries and administrators over a modem or via the Internet.

However, do *not* expect your executive to key in long reports or to create his or her own graphical presentations unless he or she has a natural inclination towards IT systems and software! Normally, the speed of input would be such that this would not be a cost-effective or sensible option. You should make sure you are the expert when it comes to presentation skills.

Audio equipment

The range of audio equipment and the features available are changing rapidly with the development of new digital systems (see below). However, given that these are still quite expensive, for some time yet you may find that you are still expected to work from the older 'tape' machines. In a large organisation, dictation can be centralised through a unit which enables authors to record documents on a main storage system (usually over a telephone with key pad) and this system then electronically distributes the recordings to those involved in transcribing dictation.

Traditional tape machines have the drawback that dictation is sequential – one document follows another – and amendments are difficult to make. Digital recording systems overcome this problem as they operate like voice processing – the dictator can go back to any mistake and correct or edit the material during creation. 'Voice prompts' can even guide the users on the type of information to dictate and when!

Digital storage and its applications

The work of transcribers is changing dramatically as digital audio systems reach the market. Philips has introduced a digital pocket memo called the SpeechPad which stores voice recordings on a device the size of a credit card. This is then removed from the machine, inserted into a PC with a voice card which then plays back the recording. The transcriber keys the information into the computer.

Even more sophisticated are two centralised digital systems. The first, another Philips system, was installed by the Radiology Department at The Christie Hospital in Manchester. It allows radiologists to speak into a microphone attached to their PCs. The reports are digitally recorded and routed via the network to speech recognition software so that their 'words' appear on their secretary's PC for editing and printing. Patient identification is carried out by a bar-code system, which is 'swiped' in by the radiologist before starting the report. The system then automatically includes the patient details on the secretary's screen.

In Scotland, Strathclyde Police installed a VDI VoiceTech digital system. All officers can record from standard telephones with the touch keypad defining the functions required. A standard voice-prompt feature, used to guide an author through the document completion, was customised into a 'voice trail' facility so that officers dictating standard reports are led through the prescribed format and a pre-recorded list of questions. This enables documents such as incident reports to be produced to a common format and reduces the likelihood of inexperienced authors including irrelevant information or omitting essential details. For security, all dictation is automatically duplicated on to a back-up disk.

If you do not have access to such modern technology, it is important that all authors follow some fundamental rules when dictating such as

- identifying who they are at the outset

- indicating the type and length of the document

- making any special requirements clearly known at the start

- speaking clearly and distinctly and at a sensible pace

- spelling technical words or proper names

- keeping a clear distinction (best through tone of voice) between dictated material and other instructions or asides (which the transcriber may easily type in error)

- following standard organisational procedures on
  - dictating punctuation
  - stating whether new paragraphs are required
  - the expected format and layout of the document (which should conform to the house style).

The task of all transcribers is to understand their equipment and the functions/features which are available and to allow for odd mistakes and mutterings even by the most experienced dictator.

Shorthand dictation

The death of shorthand has been predicted for decades and several studies indicate that it is certainly not the most cost-effective method of document production. Despite these facts, surveys undertaken by employment agencies in the mid-1990s showed that the highest salaries earned by office staff were paid to those secretaries and administrators who knew shorthand!

The reason for this was cited to be the fact that high-powered senior executives felt they needed the flexibility of a secretary/PA who could take down dictation and instructions quickly and accurately – almost anytime and anywhere – and were prepared to pay high salaries for the privilege. Today, the most commonly used system is Teeline, mainly because it is easy to learn.

If you take dictation from your boss, this has several benefits. He or she may discuss several items of correspondence with you and this gives you greater insight into the workings of the organisation. You are likely to develop a more personal working relationship as you have more 'face-to-face' contact and you will quickly learn your boss's likes and dislikes. As a new recruit, however, possibly the first strategy you need to develop is a way of coping if you cannot read three critical outlines in an urgent document when your boss has just left the office for an important business meeting. Whereas with one boss you may have the freedom to substitute your own words and phrases, this is likely to be curtailed if you work in a highly technical environment, for a purist or for a boss with a very good memory! In this case your only sensible route is to draft out the document on your word processor, save it to disk, and query the words upon your boss's return.

Discussion point

You have just started a new job as office administrator in the Sales Department of a medium–sized company. You handle document production for the sales director, and the office staff of three transcribe tapes and key in documents from written drafts provided by the office manager and eight sales executives.

Very quickly you find that the Sales office is constantly behind with its workload and that both turnround time and quality of output are very poor. Your boss tells you that it is not your job to assist the staff by doing their work for them but to identify and solve the problems. You investigate the situation by interviewing each of your staff in turn. Below are their comments.

1   *Joanne* – the most senior member of the team: 'I try to look after Ronnie – he's the office manager – because he's very pleasant and helpful to us. So I always do his work first. He also writes neatly and dictates clearly so his work is easy to follow. However, we do have a problem when Julie does anything because she normally can't be bothered to proof read it carefully so it comes back again and again.'

2   *Sarah* – the most assertive member of staff: 'I'm sick and tired of some of the sales executives. They put in technical terms we've never heard of and expect us to be able to cope – even when their handwriting's appalling and they're going to be out of the office the rest of the week. They can't spell and half of them use terrible grammar, then argue when we try to correct it. They also never identify work which is urgent and work which isn't. Two of them are OK – Brian and Sandra – but the rest aren't so good and George Gregson is dreadful.'

3   *Julie* – the newest recruit: 'I do several of the contracts and often have to type the same paragraphs in different contracts over and over again on my PC. I can't see why we can't have a system which stores these for us automatically. The problem is, even if I make a minor mistake, they come back again and again. I don't like audio so I try to type most of the written documents, but I can't always tell what people have written. When I guess, I never seem to get it right.'

As a group, and with your tutor, consider
a   the improvements which need to be made
b   how you, as administrator, could introduce changes – preferably without upsetting all the staff!
c   the systems and procedures you could introduce to help.

● The processing stage – IT equipment, software and usage

Today, the vast majority of information handled in business is processed by computer. In the same way, most documents are also created and processed using some type of IT system and software package. You are probably familiar with the difference between computer hardware (which consists of the equipment used) and software (which relates to the computer programs or packages which can be purchased). However, the type of hardware and range of software available will affect many of the decisions you may need to make as to the most appropriate way to produce and process a document.

Computer hardware

This will vary depending upon the system used in an organisation.

Stand-alone systems

A small organisation is likely to install **stand-alone systems** (Figure 14.1) where each person has an individual personal computer (PC) with a monitor, central processing unit (CPU) and keyboard. This configuration is usually known as a **workstation.** Printers may be provided for each workstation or be a shared resource controlled by a printer server or switching system.

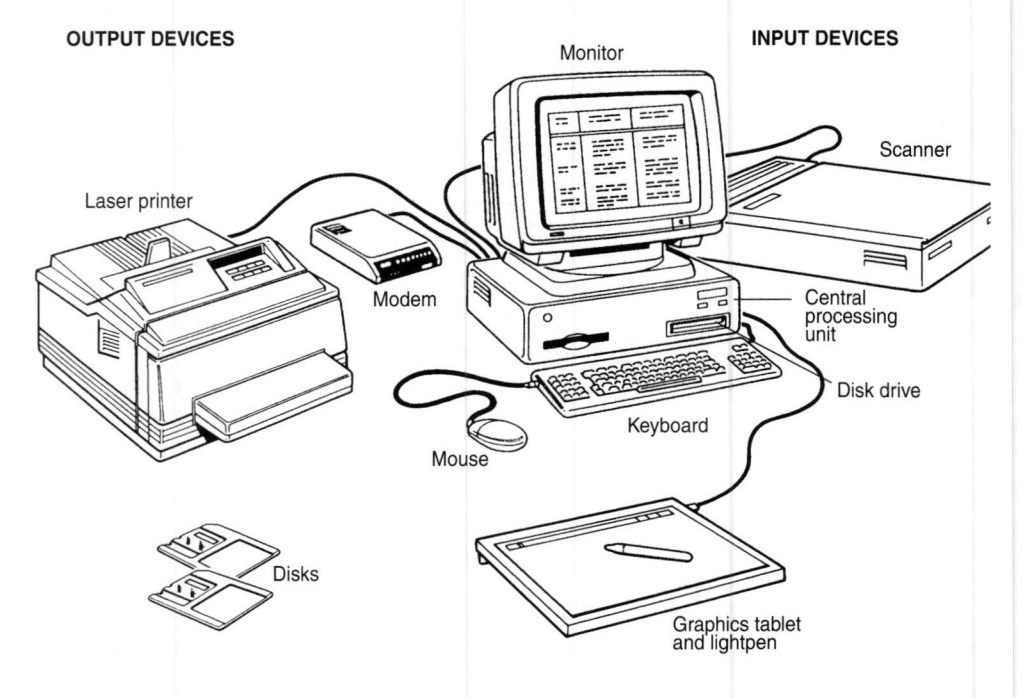

Figure 14.1 Stand-alone computer system

Computer networks (Intranets)

A larger organisation is more likely to have a **networked system.** In this case all the PCs are linked together either over a local area network (LAN) or a wide area network (WAN). A WAN is used when the computers are located on different geographical sites. Using a network means that users have shared access to software programs and company information. In addition, e-mail can be sent from one user to any other(s) on the network. Other equipment can also be linked on a network, eg fax machines and 'intelligent' (digital) photocopiers can be integrated as part of the system. A recent term used to describe organisational networks is **Intranet** – do not confuse this with the Internet (see page 302).

Most organisations which operate a networked system employ a **network administrator** who has the responsibility of overseeing both the operation and security of the system. The latter is usually achieved by ensuring that users log on to the system by entering an individual user ID and a personal password – even then the level of access to data can be restricted to different groups of users or individuals.

Network administrators also have the task of checking that users do not break copyright law (see page 326) and that software installed on the network is used legally. All software is sold with a licence agreement, which is proof that the person using the software is the accredited owner. Any user who could not produce a licence agreement when asked could be liable to prosecution.

On a network the software is usually held on a **file server** and is available to all users. To do this legally the organisation has to purchase a **site licence** from the software house which covers the maximum number of users permitted to access the software for a specified fee. The software is specifically written to run on a network and is different from the standard PC version which stand-alone systems would use.

The file server is usually·a PC which is specifically dedicated to holding and communicating all the systems and software which are required by network users. Each server looks after (or 'serves') a number of PCs in its locality – there is usually a limit to the geographical distance between a host network server and its PCs. Another part of the network administrator's job is to determine and maintain the systems controlled by each server. Figure 14.2 shows more clearly the way in which the file server is 'sectioned' to hold different types of information in different directories.

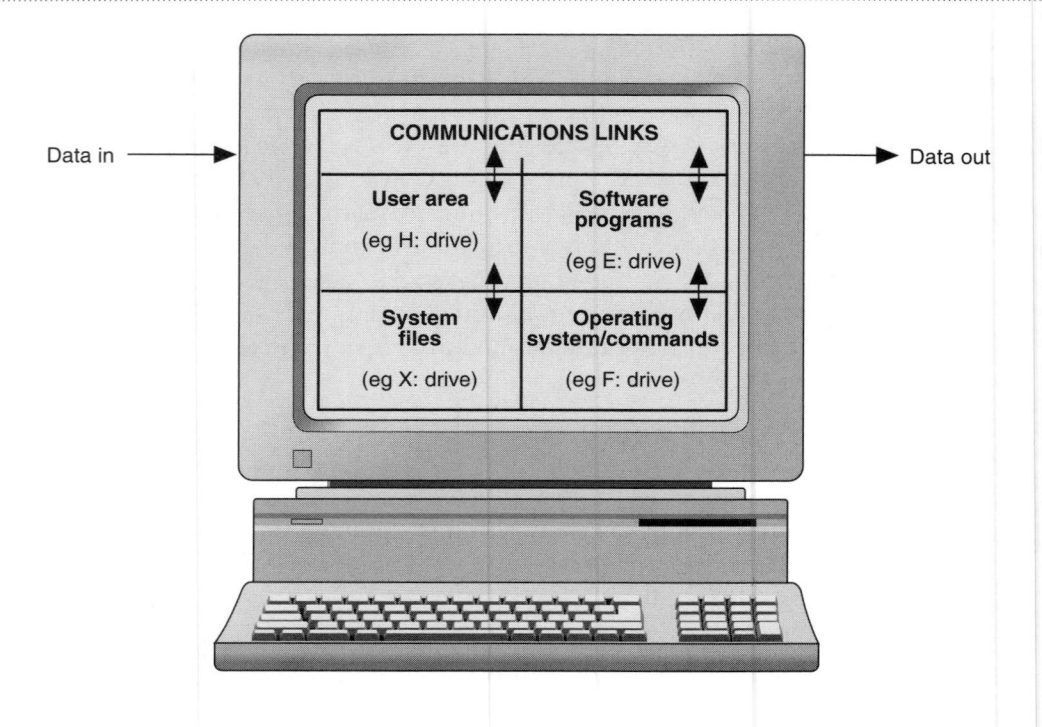

Figure 14.2 Example of areas 'sectioned' in a network file server

Mainframe systems

Some large organisations have a **mainframe system** installed. In this case there is a large capacity, high processing-speed computer used as a central resource. In addition to controlling the operation of all the individual workstations, the mainframe can be used overnight for the batch processing of company documentation, eg orders, mail-shots, invoices and payroll.

Portable systems

Finally, most people are aware that today there is a range of **portable systems** available, including laptop and notebook computers, palmtop and pen computers – some the size of a credit card! However, the smaller the computer, the more difficult it is (usually) to operate the keyboard. However, in some cases powerful laptops may be linked with a home-based screen and keyboard. In this case the laptop is simply used as a powerful processor – with a full-size screen and keyboard for ease. Most portable systems have a built-in modem so that users can communicate with the office on their travels, both to download and receive information.

In addition, as you saw in chapter 10, all organisations can take advantage of modern communications systems to link their own computer system to the outside world so that documents can be transmitted worldwide.

What's in a name?

Your computer screen is known by several different names! The original term used was VDU – visual display unit – though today this is becoming less common. Health and safety legislation uses the term DSE – display screen equipment. This book refers to the 'monitor' – the most recent term and the one you are most likely to read about in the future.

Two other terms used when referring to monitors are 'resolution' and 'colours'. Resolution is determined by the number of pixels on the screen. A pixel is a small square dot on a computer screen and the more pixels, the better the quality of graphics. Colour and shades are useful and easier to look at on-screen, but unprintable unless you also have access to a colour printer.

Input/output devices – peripherals

The term 'hardware' encompasses not just the monitor, processor, keyboard and printer but any other type of input or output device which is connected to the system. The term for such devices – which include input devices such as a mouse, joystick or scanner, and output devices such as a printer, plotter or modem – is **peripherals**; see Figure 14.1 on page 294. (Computer printers are discussed on pages 314–18).

If you study advertisements for computer systems, you may easily be bewildered by the jargon used and wonder how anyone manages to choose the best system! The choice of system is usually determined by three key features:

- memory size

- processing speed

- transfer speed.

The above features describe the speed and capability of the equipment, ie how much it can do and how quickly it can do it, which software packages it can run and which it cannot.

Memory size

The amount of data which can be processed by a computer at any one time is determined by its memory size. Memory size is measured by the number of characters or **bytes** which the computer can store at any one time. (*Note:* one byte of information equals eight bits).

The memory capacity of PCs can be measured in kilobytes (Kb), or megabytes (Mb) where a kilobyte equals 1000 bytes and a megabyte equals

1 000 000 bytes. Most business microcomputers have a base memory size of 640 Kb with optional extended memory of usually 8 Mb or 16 Mb. Extra memory chips (called SIMMs – standard in-line memory modules) can be added to many computers, increasing capacity to 128 Mb and beyond. This is unlikely to be necessary unless sophisticated graphics packages or multimedia applications are to be used. This is also the reason for multimedia computers usually being advertised with a greater memory capacity than basic business computers.

The memory capacity of mainframe computers is measured in megabytes or gigabytes (Gb, equivalent to 1000 million bytes) although the latest machines being developed now have memory measured in terabytes (1000 Gb)!

The term for a computer's 'working' memory is **RAM – random access memory.** You can access any part of the data in this memory as you are working and replace it with something new if you wish. RAM only operates on a temporary basis – when the computer is switched off data held in RAM are lost. This is why you need to use a **backing store** – usually a disk drive (see below) – to save data that you wish to access again.

Computers also have a **ROM – read only memory.** In this part of the memory you can read information but cannot change it. When you switch on the computer it already knows how to operate because a systems program has been stored in ROM. This basic program is different from the operating system (see page 303) – such as DOS or Windows – which is loaded into RAM every time the machine is started, usually from the hard disk.

Some computers also have **cache memory.** This is memory which is specially allocated to 'remember' commonly used functions. It therefore helps the computer to operate more quickly.

Transfer speed

Transfer speed refers to the speed at which information is transferred from one device to another – say from a disk drive to the processor, or from the processor to the printer. This is measured in bits per second (bps). In certain cases, this speed can be very important.

In chapter 10, for instance, you read that hi-tech fax machines will not provide any savings for their users unless the **modem – mo**dulator **dem**odulator – can transfer the data at high speed. This converts an analogue signal (eg that received over a telephone line) to a digital signal (ie that required by a computer) and vice versa. The speed of data transfer via a modem will depend on the power of the modem and the more powerful, the higher the cost. If you want to send or receive graphics, therefore, you need a fast modem, otherwise your telephone bill will be considerable as you wait for your pictures to arrive down the line, say from the Internet. Modem speeds are calculated in bps and the minimum usually recommended for the Internet and group 3 fax machines is 14.4 (ie 14 400) bps, though 28 800 bps is now becoming more widely available. Some organisations have developed a new 56K modem called 'x2', specifically for Internet applications, available since early 1997.

You may like to note that by using ISDN, which you read about in chapter 10, data can be transmitted at about 64 Kbps (ie 64,000 bits per second). Data transmitted using optical fibre (such as that installed by cable television/telephone companies) travels at even higher speeds!

Processing speed

This term refers to the speed at which the computer can process an instruction. The greater the speed, the more powerful the computer – and the higher the cost. Fast computers are usually required for graphics, CAD (computer-aided design) and CAM (computer-aided manufacturing) packages. For character-based packages, eg word processing, databases, spreadsheets and desktop publishing programs, the speed is less critical. However, if you use an applications package which is linked to a graphic operating system, such as Windows, then you will find it much easier if you are operating a computer with a high-speed processor.

Processing speed is measured in MHz (megahertz) and relates to the 'thinking time' on a PC. Generally, it takes between 1 and 10 cycles for a PC to process one instruction. MHz means millions of cycles per second. Therefore a PC which is advertised at having a speed of 75 MHz operates at 75 million cycles per second and could process up to 75 million instructions per second!

On a mainframe the speed is easier to understand because it is calculated in millions of instructions per second (mips). Most operate at about 40 mips, although the highest available is approximately 450!

Storage devices

Today all PCs are available with a **hard disk.** Until recently, all hard disks were unremovable, but some of the latest machines contain hard disks which can be taken out for use with other compatible machines. A hard disk holds a large number of programs and a vast amount of data. The size of the hard disk relates to the amount of memory in your backing store (do not confuse this with RAM!) To give you some idea of computer development, in 1990 hard disks regularly had 40 Mb capacity. Today 1 Gb hard disks and higher are on the market. Saving data to C: drive will mean your data are stored on the hard disk.

If you operate a stand-alone machine, your programs and your data will be stored on the hard disk. However, if you work on a network or are linked to a mainframe computer, you may use a computer which has no hard disk. This is because you access most programs via the file server on the network or computer system and can save data to your own home area. This is usually identified by H: drive on the system (see Figure 14.2 on page 296).

Only users who need to use individual packages on their machines within the network require a hard disk drive on which the programs are stored.

Despite the increase in hard disk capacity and networks, all computers still use **floppy disks.** The standard is currently $3\frac{1}{2}''$ double-sided, high density disks. Floppy disks are used for two purposes.

• To enable new programs to be purchased and down-loaded on to the hard disk.

• To save work stored on the hard disk as a safeguard in case the hard disk is corrupted or the system goes down.

All floppy disks have the ability to be read/write protected so that no further information can be added to or deleted from the disk. Saving data to A: drive stores your data on floppy disk.

Happy birthday to you – the chip turns 25!

In November 1996 the computer chip turned 25. A chip is the tiny device which performs calculations and executes programs inside a computer. Its creation ended the need for transistors and enabled miniaturisation to take place. As an example, the first microprocessor contained 2,300 transistors – a Pentium chip today contains 5.5 million!

Chips control the speed of operation of a computer. The higher the number, the higher the speed. You may see an older computer described as a 386 and some of your college machines may be 486s – a base standard in the mid-1990s. When Intel developed its 586 chip, it issued this under the name of Pentium for copyright reasons. Pentium has now become the industry standard term to describe processing speed and Intel has become the world's largest chip maker – which is why you may see the 'Intel Inside' sticker on most new IBM-compatible PCs.

It is simple to link the idea of MHz with Pentium chips. The P75 chip is the same as a 75 MHz machine. Today the common standard is the P120 (ie 120 MHz) and the sizes currently go up to 175. Intel, however, is far in advance of this – and currently working on developing a P600 version! Gordon Moore, one of Intel's founders, predicted 30 years ago that the number of transistors on an integrated circuit would double every 18 months – and so far this prediction has held good. Given Intel also predicts that a tenfold increase would be enough to create a computer capable of accurately recognising human speech and writing, you may like to calculate how long that will take!

The floppy disks of the future, however, are likely to be **optical disks.** These store vast amounts of information, are less prone to damage and data can be retrieved from them very quickly. Two types are in common use.

- **CD-ROM disks** are used for large databases (see page 133). In this case the user can access the information but cannot erase or replace it. Many software programs are available on CD-ROMs because of the increased storage potential, particularly if they are complex or include comprehensive graphics.

- **CD-WORM disks** are used for electronic filing systems (see page 199). In this case the user can write information to the disks but again it cannot be erased.

The disk of the future will be an **erasable optical disk** on which data can be stored and erased. The disk guarantees data for 40 years with storage capacity up to 1.3 Gb.

Discussion point

As a group, study the following advertisement for computer systems.

COMPUTER SUPPLIES LTD

BEST BUYS OF THE MONTH!

Packard Bell	120MHz Intel Pentium processor • 8 Mb RAM • 1 Gb hard disk • 6 speed CD-ROM drive • £1520
Apricot	200MHz Intel Pentium processor • 16 Mb RAM • 2.5 Gb hard disk • Optical power drive • 28.8 bps data/fax modem • £2550
Hewlett Packard	133MHz Intel Pentium processor • 16 Mb RAM • 1.6 Gb hard disk • 28.8 bps data/fax modem • £1835
Fujitsu	150MHz Intel Pentium processor • 16 Mb RAM • 2.0 Gb hard disk • 28.88 data/fax modem • 8 speed CD-ROM drive • £1740

---

1 You work as administrator/secretary to John Harper, the manager of a large retail store. Your basic requirements are for word processing and spreadsheets although you do some database work and research information for him quite regularly. You also regularly communicate with the group head office. From this information, discuss which system would be the most useful and cost-effective for your needs.

2 Write a memo to John Harper, arguing your case for an upgraded machine. Give the benefits of the system you have selected, translating the computer jargon in the advertisement into plain English for his benefit!

Accessing the Net

The Internet, commonly referred to as the Net, is a global network of computer systems. The term comes from its official title, the International Network of Computers, over which computer users can communicate in 'cyberspace'. It originated in the United States in the 1970s – today any computer user with a modem, telephone line and relevant software can gain access.

The World Wide Web (WWW), or Web, is a system that allows Net users to search for information and display pages. Therefore, the Net is the hardware, whilst the Web is the software. Net addicts use WWW to travel around the world looking for information. WWW is a hypertext system which contains links between information – you can then follow a trail of linked words – more commonly known as 'surfing the Net'.

Users go on-line by paying a fee, usually monthly, to a service provider such as CompuServe. Net access time is free with some service providers, but charged for by others. All users pay for their telephone calls to link with the Net. The user needs communications software (usually provided by the service provider) to make the link and a browser program which assembles the photos, text and audio on to Web 'pages' that appear on screen. By typing in a http:// command the user is connected to a special Net server computer that handles the data. This is like a powerful file server, communicating data to Net users via telephone lines and fibre-optic cables.

Techno-phobes unite!

Motorola, Intel's main competitor in the computer chips market, commissioned a survey of the British public and its views on information technology. According to the findings, published in October 1996, whilst 85 per cent of the population have heard of the Internet, only 9 per cent use it regularly; 78 per cent haven't a clue how to get connected; and 25 per cent are completely uninterested. It is notable that the survey questioned several top executives who held the same views!

More men than women described themselves as IT literate and knowledgeable, but there was a huge diversity in age groups. Whilst 54 per cent of 16–24-year-olds felt capable of coping with IT, only 25 per cent of those aged 45 and over took the same view. However, PC ownership is rising – and predicted to increase considerably by the millennium. The danger is that those who are poorer, older or unemployed may fall into an 'information void' in the future if society as a whole pursues computerised lifestyle options such as on-line shopping and banking.

Finally, why the 'superhighway'? Originally, this term simply described the massive potential of transmitting data through fibre-optic cables at high speed. It is still an appropriate analogy as routes to popular sites become as congested as rush-hour traffic jams – anyone trying to reach a site which supplies free software at 7 pm in the evening will tell you!

Computer software

There is a vast range of software packages on the market. However, all can be divided into two types – **systems programs** and **applications programs.**

Systems programs tell the computer how to function. Names you may hear are DOS (which stands for **disk operating system**), OS/2 (an IBM operating system which can replace DOS), Windows 95 or Unix. Another term you may see is GUI – **graphical user interface.** This is the type of interface used by all OS/2 and some Windows applications, whereas DOS applications use a textual interface.

Applications programs are those which are used for specific purposes. Typical business applications programs include word processing, databases, spreadsheets, desktop publishing packages, payroll and accounts. Many packages are sold as 'integrated' or as 'suites'. This means that you can transfer text or data easily between compatible programs (see page 306).

To link a computer to the outside world, either via a fax or the Internet, requires communications software, another type of applications program.

Choosing software

If you are searching for an applications package, remember that normally the higher the number after the title, the later the issue. Therefore WordPerfect 6.1 is an improved and later version of WordPerfect 5.1. However, the latest version of Windows is Windows 95 – in this case the year of issue has been used rather than an ordinary number. A key point when choosing software is to make sure that the software you want to buy will work on your current operating system. For instance, although you may have a Windows operating system, some software packages (eg Wordperfect Suite 7) will *only* operate on Windows 95.

You may also like to note that the term 'package' rather than 'program' is used because normally you do not just buy a disk containing the program but also a range of manuals and other documentation – all of which make up the 'package'.

The main features of the different types of business packages together with common examples of these types of programs is given in Figure 14.3. However, many of these packages are now available as a suite of programs, eg Microsoft Office, Lotus SmartSuite or Corel Professional Office. They

Type of software	Main features	Examples
Word processing	Used to produce letters, memos and reports. Enables the user to insert, delete, amend text easily. Text can be moved from one part of a document to another or from one document to another. Personalised mail-shots can be produced using mail merge. Documents can contain enhancements, such as bold or underline, different styles of text can be produced and documents can be formatted according to the user's specifications. Additional features include pagination, spell checking, access to an electronic thesaurus, footnote insertion and the creation of headers and footers. The customised design of any document can be stored using the macro facility and recalled at the press of a key.	Word Word for Windows WordPerfect Lotus Word Pro (formerly Ami Pro)
Database	An electronic filing system to store records which can be sorted to find specific information. Information can be printed out in the form of reports. Each record is designed on a database 'form' containing a number of fields in which data are entered. Data can be entered and updated – often automatically. Records can be searched and retrieved by means of 'key fields'.	Paradox Approach Access Oracle
Spreadsheet	Used for financial analysis and the production of charts and graphs based on financial information. Each worksheet consists of a matrix of cells placed in columns (down) and rows (across) the spreadsheet. Figures are entered into the cells and the results calculated or recalculated according to the inserted formula.	Excel Quattro Pro Supercalc Lotus 1-2-3

Type of software	Main features	Examples
Graphics and presentation packages	Enables graphics and text to be imported and combined in a document and printed on paper, overhead transparencies or slides. Additional images can be bought as 'clip-art' packages and most presentation packages contain guidance to the user on creating charts, expanding outline thoughts into finished documents and creating special effects.	PowerPoint Presentations Freelance Visio Coreldraw
Desktop publishing	Enables text and graphics to be combined in a poster, notice, report, newspaper or other type of 'publication'. Different styles of text fonts, lines, boxes, shadings and designs can be used to obtain a variety of effects through the use of drawing tools. Graphics can be scanned in and moved or reshaped to suit the designer.	Pagemaker Ventura Quark Xpress
Accounting/ payroll/stock control	Accounting packages enable records of all cash and credit sales and purchases to be entered in relevant accounts and for invoices and statements to be produced automatically together with other accounts such as VAT returns, bank analysis, trial balance, profit and loss account and balance sheet. Some are integrated with **payroll** packages which calculate and produce wages documentation and **stock control** packages which can be used to monitor stock usage.	Instant Accounting Sterling Sovereign

Figure 14.3 Business application packages

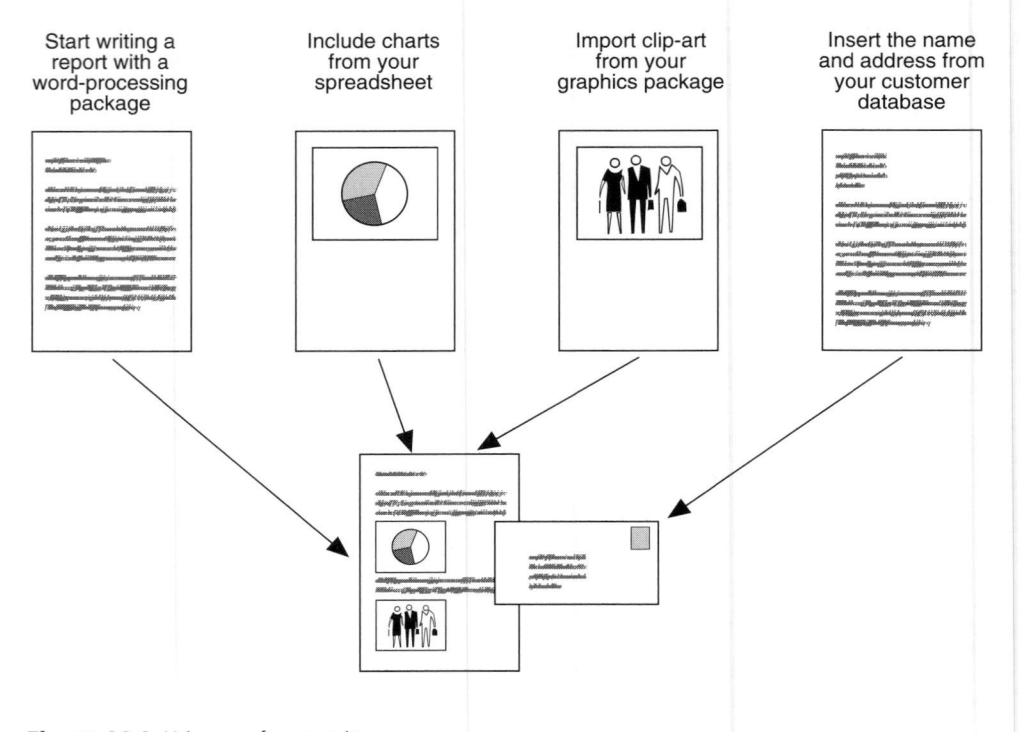

Start writing a report with a word-processing package

Include charts from your spreadsheet

Import clip-art from your graphics package

Insert the name and address from your customer database

Figure 14.4 Using a software suite

comprise a range of software packages – usually covering word processing, spreadsheets, graphics and database applications – all of which are devised so that they are compatible with each other, together with a 'manager' program. Because the programs are compatible, all or part of a document created in one program can be imported into a document created in a different program (see Figure 14.4).

Integrated packages such as Microsoft Works are a similar idea, but on a more limited basis. These offer modules for word processing, spreadsheets, drawings, databases and communications which can be used in the same way.

Using software

The only way you can become familiar with the features of different software, its capabilities and its limitations is to *use it*. It is assumed that if you are taking an administration or secretarial course, you will be learning word processing, databases, spreadsheets and desktop publishing as part of the range of skills you will need to obtain a job. However, a few useful tips are given in Figure 14.5, to help you if you suddenly find that your employer operates a different version or different brand of package to that which you followed so faithfully in college!

- Do not be put off by the number of manuals included in some suites of software. Often there are some quick reference manuals which lead you in gently!

- Be reassured that no software user ever learns – or, indeed, *needs* to learn all the possible functions on the package. Work on the 80 per cent/20 per cent rule – for 80 per cent of the time you will use 20 per cent of the functions. Learn the basics first and learn them well.

- Find out how to locate the 'help' screen!

- Make a note of commands or 'steps' you need to go through for a particular function.

- Find out if your package includes the ability to ask for a short demonstration on something new that you want to do.

- Find out if there are any **Wizards** to help you. Wizards are a feature of many Windows programs which will quickly give you a step-by-step guide to almost anything you want to do.

- If there is no 'hints and tips' section in your manuals, devise your own.

- Invest in a *short,* simple, purpose-written book which tells you how to use your software quickly. It will usually be easier to understand than the manual. Make sure it has a good index.

- Ignore any 'tutorial' manuals which insist you produce a dozen fake documents to master one simple operation.

- If the package is complicated, try to enrol on a good short course which will teach you the basics quickly.

- Never forget to read your screen – especially if a normal command is being ignored. Most software packages either include prompts to help you when you get stuck or give you visual information on your status at the moment.

- Do not become complacent once you know the basics. A quick browse through the manual – or referring to it when you want to do a particular task – will enhance your capabilities.

- Do not be frightened to experiment – but not on an important report you must get right in the next 20 minutes! If you are trying something new, then *save* the document before you experiment – so that you are covered if something goes wrong. Do not forget you have an Esc key plus an Undo or Undelete function to get you out of trouble on virtually all packages!

- Consult other users – a quick chat with them often makes an instruction understandable.

- If you are on your own and find an instruction in the manual unintelligible, telephone the software company for advice. Remember to have your licence number to hand when you ring!

Figure 14.5 Some tips on using software

Discussion point

Either through your own experience of using word processing and desktop publishing *or* after seeing a demonstration of both types of package

a   identify the main features available to the user
b   obtain examples of documents produced on both packages
c   discuss the occasions on which each package would be more appropriate to use.

The war of the cyberworld!

Few people today have not heard of Bill Gates. In case you are one of the few, Gates is the richest man in the world (estimated earnings currently $10 billion per year). He heads the Microsoft Corporation – the organisation which gave the world DOS operating systems in 1980 and Windows 10 years later.

In December 1995 Bill Gates decided that the future of Microsoft had to be linked to the Internet for its survival to be guaranteed. He then spent a considerable amount of money refocusing Microsoft's projects and products towards this objective. One early sortie was to launch Internet Explorer 3.0 – a browser program which Microsoft developed in just six months and then distributed free on Internet. The aim of this was to challenge the current market leader, Netscape. Netscape became known for its Navigator program which made finding one's way around the Internet so simple even a child could do it. The problem for users is that Navigator is not free – unlike Explorer.

Netscape is armed with a new strategy, however. It has formed an alliance with Sony, NEC, Nintendo and IBM to develop the Internet to make Microsoft Windows irrelevant. In the meantime Microsoft has developed Explorer 4 – freely downloadable to Internet users from Christmas 1996. The battle is now well and truly joined.

Data management and protection

You have already learned, in previous chapters, about the importance of file management (page 199) and data protection and security (page 220 and page 99).

However, given that as a secretary or administrator you need to be a good role model to others and to have the knowledge to advise others on these topics, below are some key points to remember.

Backing up data

Good advice is to back up your data regularly on floppy disk in case of accidents or equipment problems. Whilst this is essential, the growth in size of computer systems can make this broad ruling problematic. If you have megabytes of data on your hard drive, it could take you dozens of floppy disks to copy everything. For example, a machine with a 500 Mb hard disk would need no less than 400 diskettes to back up the work – and this would mean several hours of inserting/removing disks from the floppy drive! There are two answers to this problem.

- **Be selective** about the data you back up.

- If comprehensive back-ups are required, there are **modern systems and equipment** to help you!

Being selective means not trying to make an exact copy of your hard disk. This is usually unnecessary. Even if the hard disk breaks down, then the programs can be restored from the master floppy disks or CD-ROMs which were purchased when you bought your computer system and software packages. Therefore it is not usual to back up systems and applications programs.

The key files to back up are those which contain your created documents. These should be in folders or files (neatly labelled, remember!) in specific directories. It is then a simple matter to keep this type of data on back-up floppies. On Windows programs you can simply drag the contents of a folder to your floppy disk icon to copy it.

Modern systems and equipment can be used in two ways. Back-up programs exist which automatically detect when a file has been changed and then back them up automatically. If you *do* have the requirement to back up megabytes of data, persuade your boss to let you invest in a zip drive or tape streamer which automatically compresses high quantities of data and saves them quickly and easily. For £175 you can store up to 100 megabytes of data without spending all day loading, removing and labelling floppy disks!

Hazards and hackers

Whilst elaborate systems may be in place to provide for the backing up of key data, there are other reasons why crises occur. Murphy's Law means that it is only when you have made several important and complicated amendments to a document that the system goes down, someone pulls out the plug by mistake or there is a power failure! Programs which automatically back up your work every few minutes are very useful – otherwise train yourself to save your work at regular intervals and *especially* before you make complicated changes. Learn how to alter the defaults for this – to speed up the time delay before back-ups are made for critical work and slow it down for less important jobs.

Given that a break in the power supply can wipe the memory of every computer in the organisation, many companies invest in a type of device known as an UPS (uninterruptible power supply). This not only protects the system from fluctuations in the electricity supply but also provides back up if there is a power cut. The latest devices link with a software package which informs the computer that the mains supply has failed and shuts down the system cleanly. This can be vital if a power failure happens at night when the computer is involved in back-up routines.

However, none of these precautions will help if the system is vulnerable to illegal entry by computer hackers. Six minutes after the government joined the Internet, a man from Edinburgh University hacked into the system used by the Office of Public Service and Science and redesigned some of the pages of information. A spokesman said he was grateful – he felt the new pages were an improvement!

Protection of data

Always bear in mind that the value of the computer equipment in an organisation may be considerably less than the value of the data held in it! If nothing else, documents, files and reports which have taken hours of staff time to prepare – let alone customised software packages – would take hours of time to replace. However, in any organisation it is usual to protect both hardware and data from theft or damage.

Hardware can be protected as follows.

- Site it on specially designed workstations or in a sensible layout on a desktop.

- Install proper wire management – preferably built into the workstation itself.

- Keep movement of hardware to a minimum.

- Always close down a system properly, eg by logging out of a network using the correct procedure and always waiting until the disk light has gone out before removing a disk from the drive.

- Make sure food, drinks and other liquids are kept well away.

- Only switch off a computer when necessary. New energy-saving monitors switch themselves off – moving the mouse or depressing any key will return power to the screen. You may notice that if you are not using your computer your screen blanks out after a couple of minutes or displays a 'screen saver'. This is a screen with constantly moving images (from letters to fish swimming around the screen!). It prevents screen burn, where images are burnt on to the screen and cannot be removed.

- Keep the equipment and keyboard clean – but *always* use the right products for the job.

Equipment can be protected from theft by

- fixing alarms which sound if the equipment is moved any distance

- siting valuable equipment away from public areas, where possible

- marking equipment with a special security tag or ultraviolet pen to show the rightful owner.

Data can be protected by

- storing floppy disks in a proper disk box – and allowing sufficient space for each

- using proper disk holders for carrying disks or sending them through the post

- writing the label for the disk before attaching it to the disk

- keeping disks away from magnetic sources (such as magnetic catches on office cabinet doors!) and direct heat (such as radiators)

- never using disks in faulty equipment or saving on to a disk you have had lying in your desk drawer for the past couple of years.

Data can be protected from accidental damage in the following ways.

- Take regular back-ups of important/amended documents.

- Ensure the read/write protect notch is in position on floppy disks.

- Identify the 'protection' elements inherent in many software programs – for instance, formulae entered into a spreadsheet can be protected, as can the field titles in databases.

- Think very carefully and clearly before you embark on a program of deleting files and documents. If you are careless, you may easily delete the wrong one in error. However, all operating systems have the ability to enable users to 'undelete' a file again even if you do not have a back-up!

- Never use anyone else's disk from outside your system or a disk from an unknown source – either of which may contain a virus (see page 100). Be aware that if you download software from the Internet you could be in danger of downloading a virus too, unless you have a virus checker program installed! Good virus checkers, such as Dr Solomon, not only identify the presence of a virus and alert the user but then 'kill all known viruses'. However, virus checkers need updating regularly – as more viruses are identified and detected – to enable them to cope in most situations.

- Remember that disk manufacturers will only guarantee information on disks up to 52°C. Beyond this it is probable all information will be lost. If such damaged disks contained all the company's records and there were no back-ups stored in a separate place, it could be weeks if not months before the organisation were operational again.

Government protection warnings

The Department of Trade and Industry has issued two booklets designed to help businesses to be more aware of the dangers of information leakage. Telephones and faxes can be tapped, voice mail and telephone answering systems can be vulnerable to hacking, floppy disks and even laptops can be stolen. There is even a form of industrial espionage where information brokers obtain data unlawfully – often from disaffected employees – and offer this for sale to competitors.

Protecting Business Information: Understanding the Risks and Keeping It Confidential can be obtained free of charge by contacting the Department of Trade and Industry on 0171 510 0174 and quoting references URN 96/38 and URN 96/39.

● The output stage

Original copies of documents are usually produced on computer printers. In the majority of cases these are not suitable for multiple copying, which is dealt with on page 321. However, the type of printer you have installed will dictate the standard and type of output which is produced. You cannot expect to produce high-quality colour documents on a standard dot matrix printer!

However, in addition to knowing the type of equipment available, you also need to know how to use it effectively. This means utilising all the various features and functions of your software and your printer together in the most effective way. If you combine this knowledge with a small amount of basic artistic and presentational flair, then you should be able to obtain the maximum benefit from any system you operate.

Computer software – its output potential

As you already know, different types of software are used to produce different types of documents. For example, a spreadsheet is used to prepare a financial worksheet, a chart or a graph; a database produces a record or a listing; and a word-processing package is used to create text-based documents, such as letters, memos or reports. However, today many word-processing packages will produce charts or tables, and you may even be able to import clip-art of objects or outline diagrams. A desktop publishing package gives an even greater array of features to help you to plan and design a document containing both text and artwork.

A useful start is to check that you know how to use the software you have already got to its fullest extent.

- On a **word-processing package** for example, can you embolden, underscore and centre text without difficulty? Do you know how to reformat a document for different page width or length? Can you type in a range of fonts, ie different typefaces, styles and sizes? What other character sets can you access to print unusual characters? Can you produce tables – and will your software enable you to compile these with a range of shades and borders?

- On a **desktop publishing package,** can you design a page in different column widths and draw a thin line between each column? Can you use different fonts and types of shading? Can you reflow text around an imported graphic for effect? Can you rotate images to give a different look to a graphic?

- On a **spreadsheet package,** can you design a worksheet so it has clear headings and totals? Can you print out showing either figures or formulae? Can you change the format of cells easily or align data to right or left? Can you compress the information to print out a large spreadsheet on a small sheet of paper? Can you produce graphics with clear labels and a readable key?

- On a **database package,** can you design a clear form with sensible field lengths? Can you design or redesign a report so that it is user friendly? Do you know how to change the style of a form or report to suit your needs? Can you take advantage of all the visual styles available, such as italics, bold or alignment of text?

Usually all these facilities are clearly stated in the manual and all are familiar to professional users. If you want to be considered a professional yourself, now is the time to get to grips with them!

Computer printers

You should be aware that on many software packages you will not be limited by the options available but by the ability of your printer to support them, eg you may be able to display several different fonts on screen, but your printer may only have a limited selection.

All computer printers are controlled by software known as the **printer driver.** This makes the commands which are entered into the computer intelligible to the printer. The printer driver is usually accessed by means of a 'print set-up' command in the applications package. If you change printer, but do not instruct the driver which one you are now using, you can expect to obtain some very unusual results indeed when you try to obtain a hard (paper) copy!

On a network, a **print server** is the device used to control a group of shared resource printers. However, on some networks this function is carried out by a file server instead.

Basic issues

The type of printer you can use is likely to fall into one of the following categories.

Dot matrix printers are the cheapest option and used for payroll or other listings. The characters are created by making a pattern of small dots which means that the final result is not of a high quality. Depressing NLQ means that the printer goes over each character twice to improve the density. These printers are unsuitable for external documents and are also the slowest and the noisiest in operation.

Inkjet or bubble jet printers can produce both text or graphics but the fonts are limited unless you pay more. They work by means of tiny droplets of ink from a cartridge being sprayed on to the surface of the document. Colour printers are now available relatively cheaply (at less than £300) but different colour cartridges are required. The cartridges are quite expensive but a new service initiative is the re-filling of used cartridges. This saves money and is also environmentally friendly. (Don't be confused by the term 'bubble jet' – it is simply the trade name for inkjet printers used by one manufacturer, Canon.)

Laser printers work by using laser beams to transfer the original image on to a drum, which then transfers it on to paper. Negatively charged toner particles stick to the mirror image created on the drum and are then pressed against the paper and 'fused' by heat to produce a permanent print. Toner is simply particles of fine black dust which is contained in a special cartridge inside the printer. A variation are LED printers which use a slightly different technology.

Desktop models are becoming commonplace in many offices as their price has fallen dramatically over the past few years. The copy quality is excellent both for text and graphics. A Postscript laser printer is one that can produce very sophisticated text and graphics using a special built-in processor. Such a machine is ideal for desktop publishing work, although it may be expensive.

It is estimated that printing costs average about £6000 per laser printer installed, but this can be reduced by over £1000 a year if refillable toner cartridges are used. Laser printers are often 'paper sensitive' – therefore the latest discount offer from your local stationery store may be unsuitable for use as a means of saving money!

Other considerations

There have been several developments in the printer industry over the past few years, the most significant of which are given below.

Page printers are those which create a whole page inside the computer or printer and then print it in one go – either on single-sided pages or duplex (double-sided). This is different from inkjet and dot matrix printers which print a line at a time on the paper. This technology has been used to produce desktop laser printers at a fraction of the price of earlier models. The disadvantage is that page printers can only print in black and white. A further feature, which may be considered a disadvantage by many operators, is their speech function. If you have a computer which supports a sound card, hearing your printer announce when it needs more paper or has jammed may be amusing on the first occasion but absolutely infuriating on the tenth. Luckily, this is usually an optional feature which can easily be switched off!

Colour printing is now available on inkjet printers, and personal colour printers can be purchased relatively cheaply. Laser colour printers have been on the market since 1995 and are becoming more popular every year. It is estimated that by the year 2000 more than 20 per cent of computer systems will be supported by colour laser printers.

GDI printers were designed to have no memory and no processor but to use the Graphical Device Interface of Windows software to do this job for them. They are therefore much cheaper than standard laser printers though they can only be used with Windows software and only used successfully with a fairly powerful PC, ie 8 Mb of memory, 16 Mb for graphics and several megabytes of spare hard disk space. The printer cannot be shared between several users as it is linked specifically to one machine. Microsoft was, understandably, not too keen on its software being 'hijacked' by printer manufacturers so designed its own software called WPS (Windows Print System) which shares the job of processing the printing between the computer and the printer. For this reason WPS printers are usually better than GDI printers.

Today's printers are often advertised as **environmentally friendly** with several of the following features – energy saving, low noise levels during operation, toner saving, ozone-free processing and components which can be readily recycled.

Some of the more sophisticated laser printers have **electronic storage** facilities. They can store electronic forms, fonts and logos which can automatically be recalled and merged when printing.

The main points to consider when buying a printer are as follows.

- Whether the printer will be used for an individual user or shared between a group of users (usually called **workgroups**). Higher capacity/durability is then required.

- The type of documents which will be produced. Graphics require much greater memory than text. Without sufficient memory the page will not print, or will only partially print, unless you change the resolution (see below) or reduce the size of the image.

- Print quality depends upon the printer's resolution, ie the number of 'dots per inch' (dpi). Ordinary text is fine at the standard of 300 dpi, but large text and curved letters will be jagged and photographs will be of poor quality; 600 dpi will give much better results for graphics (you can compare this with the professional printing standard of 1200 dpi or even greater!).

- The speed of production required. Most manufacturers are extremely optimistic about speed and quote figures which no users can ever substantiate! Generally, the higher quality (or resolution) required for the document, the slower the print speed. Printer speed is normally quoted in pages per minute – anything between 4 and 10 pages per minute is usually acceptable for a 'personal' printer. As a general rule, the higher speed the printer, the higher the cost.

- The size of printer memory. Printers contain the same kind of memory chips which are found in a PC. The amount of memory required depends upon the type of document to be printed and the resolution. For text use a basic requirement could be 0.5 Mb but for higher resolution work between 2 Mb and 4 Mb is better. Insufficient memory will not only influence what you can print but what you can do whilst you are printing! If you are working with a personal printer, you may find you

have to sit and wait whilst the document is processed for printing, rather than continue with the next piece of work. On a networked system, documents are queued – and low memory can mean that your screen is frozen on a temporary basis – rather than processed and stored in the printer memory.

Printer memory can be upgraded by the use of additional chips (SIMMs) just like PCs – but it is normally cheaper to get it right first time!

Secretarial and administrative issues

Whilst the choice of printers and their usage is likely to be a key area in which you are involved, you will also be expected to monitor usage and maintenance and probably to give your recommendations for keeping costs as low as possible.

Routine maintenance of expensive printers is likely to be undertaken as part of a service contract. Smaller personal printers need little servicing and maintenance provided that they are not used beyond their maximum recommended capacity. The life of the printer should also be considered – even if the printer continues beyond this period there should be some type of replacement policy to provide for its general wear and tear. You will prolong the life of any printer by looking after it. Dust and dirt are the main enemies – and the chief villain is likely to be cheap paper which generates dust. It will also help if the printer is kept covered when not in use.

Never try to remedy problems yourself unless you know what you are doing. There is usually a trouble-shooting guide in your printer manual which will help to prevent you calling out an engineer for a basic problem (such as the machine not being plugged in or being set to 'off-line'!). Make sure that you know how to use your **print manager** – so that you can instantly stop or restart printing jobs if there is a problem or query.

There are various ways in which you can help your organisation to save money on printer consumables.

- Shop around for all the consumables you use, eg cartridges, paper.

- Arrange for cartridges to be refilled rather than replaced. A variety of organisations offer this service. However, do be careful that the printer warranty will not be compromised if you do this. Some manufacturers insist on specific cartridges being used during this period – often their own!

- Use draft or low-density print modes whenever you can.

- Switch the printer off when it is not in use (unless there is a power-saving mode you can use). However, do not be tempted to turn the printer off and on continually during the day – this is likely to cause more problems than it solves.

- Proof read all documents carefully on screen before printing.

- Never use printers for long print runs. Despite any claims by manufacturers, as yet it is cheaper to produce multiple copies on a copier than on a computer printer.

Printers and their footprints

Whilst you may have given some careful considerations to the key aspects of computer printers, such as print quality, speed, workload – and even environmental considerations, how would you cope if a sales executive told you that a key selling feature is the size of its footprint? Believe it or not, this term is not technical!

It simply means the amount of space the printer will take up on your desk. Manufacturers are now working on printers with a footprint which is less than an A4 page. The trend is to reduce the size of printers whilst improving their performance. Presumably as printers become even smaller we may start to talk in terms of handprints or even fingerprints!

Computers and presentational skills

You have already learned about the basics of document presentation in chapter 13. The next stage is to develop your skills of design and presentation of documents using a computer, software packages and an appropriate printer.

 Discussion point

1 Discuss with your personal tutor or IT tutor the different types of features you can use on your college system to improve or enhance document presentation.

2 Check that you clearly understand the meaning of each of the following terms.
   a headers
   b footers
   c orphans
   d widows
   Make sure that you clearly understand the difference between footers and footnotes!

3 Find out if the packages you use have a macro facility. This means that any formatting commands you want to enter for a particular type of document can be entered and stored as a sequence of keystrokes and simply recalled at the touch of a few keys.

Presentation options

The following hints and tips should help you to get the most out of the system you are using.

1 Do not attempt to produce documents on a page size which is incompatible with your printer! Few will produce documents larger than A4. Before you decide to make a larger version on your photocopier remember that solid black text turns grey and loses its definition when it is enlarged.

2 If you do not have access to a colour printer, find out if your local print shop has one. Enquire also if it has a computer system compatible with yours so that, on special occasions, you can obtain colour print-outs simply by giving the print shop a disk containing your document.

3 Avoid widows and orphans where single lines are separated from the main body of the text on a different page. Some software packages will adjust these for you automatically. On others you can simply define the number of pages to use and the package will condense/expand the text for you!

4 Learn how to paginate professionally. If you are producing a long report, centre your page numbers at the foot of the page and remember to number page 1. Some organisations like pages paginated at the top – on opposite sides for facing pages.

5 Find out how to insert headers and footers –using different text or styles on odd and even pages where required. Look at the way the headers used in this book change, for instance.

6 If you display text in columns do not use more than three or, at most, four columns. Use equal columns and equal spacings. Draw a thin vertical line between them for a professional look.

7 Do not mix typestyles and character sizes too much or use too much colour. Using too wide a variety looks amateurish.

8 Use bullet points rather than numbered points if you do not want to assign an order to the subsections.

9 Make sure tables and diagrams are well-balanced, easy to read, clearly labelled, positioned centrally on the text or the page and pleasing to the eye.

10 Use boxes to display important text or to indicate a graphic which is to be inserted later.

11 Investigate the capacity of your software to produce different character sets, typefaces and character sizes – and the capacity of your printer to output these!

All computers operate using one character set – usually ASCII codes. This is an international character set for computers. You often have the opportunity to use other sets which include mathematical and scientific signs, typographical symbols and foreign characters, eg Greek, Hebrew and Cyrillic letters.

The term 'font' refers to the style of typeface being used. Typeface comes in two styles – serif and sans serif. Serif has 'curly bits' whereas sans serif is 'without curly bits'! Times Roman is the most popular serif face and Helvetica the most common sans serif face.

This is an example of a serif typeface. This is an example of a sans serif typeface.

In addition, on most packages today you have a choice of typefaces – particularly those which use graphical software such as Microsoft Windows or IBM OS/2. On many printers you can purchase additional typefaces to add to the ones which are standard when you buy the equipment.

This is an example of Times typeface.
This is an example of Courier typeface.
This is an example of Helvetica typeface.
This is an example of Palatino typeface.

The term 'point' relates to the size of the text. The higher the number the larger the text, so it is quite easy to remember. You will find that on older inkjet printers you will be limited to point size – probably 20 at the most. You cannot, therefore, insert large newspaper type headlines above your text. Postscript laser printers have a much greater capability in this respect and it is worth reading the sales literature to see the different sizes you can achieve.

This is 8 point.
This is 12 point.
This is 24 point.
This is 36 point.

12 Find out about additional enhancement features on your packages, eg shading, 3-dimensional imaging and unusual alignments.

13 Read your printer manual and find out what additional facilities you could 'buy in' if you need them to extend your current options.

Methods of reproducing and copying information

Reprographic and copying systems

Copiers are a feature of all offices, although they vary considerably in their size and complexity. They are an invaluable asset because of their ability to produce an exact replica of a document in seconds.

The different types of copying systems available include

- **analogue copiers** of different sizes – from desktop models for low-volume copying to complex models with a variety of features for high-volume copying

- **digital copiers** – which use more advanced technology

- **colour copiers** and copier/printers

- **digital printing systems** – which use duplicating methods linked to digital technology.

Analogue copiers

This is the technology used for the vast majority of photocopiers in use today. It has been developed from the original Xerox machines to enable today's operators to produce clear, sharp copies at the touch of a button or key. These type of copiers operate in a similar way to a camera. The original image is projected through a lens on to a light-sensitive surface, and the image is developed using toner, transferred to the copy paper and fused through heat. Copiers have now been developed so that controls are simple to operate through touch screen displays, the machines themselves are more reliable and there are many additional features available even on the most basic models. Most machines offer automatic document feeding, double-sided copying, sorting and automatic paper-tray selection.

Typically, the functions you can expect to find on most copiers include the following.

- **Two-sided copying** – known as **duplexing** (as opposed to single-sided operation or **simplexing**) – is the most cost-saving option of all as it can halve paper costs.

- **Zoom enlargement and reduction** of originals – often 50–200 per cent or more. Reduction of documents is another money-saving device if several larger documents are reduced to fit together on one A4 page.

- **Automatic document feeder** increases the speed of input of the originals.

- **Recirculating automatic document feeder** copes with double-sided originals and passes the document through the system twice to copy both sides.

- **Semi-automatic document feeders** enable the operator to feed in one sheet of paper at a time to ensure accurate positioning of the original.

- **Sorting** allows copied pages to be stacked automatically in special 'bins'. This enables documents to be collated and a complete multipage document to be stacked in each bin.

- **Interleaving** allows the automatic insertion of index or marker pages or, in the case of OHP film copying, protective sheets of backing paper to be interleaved. On some systems this is known as chapterisation.

- **Stapling** may be on-line, off-line or both. On-line means that multipage documents can be stapled automatically after sorting, usually with a choice of staple positions. Off-line stapling enables documents to be fed manually into an electric stapling attachment.

- **Hole-punching** can be carried out automatically after sorting to prepare documents ready for filing.

- **Folding** allows A3 copies to be folded, usually into a 'Z' shape, and A4 pages to be folded to create A5 booklets.

- **Binding** is offered on the most expensive copiers and enables completed multipage documents to be finished with a professional cover (see also page 330).

In addition to the features available, organisations are mostly concerned with the speed, reliability and quality of their copying. High-volume copiers are usually described as those which can produce between 50 and 90 copies a minute (cpm). However, it is not simply the speed which is important but the machine's ability to cope with the consistent demand for copies – or volume required. 'Downtime' is the term used to describe the amount of time the machine is out of use because of a fault which an engineer needs to rectify – and is detested by all users because of the inconvenience and delays which are caused. For that reason, a machine which is highly reliable is likely to be preferred to one which has a greater number of features and operates at higher speed, but constantly breaks down!

Digital copiers

Whilst a digital copier may look similar to an analogue machine, a completely different process is involved and the range of operations is considerably greater. The original document is scanned and digitised and then stored in the copier memory. It can then be amended, edited or manipulated in dozens of different ways and combined with PC-generated documents and files. Digital copiers are claimed to be more reliable, to offer higher quality reproduction and to be able to combine several operations, such as printing and faxing. They are therefore another version of a multifunctional device, although more sophisticated.

The type of features you can expect to see on a digital copier include the following.

- **Electronic pre-collation** – where the copier itself stores the images in the correct order for collation. This means that complicated printing sequences (eg for a booklet of several pages) can be copied in the sequence most understandable for the operator and the copier will then rearrange them into the correct printing sequence.

  The copier will also select the correct paper to use and decide itself whether it should be landscape or portrait – without the operator having to choose between different paper trays.

- **Duplexing** is faster as both sides of the document are printed almost simultaneously, rather than the original being re-fed through the machine.

- **Data storage** – names, addresses, logos and headers can be stored inside the copier and automatically included on documents. This may mean the end of word-processing 'mail merge' jobs which can now be downloaded to the copier.

- **Forms storage** – forms and commonly used documents can be stored in the copier memory and recalled at the press of a few keys.

- **Editing features** allow the originals to be viewed on screen and any unwanted copy 'cut away' before copying. This enables users to omit handwritten notes from printed documents, print one newspaper article and omit the rest or collate a series of related documents on to one A4 page.

- **Image enhancement** means that the copier will automatically improve poor-quality originals – whether this is because the print is poor or the background is dense or dark.

- **Confidential copying** allows the user to instruct the copier to print from disk then, when it is convenient, walk to the copier, enter his or her confidential PIN and convert the disk copies on to paper.

- **Network compatibility** – digital copiers can be linked to a computer network for the receiving of documents, the receiving and rerouting of faxes and the storing of outgoing faxes. They are also being developed to be used as part of an electronic filing system – with documents being scanned in using the copier, rather than a conventional scanner!

As yet digital machines are quite expensive and account for less than 5 per cent of all machines sold. However, as more companies develop these machines and their price falls, the numbers of digital copiers are predicted to grow dramatically. You can therefore confidently expect to be working with a digital copier before you are too far into your career!

Colour copiers

Colour copiers are available in a variety of sizes and using both analogue and digital technology. Colour printers print documents either in black and white or in colour. Analogue machines only copy hard (paper) copy originals, but digital versions also accept copy downloaded from PCs and can be interlinked with a network system.

Colour copiers are a natural development to follow the dramatic advances in computers with colour screens, colour-capable software such as Windows and the development of cheap colour printers. There is little use producing coloured originals on a computer system if it is only possible to copy them in black and white!

Full-colour copying uses three primary colours – cyan (blue), magenta (red), yellow – and black to create a palette of millions of shades. The original is scanned at least four times to capture all the different colours – which means that colour copiers operate more slowly than black and white copiers. However, manufacturers are currently working on more sophisticated digital machines which only require one scan. Colour copiers take some time to warm up when switched on – up to 10 minutes in some cases, so they cannot be used the second someone arrives at work. Colour copies are also rather more expensive to produce than black and white copies – but are certainly cheaper to produce on a colour copier than by using an external printing service.

In addition to the range of features you will find on any modern copier, the additional facilities on a colour copier include the following.

- **Automatic colour selection** (ACS) – the machine pre-scans the document to identify whether it is a black or colour image. It then produces either a black and white or colour copy automatically.

- **Colour creation** enables the operator to change parts of a black and white document into colour using one of six 'spot' colours – cyan, magenta, yellow, green, bright red or blue. This allows black and white drawings to be reproduced in any colour, backgrounds to be patterned or coloured or spot colours to be used for headlines or titles.

- **Gradations** affect the intensity or depth of colour. These can either be selected from a pre-set range or, on top-of-the-range models, chosen by the operator.

- **Colour balancing and colour calibration** enables users to readjust colours according to their wishes and then reset the machine to preset levels and default settings automatically.

- **Image overlay** enables the operator to superimpose one image (eg a logo) over another.

- **Border erase** is used for copying originals such as maps where the image goes to the edge of the page. It enables the copy to be printed without the addition of a white border. This facility is called edge-to-edge copying on some machines.

- **Margin shift** enables the image to be moved electronically to create wider margins where required. This is particularly useful for reports or other documents which are to be bound or placed in a folder, where wider margins are required to allow for binding.

Digital printing systems

Digital printing systems combine the technology which was once used in office duplicators with modern digital technology. They do this by electronically producing a master document which is then copied over and over again automatically using an ink printing system.

The final cost per copy from a digital printing system is considerably less than that of a conventional copier, although the fact that a 'master' is produced means that the process is not cost-effective for fewer than 20 copies.

Colour printing can be achieved but it is rather slow as only one colour can be printed at any one time and the copies must dry before another colour is added. However, spot printing (where a document is printed all in one colour or with spot colours) is more easily achieved.

Most of the new types of digital printers will take instructions from a PC and produce high-speed multiple copies of a computer-generated image.

The aim of these systems is to print large-volume documents more quickly and more cheaply than can be achieved using a photocopier. They are ideal, for instance, for printing letter headings and other stationery, business reply envelopes and cards and other documentation which would normally be prepared by an outside printer. Flyers and promotional leaflets can be produced quickly, easily and cheaply without going to a print shop. They are used when the sheer volume alone (eg 100 000 copies a month!) would be far too much for a standard copier and by organisations that are trying to reduce high-volume copy costs such as schools and educational establishments.

● The law on copyright

Before you become carried away at the thought of copying everything which catches your eye – do be careful. In this chapter and chapter 9 you have looked at how to research information and how to produce it – and reproduce it. Unfortunately, if you are not careful about what you copy, you are in serious danger of breaking the law.

Colour attraction!

During 1995, 90 per cent of inkjet printers sold in Britain were colour, compared with 30 per cent in 1994, according to Romtec, a market research company.

This growth has taken place because it is acknowledged that colour not only attracts people's attention and appeals to their imagination but also helps basic understanding. People are far more inclined to read colour documents than black and white (32 per cent of people admit to this!) and 26 per cent higher retention is achieved. Before too long black and white documents may be as out of date as black and white television programmes!

However, not everyone is complacent about the trend towards colour copying. EU security requirements state that all colour copiers must incorporate anti-counterfeiting techniques to prevent the illegal copying of valuable documents such as banknotes or vouchers. In most machines this is done by invisibly marking and encoding each copy produced so that security forces can identify and locate the source copier which produced the documents. You may wish to remember this before you experiment by copying a £10 note on the office machine!

If someone writes a book or a computer program, composes a song, makes a film or creates any other type of artistic work, the law treats that work as their property (or copyright). Anyone else who wishes to make use of it (by, for instance, taking a photocopy of it or copying the program on to their own disk) must get permission to do so and – on occasions – must be prepared to pay a fee. You should note that the law of copyright *does* allow you to take *one* copy for private study or for research purposes. What it does not allow you to do is to take as many copies as you want and distribute them freely!

It will not matter if you use as your defence the fact that you did not know to whom the copyright belonged. If you infringe the owner's or originator's rights, even by accident, you could be liable to prosecution under the Copyright Act 1988 (see Figure 14.6).

One difficulty for authors and composers in the past has been how to collect the fees owing to them. Today, however, there are a number of collecting agencies which have been established to ensure that such payments are made, ie

- the Copyright Licensing Agency (CLA)

- the Performing Rights Society (PRS)

- the Mechanical Copyright Protection Society (MCPS)

- Phonographic Performance Ltd (PPL)

- Video Performance Ltd (VPL)

- Design and Artists Copyright Society (DADS)

- Educational Recording Agency Ltd (ERA).

In most cases, therefore, authors or composers will entrust the administration of their copyright to these societies in return for a percentage of the fees collected. In turn, the societies grant a licence to both public and private individuals to give them the right to photocopy certain publications on the payment of a fee. Such licences now cover most educational institutions and negotiations are currently taking place with government establishments, industry and commerce.

The most important thing to remember, of course, is that these societies act as watchdogs and protect the interests of their members by checking on both libraries and other organisations to see that no unauthorised photocopying is being carried out!

The Copyright, Designs and Patents Act 1988

Works protected by copyright

- literary, dramatic, musical and artistic works
- sound recordings, films, broadcasts and cable programmes
- the typographical arrangements of published editions (ie the layout of the printed pages of a published edition of a work)

Length of copyright period

Literary, dramatic, musical and artistic works	Copyright expires at the end of the 70th year after the year in which the author died
Sound recordings and films	Copyright expires at the end of 70 years from the end of the year in which the work was made or released
Typographical arrangements	Copyright expires at the end of 25th year after the year in which the edition incorporating the arrangement was first published

Rights of the copyright owner

The owner has the exclusive right to

- copy the work
- issue copies of it to the public
- perform, show or play the work in public
- broadcast it or include it in a cable programme service
- adapt it.

Specific exceptions

Copyright will not be infringed if the work is used for certain specific purposes such as

- research or private study
- criticism or review of a work provided the identity of the author and the title of the work are acknowledged
- the reporting of current events provided the identity of the author is acknowledged
- incidental inclusion of any work in an artistic work, sound recording, broadcast or cable programme, eg a shot in a film showing a book lying on a table with its title visible
- educational use

(*Note*: If a licence has been negotiated, such exceptions do not apply.)

- libraries and archives – specific regulations are contained in the Copyright (Libraries and Archivists) (Copying of Copyright Material) Regulations 1989
- the reporting of parliamentary or judicial proceedings, the proceedings of a Royal Commission or statutory enquiry
- abstracts – the copying of an abstract (summary) or an article on a scientific or technical subject published in a periodical containing both the abstract and article.

Other exceptions relate mainly to the use of sound recordings and artistic designs.

Figure 14.6 Details of copyright law

🗨 Discussion point

1   Visit your college library and make a note of any warnings to students about making copies of published material.

2   Nominate **one** person from your group to write to the Newspaper Licensing Agency (or to phone) to ask for a copy of the booklet advertised in Figure 14.7.

Stop!

Are you about to break the law by copying from this newspaper?

Under the Copyright, Designs and Patents Act 1988, except for single copies for research or private study, **it is unlawful to reproduce articles from newspapers without permission**. To enable you to make copies legally, your organisation must get a licence from the Newspaper Licensing Agency - set up to help you comply with the law quickly and easily.

You will find full details of the licensing scheme and an application form in a **FREE** booklet. For your copy, simply return the coupon below to: Newspaper Licensing Agency, 17 Lyons Crescent, Tonbridge, Kent TN9 1EX or phone 01732 360333 or fax 01732 360777

NLA
NEWSPAPER
LICENSING
AGENCY

- -

Please send me details of how my organisation can copy newspaper articles legally.

Name (Mr/Mrs/Ms)..

Job Title..

Company Name...

Address...

....

....Postcode.........................

Tel...Fax................................

Nature of Business...

Figure 14.7 Information from the Newspaper Licensing Agency

3   You have been appointed as administrator in an office where no one seems to have any appreciation at all about copyright legislation. Write a memo to all staff, summarising the main points of the Copyright Act and emphasising its importance.

The rights and wrongs of copyright

Until recently, copyright laws covered a creative work for 50 years after the death of the author. Today, because of an EU directive, this protection has increased to 70 years. This means that the copyright on this book, if the author lived for another 40 years, would not elapse until 2107! This is despite the fact that by then, everything it contained would be completely out of date!

The situation is even more ludicrous in relation to computer software – which is also covered by the same ruling – yet can be obsolete within six months! There has also been no consideration that the growth of the Internet, for instance, is increasing the amount of information which is held in the public domain. This may mean hundreds of test cases in the future as authors, writers and software creators argue about whether information accessed on the Net is infringing copyright on their own creations.

One vulnerable group is the manufacturers of 'shareware' where prospective customers are invited to download and try out the software programs and to send a registration fee to the author if they wish to continue using it. This way they become entitled to support and upgrade information. There was a recent outcry when CompuServe tried to introduce a new clause into its agreements allowing it to adapt and modify any software or files which are on its system. Shareware manufacturers considered this would infringe copyright and CompuServe has since backed down. However, experts consider that the growth of the Internet could exert considerable pressure in the future as the creators vie with the public to determine their rights of access and usage.

The finishing touches

Whilst this chapter has covered a wide range of processes and equipment related to document production, there are some final considerations for you to think about. These involve the finishing touches you can add to documents to give them a professional look which will impress even the most discerning of bosses and customers!

Paper-based documents

Multipage documents are usually stapled for internal use but are better bound if they are being used in formal presentations.

Thermal binders use a heat process which attaches the papers to the cover by melting glue down the spine and attaching the edge of each paper to it. Covers are available in a range of sizes and widths, colours and designs.

High-quality printed covers are available at very reasonable rates to customise the presentation.

Comb binders can also handle a variety of document widths and are more sturdy for very bulky documents. Using this system a metal or plastic comb is inserted through the spine of the documents. This system also enables even very large documents to be opened out flat on the desk. Special presentation covers can also be purchased for use with these systems.

Laminating machines can be used to cover IDs, documents and binders with a plastic film. They are ideal for valuable papers, menus and documents such as instruction sheets which are handled frequently. Laminators can be purchased which will cover papers up to A3 size for signs, charts or even street plans.

Two final points. Never try to staple very thick documents with an ordinary stapler – it simply cannot cope. Photocopier stapling facilities may be usable off-line, otherwise you will need to buy a heavy-duty stapler for the job. Secondly, never forget that bound documents need wide margins at the inside edges – otherwise you will cut off the edge of the text.

Multimedia presentations

These presentations are a mix of sound and graphics using computer-based presentation and video. They are the method used by businesses to make professional presentations both in-house and to clients. Computer packages such as Powerpoint have been designed to assist with this process. The type of equipment which may be available or used for such a presentation includes a

- rear projection screen

- video projector

- slide projector

- VHS recorder and large screen TV

- OHP foil feeder into which OHP masters are placed and fed through at the touch of a button.

These are in addition to OHP screens, flipcharts and whiteboards.

A later innovation is the electronic copyboard where notes can be made – either at the time or in advance. The copyboard can rotate to show a clean surface and presentation material can be unveiled one step at a time if required. Probably the most useful feature is that of 'print-out on demand'. Notes made on the copyboard can be printed out at the touch of a button so that all delegates receive a hard copy at the end of the presentation.

If your company does not have these facilities in-house (and few small firms do), then most large hotels which offer conference and seminar facilities will provide them on request.

Discussion point

1   As a group, decide upon the process (including software) and equipment you would use to produce each of the following if you were employed by a large organisation with a wide range of equipment and facilities.

Then discuss how you would modify your ideas if you were employed by a small firm with only a modest computer system and copier but with a helpful (though quite expensive) print shop around the corner.

a   Handouts for your class prepared by your tutor.
b   A health and safety booklet for the use of all new employees.
c   A report giving the latest sales figures and trends for presentation to the board of directors.
d   A 40-page business proposal for a new contract which includes detailed calculations.
e   A newsletter for all staff.
f   A sales presentation to be made to a potential new customer.
g   A price list for customers which includes illustrations of some new products.
h   A mail-shot to existing customers telling them of bargain discounts.

2   If you were employed by **each** of the following small organisations, which type(s) of software and equipment would you recommend to be bought to produce the items below?

a   An estate agent who wishes to produce leaflets showing an illustration of the property for sale together with a description and a floor plan with measurements.
b   An interior designer who wishes to produce advertising material showing how a room can look with effective colour coordination.
c   An employment agency which wants to produce up-market and attractive job advertisements for its window display.
d   A financial adviser who wishes to produce
    i   an attractive sales leaflet showing his or her services and the trends of current investments
    ii   regular information bulletins on investments for clients
    iii projected calculations on the return from different types of investment.

Revision practice

Short-answer questions

1 State four principles of effective communication.

2 State three reasons why the tone and style of a document is important.

3 Identify three differences between a memorandum and a letter.

4 Give six reasons why letters may be sent in business.

5 Clearly differentiate between a bar chart, a line graph and a pie chart.

6 Identify three occasions when graphics should be included in business documents.

7 Identify three advantages of using an integrated computer system.

8 Explain four methods of enhancement you could use effectively on a business document prepared on computer.

9 Identify four precautions you would take to protect data stored on your computer system.

10 State four features found on most modern photocopying machines.

Essay questions

1 You have been asked to produce the text for a booklet about your organisation which will be sent to all your customers. The first section is a brief introduction to the organisation and its history, the second gives details of customer service staff, the third gives details of the services offered.

The text will then go to the Graphics Design Department of your organisation before being printed in-house.

   a Explain the advantages of preparing the text on a modern word-processing system.

   b What graphics would you recommend as suitable for inclusion in each section?

   c What type of equipment would you consider should be available in an organisation for such a booklet to be produced in-house, rather than sent to a professional printer?

2 There is considerable concern in your organisation about the security of expensive computer systems and the data held on them. Draft out an information sheet for staff which will give guidance on good practice to minimise damage or loss to both hardware and software.

3 Identify the advantages to an organisation of installing modern computer systems and up-to-date printing and copying equipment.

4 Identify and give a brief explanation of
   a three types of internal communications, and
   b three types of external communications

   which would be used by an administrator or secretary during an average working day.

5 Your employer, Peter Hudson, is concerned about the standard of written English of many young people and wants to devise some way of testing these skills at interview. He has asked you to send him a memo in which you recommend
   a the type of questions which could be given at interview to check if a junior employee has the basic skills for employment in an office
   b the additional skills which should be possessed by applicants for secretarial and administrative positions – and suggest how these, too, could be assessed at interview.

Case study
You are employed as administrator in the fund-raising office of a large children's hospital in your area. You recently attended a meeting on fund-raising activities where the following points were agreed.

- Fund-raising must be undertaken more professionally given the number of charities competing for funds.
- The hospital should introoduce an 'angel scheme' and appeal to local people to become members by paying a minimum subscription of £10 per year. In return each person would receive a four-page newsletter on hospital activities and successes three times a year.
- 'Little angels' could be recruited, who would be asked to give a minimum of £1 a year from their spending money. This could be targeted at local schools. A member of staff would visit the school to give a brief presentation about the scheme and there would also be the offer of members of staff visiting to give talks about health, exercise and diet.
- The increased money would be used to buy new scanning equipment and to provide accommodation for parents who wished to stay with very sick children.
- Costs would have to be kept down but, at the same time, it would be cost effective to invest in a new computer system and printing/copying facilities to enable the newsletters to be prepared in-house – preferably in colour.

Following the meeting you have been asked to undertake the following tasks.

1   Draft a circular letter, to be sent to all local primary and secondary schools, informing them of the Little Angel scheme and saying a member of staff will contact them shortly to discuss the project further. You are obviously expected to promote the scheme as much as possible.

2   Investigate the cost of buying a modern computer system together with software which will enable letters to be produced, a list of Angels and Little Angel members to be kept and incoming and outgoing expenditure to be recorded and analysed. In addition, ascertain the cost of purchasing a colour printer and colour photocopier.

    Present all the costs and benefits clearly in a report, together with your recommendations.

3   In a memo, suggest a procedure which should be implemented to reduce wastage of photocopied documents. It has been suggested that a sensible first step would be to find out the various ways in which modern photocopiers incorporate facilities for checking usage by individuals and then to build on this information in devising your procedure.

4   Assuming that the equipment is purchased, the letters sent and the project is 'up and running', give details of the action you would take if
    a   you received a letter of complaint from one headteacher saying that young children should not be targeted in this way – particularly as many of his young pupils came from very deprived backgrounds themselves and did not receive any spending money
    b   you find a junior member of staff has included an extract from a national newspaper in the next draft of the newsletter
    c   the fund-raising manager asked you to investigate how he could use modern technology to improve the quality of his presentations to schools and other groups.

● Relating to others

The previous sections have been designed to help you to cope with the tasks with which you will be involved when you start work. However, unless you work in a very unusual type of enterprise, it is likely that you will be trying to accomplish these tasks alongside other people. Some of these will be helpful, friendly and cooperative. Others will not. Whilst you may be able to choose your friends, you cannot choose the people you work with – at the same time you are paid not only to tolerate them but also to work with them positively and to get the best out of them. This may mean asking people to undertake specific tasks – and ensuring they do them happily, which is far more difficult!

'People skills' or 'personnel management' as this area is often called, can be among the hardest skills to acquire. Many highly paid executives fall at this hurdle. They may be excellent at achieving their own goals, but much less effective at motivating other people and building a good team. However, this attribute is invaluable in achieving results – both for yourself and for your organisation. You know yourself how easy it is to help someone whom you admire and who will always lend *you* a hand when you have a problem. You know, too, how you feel if someone lets you down, is sarcastic, two-faced or constantly moody and difficult to cope with.

The aim of this section is to examine the strategies you can use in your own career to develop constructive working relationships so that you can obtain the cooperation of those with whom you work – and to cope when you meet someone who is difficult to handle.

The theoretical aspects of motivation and leadership are covered in the companion book, *Business for Advanced Secretarial Students.* This section covers the practicalities of working with other people both inside and outside the organisation. It focuses on developing and maintaining working relationships, team-building, dealing with other people in meetings and at interviews.

It also concentrates on the secretary/administrator's role when making arrangements which frequently involve external contacts – customers, clients and others. These may include making outward or inward travel arrangements, organising hospitality and social events, arranging conferences and seminars. The public relations (PR) role of the administrator or secretary is one which becomes more important as his or her career progresses and there is greater involvement with important outside contacts.

Working relationships

15

● Introduction

In your professional life you will form working relationships with everyone with whom you come into contact as part of your job. This is likely to involve a wide range of people – both within and outside the organisation. An important aspect of your ability to succeed at work will be the *type* of relationships you form with each person as *their* perception of you will also be important for several reasons.

Firstly, it is quite natural that you will want your colleagues to like and accept you as a member of the group. Secondly, you will want your boss to consider you a hard and efficient worker, particularly if you are hoping that he or she will help you to advance in your career. Thirdly, you would be unusual if you did not want those outside the organisation to respect you as a professional and to speak about you in glowing terms – as someone who can get things done and is always pleasant and helpful.

An important aspect of having a professional relationship with someone, rather than a personal one, means that your individual views and feelings are secondary to getting the job done without rancour or ill-feeling. When you deal with any external contacts in business – such as customers or suppliers, you are representing the organisation rather than yourself. This should therefore influence the way in which you speak and react to them.

Quite obviously, the situation is rather different with your office colleagues! However, there should always be a slight difference in your behaviour at work, which prevents you from indulging in certain types of conduct which may be acceptable to (or at least tolerated by!) your close friends and family. As an example, you are paid to be pleasant and agreeable, no matter how you feel or how late you went to bed last night! This will be easier with some colleagues than others. There may be some people to whom you take a personal dislike or with whom you find it difficult to relate. Again, however, you are not paid to indulge your personal feelings. In addition, it is very rare that a person has *no* good points – and it may be up to you to find them!

Your contacts at work can be divided into different categories.

* **Within the organisation** – your internal contacts will include your superiors, those who are at the same level as yourself (your peer group) and those who are below you. At the start of your career it is usual to find that most people are senior to you in the organisation structure but, over time, this is likely to change.

  Some of your relationships at work will be formally recognised – you will operate as a member of different working groups or teams. Other relationships may be more informal – contacts made as a result of a common interest or friendship. In addition, you will deal with your contacts in both formal and informal environments – from an interview or committee meeting to the Christmas party!

- **Outside the organisation** – your external contacts will include those who are existing or potential customers and those who are existing or potential suppliers. This includes those who work for organisations which provide a service to you in any way – from the photocopier mechanic to the travel agent. In addition, there may be other contacts you make on a more fleeting basis – to obtain or exchange information, for instance.

  You may also be expected to represent your organisation at external events or to act as host at a company event for external clients. At executive secretary/PA level you may be expected to meet, liaise with or even entertain clients in your boss's absence.

● Internal contacts

Your range of contacts at work may include the following.

- **Senior executives** – from the managing director or chief executive to other managers or directors. With the exception of your own line manager, it is unlikely that you will have much contact with this level of personnel – unless you work in a very small organisation.

- **Senior colleagues** – those who have worked in the organisation for some time and/or hold positions senior to your own, even if they are not in a management position. In your own area your contact with this group may be frequent. As a newcomer you would be expected to respect their position and experience, particularly if they are much older than you. In many ways, you have to 'earn your stripes' with this group of people and cannot rush the process.

- **Other colleagues** at the same level as yourself. You are likely to relate most closely to this group as they are likely to 'experience' the world of work very much as you do – and this will create a natural bond. However, if there is a large group, then you may find that you have a natural affinity towards some people more than others – and, if you are sensible, you will have to guard against letting this show.

- **Subordinates or juniors** – whether or not you have any direct control over them. To this group you should be a **role model** – someone who shows them how they should behave. You will find this easier if you do not try to 'belong' to their group and always treat them with fairness and impartiality. If you were ever in a position of having to reprimand a junior member of staff, you would find this difficult if you had become too friendly.

- **Other contacts** – those who are not your direct colleagues but with whom you come into contact regularly, either to seek their cooperation or because they have some reason to seek yours, such as someone who works in another department. In some cases you may find that some of these people have professional power over you. An example would be a security guard who can insist you follow certain rules and procedures whether you like it or not or the canteen manageress whose cooperation in agreeing to provide refreshments at the last minute can be invaluable if important visitors arrive unexpectedly!

A word of warning. Remember that all people are different – there are therefore inherent difficulties in putting people into groups as there will always be exceptions. You may, therefore, find yourself in the fortunate position where you are almost 'adopted' by kindly senior colleagues or have a boss who has a regard for you and is concerned about your welfare. However, do not count on this throughout your career!

● External contacts

Customers are the lifeblood of all organisations. Without them the organisation will go out of business. However, the range of customers with whom you may deal can vary considerably – depending upon your organisation and the job you carry out. At one extreme, you may be dealing in a large retail organisation with an elderly person, at another you may be in contact with a senior director of a multinational company. Whilst you should obviously adapt your behaviour to that which is particularly appropriate to individual customers, some general rules apply – such as politeness, courtesy, efficiency and honesty (with diplomacy!).

However, you are likely to find that private customers will expect a less formal response than business customers and long-standing customers will expect you to remember who they are (and know their names!) and there will be more informality with the relationship than when you are dealing with new customers.

Suppliers, on the other hand, are obviously interested in pleasing you as your organisation is their customer. However, this does not mean that you should develop a reputation as someone who cannot be bothered to help them or who expects them to drop everything to come to your assistance as and when required! You are far more likely to obtain their help and assistance quickly if you have always been helpful and courteous to them!

Most organisations recognise that they are likely to obtain better service from their suppliers if they work with them and develop a positive relationship rather than 'shop around' and prove they do not really need them! However, the policies of your organisation may change – therefore it is sensible if you always keep your relationship with any suppliers on a professional and relatively formal basis in case, through circumstances beyond your control, you are suddenly expected to stop dealing with them. Remember too, that you should *never* accept any type of inducement (financial or otherwise) for placing an order.

Miscellaneous contacts include anyone else with whom you make contact in the course of your job. This could be the librarian in the local reference library, a trade union official, a member of the emergency services or someone in a government department. It might even be the shareholders of your company or a local commercial organisation – from a dry-cleaning firm to a car-hire company, from a locksmith to a florist. Frequently, you may be in the position of trying to obtain information or guidance. Generally, your contact with this type of person will be temporary and for a specific purpose. However, try to make sure that he or she will remember you positively – if only because you never know when you may wish to contact that person again!

Note: External contacts and the PR role of the secretary/administrator are covered in chapter 17.

● Establishing a working relationship

There are some fundamental attributes which will always make one person more approachable than another. These include

- a pleasant and helpful disposition

- a positive attitude

- an air of efficiency and purpose

- an open and friendly personality

- a sympathetic nature

- a tactful and sensitive approach.

Whilst this may seem a tall order, it is almost second-nature for us to try to seek out people with these characteristics rather than someone who is uninterested, negative or aggressive.

However, in any job you will find that there are limits within which you are allowed to operate. These will probably be specifically designed in relation to external contacts to protect both you and your organisation. They will consist of systems and procedures which you must follow and boundaries within which you are allowed to operate. A typical example concerns credit. You may not be allowed to offer further credit to a customer who has not paid a debt, regardless of whether you like the customer or not! Equally, you may be severely constrained as to the value of orders you can place without your boss's authority. There are likely to be specified procedures for dealing with visitors and handling customer complaints. If you value these as useful parameters rather than irritating constraints, you will be less likely to become annoyed by them – and find fewer reasons to challenge them!

The limits of your dealings with internal contacts will be less prescribed. In many ways it is in this arena that you are left more to your own devices, though your ability to form a constructive working relationship with a wide variety of people can have definite benefits. Quite apart from the fact that getting along with people improves the quality of life generally, the cooperation of some individuals will be essential if you are to operate effectively. You may think that if you are always pleasant and helpful people will always be the same to you. Unfortunately, this is not always true. Understanding why this problem occurs is often a first step towards developing greater insight into the whole subject of human and working relationships.

Identifying your contacts

There are various ways in which you can identify and classify the groups of people with whom you work.

- **By formal groupings** – generally, you will see more of people if you are grouped with them formally in some way, eg
  - you work in the same office, unit or department
  - you are part of the same cross-organisational group, such as a quality group, equal opportunities group or the health and safety committee (see also page 356)
  - you are part of the same team, which may have been formed for a particular purpose (see page 357)
  - you have the same boss.

- **By geographical closeness** – you are apt to have more frequent contact with people who work in and around your office than with those at the other end of the building or on a different site.

- **By power and influence** – this involves understanding the ability of different individuals to influence your own effectiveness, quality of life or job content.

Whilst the ideal is to try to get on with everyone, this is normally impossible all the time. However, you can attach degrees of importance to people for your own peace of mind. It is obviously more critical, for instance, that you develop a positive working relationship with someone whom you see constantly and whose cooperation you need on a day-to-day basis rather than someone whom you only see once a month and whom you can bypass easily if he or she is awkward or difficult.

One technique for identifying the people who are the most important to you is to work out your own role set. This can be done for both internal and external contacts.

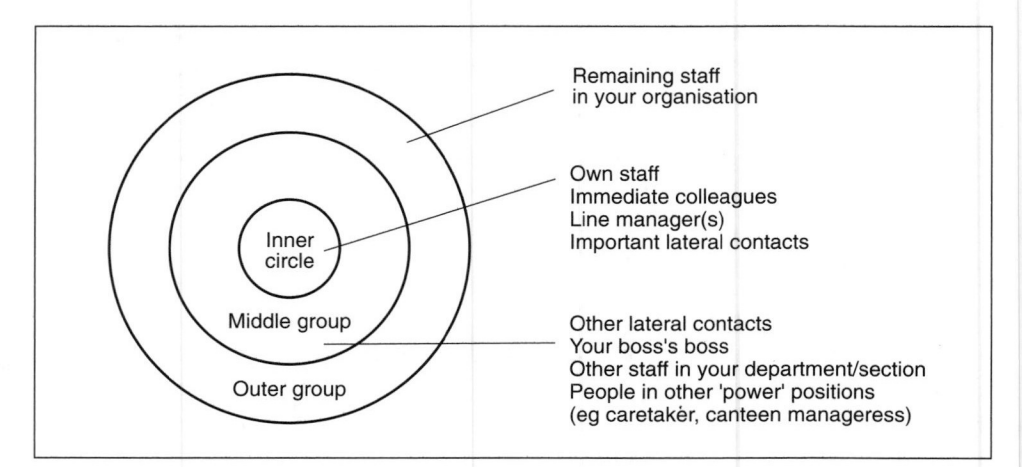

Figure 15.1 Groupings of colleagues

Figure 15.1 shows the different internal contacts of Tina Watson, an office administrator. She has divided these groups into

- an inner circle with whom she deals daily

- a middle group who are important to her, because she needs their cooperation

- an outer group of people with whom she only has distant contact.

In Figure 15.2 she has expanded this idea by identifying her actual role set. This is her inner circle and the importance of each person she deals with is indicated by the different-sized circles. The closeness with which she works with them is indicated by the length of the lines.

Tina has also taken the idea one stage further. She has put a tick in the circle of everyone she finds easy to deal with and a cross in the circle of those she does not.

Tina now decides to analyse her relationships with the people in her role set to see if she can improve her working relationships in any way. She has identified problems with three individuals.

a Kenny, the head of the Central Reprographics unit, is terse and abrupt with her and frequently tells her urgent work cannot be done in time when she thinks it could.

b Gerry, the assistant office manager, is perpetually disorganised, rarely gives Tina information when she needs it and, she suspects, often criticises her behind her back to the office manager.

c Julia, the assistant administrator, who Tina knows wanted her own job but failed to gain promotion.

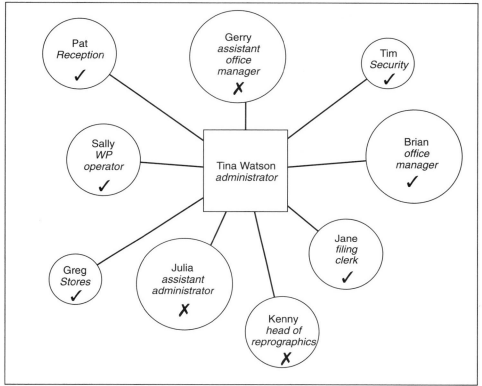

Figure 15.2 Tina's role set

Discussion point

As a group, discuss with your tutor

a   the *reasons* why you think each person may be antagonistic to Tina
b   the *degree* to which you think it is Tina herself who might be a problem – or whether you think anyone doing her job may have similar difficulties
c   whether you consider Tina can do anything to improve matters.

Be prepared to revise and review your thoughts after you have read the next few pages!

Could your group sing for its supper?

If you think that being part of a company football or netball team is a waste of time and nothing to do with work, then you are wrong! Many organisations actively promote and support this type of activity to help people to get along together better.

In any organisation you will find **informal groups** in operation – consisting of people who meet because of a common interest or personal relationship. On Tuesday night one group may go to aerobics, on Friday another group always lunches together and so on. Such groups are useful because they encourage an exchange of views and communication across the organisation. They provide peer support, friendship and security and allow employees to discuss and solve both work-related and personal problems. The only worry for managers is if the values of the group go against those of the organisation as a whole.

For that reason, the organisation may encourage groups which can support and further the interests of the organisation. In the United States, a popular way of doing this is to form a company choir or chorus. 3M, a large American corporation, has a chorus which travels all over the country performing at different events. The management considers this ideal for enabling all ranks of employees to mix together and make friends. In Britain, even more popular are sports teams – including golf, netball, darts and football.

● Work roles and responsibilities

Every person employed by an organisation has a formal job role which determines the jobs and tasks they are expected to perform. The content of the job is usually specified in the job description and this alone starts to determine the expectations of other people. You would expect a receptionist to deal with visitors in a pleasant way, a manager to organise and control the work of a department, the caretaker to keep the building secure and clean and so on. There will obviously be problems if someone is employed in a job and fails to carry out his or her tasks in a satisfactory way. In some cases this can result in counselling if someone cannot cope with the job, or disciplinary action if the failure was deliberate.

The job content and responsibilities of each person will determine his or her priorities in relation to the work which must be done. Unless you *know* (or at least appreciate) these priorities, it is impossible to try to work out how these can link (or conflict) with your own.

Work roles and expectations

The job a person is appointed to do also affects that individual's work roles. A role relates to the set of activities a person is expected to carry out and the type of behaviour which is expected of him or her. For instance, managers would be expected to be good at representing their staff, motivating team members and passing on information. If you consider all managers should be good at making decisions, then you will be disappointed if your own boss is not competent in this area – because your boss will not be carrying out the management role in the way you expected. Similarly, if your boss expects all administrators/secretaries to be neat and tidy, he or she will be disappointed if your desk is always in a mess.

Misconceptions and disagreements about role can lead to various problems – often known as **role conflict.**

Role conflict

Role conflict is important because it is a key factor in determining stress at work. It can result in minor ailments, various illnesses and days lost through absenteeism.

- **Role ambiguity** occurs when you are not sure what you are supposed to do or why. This may be because no one has told you what is expected of you. In this case you may try to please but never succeed because you are not certain what type of behaviour is acceptable and what is not.

- **Role incompatibility** is very common and often experienced by administrators or secretaries who have more than one boss. In this case they could easily be given conflicting or even contradictory requests or instructions. Another example would be instructions from the boss which the administrator knows will be unpopular with staff. In this case you cannot be loyal to both, so there is obvious conflict.

- **Role overload** occurs when you have too many people to please and all have different expectations. This is a game no one can win. Bear in mind that this is different from work overload when you simply have too much to do.

- **Role underload** means that your expectations about your role are not being fulfilled. This could be because you see yourself as capable of taking on far more responsibility than you are being given.

The psychological contract

The expectations of people at work come together in what is often termed **the psychological contract.** This is an unspoken agreement about what is acceptable and what is not. You will have a psychological contract with each person with whom you work. If either of you breach this contract, then the relationship can deteriorate rapidly. For instance, if you had an agreement with a colleague that you would both help each other out when one of you is very busy, so you could both leave on time, this agreement would probably work very well. If, however, the next time you are overloaded, your colleague refused to help you for no apparent good reason, you would most likely withdraw your own help when your colleague is next busy. In other words, you have redefined the terms of your unspoken agreement.

Discussion point

As a group, and with your tutor, discuss your perception of the 'role' of tutor and student.

1   How does this perception influence the expectations each has of the other's behaviour?

2   What *additional* roles might a student expect of a tutor besides being a teacher of knowledge/someone who imparts information?

3   Can you think of any occasions when a tutor's different roles may conflict in some way?

● Working relationships – the reality

No matter how much you study people's job descriptions or think about their job role, this will never totally explain people's behaviour. This is because, in the real world, various factors complicate the situation and result in

• people not behaving as you would expect

• people appearing to have illogical or irrational reactions to situations and events – or making what appear to be unreasonable demands on others

• some people appearing to have undue influence over others – for a variety of reasons.

The problem is that you have to learn to cope with people as they are, not as you wish they would be! Saying 'someone must change' because you want him or her to do so is normally useless. People can adapt their behaviour but cannot usually undergo a complete change of personality to suit you. Therefore, any changes must start with you, rather than them!

Perceptions and self-fulfilling prophecy

Our perceptions about particular people are based on several factors including

• our personal history and experience

• people and situations we have met before

- our beliefs, values and attitudes

- our own confidence and inner security

- our personal history of that person.

All these will colour our view of someone and once we have 'accepted' that view, then we will struggle to change it. Indeed, we will actually seek to find ways of reinforcing our views rather than accept evidence which contradicts our opinion. You will find this, for instance, if you meet someone who is sexist or racist. No matter how much evidence you provide to the contrary, a person who has set his or her mind against a group of people will always use the arguments which substantiate those views. This is sometimes called a **self-fulfilling prophecy.** It might also mean that individuals may have formed an opinion about you before they have even met you – if you fall into a group of people about whom they hold fixed views.

For instance, if a manager considers all young people are lazy and have little interest in work, then he or she will have low expectations, usually give them routine work (which they will find boring) and look for mistakes to criticise. Conversely, a manager who considers that young people are generally keen to learn will work hard to motivate them and challenge them to do their best. The behaviour of each manager is therefore likely to bring about the very results he or she expected – which will reinforce his or her initial beliefs and continue to reinforce that behaviour.

Reality shock syndrome

This is a term devised by an American writer, Douglas Hall, to describe the reaction of many people at work when they discover that there is a difference between the reality of the workplace and their initial high expectations. This can affect behaviour in several ways.

For instance, a new member of staff may be keen and eager to please, but then finds after several years of hard work that he or she is constantly passed over for promotion. A young manager may be disappointed because he or she is rarely given much responsibility and the job is not all it was made out to be.

People react differently when faced with problems and difficulties in their career. Those who are rewarded for their hard work usually continue to be loyal to the organisation and to support its aims and objectives. Those who have not may rebel – they may become bitter and difficult to work with or voluntarily leave to work elsewhere. Some will be selective about those parts of the organisation's aims and values they agree with and accept and those which they reject. In effect, they have redefined their psychological contract with the organisation.

Given that you do not know everybody's history you cannot therefore make judgements on what will appear to be logical and sensible reactions to *them*.

Operational style and values

Organisations vary in their culture and values; managers vary in their styles. The two together can influence the behaviour of staff in an organisation. In one company, for instance, there may be an ethos where people work together, are open about their feelings and are friendly and helpful. In another, staff may be expected to be competitive, to obey orders without question, to cover up for the boss if there is a problem. All these factors will influence the way in which people relate to one another.

Power and influence

Power is the ability to make decisions about work and people – and is given to those who hold responsible positions in the organisation. However, power and influence are different. A person may not be powerful, but may be very influential – the managing director's PA, for instance, may have little formal power but tremendous influence. If you work alongside the chairman's niece, then you are likely to find out very quickly the difference between power and influence – and this would doubtless affect what you said and did in her presence!

In addition, in any organisation you will find that a number of people have relationships with one another which can affect the balance of power and influence in an organisation. These relationships can occur for a variety of reasons, including

*   historical links, eg the marketing manager and the managing director went to university together

*   social links, eg the administration manager's sister is married to a member of the technical support team

*   current priorities, eg the managing director is keen to cut costs and has hired a whizz-kid accountant who, although disliked by the rest of the staff, is telling the managing director what he wants to hear and so is very highly regarded.

Do you say what you mean or mean what you say?

Chris Argyris, a sociologist, identified a contrary characteristic in many people. He found that many people say one thing but mean another. You may have suspected this for years, but never knew that anyone had formally studied it!

He called what people say their 'espoused theory'. This is what they say they believe in. However, their 'theory in use' is their *real* belief which influences their actual behaviour. This explains why parents may argue that

freedom for young people is essential if they are to grow up as responsible adults, at the same time as they enforce a strict curfew on the time their own offspring have to be in each night!

At work, your boss's or colleague's theory in use may be less obvious. However, Argyris' findings will explain why your boss may agree that you can leave early one night despite the fact that there is some important work to complete – and then be annoyed with you the following day for doing so!

● Building constructive relationships

You may think that with all the complicating factors at work, it is impossible to build or foster good working relationships. However, you would be wrong! The aim of everything you have read so far is to help you to appreciate that people have *reasons* for behaving in the way they do. Whilst these reasons may be unknown, irrelevant or unimportant to you, they are certainly not to the individuals concerned! Understanding that they exist, even if you cannot change them, should help you to tolerate a broader range of behaviour than you otherwise might, to make allowances for how they act and to develop strategies for coping with them.

A good starting point for building a constructive relationship is to review your own expectations about other people and to check that these are reasonably realistic! Then think about the traits in other people which bring out a positive response in you – and decide to what degree you would like to work with yourself! Finally, use the information you have read so far to identify all the reasons people have for behaving in ways which may seem strange or unreasonable.

Discussion point

As a group, carry out each of the following tasks.

1   Identify 20 attributes which you consider would make someone
    a   a good colleague
    b   a good manager.

    Then rank these in order of importance.

2   Work through the hints and tips shown below and discuss them
    with your tutor. Try to identify those areas which you would find
    particularly difficult.

3   Turn back to page 344 where Tina listed the problems she was
    having with three of her colleagues. Identify as many reasons as you
    can *why* each person might be acting in that way. What suggestions
    could you make to Tina to improve each situation?

Hints and tips on building and maintaining constructive relationships

Although there is no infallible guide for dealing with everyone, the following
lists may give you some ideas of the main areas on which to concentrate so
at least *you* can be considered a great person to work with!

With all your contacts

1   Remember that 'please' and 'thank you' cost you nothing, yet can make
    all the difference.

2   Do not make excuses if something goes wrong – admit your mistakes.
    You would not be human if you did not make any. Do not be
    aggressively defensive, do not blame other people but do not grovel
    either. Simply admit the error, apologise and offer to help put it right.

3   Do not boast about your achievements – particularly when things are
    not going well for everyone else.

4   Make a habit of looking pleasant – do not frown or glare at people (even
    unintentionally when they interrupt you!).

5   Do not issue orders when you should be making requests.

6   Do not interrupt people to put forward your point of view.

7   Put tact and diplomacy at the top of your list.

8   Learn to keep a secret

9   Never take credit for anyone else's idea.

10 Never talk about individuals behind their backs.

11 Learn the difference between assertion (putting forward your point of view) and aggression (attacking other people to defend yourself). If you are right, why be aggressive?

12 Help new staff (or the latest temp) to fit in. Check they know where to find the cloakroom, toilet and coffee machine. Invite them for a sandwich at lunchtime. Do not save up all the nastiest jobs for them to do.

13 Keep an eye on those you work with for serious signs of stress – increase in irritability, no sense of humour, violent mood swings, poor concentration, even heavy drinking or workaholism. Recognise professional help is required if the situation is serious and find out what stress counselling is available.

14 Make time to listen when someone needs it.

15 Never make promises you cannot keep.

16 Do not gossip, spread rumours, speculate or tell lies.

17 Learn to spot hidden agendas. This is the hidden motive behind the actions and intentions of many people.

18 Do not expect to get your own way all the time – no general won every battle! Be prepared to lose the odd battle to win the war – in other words, identify what you *really* want to achieve and be prepared to lose something in order to achieve it.

19 Be unswervingly loyal – even when it is difficult.

20 Be consistent and even-tempered. Moody people are always kept at arm's length.

With your boss

1 Make his or her priorities *your* priorities.

2 Do not be an alarmist and magnify problems and disasters, and do not offload your problems – always offer solutions. See every problem as a potential opportunity.

3 Take a positive attitude when times are tough – and stay cheerful (but do not overdo it!).

4 Try to develop a balanced relationship – not 'crawling' or obsequious but giving due respect for seniority and status.

5 Separate facts from opinions. State the facts, only add your opinions if asked to do so.

6 Be prepared to be constantly interrupted.

7   Do not take it personally if your boss is having a bad day or arrives in a terrible mood. For all you know he or she could have personal problems.

8   Learn to pick your time.

9   Learn how to summarise and impart important information quickly.

10 Learn to tolerate his or her blind spots and work round them. If your boss is convinced a member of staff is invaluable and you think otherwise, do not waste your time trying to change your boss's attitude.

With your colleagues

1   Allow for their strengths, weaknesses, individual personality traits and personal histories and backgrounds.

2   Accept people for what they are, not for what you would like them to be.

3   Remember that their priorities may not be the same as yours – in other words, they will be more interested in getting their own job done than yours – because that is what they are judged on.

4   Do not interrupt them with inessentials when they are busy.

5   Offer to roll up your sleeves and help when a crisis occurs or there is a lot to get through.

6   Do not expect instant action to last-minute requests.

7   Repay favours.

8   Give individuals space and time if they do not accept you easily. Do not force yourself upon them. Only consult them on business matters, stay polite, courteous and calm.

9   Learn to tolerate someone you do not like. Avoid open conflict. Try to find some kind of common interest (a film, music). Even working with someone creates a common interest over time.

10 Expect other people to have different points of view to yours. Learn to live with these, even if you do not agree.

With your subordinates

1   Be firm but fair.

2   Guard against having favourites.

3   Praise and reward at least as much as you find fault.

4   Criticise constructively, not to put someone down. This means helping someone to see how something could be done better.

5   Avoid getting at them because someone is getting at you.

6   Learn when to give support and when to stand back. Encourage initiative.

7   Make it clear what you want, how it should be done and the standards you expect.

8   Do not talk down to them.

9   Give reasons for what you want them to do. The more logical the reason, the better!

10   Be consistent in what you do, say and in your behaviour so they will do what you ask because they want to please you, not because they fear you.

● Building bridges – a word to the wise!

A key aspect in the formation of any type of working relationship is not to rush things! It can be an easy matter, especially as a new employee, to join an organisation full of enthusiasm and expect everyone to be delighted to see you. Whilst such enthusiasm should be encouraged, unfortunately this approach is a little naive and you might find you have several disappointments.

Remember that all the people you meet already know each other, have their own perceptions of the organisation and their boss (true or false, but true to them!) and have lots of personal 'baggage' which will affect their attitude and their views. You cannot hope to be accepted immediately, except on face value. Develop coping skills as follows.

- Remain the outsider until you have been accepted as one of the group. This will take less time with some people than others.

- Keep your own counsel. Do not confide in anyone at the outset unless you are sure you can trust that person.

- Listen to everything you hear but remember that it is each person's perception you are hearing – which may not be the same as someone else's, and both may be different from yours!

- Accept gestures and offers of friendship and assistance – but do not depend on these people for lifelong support.

- Make a note of those approaches you find helpful and those which you do not – and vow to help other new staff who follow you by putting into practice everything you have learned!

- Find a mentor – someone who you can trust and in whom you can confide – who will help you over the hurdles of the first few weeks and help you to understand why you are having problems with certain people.

- If possible, avoid those who make your life a misery. In a large organisation it is unrealistic to expect to get on well with every single person all the time.

● Groups and teams

More jobs today than ever before insist that applicants must be 'good team players' or 'able to work as a member of a team' or 'appreciate the value of team working'. What are teams? How do they differ from groups? How can you help to build a team, foster team working and give support to your own team?

Working groups

You have already seen that you are likely to be a member of various formal and informal groups. A group of people is any set of people which has common characteristics – and the first group to which anyone belongs is usually the family. In the same way, you can group people by age, gender, race, marital status or in dozens of other ways.

Working groups have some common characteristics.

- They are usually dependent on each other in some way.

- They have a reason for being together.

- Each member knows he or she is part of the group.

- Different members of the group will undertake different roles or take on different responsibilities.

- There is usually an assigned group leader.

Groups will differ however in

- their size and strength – small groups are usually closer with the same ideals; strong groups may impose sanctions against members who do not conform with the norms of the group as a whole

- their structure – some are tightly structured and everyone has specific tasks to undertake; in others roles and relationships vary and the structure is far more flexible

- their cohesiveness – groups which are small and have been together a long time are more likely to 'stick together' if there is a challenge from outside the group

- their style – whether all members are equal or one leader predominates, whether the atmosphere is informal and relaxed or aggressive and confrontational.

Working groups are formed for a variety of reasons. Some are permanent and some are temporary. Permanent groups include all the units, sections and departments which are shown on the formal organisation chart plus any standing committees – from the board of directors downwards. Temporary groups are normally set up for a specific purpose – when the purpose has been achieved, the group is disbanded. They may be known as a working party. An example would be a group of employees who are asked to solve a particular problem.

Working teams

A team is different from a group. Whilst, like a group, it may have a common purpose, leader and identity, the team will work together to accomplish a communal goal. This then becomes the predominant factor and is more important than the needs of the individual team members. The team will therefore subjugate individual wishes to achieve the team objective – and will use the strengths of each person to the best effect to achieve this objective. This is easy to appreciate if you think of sporting teams. A football team has the objective of winning the match. No one is interested in the aspirations of individual members of the team; everyone expects the players to give their all to win. Everyone also takes for granted that the role of the manager will be to use the strengths of the team to undertake certain roles. Therefore one person is the goalkeeper, certain others are 'strikers', others play in defence and so on.

Teams have become important in business because productivity is crucial to organisational success. The belief is that the team is greater than the sum of its players – therefore collectively the team can achieve more than a set of disparate individuals. They will work together to achieve the productivity objectives set by the company and will encourage and support each other to do so. They will collaborate with one another and take joint responsibility for the success of the team and for its achievements. They will be effective because they will bring together a 'mix' of different skills and abilities so that *between them* the members of the team can cope with a variety of tasks and problems.

Team working and empowerment

Many organisations have developed teams and given them more responsibility for coping with problems and making decisions than would normally be expected. This is often called **empowerment.** The philosophy of team working even results in different job titles.

McDonald's, for instance, does not have staff or employees, it has 'crews'. If you work in your local McDonald's restaurant you will become a 'crew member' and will be expected to deal with customer enquiries, problems and difficulties, wherever possible, without referring them to your manager. TGI Friday's also has the young team philosophy. The restaurants (the name comes from Thank God It's Friday) have waiters – who form the teams – and a coach, who is team leader. Waiters are expected to handle customers and can make a range of decisions without referring them to the coach – such as giving complimentary drinks. There are no managers – the coach is all!

Team-building

Successful teams have a clearly defined purpose and an effective leader. Team-building techniques are used to turn a group into a team – to bring together people with a common interest and to help them to identify the most effective way in which their strengths and abilities can be combined to achieve a common objective.

Some organisations arrange for teams to be sent on outdoor courses where the whole team is given a range of problems to solve. This can be anything from crossing an imaginary marsh with two oil drums and two planks to getting the whole team over a high wall to agreeing which are the essential items (from a fairly wide range) to survive in the wilderness! Team-building experts are not as much interested in whether the team achieves its objective but the way in which individual members interact with each other – often known as **group dynamics.** Some members may be the most vocal – and shout down others who may have better suggestions. Others may have high-level thinking and analytical skills but be wary of putting their views forward for fear of rejection or criticism. Another group may think of good ideas but want to hoard information or resources rather than share them – preferring to have personal success and security rather than put the aims of the team first. The role of the leader is to help members of the team to identify the roles individuals should play, the roles they can play and the best way to link together. For that reason, one of the most important parts of team-building is feedback and analysis of performance.

Many people argue that it is the calibre of leadership which makes a successful team. The team leader should be responsible for removing barriers which prevent people operating effectively and give them ideas for contributing positively and imaginatively. This is not easily achieved. It implies providing practical support, sharing responsibility for performance with the team and having a clear idea of where the team should be headed. Many teams feel they are not performing adequately when the reality is that no one ever praises their achievements. In other cases, people rush to put a team together without thinking of the implications. Many people struggle to put team values first if they are used to being rewarded for individual achievement.

May the best team win?

Some organisations have decided to focus on team rewards and bonuses for performance rather than individual rewards. Rank Xerox has introduced team bonuses for about 2000 staff, management and engineering staff, linking team performance to the company goals of customer satisfaction, sales revenue and market share. Bonuses range from 15 per cent on basic pay for managers, to £1600 for engineers and £2000 for sales people. A sales person in a good team can earn an extra £160 a month.

Sun Life pays its brokers team pay, based on a customer service index. This shows how efficiently teams deal with their customer requirements in terms of speed, time and quality. The 1400 employees covered by the scheme can earn up to 10 per cent of their basic pay if they operate in a successful team.

Those who advocate team pay schemes claim it encourages team working, persuades people to share ideas, enhances flexibility and motivates ineffective workers to improve.

You work for an organisation which pays its successful teams a bonus.

1   What advantages and disadvantages can you think there might be for you as a team member?

2   What would you do if you were placed in a team which did not perform well?

3   How do you think the members of a team might react if the team was continually successful and management increased its targets for performance every year?

Discuss your answers as a group.

Maintaining constructive relationships

This chapter has focused upon the different types of people you will work with in an organisation, their aims and objectives, personal needs and differences, groupings and structures. Hints and tips have been given on establishing constructive relationships.

Over time, it is generally true that most working relationships improve. Either they improve because you genuinely like someone and enjoy working with them or because you have learned to 'rub along' with those whom you found difficult to work with in your early days. You have become used to people, they have become used to you. However, a variety of circumstances can upset the situation. Identifying these, and using your common sense to help you cope (and your new-found 'people skills') will usually help.

Examples of difficult situations can include

- having to pass on information or instructions which are unpopular with staff

- disagreements or conflicts between people you work with

- personal or work-related problems which affect the performance of one person or of the team as a whole

- having to reprimand or discipline a member of staff

- saying the wrong thing to the wrong person or at the wrong time

- being accused of something you did not do – when telling what happened would involve blaming someone else

- being asked to divulge a confidence by someone senior.

There are no golden rules to coping with such a diversity of situations. It will clearly help if you have a reputation of being someone who is honest, loyal and helpful. It will also help if you have good verbal communication skills – so that you can state your case clearly and unambiguously – and are prepared to listen to the other person's point of view.

Supporting other staff

Quite often the best way in which you can support someone else is by listening to that person. People frequently feel better for just talking about a problem – it is almost immaterial whether you can offer practical assistance.

A key attribute to being a good listener is not to jump to conclusions at the beginning of the conversation, impatiently wait for the other person to pause and then rush in with your own solution. What may be the answer for you could be catastrophic for someone else!

Be prepared to vary your approach depending on the person who is talking to you. For example, your boss may simply want to 'let off steam' to a sympathetic ear – without expecting you to offer a solution. A colleague may want to talk about a problem to someone who will listen and understand. A junior member of staff may want to talk about something of concern – and may welcome practical support and guidance about what to do. This is particularly the case if the problem is connected with work.

Adult, parent or child – which are you?

The technique of transactional analysis was developed by Eric Berne. Berne considered we all speak and act in one of three ways – either as an adult, parent or child. If we choose a way which 'crosses' the way in which someone else is speaking, this can lead to problems.

As an adult, we are either 'rational' or 'primitive'. When we are rational, we answer objectively and analytically. When we are primitive, we are following our inner feelings and vibes. As a parent, we are either 'critical' or 'nurturing' – we may patronise someone or be protective and give advice. As a child we can be 'rebellious', 'free' or 'adapted'. As a rebellious child, we want to hurt someone or hit back. As a free child, we are excitable, emotional and want our own way – we yearn for escapism. As an adapted child, we will do anything to please.

Whilst we cannot alter the way other people speak to us, we can change our own 'mode' of speaking. This helps us to choose the right way to respond in a situation.

🗨 Discussion point

1 You are about to attend your first meeting and take the minutes. You are understandably nervous. Your boss has arranged for a senior PA to accompany you on this occasion. Using Eric Berne's system of transactional analysis, what 'mode' would you consider she is in if she greeted you with *each* of the following remarks? In each case, suggest a reply which would please her – and one which would upset her! Then try to identify which mode you would be in if you made either remark.

    a 'Sit still, say nothing and leave it all to me. I do not expect you to do very well at all the first time you attend.'

    b 'Forget the meeting, they never talk sense. Did you know I'm off to New York for a week on Saturday?'

    c 'Here is the agenda, they'll use this as their guide. Mr Barnes is chairing it and you'll find he's very good.'

    d 'I'll help you if you get stuck, I'm sure you'll do very well.'

    e 'I know I'm late but blow them! They seem to think you're on the end of a string at this place.'

    f 'I know exactly how you feel. I won't give you too much information now, we can talk about it all afterwards.'

    g 'Whatever you do, you must make a good impression. Jump up and pour the coffee when it arrives, smile at everyone, write neatly and do not say anything at all.'

2 Look back at the problem situations you may face as you try to maintain constructive working relationships (see page 360). Discuss as a group, and with your tutor, the best way of coping in each

● Job roles, training and development

Work roles have already been discussed on page 346, and the changing job roles of administrators, secretaries and PAs were considered in chapter 1. You can usually divide any job into three main areas, all of which require a certain level of skill and expertise.

- **Conceptual content** – this area identifies intellectual ability and ways of thinking. Different jobs require different levels of academic ability.

- **Vocational skills** – this area relates to the technical skills required. The skill level will vary for different jobs and different skills. Key skills for a job (such as keyboarding for secretaries) may be required at advanced level, whereas for additional skills (such as desktop publishing), beginner's level may be acceptable as a starting point.

- **Personal skills** – this area covers a wide range of abilities, from communication skills to team working and from assertiveness to time management. Organisations will usually support staff who wish to achieve personal skills directly related to their work role.

Analysing job roles

It is possible to analyse the job roles of both yourself and any staff with whom you work to identify the degree of expertise and the type of skills which are required. This information helps to inform job descriptions for staff, person specifications for new applicants and to help in the compilation of a skills audit for the organisation. This shows the type and level of skills owned within the company, and can be used to identify when new skills need to be brought in or when existing staff should receive additional training, and in what areas.

The steps to take in analysing a job role are to identify

- the tasks which must be carried out by the job holder
- the skills required for each task to be undertaken successfully to the required level
- the degree of responsibility for each task (partial or total)
- whether the job holder is responsible for any subordinates
- the additional attributes required for the job to be carried out successfully
- the degree and level of previous experience required.

At this point it is usual to separate skills, attributes and experience into those which are considered essential and those which would be desirable.

 Discussion point

Figure 15.3 shows an advertisement for an assistant administrator/secretary to work in a college of further education.

1   As a group, identify from the advertisement
   a   the skills which you think are essential for the job holder
   b   the skills which you consider are desirable
   c   in which areas training is offered.

2 Divide the skills you have identified as essential and desirable into three different areas – conceptual/intellectual, vocational and personal. Discuss with your tutor

    a what qualifications you would expect the job holder to have on appointment

    b what personal attributes would be useful in this job role.

3 Assume the Marketing Department grows in size over the next few years and the job holder is promoted to senior administrator/PA. He or she is now made responsible for three other staff.

    a What additional skills and abilities do you now think would be desirable?

    b Assuming the job holder is ambitious, discuss with your tutor the type of additional qualifications he or she may wish to hold.

ASSISTANT ADMINISTRATOR/SECRETARY

required for varied role in Marketing Department of busy College of Further Education.

Applicants must have good typing speeds and up-to-date knowledge of computer packages – preferably word processing (ideally Word for Windows 6) and presentation packages. Database and spreadsheet experience useful but training will be given.

Must be well organised, an excellent communicator with a good telephone manner and a flexible attitude.

The successful applicant will be expected to organise the work of the marketing section in addition to giving secretarial support to the marketing manager. In return we offer full training in marketing techiques and procedures and good career prospects. This is an ideal opportunity for a newly qualified administrator or secretary to broaden his/her experience.

Salary approximately £11 000 depending upon age and experience.

Apply in writing for application form to

The Staffing Officer
Hightown College
Riverside Place
HIGHTOWN
HG2 9MD

Figure 15.3 A job advertisement detailing the skills required

£7 billion a year stress bill

The Institute of Management issued alarming figures on the effects of stress in the UK. Stress, it argues, costs £7 billion a year with 270 000 people absent every day and 40 million lost working days a year.

A major reason for this has been the increased concentration on productivity. Stress occurs when the level of demand is high and the individual is unable to cope with the demand with the resources available. However, people's reactions to stress vary. One person may thrive on it, whereas another person may quickly become physically ill. People therefore need to be able to recognise their own tolerance levels and to find coping strategies to help them to deal with stress.

There is now a move towards giving managers training in helping to identify the symptoms of stress – both in themselves and in their employees. The aim is not just to reduce the number of working days lost but to reduce the number of errors caused by stress, the opportunities lost if staff are too exhausted to cope and the number of good employees who leave the organisation simply because of stress.

Offering training and development

Most organisations expect staff development to be a two-way process. In other words, employees are responsible for identifying their own training needs in accordance with their individual aspirations and discussing these with their line manager. The line manager's task is to examine people's personal needs and ambitions and link these to the needs of the organisation. This is usually a major function of **appraisal interviews** – which focus on helping staff to develop in ways which will mutually benefit both the company and the employee. Most organisations are prepared to support their employees to an extent, but also expect some commitment from them. So, for example, they may agree that employees can attend a course partially in work time and partially in their own time (say one afternoon and evening a week). In another case, they may agree that one employee can attend a short course provided he or she cascades or passes on the knowledge to other people in the organisation. This reduces the cost and ensures that several people benefit.

Training needs can also be identified in other ways. Observation of work performance will usually show whether people are competent or are lacking in certain areas. Change is a key area which can bring the requirement for new skills and knowledge. This can occur because of the introduction of new software or equipment, through new job roles after staff reorganisation, and legislative changes, such as those relating to health and safety at work. In addition, more enlightened organisations will arrange support for staff who are under greater pressure through change or reorganisation by offering courses such as time management or dealing with stress.

Investing in people – good or bad?

Two reports on the results of the Investors in People (IIP) initiative were published in 1996. IIP was launched by the government in 1991 with the aim of encouraging employers to improve skills levels and to develop employees in line with business goals.

Report 1, published by the Institute of Employment Studies (IES), showed that the main beneficiaries of training are the companies, rather than the employees, with tangible benefits in the skills of the workforce, employee morale, identification of training needs and financial performance of the company through increased productivity.

Report 2, called *Making People Your Business,* and carried out for the government by consultants Coopers & Lybrand, found that whilst 80 per cent of company chief executives considered IIP to have been successful, their employees did not. Managers claimed employees had been involved through team meetings, staff briefings, newsletters, presentations and annual reports. In reality only 25 per cent of employees felt they had actually benefited. A spokeswoman for Investors in People UK said that this would only be remedied if, in addition to training, staff were given encouragement to develop themselves and provided with the opportunity to do so.

Note: Further information on IIP, appraisal interviews, job descriptions, person specifications and training and development is given in the companion book, *Business for Advanced Secretarial Students.*

Discussion point

1   As a group, and with your tutor, identify the different skills and abilities which you think would be
    a   essential, and
    b   desirable

in each of the following members of staff. You may find it helpful to reread in chapter 1 pages 6–12 before you start to answer this question!

- • an accounts clerk
- • a receptionist

- a trainee administrator
- a word processor operator
- a junior secretary

2 Figure 15.4 shows a list of training activities and courses on offer at your local college. Select three which would be applicable for each of the staff listed above assuming that each has the essential skills you have identified but none have all the desirable skills.

TRAINING ACTIVITIES AND COURSES

Short courses

Assertiveness training
Customer service skills
Public speaking
Interpersonal skills (working with others)
Minute-taking
Health and safety training
Team-building
Employment law
Stress awareness/management
Telephone selling
Sign language
Understanding equal opportunities
Managing change
Problem solving
Quality management
Reception management
Counselling skills
Running induction programmes
IT training and the Internet

Time management
Making oral presentations
Project management
Managing your boss
Confidence building
Managing the office team
First aid
Negotiating skills
Creative thinking
Personal safety training
Leadership skills
Coping with change
Business writing skills
Telephone skills
Appraising staff
Organising the office
Windows 95
Word for Windows 6.0

Professional development/vocational skills

IT qualifications (WP, DTP, CLAIT, IBT 2, NVQ 2/3 IT)
Shorthand or Teeline/audio/keyboarding skills
NVQs – Customer Service, Administration, Accounting
LCCI Private and Executive Secretary's Diploma
IPD Certificate of Personnel Practice
Association of Accounting Technicians courses
Institute of Purchasing and Supply courses
Certificate/Diploma in Marketing
Language courses
Supervisory Management (NEBSM)

Academic development

GCSEs and A-levels
HND/HNC in Business with Finance, Marketing or Personnel
Certificate in Management Studies (CMS)
BA degree in Business Administration or Business Studies – or Open University degree in relevant subjects (BA/BSc)
Diploma in Management Studies (DMS)
Master in Business Administration (MBA)

Figure 15.4 Training activities and courses offered at a college

● Introduction

Meetings and interviews are both occasions on which people get together face to face to discuss an issue or a range of issues. The reason for the discussion may vary considerably, as may the participants and the way in which the session is structured. The event may be formal or informal. The major difference, of course, is that an interview is usually between a small group of people and the discussion will be of a more personal nature, whereas a meeting is held with a larger group and will relate to more general issues. However, there are certain common elements.

- There is a purpose or reason for holding the event.

- The event is held on a specified date and time and in an appropriate location.

- All those involved are notified beforehand.

- The proceedings are planned and structured in advance so that people know what to expect and time is used to the maximum advantage.

- There should be no interruptions to the proceedings.

- A record may be kept of the discussions and decisions made.

Administrators and secretaries are usually involved in making the practical arrangements which surround meetings and interviews. There may, however, be occasions when they are personally involved in the proceedings. For that reason, it is not only important that you should know how to prepare for such events but also how to participate effectively.

● Preparing for meetings

Types of meeting

Meetings can be broadly divided into two types – formal and informal – although the degree of informality may also vary!

Formal meetings include all those which must be held by law – such as the Annual General Meeting of a public limited company, meeting of the Board of Directors, committee meeting at your local town hall or governors' meeting at your college. In this case there are very clearly laid-down procedures which must be followed to ensure that the meetings are held according to the official documentation relating to them – such as a company's Articles of Association or the standing orders for that particular type of meeting (which set out the rules governing the way in which the meeting should be run).

Less formal meetings include those which occur regularly to transact business for specific purposes, eg the health and safety committee or a management team meeting. These are not as formal as statutory meetings but still must be arranged and recorded officially.

Informal meetings are held frequently in most organisations – some will be held at specific intervals, others will only be held when necessary. Examples include departmental meetings, meetings held to plan for or organise specific events or to solve a particular problem and so on. They will often be held at quite short notice.

Occasionally, a large meeting may be held – for instance, if the managing director wants to address all the workforce. However, these are relatively rare – particularly in large organisations – and normally take place to impart information or report back on a particular activity. There are usually no notes taken at such an event.

There are often specific terms used for different types of meetings and committees and a summary of these is given in Figure 16.1.

Annual General Meeting (AGM) – the annual meeting which all public companies must hold and to which shareholders are invited

Extraordinary General Meeting – a meeting called to transact business which cannot be held over until the next AGM

Board meeting (EGM) – the meeting of the board of directors at which company policy is discussed and decided

Committee meetings – committees may be appointed to carry out certain delegated tasks and duties covering specific areas of the organisation, eg production planning, health and safety, equal opportunities, etc.

- An **executive committee** has the ability to make decisions which are binding on all members.

- An **advisory committee** has only the ability to make recommendations, not binding decisions.

- A **standing committee** is one which has a permanent existence.

- An **ad hoc committee** is formed temporarily for a specific purpose. It may comprise a **working party** to organise a particular event.

- A **sub-committee** is formed as part of another committee, eg the production planning group may have a sub-group which concentrates purely on machine maintenance and scheduling.

- A **joint committee** is formed to coordinate the activities of two or more committees, either temporarily or permanently.

Whereas the term 'committee' is common in public-sector organisations, it is less widely used in the private sector. This does not, however, mean that meetings are held any less frequently!

Figure 16.1 Types of meetings and committees

Meetings documentation

There are up to four documents associated with holding a meeting, though most meetings today require the use of only two.

1 **Notice** of the meeting. This tells everyone when and where it will be held.

2 **Agenda.** This states the items which will be discussed in the order in which they will be dealt with.

Usually, these two documents are combined into one for ease. The only exception would be if you were asked to call a meeting but the agenda had not yet been prepared. You could therefore send out the notice to warn everyone in advance to book the meeting in their diaries and then follow with the agenda nearer to the event.

An example of a combined notice and agenda is shown in Figure 16.2. Certain items appear on every agenda (unless it is the first meeting in a series, or one held on a specific issue, when the first three items would be omitted). Information on the reason for each of these permanent items is given in Figure 16.3.

TOWNSEND ELECTRONICS PLC

NOTICE AND AGENDA

15 January 199–

The next meeting of the Safety Committee will be held in the Board Room at 1430 hours on Wednesday, 23 January.

J Wilcox
Secretary

A G E N D A

1 Apologies for absence

2 Minutes of the previous meeting

3 Matters arising

4 Correspondence

5 Safety Officer's annual report

6 New safety regulations and implications

7 Review of fire training procedures

8 Safety exhibition

9 Any other business

10 Time and date of next meeting

Figure 16.2 A combined notice and agenda

The Notice – must include the date, time, location and type of meeting.

The Agenda – standard items include the following.

- **Apologies for absence** – names of those who could not attend are recorded.

- **Minutes of the previous meeting** – these are read and agreed. Any factual errors cannot be altered but the amendment would be recorded in the minutes for the current meeting.

- **Matters arising** – this enables comments to be made on action taken since the last meeting and other developments appertaining to those items which were discussed and recorded.

- **Correspondence** – this item is omitted from those meetings where correspondence is not a feature. Otherwise it draws the attention of the meeting to any relevant communications received since the last meeting.

- **Specific items** – usually given in order of importance. The most crucial are listed first. It is unwise to include too many items.

- **Any other business** (AOB) – allows members to raise subsidiary matters which may be of general interest. Note that an important issue would not be discussed under AOB but should be put on the next agenda.

- **Time and date of next meeting** – usually the last item unless it is possible that time may run out or people may have to leave early, in which case it may be agreed earlier in the proceedings.

Figure 16.3 Notice and agenda – customary items

3 **Chairperson's agenda.** This provides space for the chairperson to make notes during the meeting. It simply lists the main agenda at the left-hand side with space alongside for comments, as is shown in Figure 16.4.

A chairperson's agenda is not usually prepared for informal meetings.

4 **Minutes.** This is the term used for the record of the proceedings. Minutes are usually very short – and may even be as brief as a series of action points. The object of minutes is to record the decisions which were reached at the meeting and to identify the action which is now being taken and by whom. For this reason it is usual to include an action column as shown in Figure 16.5.

Minutes are always written in the past tense and in the third person. They are signed by the person who chaired the meeting and are clearly dated. A copy is sent to everyone who attended the meeting. These people are listed at the top of the minutes, usually in alphabetical order, with the chairperson named first.

CHAIRPERSON'S AGENDA

Safety committee meeting — 23 January

AGENDA ITEM	NOTES
1 Apologies for absence — note K Watts abroad on business	Brian Kay absent also
2 Minutes of previous meeting	✓ OK
3 Matters arising — quote for new emergency lighting is £12 500	=from Brands Electrical ? Other 2 quotes? - chase up (JW)
4 Correspondence — letter from chief fire officer	→ must notify fire officer when planned fire drill - circulate
5 Safety officer's annual report — hand over to JW	Acc. figures ↓ 15% this year
6 New safety regulations and implications (JW)	Carried forward (not yet rec'd)
7 Review of fire training procedures — see staff survey on previous in-house event	Poor report on consultants session. Private co. doing upbeat sessions BD to investigate
8 Safety exhibition — at NEC on 16/17 February	JW & K McG to attend
9 Any other business	Probs with signs at depot - JW to check
10 Time and date of next meeting — suggest 12 February	✓ 14.30

Figure 16.4 A chairperson's agenda with notes

MINUTES
Minutes of the Safety Committee held in the Board Room at 1430 on 23 January 199–

PRESENT

Pamela Butterfield (Chairperson)   Bill Davies
Philip Arnold   Kay McGregor
Georgina Case   James Wilding (Safety Officer)

ITEMS   ACTION

Apologies for absence
Apologies were received from Keith Watts and Brian Kay.

Minutes of the previous meeting
These were agreed as a true and correct record and signed
by the Chairperson.

Matters arising
The Chairperson reported that a quotation had been received
from Brands Electrical for new emergency lighting at a cost
of £12 500. Two other quotations were still outstanding.
JW agreed to obtain these speedily.   JW

Correspondence
A letter had been received from the Chief Fire Officer
regarding new procedures for notifying the local fire
station in the case of a fire drill. Copies were given to
all present. JW to inform all fire marshals.   JW

Safety Officer's annual report
JW circulated copies and outlined key items – in particular
accident figures which were down by 15 per cent from the
previous year.

New safety regulations and implications
Details had not yet been received from the HSE. This item
was therefore carried forward to the next meeting.

Review of fire training procedures
It was agreed that the consultants brought in to organise
the last staff training session were disappointing – the staff
survey showed most attendees had felt the session
inappropriate. Bill Davies mentioned a practical training
initiative being developed by a private company and agreed to
obtain details.   BD

Safety exhibition
The Chairperson reported that this event would be held at
the NEC on 16 and 17 February and suggested at least two
staff members should attend. It was agreed James Wilding and
Kay McGregor would visit the exhibition and report back to the
committee.   JW/KMcG

Any other business
Philip Arnold reported that he had recently visited the
depot at Northfield Road and noticed that several safety
signs had been vandalised. James Wilding agreed to
investigate.   JW

Time and date of next meeting
It was agreed this would be held at 1430 on Monday, 12 February.
.... Chairperson
.... Date

Figure 16.5 Minutes of a meeting showing an action column

The role of administrator/secretary

It is the job of the administrator or meetings secretary to make all the preparations for the meeting. The amount of work involved will depend upon the reason for calling the meeting, its formality, the number of people involved and the venue. There is clearly a considerable difference between organising an Annual General Meeting at a large hotel where the media will be present and arranging for a group of four colleagues to meet in the office down the corridor for half an hour!

For the vast majority of meetings, however, the following guidelines will be sufficient.

Before the meeting

For any type of meeting you should follow the procedure outlined below.

- Book the accommodation allowing sufficient time (say 15 minutes) both before and after the meeting. This gives you the opportunity to check the room is tidy beforehand and also means that if the meeting overruns the next occupants will not be kept waiting.

- Prepare and circulate the notice and agenda. Attach any additional papers which must be sent out and the minutes of the last meeting if these have not been circulated previously.

- Keep a record of any apologies you receive for people who cannot attend. Some may wish you to record their views on certain items to give to the chairperson.

- Check any refreshments which are required and book these. Tea/coffee and biscuits are usual; lunchtime meetings may mean you will need to order sandwiches.

If the meeting is formal, then you might have to undertake some additional tasks.

- Prepare a seating plan and name places. You also may need to prepare an attendance list for people to sign as they enter, particularly if a large number is expected.

- Supply pens, stationery and carafes of water and glasses. You may like to note that if the meeting is to be held at an external venue, such as a hotel, these will usually be provided.

- Check on any equipment which is required, such as an overhead projector or flip chart. This will either have to be booked and moved into the room immediately before the meeting or you will have to notify your contact at any external venue of your requirements.

On the day of the meeting

- Make sure that you have adequate supplies of all relevant papers – someone is bound to forget them!

- Make sure that switchboard or reception staff know where to direct people and that they should take messages during the duration of the meeting.

- Check the room is tidy, there are sufficient chairs and everything which has been booked is in place.

- Greet people on arrival.

- Take notes of the proceedings, if this is part of your job. Bear in mind that if you do this, it is not sensible to have also nominated yourself as the server of tea and coffee. At most meetings it is sensible to have this available as everyone arrives, so that they can help themselves.

After the meeting

- Check that no one has left anything behind and that the room is left tidy.

- Draft the minutes and check them with the chairperson. Once they have been signed, copy and distribute these to all those who were present or should have been present.

- Check that all paperwork is up to date and filed correctly and that the date of the next meeting is in both your diary and the chairperson's diary.

Participating in meetings

Meetings are always held for a reason. Regular meetings usually involve ongoing discussion about specific matters. Members are invited to contribute to the discussion as their knowledge and expertise is valued. On other occasions members may be asked to present ideas or make suggestions, to give their views on certain issues or to report back on an action they have carried out. The aim is that the final decisions reached will be better because there have been a variety of contributions. This is the theory. In practice, several things can go wrong to prevent this occurring. For instance

- the meeting may have no clear purpose or direction so no one knows what they are supposed to be doing

- those who arrive may know little about what is being discussed and show even less interest in the proceedings

- the chairperson may be poor at organising and controlling the meeting, so there is much talk but little action

- the meeting may be 'commandeered' by some members who hold strong views and who overshadow the others

- the decisions reached may be poor because they were made for the wrong reasons (see page 380)

- there may be no follow-up so that people who promise to take action fail to do so.

Chairing a meeting

Chairing a meeting is a skill which must be learned. If you were holding a staff meeting and had the job of running the meeting and controlling your staff, then you would quickly learn to admire the skills of an adept chairperson who not only keeps everyone's mind focused on the key issues but who also makes certain that everyone contributes and that the best decisions are reached. A strong chairperson, who is firm but fair, is respected for his or her ability to keep the peace if there are any disagreements among those present and to review and evaluate the advantages and disadvantages of different courses of action.

Some useful strategies include the following.

- Nominate a chairperson who has enough power and influence over those present to ensure that, at least on the surface, they fulfil the requirements of membership.

- Avoid overloading the agenda, which results in inadequate time to discuss important issues properly or the meeting running out of time before the business has been completed.

- Send out complicated papers in advance so that they can be studied by members but do *not* overload them with detail. No one wants to plough their way through 30 pages of detailed information and then have to remember it whilst it is being discussed!

- Arrive before time and expect the meeting to start promptly. Latecomers should find the meeting in progress, not everyone sitting around sipping coffee.

- Insist that all present 'address the chair' rather than talk to each other. It is impossible to keep order at a meeting if three different conversations are taking place at the same time!

- Start the proceedings by going through the minutes of the last meeting, with particular emphasis on the action points which were agreed and check the action which has been taken by named individuals.

- Introduce each new topic, give a lead (such as relevant background information) and then keep quiet whilst discussion develops.

- Praise good ideas and suggestions, but do not commit everyone to any action until everyone has had a chance to speak.

- Keep people to the point and firmly discourage interruptions.

- Guillotine (ie cut short) discussion after all the main points have been raised. Otherwise some discussions would go on for ever! A good meeting is brisk and focused.

- Summarise the main points which have been raised and the action which has been agreed. If this is still in doubt, then the chairperson often has the ability to sway the meeting provided that he or she can give a good reason why one action is preferable to another.

- Make sure everyone is clear about what has been agreed.

- Follow this strategy until all the items on the agenda have been discussed.

- Close the meeting promptly and formally so that everyone is clear that the meeting has ended.

Although you are unlikely to chair a formal meeting, you should be aware that on these occasions the chairperson's role includes

- being completely familiar with the standing orders which govern the meeting – in case there is a dispute about procedure

- maintaining order, even with a large group

- giving the **casting vote** in the case of a 'tie' – however, it is usual to vote to preserve the 'status quo' in this situation, that is, keeping the existing state of affairs

- adjourning the meeting if, for instance, there are insufficient members present to form a **quorum** (see Figure 16.6).

The chairperson – and the meetings secretary – also needs to be thoroughly familiar with all the special meetings terms used on these occasions. A glossary of the main ones you may encounter is given in Figure 16.6.

The art of decision-making

Everyone has to make decisions. Some decisions are basic, simple and easy to make whilst others are much harder and more complex. Deciding which film to see with three friends is obviously easier than deciding whether or not to change your job or leave home because the *implications* of making the decision are much simpler. All you have to lose by seeing a dreadful or boring film is one wasted night out. If you made a mistake changing jobs or leaving home, then there are several implications. You might be very unhappy, miss your friends, earn less money, spoil your career opportunities in your current job and so on.

Normally, decisions involving people are considered to be more complicated than those involving tasks. For instance, deciding which type of computer to buy is easier than deciding which person to promote.

Address the chair   To speak through the chairperson.

Adjournment   The discontinuation of a meeting until a later date. The adjournment may be **sine die,** ie without another date being agreed.

Amendment   A suggestion to change or amend a **motion** – usually to improve it.

Casting vote   The 'second vote' held by the chairperson if there is an equal number of votes for and against a motion.

Clear days   The number of days between serving notice of a meeting and the date on which it is held.

Coopted member   A person invited on to a committee because of his or her specialist knowledge or expertise.

Ex-officio   A person entitled to serve on a committee as a right because of his or her position in the organisation.

In attendance   A person invited to be present for a specific reason but who has no voting rights.

In camera   In private.

Lie on the table   The agreement that no action should be taken on a particular issue at present.

Motion   A proposal put before the meeting.

Nem con   No one contradicting a vote, however some members may have abstained from voting.

Opposer   A person who speaks against a motion.

Point of order   A query as to whether the correct procedures are being followed.

Proposer   A person who puts forward a motion.

Quorum   The minimum number of people who must be present for the meeting to be valid (note **quorate** and **inquorate**).

Resolution   A decision made and passed at a formal meeting.

Rider   A suggestion to add to a **resolution** after it has been passed.

Right of reply   The right of a proposer to speak again after a motion has been discussed.

Seconder   A person who supports the motion or proposal.

Substantive motion   A proposal which includes one or more amendments.

Unanimous   Everyone in favour.

Figure 16.6 Formal meetings: terminology

However, no matter how difficult the decision is, the consequences of doing nothing may be worse. In any organisation, decisions have to be made regularly as delay and inaction may be the worst choice of all. A company which is trying to decide whether to spend most of its marketing budget on television advertising or press advertising would be ill-advised to do nothing and not advertise at all!

Discussion point

You are chairing a meeting of the administrative staff and have two problems to solve.

1 The photocopier is constantly breaking down in the office and is now considered almost beyond repair. The staff are keen to replace it with a larger model which will undertake more functions automatically. Your line manager has informed you that if you do this, there will not be sufficient money in the budget for the two new printers required in the office and the purchase of these will have to be delayed for 12 months.

2 The staff have submitted their holiday dates, but there is considerable overlap. Your line manager has informed you that a new head office directive requires that at least two staff are on duty in the office throughout the summer and no one must take more than two consecutive weeks without special permission. This will mean either two members of staff rearranging their plans or the other staff working around them. Your line manager has insisted that a revised schedule is submitted in five days' time.

As a group, discuss

a which problem would be the easiest to solve and which the most difficult
b the steps you could take to solve the easy problem
c the difficulties you would encounter in solving the harder problem. To do this consider
    i the attitude of those involved
    ii the possible ways in which you could introduce the topic
    iii the range of reactions you might face
    iv the strategies you might use to obtain some agreement.

Discuss your answers with your tutor.

(*Note*: You may prefer to role play the above in a meetings situation with the rest of your group!)

Assisting decision-making

If you accompany your boss to a meeting – or represent your boss – then he or she will expect you to 'toe the party line'. This means arguing for the cause your boss believes in or supporting him or her to help the team to reach agreement. If you are chairing a meeting yourself, then you have an even harder job – particularly if the direction being taken by staff is not likely to be popular with your boss! The following should help you to overcome this difficulty.

First, you need to accept that there are some things in life which are changeable and some things which are not! It is therefore useless spending valuable time discussing something you cannot do anything about. In the example above, team members may be tempted to argue for hours that the remit from head office is unfair. This is a separate issue and not one they can do anything about. To assist the decision-making process you would need to concentrate their minds on what *can* be changed – not what they would like to change!

Taking a positive view means that you can influence the action; shrugging your shoulders and saying 'typical' means, in effect, you 'opt out' and are hardly in a position to argue if you do not agree with the final decision.

In each case you should try to identify

- what is the best you can achieve
- what you can live with
- what could be the worst outcome.

Aim for the first, but be prepared to settle for the second.

It is essential to recognise that people reach decisions for different reasons. They may

- only be interested in their personal situation and want the best for themselves
- be very logical and rational and put information and results before people's feelings
- want to 'play safe' and follow rules and regulations
- not want to challenge their colleagues but to agree with the 'popular vote'
- be a strategist – this may mean deciding to play a 'waiting game' to see if the situation improves
- have a 'hidden agenda' (secret reason) for not following an expected course of action. This could be, for instance, because they want to gain more power, get their own back or outmanoeuvre someone.

Therefore the thought processes of those involved in a meeting can be very complex indeed!

A sensible rule of thumb is to find out how your boss is thinking and only dispute this in private! He or she will expect your support in public. If you talk through the implications, you can identify your range of acceptable actions before you begin. You can then look for ways to present your boss's case – as well as your own – in a way which will enable a sensible decision to be made.

Theory	Method	Advantages	Disadvantages
The rational approach	Collect all information Analyse it Make rational decision based on data Evaluate possible outcomes Propose action	Easy to defend	Impossible to collect all relevant data Apt to favour data that prove own view!
Limited rationality	Collect as much information as possible Add to this with own opinions and views Obtain 'best possible' decision in time available	Allows for 'grey' areas Recognise personal input	Relatively inflexible method How good is 'best possible' decision?
Rules and precedents	Refer to similar past cases Look at precedents Find out organisational rules which apply Give ruling	Easy to justify People expect to follow rules Simplest method	Some cases have no precedent Few problems are exact repeat of others No staff input
Symbolic action	Obtain views of colleagues Interpret how they will react Take action which accords with popular view	Includes staff input/beliefs Usually popular choice	Often a compromise solution Time-consuming May not be best answer
Garbage-can analysis	Only solve problems when need to (too busy to solve those which are not urgent) Problems and information arrive in random order Match together in best way possible	Often accords with what really happens! Saves time working on problems which may solve themselves	Haphazard approach Some problems may be overlooked

Source: J G March, *Theories of Choice and Making Decisions*

Figure 16.7 Theories on decision-making

🗨 Discussion point

Figure 16.7 outlines some interesting theories on how people make decisions, although other examples were discussed above. Study each theory carefully and then answer the question below.

You have five good friends and next summer you intend to go on holiday together. Various suggestions have been made – from camping in France to an apartment in the Algarve. The only thing everyone seems to agree on is that the holiday must be reasonably cheap and the weather must be good!

Assume your friends each operate according to a different theory of decision-making. How would this influence their behaviour and the possible outcome if you met to make a decision? Discuss your ideas with your tutor.

The value of win/win

In any disagreement there are potentially different outcomes depending upon the degree of cooperation and assertiveness shown by the different parties. Both may 'lose' (I lose/you lose) so both are unhappy, or one may give in or compromise (I win, you lose or you win, I lose). However, the aim should be for both sides to win.

How can you achieve 'I win, you win'? Suppose, in your holiday discussions, one person wanted to visit the United States, whilst another longed to see Greece. A compromise may be to go to one of these (and one person loses) or to go somewhere completely different (both may lose) (see Figure 16.8). Win/win occurs if

- you both find another location which really does suit you equally

- I convince you (or you convince me) that we genuinely would really enjoy either the USA or Greece.

Win/win is a state of mind. The ideal outcome is when both people are pleased with the result because both have achieved something.

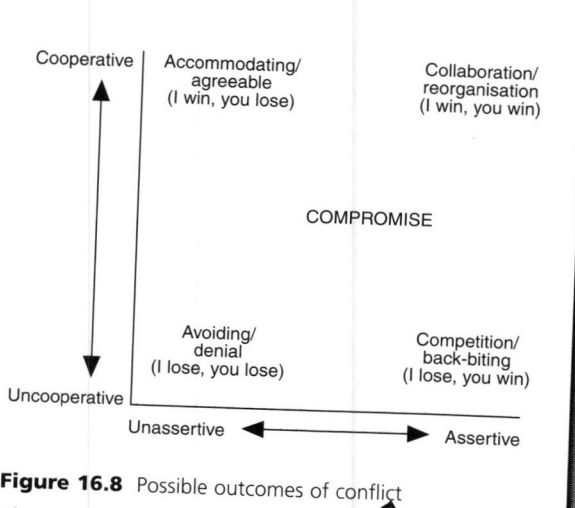

Figure 16.8 Possible outcomes of conflict

● Interviews

Interviews are held for a variety of reasons. The term 'interview' can be used for any occasion where a few people (often only two) meet for a private discussion about an official matter. Typical examples include

- job interviews
- promotion interviews
- appraisal interviews
- counselling interviews
- grievance interviews
- disciplinary interviews.

If you are involved in interviews, you may be asked to

- make the arrangements
- attend such an interview (eg if you apply for a job)
- conduct an interview.

Making the arrangements

If your boss is involved in job, promotion or appraisal interviews, then there are often several people to see, often over a short space of time. Scheduling the interviews then becomes important, as does making sure that everyone involved is notified in good time.

Counselling and disciplinary interviews are more specialised. In this case there will normally be only one person involved, although he or she may choose to be accompanied by a colleague or a trade union representative.

Two important points to remember are that the discussions will always be confidential (as will any subsequent paperwork) and that arrangements must be made to ensure that there are no interruptions.

Given that job interviews are probably the most common type of interview, below is a checklist of the actions which should be taken when making the appropriate arrangements.

- Assemble all the relevant documentation in a file for your boss. This would include the job description, person specification, terms and conditions of employment and shortlisted application forms.
- Ask your boss to inform you which date is most suitable. Draft out an interview schedule with sufficient time between candidates and agree this with your boss.

- Book an interview room and a waiting room, if appropriate. Arrange refreshments.

- Notify candidates in writing of interview arrangements. If your premises are hard to find, include a map, and, if appropriate, arrange car parking spaces. Make sure candidates travelling a long way are given information on expenses which can be reimbursed and how this will be done.

- Take up references of candidates (if done at this stage) and add to file.

- Prepare any tests to be given. If required, make sure a separate room is available with any equipment.

- Put the file in order for your boss so that the interview schedule is attached to the front and application forms/references are in time order inside the file. Prepare duplicate files for other interviewers.

- Inform security and reception so that candidates are directed to the correct place.

- Greet interviewees on arrival and take them to the waiting room. You may have to do escort duty for the day to and from the waiting room and interview room or show people around the premises.

- After the interviews, send out an offer letter to the successful candidate and, upon receiving confirmation, send rejection letters to unsuccessful candidates.

- Send out official confirmation of appointment to the candidate and arrange an induction programme.

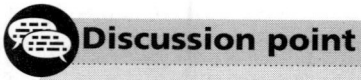**Discussion point**

Make suggestions as to how this schedule would be different if
a   there was a mixture of internal and external candidates for a job
b   you were arranging appraisal interviews for departmental staff with your boss
c   it was a disciplinary interview with a member of staff and the individual's trade union representative.

Attending an interview

No matter what type of interview you are attending, you may be rather apprehensive or even very nervous beforehand. Usually, it helps if you make adequate preparations which at least should minimise last-minute problems or disasters!

Check you are clear about the time of the interview, where it is to be held and the length of time it will take you to get there. If you are travelling any distance, allow for unexpected problems or delays. If the interview is internal, do not keep working until the last minute so that you end up sprinting from one end of the building to another in a panic!

Prepare mentally for the interview by thinking in advance what is likely to be asked and discussed and what your own contribution should be, eg

- for a job or promotion interview, you should think carefully about the requirements for the post and your own best points and strengths (and weaknesses!)

- for a job interview, you should also find out something about the organisation itself

- for an appraisal interview, you should think about the work you have carried out over the last year, your achievements and disappointments, your planned career development and what you could do to achieve your ambitions

- if you are seeking counselling, then you will help your counsellor if you have thought through your problems or difficulties beforehand and can talk about these reasonably fluently

- at a grievance or disciplinary interview, you will be given the opportunity to present your case. You may also find it helpful to have someone with you. This person will also be a witness in case there is any later dispute about what actually took place.

Think about your appearance. We all gain confidence from feeling we are dressed appropriately and look business-like.

Try to relax! Whilst this may be difficult, deep breathing exercises can work. Interviewers will expect you to be nervous and a professional interviewer should try to reassure you – not make you feel worse!

Make sure you say what you want to say! Many people leave an interview annoyed because they did not ask an important question or make a crucial point. Asking questions is usually encouraged because it shows you can assert yourself in such a situation. Always make sure you clarify anything you are not sure about before the end of the interview.

Conducting an interview

It is unlikely that you will be asked to conduct disciplinary, grievance or counselling interviews at this stage in your career. However, you could be involved in an informal counselling session with one of your staff if he or she is particularly upset or stressed. If the situation is serious, you should always recommend that the staff member obtains professional help.

Counsellors are specially trained to assist people in these circumstances – and an over-enthusiastic amateur may do more harm than good.

The key skill in conducting any interview is to be able to **listen.** The interviewer should only speak for about 15–20 per cent of the time. Another important attribute is to have an open mind and not judge candidates too hastily or on the wrong criteria. Expert interviewers are also adept at asking the right questions to find out information about the interviewee. All these skills mean that many organisations insist that staff involved in interviewing job applicants or appraising other staff receive professional training. However, if you work for a small firm you may be expected to conduct 'first-stage' interviews with job applicants before your boss conducts final interviews. You may also be expected to appraise your own staff.

- Good interviewers always prepare well in advance. They make sure they have all the relevant paperwork to hand and that they will not be disturbed during the interview. They also think carefully about the questions they will ask and the structure of the interview.

- An appropriate way to open an interview is to greet the person and then explain the format of the interview. This puts the interviewee at ease.

- Interviewees are encouraged to talk if they are asked 'open-ended' questions – those to which someone can answer 'yes' or 'no' are usually inappropriate unless they lead to a second, more open question.

- Points of interest should be developed and discussed.

- People vary in their ability to answer questions and the way in which they answer them. One may think a long time before speaking, another may give very long replies! Good interviewers are not afraid of silence and very good at tactfully terminating answers which are too long or refocusing those which drift off the point!

- At a job interview, the interviewer is responsible for making sure that all candidates are
  - asked the same questions
  - told about the duties required
  - informed about the terms and conditions of employment.

- Check if the interviewee has any questions to ask, review the main points discussed and explain what follow-up action will be taken.

- Thank the person for attending the interview.

- Write up any notes immediately afterwards.

Beware the halo effect!

Alarmingly, a survey of interviewers found that 75 per cent judge the candidate mainly on appearance, 17 per cent on background and qualifications and only 8 per cent really listen to what the candidate is saying!

Some interviewers were very impressionable where the candidates' clothes were concerned – women who 'power dressed' were considered to frighten some male interviewers, men who arrived with a sweater under their jacket were discounted at the outset. Apparently, the most effective outfit for female secretaries was a dark suit and light-coloured blouse!

Interviewers were also guilty of preferring candidates who had a similar background to their own – whether the same school, college, qualifications or home town.

The 'halo effect' occurs when an interviewer is so impressed with a candidate at the outset because their application, appearance and background all appeal, that they then look only for information to reinforce that view. Any replies which are unsatisfactory can be ignored or not investigated as the interviewer simply looks for evidence to substantiate his or her initial views. All professional interviewing courses teach interviewers to guard against this.

Discussion point

1   Discuss your interviewing experiences with your tutor and the rest of your group. Try to identify the characteristics and attributes of interviewers you have found easy to talk to and pleasant to meet.

2   Discuss the format of an appraisal interview with your tutor and the role of the interviewer in this situation. Further details on appraisals are given in *Business for Advanced Secretarial Students,* the companion book to this.

Introduction

Many administrators and certainly a considerable number of secretaries and PAs frequently liaise with external contacts. In some cases they represent their own and their organisation's interests; in others, they represent their boss. They may be involved in making arrangements which involve external contacts or in attending functions at which they will play an active public relations role for their organisation.

The type of arrangements and events with which they may be involved include

- travel arrangements – either for their boss, other executives or for external contacts visiting the organisation

- entertainment and hospitality arrangements

- organising other events – such as training days, seminars and conferences.

On all these occasions, administrators/secretaries are likely to be the interface between the external contact and their organisation. They must ensure that everything runs smoothly, that everyone knows what arrangements have been made, that at an event no one will be left feeling disappointed or neglected. The skills involved therefore go beyond basic organisational abilities to include the skills and ability to deal with a wide range of people sensitively yet efficiently.

Making travel arrangements

Outward travel

If you are involved in this activity, you will be mainly considering your boss's needs. However, no business person travels without a reason! Therefore, at some point on the trip he or she will meet other people and attend events. Your role is therefore likely to encompass liaising with these people to ensure that the arrangements made are mutually convenient.

Making outward travel arrangements may include all or some of the following activities:

- planning and scheduling trips in this country and/or abroad

- organising passports and renewals, obtaining visas, arranging inoculations and giving other health information prior to an overseas trip

- making airline, rail, car hire, ferry or hotel reservations – or arranging these through a local travel agent and/or a hotel booking agency

- arranging travel insurance (unless there is an overall company policy)

- obtaining foreign currency and traveller's cheques

- negotiating and confirming appointments with external contacts in the UK or overseas

- preparing itineraries.

All the above tasks must be undertaken according to any official policies or procedures for travel laid down by your organisation. In some companies bookings are made through a central travel section and there may be standard forms to complete. In others, individuals can make bookings provided these are all handled by a nominated travel agency. In a small firm you may have more scope to make your own choices. There are always, however, likely to be some policies in force on the amount which can be spent to prevent costs escalating. This will affect class of travel, type of hotel and room, size of car you can hire and so on. Whatever the policy in force, you are always in a better position if you have the knowledge to plan the arrangements yourself, rather than simply relying on the word of a travel agent. If nothing else, you know which questions to ask!

Wherever you work, however, you are likely to have to consider the preferences of your own boss or those for whom you make any bookings. Executives who travel frequently rapidly develop individual preferences for certain airlines, routeings, hotels and modes of transport. In addition, your organisation (or your boss) may participate in a Frequent Flyer Programme with a particular airline or a Frequent Visitor Programme with a group of hotels. You will then usually be expected to use these where possible to take advantage of the benefits offered.

Organisations such as Reed Travel offer special training to secretarial staff involved in making travel arrangements, and today there is no need to keep dozens of reference books when planning a journey overseas. Subscribing to the Official Airline Guide's FlightDisk or to an Internet service provider who gives access to timetables and reservations means you can custom-build a flight itinerary through your PC! Current timetables for frequently used services are a must, however, together with the names, addresses and phone and fax numbers of useful contacts including

- the name and address of your travel agent

- favourite hotels in the UK and abroad plus at least one hotel booking agent, such as Corporate Reservations Services Ltd in Hounslow (such organisations are able to make a booking almost anywhere in the world for the price of a phone call or fax message)

- the information desk at your local airport

- your local BR station(s) and the British Rail Business Travel Service

- local car hire firms – particularly those which allow drop-off at a different destination from the point at which the car was collected

- your local passport office and consulates of frequently visited countries

- any overseas representatives or agents contracted by your company

- your boss's GP and either MASTA (the Medical Advisory Service for Travellers Abroad) or the Thomas Cook Medical Centre in London. You should also have a copy of the latest Department of Health leaflet on *Health Advice for Travellers*.

Ticket? No, sir!

Ticketless travel is likely to be a feature of the future. Firstly, you make the electronic booking; secondly, you pay by plastic card; thirdly, you show your card at the airport to claim your seat.

Some airlines are already experimenting with this system. British Airways successfully trialled the introduction of ticketless travel between Gatwick and Aberdeen and by 1997 plans to abolish paper tickets for all domestic flights (ie those within the UK).

Hints and tips on outward travel

The intricacies of planning and costing complex business trips is beyond the scope of this book. If you are pursuing your studies to PA level or taking a PA option as part of your award, then you will need to increase your expertise in this area. However, the following are useful guidelines to help you to guard against some of the pitfalls of making travel plans.

- Open a separate travel file for each trip.

- Make sure you obtain as much information about the trip as possible. You will need the individual names of all travellers, dates, organisations being visited and contact names, preferred routes/times of travel. Bear in mind that tickets issued in one name are often not transferable.

- Draft the itinerary showing proposed travel options. Make a note of which arrangements have been confirmed and those which are still pending.

- Try to book direct air routes wherever possible or put your boss down on the waiting list for one. This will mean an automatic transfer from an indirect route if a seat becomes available.

- Confirm all accommodation arrangements, other bookings (eg hire car) and all appointments in writing – fax is usually best. Put copies in the travel file.

- When booking hotel accommodation make sure the hotel is aware of your boss's estimated time of arrival (ETA), particularly if this is likely to be late in the evening.

- When booking car hire check the insurance details. The basic charge includes insurance against passenger liability and third party risks but there is usually an additional charge for collision damage waiver (which covers the actual vehicle) and for personal accident insurance.

- If you are discussing payment by credit card abroad, use the terms Visa and Mastercard. Chargecards which are acceptable in most countries include American Express (Amex) and Diner's Club. A BT Chargecard is also useful for making calls back to the UK.

- Type an emergency list of special telephone numbers for your boss to take on the trip, eg the card protection agency, alternative hotels in the area, company agents and representatives, bank number in case traveller's cheques are lost or stolen.

- Produce two itineraries – a short one with travel details on a card for keeping in a pocket and a longer one for the file which gives full details of all appointments and enclosed documentation.

Discussion point

Figure 17.1 shows the type of information which would be included, for reference purposes, in a detailed itinerary. Discuss which information would be included on a shortened version for the traveller's quick reference. Check your ideas with your tutor.

Inward travel

This involves making arrangements for other people to visit your organisation. You are unlikely to be asked to make any airline reservations (unless for travel within this country) but you are likely to be asked to liaise with visitors over

- meeting arrangements at an airport or BR station

- transporting them to your organisation

- booking hotel accommodation

- dealing with other details during their stay.

The type of arrangements you make will usually be determined by the importance of the visitor. The most important foreign client may be met by a uniformed chauffeur and accommodated at the best hotel in your area. The

```
                TRAVEL PROGRAMME FOR MARTIN GREGSON


VISIT TO EUROPE - 12-15 MARCH 199-
Monday 12 March

1300        Company car from office to airport

1400        Check in Manchester, Terminal 1

1500        Depart on flight BA236

1600        Arrive Paris, Charles de Gaulle. Met by Pierre Lefevre,
            French representative

            Accommodation reserved at Royal Hotel, 33 Avenue de
            Friedland, 75008 Paris for nights of 12 and 13 March
            (confirmation attached)

2000        Dinner with Jacques Lacroix and Jules Carriere of Mondial
            Associates et Cie. Arrangements made by Pierre Lefevre

Tuesday 13 March
0930        Meeting to discuss proposed contract at Mondial Associates.
            Transport arranged by Pierre Lefevre. Relevant documentation
            attached

            Remainder of day in French office

Wednesday 14 March
0800        Taxi arranged for journey to Charles de Gaulle airport

0845        Check in at Air France desk

0945        Depart flight AF590

1045        Arrive Rome airport

            Accommodation reserved at Hotel Atlante Star, Via G
            Vitelleschi 34, 00193 Roma. Courtesy car will collect you at
            airport

1400        Meeting with Carlo Pontelli of Elettronica de Roma regarding
            proposed patent agreement. Documents in file attached

1700        Dinner at Ambasiatoria Palace Hotel. Black tie. Invitation
            attached

Thursday 15 March
1000        Meeting at hotel with Julio Fernandez - proposed agent for
            Italy, Spain and Portugal

1400        Courtesy car to airport

1500        Check in at British Airways desk

1600        Depart on flight BA381

1830        Arrive Manchester, Terminal 1 - met by company car

£400 in sterling traveller's cheques
£200 cash in French francs
£200 cash in Italian lira
```

Figure 17.1 A detailed travel itinerary

situation will be rather different for one of your own overseas representatives who is visiting for a month! However, you can still do much to help on these occasions.

Hints and tips on inward travel

* Liaise with the visitor's own secretary or PA regarding his or her preferences, mode of transport, exact time of arrival and other information. Make sure you both keep each other fully informed, particularly if there are any last-minute changes to the arrangements.

* Check to find out the exact details of any inward travel arrangements. It is not enough to know which airport or which city! For anyone arriving by air, you need to know the flight number, ETA and terminal number. For anyone arriving by train, you need to know which station!

* Book the most appropriate form of inward transport. Several taxi/minicab companies have a range of vehicles from basic to luxurious. If you work for a large organisation, you may have a central transport section with its own drivers. In either case, someone needs to check with the airport (or BR) before setting off to ensure there are no delays. Make sure you know whether this is your responsibility or will be done by the driver.

* If the traveller is visiting you 'in transit' or is arriving urgently for a meeting, then make sure there is a secure place for leaving luggage and other personal belongings. Otherwise it is more usual for the driver to take the visitor to his or her hotel first and then wait or call back to make the transfer to the organisation.

* If you are booking accommodation or making meal reservations, check if the visitor has any particular preferences or special needs. This could range from a non-smoking hotel room to special dietary requirements. His or her secretary/PA will be your contact for this type of information.

* Be prepared to provide other types of information and assistance. This can range from arranging for an interpreter or for express dry cleaning to providing information on local shopping or visitor attractions or making telephone calls or sending faxes on the visitor's behalf.

* If you are *personally* asked to collect a visitor, escort him or her to the hotel or even escort the visitor's partner to a particular place, be aware that you are doing this in a professional capacity. You would be well advised to keep any conversations about your organisation and your job very general and concentrate instead on neutral topics. If the visitor is from abroad, useful social courtesies usually involve enquiring about the journey and showing interest in where he or she comes from.

🗫 Discussion point

Many novice secretaries think that the absence of their boss on a trip abroad will mean they will have an easy life for a week or so! Experienced secretaries and PAs will soon tell you this is not the case.

As a group, and with your tutor, discuss the responsibilities which you would have to undertake when

- handling correspondence which arrives during that period
- dealing with emergencies (try to think of some examples!)
- dealing with unexpected visitors and callers
- covering for scheduled meetings your boss would normally attend
- passing on information to your boss
- catching up on other jobs
- organising outstanding paperwork and documentation for your boss's return.

● Entertainment and hospitality arrangements

Entertainment and hospitality can range from organising drinks and nibbles in the boardroom to arranging a day out for 25 VIPs at Ascot or Wimbledon! Indeed some major organisations have considerable budgets for corporate hospitality – all with the aim of building and furthering business relationships.

Unless you are working at a high level as an executive secretary or PA, it is likely that you will be given a fairly detailed brief for such an event. However, it is not unknown for a worried boss to expect his secretary or administrator to come up with some good ideas if he or she is suddenly given the responsibility of entertaining four foreign visitors over a weekend!

If you are given specific instructions then life is obviously very much easier. The majority of events are likely to be relatively routine and are likely to centre around organising drinks and booking restaurant tables. Often an organisation will have standard procedures for booking hospitality (again, to monitor the costs) and this will limit your ingenuity! The situation is rather different if you are involved in arranging a major hospitality event.

If you are ever involved in arranging a special event for a number of guests, a golden rule is to make all the arrangements before you arrange for letters of invitation to be sent. This then enables you to give the guests the fullest possible information on the day's or evening's activities – and prevents people arriving wearing unsuitable clothes or with unrealistic expectations. It also gives people the opportunity to make a suitable excuse if your boss's idea of a 'great day out' for customers does not coincide with the opinions of some of those invited!

Hints and tips on hospitality

- Either use your organisation's specified firm of caterers or obtain a range of quotes and involve your boss in making the selection. Again it is important you cater for individual dietary tastes – particularly vegetarian needs which are very common these days.

- Outside caterers usually provide table linen, crockery, cutlery and glasses if requested, but make sure the provision will match the occasion.

- If you are regularly expected to buy sandwiches and drinks locally, persuade your boss to invest in some suitable crockery, a good bottle opener and other accessories.

- Keep a file with names/telephone numbers of recommended and preferred local restaurants. Mark those which provide a rapid/prompt service – in case the meal has to be squeezed in between business discussions.

- Keep a list of local events/places which would be interesting to visitors to your area, together with times/dates of opening. If you are frequently asked to arrange entertainment events, then a list of theatres in your area and the telephone number of a good booking agent can be invaluable.

- Always think about the profile of your guests. Bear in mind that the needs of the old/young, sporty/intellectual will vary. Women are still likely to have different preferences from men. Therefore you may decide to offer a choice of activities as part of a 'partner programme'.

- Hospitality events take place during the day or the evening and are either active or passive. Usually, the older or more senior the guests the more likely they are to prefer passive (ie spectator) events. A good starting point is to obtain a list of major events (sporting, musical and general) in the area and the dates on which these take place. A major corporate hospitality event could then be linked to one of these dates. Particularly popular, for instance, would be the Open Golf championship, British Grand Prix or Henley Royal Regatta – locally you may have river trips, a famous historic building or ice hockey matches, football games and horse racing events. Participatory activities can include anything from sailing to hot-air ballooning. The important aspect is to check the budget for the whole event before making any bookings!

- Think carefully if foreign or multilingual visitors are invited. What may appeal to an all-British group may have less interest (or more!) for an international group. Be particularly wary of any event where language skills would be important – a play or a murder mystery weekend may be inappropriate in these circumstances.

- Make certain that you know about any health conditions or disabilities of your guests if a planned event will be at all strenuous or if special access or facilities will be required.

- Find out if corporate souvenirs will be given and what type/how many will be required. These may range from glasses and pens to ties or golf umbrellas!

- Finally, be aware that special agencies and organisations will help you if you are ever put in the position of organising a major event yourself. Your local library should keep a copy of the latest edition of the *Corporate Activities and Venues Directory* which may give you ideas. The Sports Council will give you details of planned sporting events. Red Letter Days is an organisation which produces a catalogue of activity-based ideas which they will arrange for single or multiple guests. Finally, organisations such as Page and Moy marketing consultants specialise in arranging large-scale events for corporate clients.

Discussion point

Your boss has just informed you that a party of five important directors from your US head office will be visiting your organisation next month and the managing director has decided to combine their visit with a corporate hospitality event for 50 of your most important customers.

As a group, brainstorm the best way to provide entertainment in your area if

a   the event will be held on a weekday

b   the event will take place on a Friday evening

c   partners will be invited.

Organising other events

Every organisation holds a number of standard events each year and most secretaries and administrators are involved in making arrangements for these. Events may range from a small, internal gathering (such as a departmental training day) to a large event held at an outside venue.

Examples of events which you may be expected to organise include seminars, conferences, staff social events, workshops, training courses, open days and exhibitions.

To a considerable extent, the type of events with which you are involved will depend upon the type of business undertaken by your organisation and your area of responsibility. If you work in Human Resources, for instance, you would probably be involved in arranging internal training courses. If you are employed in Marketing or Sales, then you may take part in organising seminars, exhibitions or even conferences.

Your ability to make appropriate arrangements and to ensure everything runs smoothly will very much depend upon your planning and organisational skills. Whilst these are covered more generally in chapter 19, page 427, this chapter focuses particularly on the type of preparations you would need to make if you were asked to organise an event by your boss.

Hints and tips on organising an event

If the event is small, you will probably be expected to make all the arrangements yourself. If it is on a large scale, such as participation in an exhibition overseas or a conference with 100 delegates, you will be more likely to be part of a larger team of people working on individual aspects of the event. Overall, however, the main points to be covered are given below.

- For each event open a special event file into which all documents, checklists and confirmation letters are placed.

- Check that all the major details are covered when the initial plans are made. These include the type of event, likely number of participants, date(s), venue (or suggested venues), types of refreshment/meals required, materials and equipment which will be needed, essential papers and documentation. If the event is on a large scale, responsibility for each of these areas should be delegated to different members of the team with a deadline date for the completion of the different tasks. It is useful to draft this in the form of an action plan or checklist and issue a copy to everyone involved (see Figure 17.2).

- If you are inviting any important guests or speakers, check they are available for your suggested dates before you make any firm arrangements, particularly if the success of the event is dependent upon their attendance.

- Make a comprehensive list of everything which is required and check you either already have it or know where to obtain it. Your list may range from name cards and a lectern to a large screen video or exhibition display stands!

- For a major event it is advisable to contact a hotel or other venue which is used to hosting this type of activity. The responsibility for providing all

```
                    TOWNSEND  ELECTRONICS


SALES  CONFERENCE  -  15/16  APRIL  199-
ACTION  PLAN/CHECKLIST

Guest lists                                                      JL
•   invitations to all internal sales staff and representatives
•   dinner - additional invitations to John Morrison and
    Kate Stevens from advertising agency

Confirmation of attendance to be received by 28 February

Accommodation/catering                                        PT/JL
Book accommodation at Foresters Hotel, Grosvenor Way
•   10-15 single rooms (final number to be confirmed)
•   meetings room for up to 25 (both days)
•   equipment required - overhead projector, flip chart,
    video recorder and large screen TV
•   arrange buffet lunch first and second day, book
    dining room for private dinner 8 pm on first day

All arrangements to be completed and confirmed by 10 March

Documentation/printed literature                              ST/JP
•   programme of events
•   schematic diagrams for new SNTP unit
•   revised sales literature and brochures

All printing to be completed by 7 April

Additional equipment/requirements                                JP
•   miniature prototype of new SNTP unit
•   video of planned sales campaign

To be taken: available for transporting by 14 April
```

Figure 17.2 An action plan for a sales conference

the facilities is then firmly in its hands – provided you make sure you cover for all eventualities.

• As soon as possible, send out notification of the arrangements, either in a formal invitation or in a letter or memo, depending upon the type of occasion. You may decide to include a map (if appropriate), a programme of events and any other relevant information with the original notification of the event (eg for an internal sales conference) or only issue this when the invitations have been accepted (eg for a major event including internal and external visitors).

• Ensure that you make adequate arrangements for people to be dealt with professionally on their arrival. This may mean
  – arranging transport for guests (eg from a local station)
  – making certain that there is adequate parking available
  – arranging for a separate reception area to greet guests, check them in and issue name badges/event documentation (usually placed in a special folder).

- Check that any equipment which is being transported has been listed and is insured against damage or theft. It might also be your responsibility to check it is in working order once it is in place and to make sure it is returned afterwards.

- Be prepared to mingle with guests and to socialise during evening events. Your attendance may be required at anything from a formal dinner or an informal buffet. Although this may seem nerve-wracking at first – and it may be tempting to cling to one or two people you know – try to avoid this if you can. A useful first step is to socialise with external guests alongside one of your colleagues. It is important, however, that you retain your professional image! This means dressing conservatively, guarding against being indiscreet or too informal and *never* having too much to drink! Keep in mind, too, that if you are one of the organisers of a two- or three-day event, it is very likely you will have an early start the following day!

A new type of venue – the purpose-built alternative

Today there are a variety of different venues to choose from if you are trying to organise an external event. Hotels, country houses and universities now face intense competition from purpose-built centres which provide a range of facilities for their guests at very competitive prices. In addition to bedrooms, meeting and conference rooms, some such centres also offer leisure activities including a swimming pool, golf course and gymnasium!

Many organisations rent out conference or training rooms for specific periods and will arrange a wide range of facilities – from computer networks to presentation aids – and are specifically focused on serving the needs of corporate clients. This means less likelihood of finding that the local hotel has moved you to a smaller room because of a wedding booking, or that your arrangements must be restricted to the most convenient times for the hotel, rather than your company.

Discussion point

Many organisations today have been able to reduce the number of overseas visits and meetings they undertake because of the alternative of **video-conferencing**. As a group, find out as much as you can about this option and decide the main advantages and disadvantages of this approach, as opposed to face-to-face communication.

● The PR role – an overview

The public relations role of a senior administrator, secretary or PA cannot be over-estimated. Ideally, it should be just as acceptable for any external customer or client to deal with you as with your boss – though you will only gain this honour if you are able to impress callers with your courtesy *and* efficiency. Even then, there will always be those who are status conscious and refuse to deal with a secretary.

The degree to which you are given the responsibility of dealing with important external contacts is likely to increase as you move up the ladder and, on the part of your boss, is a clear indication that you are trusted to promote the aims and values of the organisation. No boss would let anyone near an important client if he or she might ruin the business relationship!

Whilst dealing with external contacts may be nerve-wracking in the early stages of your career, developing the necessary skills should be one of your major aims. Having the confidence and ability to deal with a variety of different people – including complete strangers – making people feel important, remembering their individual likes and dislikes (even if you have to keep a record!) and having a friendly and positive approach are all attributes which will be noted and valued. Not only will the 'social side' of your job mean that your work becomes more varied and enjoyable but it also gives you a clear indication that you are developing the skills to move onwards and upwards in your career!

Revision practice

Short-answer questions

1   Identify
    a   three types of internal contacts, and
    b   three types of external contacts
    which are likely to be made by an administrator or secretary.

2   Explain briefly how role conflict can cause problems in an office.

3   You have recently started work in an organisation. Give four points you would bear in mind to help you to form good working relationships with the existing employees.

4   A new recruit has started work in your organisation. State four actions you would take to help her settle in as quickly as possible.

5   Your boss has a highly pressurised job. Give three examples of actions you could take to help him to stay calm on a particularly difficult day.

6   You have recently been promoted to administrator and will be supervising the staff who were once your colleagues. Identify the dangers you would have to guard against in this situation and state briefly how you would do this.

7   Identify three differences between a group and a team.

8   Explain the main components of an agenda for a meeting.

9   State four actions a secretary should take when preparing for a meeting.

10   Identify four considerations you would bear in mind if you were arranging hospitality for a small group of clients.

Essay questions

1   Your friend is an administrator in another organisation. She is having problems in managing the six staff for whom she is responsible and comments that they are always antagonistic to each other and there is little team spirit.
   a   What are the advantages of promoting team spirit within the group?
   b   Suggest how this could be achieved
      i   on a day-to-day basis
      ii   through formal training and development.

2   Your organisation has just introduced a system of appraisal interviews.
   a   In what way would you expect appraisals to be linked to job roles and the training and development of staff?
   b   If you were organising appraisal interviews for your boss, with the 20 members of staff in your department, what arrangements would you make?

3   Your boss is visiting Berlin for a week on a sales trip, meeting customers and prospective customers.
   a   Briefly explain the arrangements you would make for this trip.
   b   What actions would you take to plan for her return?

4   You have recently arranged for next month's sales conference to be held at a nearby hotel. This morning you learn that it has suffered a serious fire and will no longer be available.

   State clearly the actions you would take.

5   You have received an internal promotion and are working as secretary to the technical manager. You are happy in your new job but disturbed at the attitude of the production controller, who is very difficult to deal with. Unfortunately, you cannot avoid him as you frequently need to liaise with him about important information.

During the past week he has shouted at you in front of three other staff, refused to give you some urgent information because he said you should have given him more notice and pointedly refused to answer any of the numerous e-mails you sent him.

a What suggestions can you make to account for his behaviour?

b What initiatives could you take to try to influence or change his behaviour?

c What would you do if your initiatives did not work?

Case study

You are employed as administrator in a large firm of solicitors. Once a month, you hold a meeting for the 15 clerical and secretarial staff and it is agreed that this should be held on the last Thursday in the month between 8.30 am and 9.30 am, provided one person is left to cover reception and the switchboard.

At a recent meeting of the partners, the suggestion was made that all administrative and secretarial staff should wear a uniform in the firm's colours of pink and grey. It has, however, been agreed that the style and design of the uniforms can be decided by staff. Whilst this will be the main focus of the forthcoming meeting, you have two other items of information for staff – the refurbishment of the front office which will start in three weeks' time and the fact that the partners have agreed all staff can have a day's leave for Christmas shopping this year. You should note that correspondence is not usually an item at these meetings.

1 Prepare the notice and agenda for staff.

2 During the meeting, there is considerable dissent about the issue of the uniforms. Some members of staff are totally opposed. To make matters worse, the staff are a mixture of ages and sizes and cannot agree on a standard design. One redhead is horrified about the idea of wearing a pink blouse.

State the strategies you would employ to facilitate decision-making amongst the group so that you have a consensus to take back to the senior partners.

3 What action would you take to ensure that the one missing member of the group has her views taken into consideration?

4 It is eventually agreed that staff will accede to the proposal and most have suggested a grey suit with pale pink blouse. However, they wish to vary the design of the blouse in summer so that the uniform will comprise a summery top and skirt. They also want to decide their own length and style of skirt. They have asked you to make these views known.

Prepare the minutes for the meeting assuming that

a only Sarah Taylor, who was on the switchboard, was absent

b under 'any other business' staff asked if information on the staff Christmas social could be available earlier this year as last year many had made other arrangements by the time the date was announced

c the meeting went smoothly in all other respects. The information on the refurbishment was accepted without comment though staff were very pleased about the extra day's leave for shopping.

The administrative control function

● Introduction

So far this book has discussed the various aspects of working as an administrator or a secretary in a modern office. You now know how to research information, write and produce documents, use a computer effectively, greet visitors, balance the petty cash and prepare for a meeting – to name but a few of the tasks covered! However, there is a danger in seeing these as isolated and discrete activities which take place in a random way, whenever someone appears in reception, suddenly wants a letter producing or decides to hold a meeting. Whereas some activities will always be a response to a situation, the majority are routine requirements which are fundamental to the day-to-day successful operation of the business. For that reason they are part of a planned operation with each person taking his or her part in order to achieve specified objectives.

This integration, coordination and organisation of activities does not happen by chance. It is tightly planned, scheduled, monitored and controlled. It utilises the abilities and strengths of different members of staff and individual teams together with the resources of the enterprise to the best advantage. The more effectively this is accomplished, the greater the likelihood that planned activities will be undertaken successfully within the time constraints and budget allowed – and the easier it is for members of staff to see the individual contributions they have made – which leads to greater job satisfaction.

Your role in this process, as an administrator or secretary/PA, is considerable. If, having the skills to undertake the tasks you have to carry out is 'the administrative cake', then the ability to plan, organise and deliver to time is the 'icing'. These skills will mark you out as a true professional who can identify with the needs of managers to deliver results in the most efficient and effective way.

This section concentrates on helping you to develop these skills by reviewing the importance of systems and procedures (first introduced in Section 2) as invaluable methods for controlling the standards and output of a variety of activities – and learning when and how to instigate and implement these. It then examines how to develop the skills of planning and prioritising of work, managing your time and resources and organising your own working environment as well as controlling other aspects of work for which you are responsible.

Again this section gives you practical guidance. The theoretical approach to administrative work, systems and procedures and coordination and planning is covered in the companion book, *Business for Advanced Secretarial Students.*

● Introduction

For a moment forget about offices and business. Imagine two groups of friends, all of whom are having a 21st birthday in the next few months. The friends in each group decide to pool their collective abilities so each will help the others to organise their celebrations.

The friends in Group A realise that if they get it right the first time, the subsequent parties will be very much easier as they can use their masterplan over and over again – although they may make improvements based on experience. They spend some time working out their budget and then planning the food and drink they can afford. They buy carefully, according to their plan, and shop around for the best buys. They work out how long they will need to prepare the food and start work in good time – with each clearly knowing what he or she has to do. All their equipment is to hand, everyone knows where the various items are stored. Sometimes each person works alone, for other tasks they join together. Complicated dishes are created by the most talented member who has brought along her tried and tested recipe book. The leader of the group keeps an eye on the time to check everything is going to plan. An hour and a half before the event is due to start everything is completed and set out for the guests and the friends disappear to get ready.

Group B has a similar idea to group A, but the friends decide to take a more individual approach. They prefer not to plan and since they have little time to meet beforehand, decide that each person should turn up on the day with a range of groceries to make their favourite dishes.

Discussion point

Discuss as a group and with your tutor

a   which group will be the more successful

b   the likely consequences of the Group B approach

c   the type of improvements Group A might make if the friends have a review session between the first and second parties

d   the importance of the Group A approach if the friends decided to become professional caterers.

● The importance of having a system

Group A took a systematic approach to the task of catering for a large number of people. This immediately meant that it was better organised from the outset. Group B, by contrast, took the random or haphazard approach. The benefits of planning what to do and making sure all group members knew their own jobs were as follows.

- Everyone was clear about what must be achieved.

- Each person clearly understood his or her responsibilities and duties.

- There was no unnecessary duplication or overlap of items purchased or activities.

- Fewer mistakes (and accidents) were likely to happen.

- The workspace could be used more effectively.

- Equipment could be shared more productively.

- Everyone knew how much they had to produce and the time scale involved.

- Set procedures could be followed for complex operations (eg as given in the recipes).

- Quality of output could be controlled and guaranteed to a higher degree – even if someone else had offered to join the team at the last minute.

Group A had a clear system which everyone knew about and could follow. All systems are designed to enable a large number of people to undertake different activities with each knowing what they must do and when. This means that coordination is relatively easy (people do not need to be told over and over again what to do), the results can be forecast more accurately and the quality of the 'end product' can be controlled and standardised to a greater degree.

One of the most elaborate systems with which we are all involved is the UK traffic system. This has been designed to enable a large number of people and a variety of vehicles to use the same roads, at the same time, with a high degree of safety and the minimum of delays and inconvenience. Generally, it is only when people do not follow the system (eg drive through red traffic lights) or there are interferences (eg roadworks) that these objectives are not achieved.

To support any system it is necessary to have set procedures. You follow various procedures, as a road user, when you cross a road, or negotiate a roundabout. All these procedures are clearly documented in the *Highway Code* which drivers must prove they know before being given a full driving licence.

From this analogy we can see that

- a system is developed to control the behaviour of users and help to guarantee results

- a system is required when there are **clear objectives** (results) to be achieved – usually to obtain quality of output with limited resources (including time)

- setting up a system means that users follow a **sequence of activities** which are determined as part of the system

- **procedures** specify these activities which are designed so that the input of individual users will be standardised and are integrated into the system as a whole

- anyone using the system must know the procedures they have to follow and it is normal to **document** these in some way so they can be kept for future reference.

A further point you may like to consider is the degree of control required. With some procedures there are tight controls – you would be prosecuted, for instance, if there was evidence that you had driven through a red light. With others there is less control – the procedure may simply be a *recommended way* of doing something. For instance, you are advised to show a warning triangle if you break down and to stay with your car – but you would not be prosecuted if you failed to do so. The degree of control should correspond to the seriousness of the problems which would be caused if the procedure is not followed. Tight controls on marginal activities are apt to annoy people, who feel constrained and restricted by them.

Discussion point

Systems and procedures have been discussed in various chapters of this book. In each of the systems listed below, identify with your tutor

a why a system is required

b the type of procedures which would support each system

c the type of procedures which would be closely controlled and those which would be only recommendations.

You may wish to look back at the relevant pages before you answer this question.

A system for

1 dealing with visitors (pages 51–8)

2 handling petty cash (pages 81–3)

3 delivering incoming mail (pages 31–40)

4 controlling stationery stock (pages 68–74).

● Identifying the need for a system

It is fairly easy to see that you will need some sort of system whenever you have a specific objective to achieve and several users participating in the operation. Otherwise everyone will 'do their own thing' and there will be no coordination, organisation or integration of the different activities. Neither can quality be guaranteed. Any new system should be designed to

- make jobs easier for staff

- enable time or money to be saved

- deliver benefits in improved service to customers and clients

and preferably, all three! Usually you can quickly identify the need for a system if you see that there would be obvious benefits to users and the company as a whole if there was a standard way of doing something.

In some cases a system can be in place but can 'break down' because it is out of date or no longer has any relevance to achieving the objective. For instance, the office of the future is unlikely to have the same type of system and procedures to deal with incoming mail as we have today because of the growth in e-mail and faxed messages. In other cases, a system – or a set of procedures – can be amended or developed because users suggest sensible improvements which can be made (such as would have been made during the review meeting after the first 21st party was held).

In some organisations a **systems audit** is carried out at regular intervals which identifies the types of systems in place, and what they aim to achieve, and also investigates their usefulness as well as the degree to which they are followed by users and achieve their objectives. A review of a system is carried out if it is failing in some way. This may mean it is scrapped altogether (if there is no longer any need for it) or replaced by a redesigned and updated system. In other cases, a systems audit may show that there is no system in place for a new objective which must be achieved.

The need for expert advice

Do be careful that you are not tempted to introduce and develop a procedure relating to a specialist area without obtaining expert advice. For instance, if your boss wished to introduce a procedure for dealing with claims of sexual or racial harassment, then you would need to make sure that you were operating within current employment legislation. If you were asked to introduce a system to ensure that all computer staff complied with the requirements of the Display Screen Equipment Regulations, you would need to know what these were. If you were reviewing the current procedure for fire drills you would find it beneficial to study the current Fire Regulations.

Given the complexity of many aspects of the law, you would be sensible to obtain the views and guidance of an expert. Large organisations usually employ a human resources manager, a computer services manager and a health and safety officer, all of whom would have a wider view of the implications than you are likely to have. If you work for a small organisation, then you may have to contact outside experts. In this case, you may obtain helpful assistance from the Trades Union Congress (TUC), Health and Safety Executive (HSE) and local fire officer, respectively.

Case study on systems and procedures: stage 1

You work for JA Computer Services, an organisation which has grown in size considerably over the past few years. This has resulted in many activities being undertaken without formal systems and procedures, simply because initially they were done by one person or could be controlled easily by one of the managers. You have recently been appointed as administrator to sort out these problems and to design and introduce systems and procedures where they are needed. At the first planning meeting with your boss, he identified two priorities which are given below.

1   There is no formal system for staff to book their annual leave entitlement or personal days. All staff are entitled to 25 days' annual leave, including statutory days, which rises to 30 days after 3 years' employment. At present staff simply check with their line manager before taking a day off or a week's holiday.

2   The filing is chaotic. There are several horizontal cabinets in various offices and many papers are duplicated in different cabinets or are completely out of date. In particular, your boss wants to make sure that, as a top priority, the customer files are sorted and kept in one

place so that important documents can be found quickly. As it is, you would have to make a round trip of five offices to collect all the paperwork relating to one customer!

As a first stage, identify, with your tutor and your colleagues, the **benefits** which would accrue to the company if a proper system was introduced in both these areas. Keep your suggestions safely on one side until you have read the information in Stage 2 below.

Developing a system

The need for a new or updated system may be identified by you, your colleagues or your manager. Of course, if you work in a very well-organised company, which believes in the benefits of systems and procedures, you are likely to find that you have to follow procedures yourself to ensure that you set up the system correctly. For the first time, then, you may see the benefit of having procedures which can act as guidelines so that you have less scope for making mistakes! An example set of procedures for developing a system is given in Figure 18.1. It is then possible to follow these procedures to examine the implications of each stage of the process.

Need for system identified

If you identify the need for a system, you should obtain your boss's permission before you start planning in detail. Otherwise you may find yourself undertaking a considerable amount of work for no useful purpose! In addition, your boss may already know if there is a similar system in force elsewhere in the organisation and/or the best people you could ask for expert help and guidance if this is required. You should therefore think out the requirements for the system thoroughly before approaching your boss – as you are likely to be asked to identify the possible benefits and the main objectives at the outset.

If you are acting on instructions from your boss in the first place, it is likely he or she will have given considerable thought to these aspects first and, quite obviously, you have no need to seek any other official approval for the preliminary investigations you will be expected to make.

Undertake feasibility study

A feasibility study is undertaken to determine

- whether it is financially worthwhile to implement the system

- the most cost-effective system to introduce, if there are several alternatives.

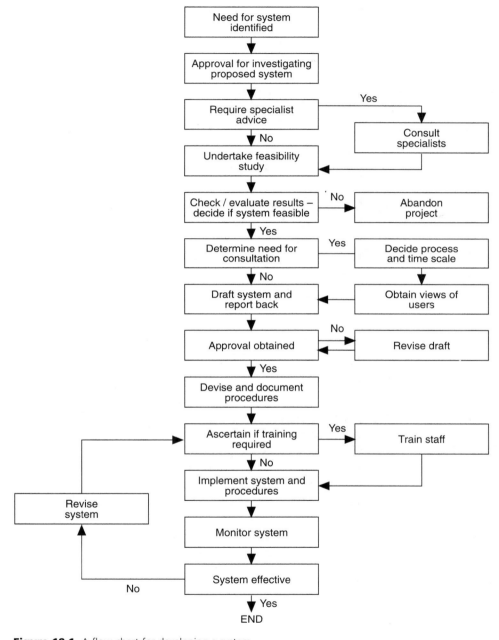

Figure 18.1 A flow chart for developing a system

This is done by identifying the possible and projected benefits and comparing these with the costs of implementation for the alternatives available. For this reason, people often talk about undertaking a **cost–benefit analysis** to decide whether it is worthwhile proceeding with the proposal.

Identifying benefits

You have already identified benefits from the case study given on page 411. From this you should be able to see that

- a benefit is always positive

- some benefits are financial – they relate to the more effective use of materials, equipment, staff or money

- other benefits relate to the advantages to be gained by users of the system or other people. These are often termed **social benefits** – and are harder to quantify (ie put into numerical or financial terms).

Identifying costs

In the same way, the 'costs' of introducing a new system are not just financial. You should note that

- a cost is always negative

- costs can also be financial and social

- financial costs usually relate to the increased use of materials, equipment, staff or money

- costs can usually be quantified (ie translated into monetary terms), but not always.

Comparing benefits and costs

For a system to be worth introducing, the benefits must outweigh the costs. However, alternative proposals may have different costs and benefits – but achieve similar objectives. For instance, in our case study, JA Computer Services has a chaotic filing system. The degree to which the filing is reorganised and the amount of expenditure on new equipment would affect costs. So would a decision to introduce electronic filing. The higher the costs, the greater the perceived benefits must be. However, if the organisation is still increasing in size it is normally cost-effective to consider the potential requirements rather than the existing ones. It is wasting money to set up a system which would need revising drastically in a very short time.

To save time, it is usual to obtain details of the costs of various alternatives before submitting any ideas or recommendations. A decision can be made as to which option would be most appropriate given the resources available and the likely benefits.

Social costs include the amount of disruption to staff, annoyance and inconvenience whilst new procedures have to be learned and followed and the degree to which staff may object to new controls over areas in which they previously had more freedom to operate. These 'costs' can usually be minimised if staff are involved in the discussions about the new proposals and, where appropriate, consulted for their ideas and suggestions (see below).

Case study on systems and procedures: stage 2

1. Identify all the social costs involved in devising a strict system to check staff holidays and leave entitlement. What objections do you think may be raised by staff and how do you think these could be overcome?

2. Divide into two groups and research the costs of
    a. modern equipment to hold paper files
    b. electronic filing systems.

3. As a group, identify the likely costs and benefits of implementing a filing system which
    a. uses the existing equipment where possible but reorganises its location so that customer files are kept centrally by you, as administrator, and your assistants
    b. sets up a completely new centralised unit for customer files with specialist equipment and a new member of staff to oversee the system
    c. introduces an electronic filing system for all customer files
        i. where documents are scanned in by an agency
        ii. where documents are scanned in-house.

The need for discussion and consultation

If you have undertaken the exercise above, you will already have had some types of discussion and consultation – in this case with those who manufacture or sell filing equipment and electronic systems. This is another example of obtaining expert advice and information, which was mentioned on page 411. However, be careful when contacting suppliers, as obviously each will concentrate only on the likely benefits to be gained by their own equipment – not the costs! It is therefore sensible to get several quotations and to compare the costs of different systems yourself.

Once a new system has been decided in principle, however, an important step is to consider the needs of those people who will have to use it and follow the procedures you devise. You also need to consider the views of other people who may be affected – this is likely to include your boss, and may include other departments and possibly even other organisations. You then need to decide whether to go ahead and **inform** people about the new system or whether to **consult** them first.

Giving people information

Telling people is usually better than consultation if there is no useful contribution that they could make to designing the system or influencing the procedures. People become annoyed if they are asked for advice which is then simply ignored. It is therefore more suitable to inform people if you are introducing a system or procedure which

- has been designed in accordance with legal requirements
  (eg the procedure to use in case of emergency evacuations)

- has been designed by experts to solve a particular, serious problem
  (eg a procedure to minimise the risk of computer viruses)

- has been imposed upon you from above (eg to follow a new government
  regulation)

- no one can do anything about (eg if your company is moving offices next
  week and all the furniture must be out by Friday)

- is fairly standard and routine and which staff would expect to follow
  (eg a procedure for submitting overtime claims) ·

- has to be introduced in a hurry – so that there simply is not time for
  consultation at this stage.

Consulting others

Consulting potential users, however, has several benefits because

- they will often have a wider range of knowledge and experiences than
  you and you will benefit by drawing on this expertise

- staff will be more likely to follow a new system – and understand it – if
  they have contributed to its design and feel some 'ownership' of it

- you may gain knowledge of possible consequences you had not even
  thought about

- people who do something every day usually resent an 'outside expert'
  telling them how they should do their job

- you will usually obtain more support for your ideas

- several heads are usually better than one – different contributions enable
  you to see things from more than one perspective.

However, there can be problems with consultation:

- It can be time consuming, particularly if you want to ensure everyone
  has an equal say.

- Some people feel they must make some sort of suggestion – otherwise
  they will be seen as someone without an opinion. They may therefore
  make suggestions which are unhelpful, naive or even negative and
  destructive.

- You may end up with several conflicting suggestions.

- People are apt to be annoyed if they make, what is to them, a reasonable
  suggestion to find later that it has not been taken into account. This may
  make them negative towards the whole new system.

You can usually prevent these problems if you restrict your consultations to those who have some expertise on the issue, will have to follow the new system and/or will be affected by its implementation. It is also useful to have a clear outline of your proposed system in your mind before commencing consultation (at least know what is and is not feasible!) which at least sets the parameters of the discussion – even though you should keep an open mind about the details. It is then sensible to try to include some – or at least one – of the suggestions you receive into your specification for the new system and give reasons for the rejection of other suggestions. Another useful strategy is to implement the proposed system for a 'trial period' and then obtain feedback on the results.

Making savings through consultation

Companies which do not consult their staff often waste money in an attempt to please them. This was the finding of one consultancy, Hays Personnel Services, which carried out a survey to find out what type of 'perks' made staff happy. The consultancy found, to its surprise, that many could be provided by companies with little cost and that most staff preferred fresh coffee, cold drinks and free snacks to the use of a company car!

The most popular perk of all was found to be the staff biscuit tin. Others included birthday cakes, fans in summer and Christmas gifts. Even

cheaper – or virtually free – options included being able to miss the rush hour traffic by leaving early on Friday, having a day off for Christmas shopping or on their birthday and being able to dress more informally on a Friday.

Some companies introduce additional perks to avoid giving a pay rise or are re-evaluating staff perks to save costs. Another, more positive approach, is to revise and reformulate these – in line with staff suggestions – to improve staff motivation and encourage a positive response to changes in working practices.

Drafting the system and reporting back

If you have followed the procedure outlined so far, you will now have obtained a variety of suggestions which can be used to inform your initial ideas. At this stage you should be able to refine your ideas and consider a suitable system which you could recommend to your boss. It is usual to present your recommendations in the form of a report which takes into consideration all the key aspects. The main points to consider include

- the aim of the system, ie what are the objectives it is trying to achieve

- the different alternatives you have considered – and the costs/benefits of each

- the resources which would be required for your recommended system

- the possible side-effects which may result from its implementation, both positive and negative

- the needs of the users and how much training they will require

- the procedures which will be required to support the system and how these should be documented

- the time scale over which the system should be introduced

- the measures you will use to check the system is effective, ie achieving its objectives.

You should remember that you have already undertaken report writing in chapter 12 – and that this was specifically concerned, even then, with systems and procedures (otherwise turn back to pages 246–8 to refresh your memory).

Case study on systems and procedures: stage 3

1 During your initial discussions with your boss, he informed you that he saw no reason why staff should be consulted about the proposed system for logging their holidays as everyone knew their official entitlement and he had no intention of renegotiating this.

   What do you consider are the strengths and weaknesses of this approach?

2 Your investigations into a possible system for logging holiday entitlement have led you to make several notes, shown in Figure 18.2.

   Use these to prepare a short report, giving your recommendations. Make sure that you cover the main points as outlined above.

3 As a group, discuss the possible range of responses you are likely to receive from staff if you decided to consult them about your proposals for a centralised filing system. In what way(s) do you think their input may affect your eventual recommendations?

Obtaining approval

It is possible that your report may be accepted in its entirety and your recommendations approved. However, it is more likely that your report will be returned with queries, suggestions or requests for additional information,

NOTES ON INVESTIGATIONS

Terms of ref: report requested by MD

Procedure: Investigated current practices - no formal system for requesting / booking leave

Findings   - most make request to line manager - out of courtesy
            - no records kept
            - most mgrs think leave entitlement abused by some staff
            Leads to difficulty locating / tracing staff

Conclusion - current practise open to abuse
              system urgently required

    Rec   - leave form produced showing name, years worked, leave entitlement
            - staff negotiate dates with line manager & enter on form
            - line manager approves form (bearing in mind cover for duties) & submits (to me?)
            - check & record on wall-mounted holiday planner

    Advs   - cheap, simple to use

    Disads- what about emergencies eg personal leave for funerals, family illnesses etc? Need to
            discuss this.

Implement immediately - inform staff by memo & attach form. 14 days to complete / agree /
submit.

Obtain feedback from line managers on success of new system after 6-8 wks.

Figure 18.2 Notes on a possible system for logging holidays

particularly if you included little information on costs or glossed over the resources required! Your boss is far more likely to be interested in 'the bottom line' (ie how much it will cost) than in how the staff should be trained. Time and again, however, people submit reports which give maximum emphasis to the 'softer sections' which contain more woolly information. Wherever possible you should guard against this as you will simply find that you are asked to provide more details the second time around.

You not only need approval for your idea overall, but also agreement on the time scale for implementation, the expenditure required – and support for when you notify staff. This is particularly the case if the users extend beyond staff for whom you are personally responsible – as you will need your boss's authority before they will comply. If he or she notifies them about the new system, this will obviously carry more weight, and mean that serious objections or arguments are not referred to you.

Devising procedures

The key consideration for users is the procedures that they will have to follow. Frequently, people lose sight of the overall system, or what it is trying to achieve; all they concentrate upon is the tasks they must do. You know this yourself – how often do you use the roads and think about the system as a whole? Probably, never! Yet most procedures you know by heart.

Procedures are usually documented in a number of ways.

* By a step-by-step approach which states the sequence of activities that must be followed. An example relating to dealing with visitors is given in Figure 18.3 – other examples were included on pages 36 and 45.

COMPANY PROCEDURE FOR GREETING VISITORS

(To be kept in reception at all times)

1 Greet visitor(s) courteously.

2 Find out if visitor has appointment and/or the person he or she is visiting.

3 Ask visitor to complete visitor book.

4 Notify member of staff by telephone of visitor's arrival.

5 Check all sections in visitor's log have been completed by visitor.

6 Tear off bottom section of visitor log (top copy only) and give to visitor. This is his or her official pass. Inform visitor that the pass must be handed in to reception upon departure.

7 Ask visitor to wait in reception until collected by member of staff.

8 Remind member of staff if visitor still in reception after 10 minutes.

9 When visitor leaves, collect pass.

10 At end of day check that number of passes handed in matches total number of visitors into building. Report any discrepancy to the office administrator.

Figure 18.3 A step-by-step approach to documenting a procedure

* A flow chart includes alternative actions which can be taken. An example was given in Figure 18.1.

* Through the use of graphics – this is usual if equipment or machinery is involved as a graphical representation is easier to understand. Virtually all photocopier and fax manuals show illustrations to guide the user in the correct procedures to follow.

If several procedures relate to the same system, it is usual to combine these in a **procedure manual** which includes clear instructions for users. An example of a procedure manual would be the user guide you receive when you buy any item of new equipment or computer software – whether at home or in an office. If you have ever seen some user guides or software manuals, you will appreciate that the length can vary considerably, but there are some golden rules you should follow!

- The procedures should be clear and straightforward so they are easy to follow.

- They must contain sufficient detail for all users to be able to follow them without having to ask for additional information.

- They should specify what has to be done and, if appropriate, by whom it must be done, how it will be done, where and when it will be done! This can often result in the drawing up of a specification for all involved. An example is shown in Figure 18.4 – this time it involves the procedure for dealing with interview candidates which requires the coordination of several people's activities to run smoothly.

Action	By whom	Location	Time
Greet candidates and direct to waiting room	Receptionist	Reception	Upon arrival
Notify administrator of number of arrivals	Receptionist	Administrator's office	At nominated time for start of interviews
Greet candidates and give brief introduction to company and interview procedure	Interviewer	Waiting room	As above
Escort first interviewee to interview area	Interviewer	Interview area	At appointed times
Candidates to be taken on tour of building	Admin. staff	Waiting room	At pre-arranged times
Candidates to be served coffee	Canteen staff	Waiting room	At pre-arranged times
Candidates to be notified individually of result	Interviewer	Own office	At end of session

Figure 18.4 Specification for dealing with interview candidates

- The procedure manual should contain details of the system to which the procedures relate, the originator of the system, the person who approved it and the date of implementation. This way users know who to ask if they have a query and can also tell whether or not the procedures are currently in force. In a large organisation this may be essential.

- A copy of the manual should be kept in all offices where users are based, so that it can be used for reference.

Hints and tips for writing procedures

When writing a procedure, start by dividing it into simple steps. If you find yourself writing a very complicated instruction, consider whether the use of graphics would be appropriate and assist understanding. Finally, think about whether any alternative actions are involved and how to show these. Wherever possible keep your procedure simple and to the point – if required you can always attach explanatory notes for first-time users.

At this point you need assistance. It is always the case that we can understand our own instructions more easily than other people's – because we know what we meant to say (even if we did not explain it very well!) You therefore need to test your procedure on several potential users to check whether

- they can follow your instructions

- the procedure works

- the procedure achieves its desired objective(s)

- there are unexpected or problematic side-effects or consequences.

Bear in mind that the degree to which procedures *must* be watertight does vary. Some procedures must be written to fulfil their objectives 100 per cent of the time. This would obviously be the case if you were designing an emergency evacuation procedure. However, in other cases such a requirement would be unrealistic. For instance, you are unlikely to develop any procedure for handling customer complaints which would result in 100 per cent satisfaction of all customers all the time!

Always be prepared to amend your procedure when you receive feedback. If several adjustments have to be made, it is sensible to test your revised procedure. If you are new to writing procedures, then you can expect several redrafts before you obtain the best result. Remember you will never look foolish consulting people to obtain their opinions – you *will* look silly if you insist on implementing a procedure which clearly does not work!

Case study of systems and procedures: stage 4

1   There are various procedures in which you are involved in your
    personal life or as a college student, eg
    - how to enrol as a student
    - how to log on and log off your computer system
    - how to make a photocopy
    - how to answer a telephone.

    Select any one of these examples (or substitute an idea of your own
    if your tutor agrees) and write a simple, step-by-step procedure for
    other users to follow. Then test your procedure by asking other
    members of the group for their opinion!

2   You have received the memo shown in Figure 18.5 from your boss,
    which gives approval to your recommendations for a system for
    logging holiday requests, together with a suggested procedure.
    Expand this into a flow chart as requested and compare your
    attempt with those of other members of your group.

3   As a group, decide the type of procedures and instructions which
    would be included in a procedures manual to support the new
    centralised filing system. Then divide these between you and write
    one each for your tutor's approval.

● Implementing the system

Before your system 'goes live', you need to make sure that everything has
been prepared – including the staff! This may mean arranging training
sessions for both users and those who will administer the system. Often a
timetable for the introduction is devised, showing what is planned to happen
and when. Needless to say, you will need all your documentation to hand
before any training sessions start – so that people have the correct
paperwork.

The way in which you introduce the system and train staff will depend
largely upon the type of system being introduced, its complexity and the
number of potential users and administrators involved and their previous
experience. You may have the choice whether to

- arrange formal training sessions

- issue guidelines in memos, leaflets and help sheets

- provide policy documents and instruction sheets

- give demonstrations

- hold discussions with key groups of staff.

MEMO

TO   You

FROM   Your boss

DATE   (today)

PROPOSED STAFF LEAVE SYSTEM

Thank you for your recent report giving your proposals for the above system. I have considered this in some detail and feel that it is suitable for implementation.

I appreciate, however, the concern you express for coping with last-minute emergencies, such as personal leave for family illnesses, the funerals of close relatives, weddings and the like. I have decided to allow all staff up to 3 days' personal leave a year for this type of event, above that the time must be taken from the holiday leave entitlement. Serious family crises and illnesses will be considered separately, with counselling where required.

I will prepare guidelines for all staff, giving them the information they need and we can issue this in conjunction with the memo advising them of the new system.

I suggest staff follow a procedure whereby

- they log their leave for the year (1 April-31 March)
- they agree their requests with their line manager
- if this is not granted (because of clashes with key staff), then they will have to revise their request
- when the form is agreed, the manager signs it
- you receive the form and note the leave on the central wall planner
- if an emergency occurs staff use any remaining days, if possible + up to 3 personal emergency days
- staff who have used up their allowance must see their line manager before having any additional time off.

Is there some way you could convert this into a flow chart for them?

Thank you

Figure 18.5 A memo from your boss

Training methods should, wherever possible, be linked to the ability of staff and their needs. You would therefore not use the same method with a group of users who are senior members of the organisation as you would with two junior members of staff who have just been appointed and whose jobs will be concerned with the operation of certain aspects of the system.

You will also need to provide some back-up facility to help new users in the first few weeks (such as a help line or help desk), particularly if the system is complex or if there are many people involved. For that reason you usually find that organisations which change their computer systems operate such a facility until everyone is clear about what they are doing.

Different types of implementation

Some systems are so vital that even when a new system is introduced, the old one continues for some time – just in case there is a disaster. Examples in business include the installation of a new computer system or the changeover from a manual to a computerised pay system. The potential problems inherent if things go wrong on a large scale are so horrendous that it is considered safer (albeit more inconvenient and expensive) to operate both systems together for a trial period.

Another way of minimising problems is to 'phase in' a new system. This can mean it is introduced either in stages, over a period of time, or geographically – one area at a time.

This is the case when it is impossible to resource an immediate changeover (say, because of the number of staff involved and because of the amount of organisation necessary). An example is the introduction of the Channel 5 broadcasting system which requires the re-tuning of millions of customer videos all over the country.

When such phasing is impossible, for instance, with the introduction of a new system of dialling codes, a back-up system is usually available to users until everyone gets used to the new system, eg BT puts voice prompts on the line if a code is changed, to advise users who have dialled the old code to redial.

● Monitoring the system

Even when a system has been introduced, and users have become familiar with the procedures involved, it is sensible to check that it is still meeting its objectives over a period of time. This can be undertaken officially – through carrying out a systems audit – or unofficially – by asking people their opinions. Often monitoring the results is the key determinant. A system which still meets its objectives and is considered to be good by all those who use it should be left well alone! However, if it is constantly failing to achieve what it was set up to do, and there is widespread user dissatisfaction, rapid revision is usually required.

Case study of systems and procedures: stage 5

1　Although you introduced the system for logging staff holidays some time ago, and issued information on the procedure to follow to all staff, one particular group of staff is failing to follow it. Last week you found out by accident that two members in the section had booked a day's leave each for this week and not bothered to notify anyone.

　　As a group, discuss the actions you could take to solve this problem and the problems you are likely to encounter if you do nothing!

2　The equipment has arrived for the new centralised filing system and the office area designated for it has been redecorated. The procedure manual has been completed.

　　As a group, decide how you would

　　a　train the managers who will release customer documents for filing
　　b　train their secretaries, who will need to retrieve these documents
　　c　train the two new filing clerks who have been appointed to run the system, under your overall control.

3　Three months after the implementation of the system your boss informs you that he has received the following complaints.

　　a　There are long delays providing documents – even in an emergency.
　　b　When an important contract was lost recently, each filing clerk blamed the other. The contract was later found in another office.
　　c　When one filing clerk was absent with flu, the other struggled to cope.

　　As a group, decide what you would do to answer these criticisms.

● Introduction

There is little point in being able to design and implement systems and procedures which must be used by other people to control office activities and output, if you cannot plan, organise and control your own work! Although it may seem tempting, not everything can be controlled by devising a system or procedure – indeed, if it could, this would remove much of the spontaneity and enjoyment from your job! Generally, the more senior your position, the more you will be expected to cope with the unexpected and the different – often at the last minute and frequently simultaneously! This ability to 'keep several balls in the air' and still look serene is a skill which must be learned and developed – few people are born with it. Usually, as a rough rule of thumb, the more balls you can keep in the air simultaneously then the higher your pay! It is therefore a skill which is well worth learning.

Your ability to deal with a wide variety of different tasks, with different priorities and time scales, as well as the routine aspects of your job, will depend upon the following factors

- Your ability to plan, schedule and prioritise work.

- Your ability to manage your own time.

- Your organisational skills (and memory!).

- Your attention to detail.

- Your ability to deal with the unexpected.

This chapter develops these areas in more detail (time management is discussed in chapter 20) as well as giving you practical guidance and hints and tips on what to do – and not to do!

● Work planning methods

There are various ways in which you can plan the work you have to do. Much will depend upon your own personal preferences and the type of activities you undertake. At the college at which you are a student, for instance, different methods will be used to plan

- a new course which is to be held next year

- the timetables for students and staff

- the order in which topics should be taught on a course

- the number of assignments students on certain courses must submit, their content, and the final date for assessment of each.

This is because each of the objectives shown above has different components and different implications – as you will see below.

● Target setting and action planning

If the task with which you are involved has a clear target, the most likely method you will use is an action plan. If the target is the goal, then the action plan is the route you will take to achieve that goal. The route may be long or short – depending upon how far you are away from the goal at the moment.

An action plan is a list of activities which you will undertake, usually in time/date order, which will lead you towards your goal. If several people are involved, it is usual for each person's name to be entered on the action plan alongside the particular activities for which individuals are responsible. The activities are usually listed in sequential order and progress meetings can be held to check that everything is going 'according to plan'.

Bear in mind that an action plan is normally suitable only if there is a single target to achieve. Multiple targets usually mean a different approach is required.

Discussion point

1   Figure 19.1 shows an action plan for a new course to be offered by your college. Note how each activity has been identified and listed with the target date for completion alongside – plus the name of the person responsible for the activity.

2   Assume you wish to plan a holiday in the United States for next summer with three friends. Make out an action plan which shows the series of activities you will have to undertake and compare this with the attempts of other members of your group.

3   Discuss with your tutor the action you would take if a member of your team frequently 'forgot' to undertake activities for which he or she was responsible.

```
ACTION PLAN FOR NEW LEGAL COURSE

1   Complete costings                AG      7 Jan

2   Complete approval form           DK      14 Jan

3   Submit to approvals committee    TY      20 Jan

4   Prepare submission               Team    28 Feb

5   Submit for internal validation   TY      13 March

6   Submit for external validation   TY      5 April

7   Organise staff development       DK      1 May

8   Advertise course                 MP      June-August
```

Figure 19.1 An action plan is a list of activities in date order showing who is responsible for each

Scheduling

Probably one of the most complex planning activities which anyone can imagine is that undertaken by airlines at the height of the summer season! Imagine trying to plan in detail the number of planes, the routes and destinations, the crews, the take-off and landing slots and to keep in mind, at the same time, that planes earn money only whilst they are in the air and not on the ground!

Scheduling is used when you have a variety of objectives and a number of resources. It is used in your college to decide your timetable. Here the resources involve staff, rooms and groups of students. All have to be brought together in the most effective way to make maximum use of rooms, the best use of staff expertise and qualifications and without making students attend one class from 9 am to 10 am and then have a break until 3 pm!

Scheduling takes longer than action planning because, by its very nature, it is more complex. There are far more variables to consider. In some cases there are computer programs to help but not always. You will often find that the worst aspect of scheduling is knowing where to start! The best way is to

- read carefully any criteria which will affect your schedule (eg days people are/are not available)

- make a first attempt in *pencil*

- identify all the areas where there is a mismatch or a gap and shuffle everything around where necessary

- re-read the criteria to check you have allowed for/covered everything

- try to improve the schedule as best you can – checking that you have met all the criteria.

💬 Discussion point

As a first attempt at scheduling, try the exercise below. Then compare your final attempt with those of other members of your group.

Margaret Stephens, the health and safety officer in JA Computer Services, is arranging for all members of the Human Resources staff (except herself) to attend a two-day fire safety course. The course will run on Monday/Tuesday, and Wednesday/Thursday over the next two weeks. All staff *must* attend, but only two can attend at the same time to prevent a backlog of work occurring in the office. To complicate matters, some staff have other arrangements over the next fortnight which must be taken into consideration.

You have been given the course rota and asked to enter names on the most appropriate dates for attendance. Below is a list of staff commitments during the two weeks, which must be considered when the rota is drawn up. From this information, copy out the rota shown in Figure 19.2 and complete it in the best order possible.

Staff commitments

Gerry Pugh and Sylvia MacGregor go to college every Tuesday so cannot attend on that day. You go to college every Thursday.

Karen Felix is in London throughout the second week.

Mohammed Patel can attend only on 13 and 14 November.

Amina Hussein takes the minutes of the weekly meeting every Thursday and wants to attend the course during the second week.

Frank Blower is running a training course all the first week.

Vivien Carr can attend only on 6 and 7 November.

Gerry Pugh must attend the second week.

FIRE SAFETY COURSE ROTA		
Members of staff are scheduled to attend as shown below:		
Mon/Tues 4/5 Nov		
Wed/Thur 6/7 Nov		
Mon/Tues 11/12 Nov		
Wed/Thur 13/14 Nov		

Figure 19.2 An outline rota for completion

● Prioritising

Prioritising sounds like common sense. It involves doing the most complicated, important or urgent activities first. However, there are times when even these criteria conflict, eg

- how do you cope if some items are urgent and some are important

- what do you do if your boss has some items which are also urgent and important

- what strategies should you use if, during a particularly hectic day, even more urgent items arrive?

If you take each stage a step at a time the situation becomes easier to deal with.

Every administrator and secretary has an in–tray which *should* (if you are organised!) contain the papers which must be dealt with. Add to this

- the notes for letters, memos and telephone calls in your notepad

- e-mail messages to which a response is required

- ongoing jobs which must be done daily or weekly, eg filing, completing records, etc.

There are few people who believe that the most sensible way of undertaking these jobs is to process the tasks in the order in which they were received! A task which you were given at 9 am may not be required for a fortnight; the one you received 10 minutes ago may be needed in 5 minutes' time! For that reason you should process tasks by order of requirement, not arrival.

A useful guideline is to divide tasks into

- those which must be done immediately (ie urgent tasks)

- those which must be done as soon as possible (ie important tasks)

- those which *should* be done

- those which *could* be done.

Generally, your boss's ideas of priority should come before yours. However, if you have a practical and sensible working relationship and, on a particularly chaotic day have far too many urgent jobs to cope with, you have two options. Either

- consult your boss to see which he or she advises should be left, or

- delegate some jobs to your assistant.

The second option presumes, of course, that you have an assistant! If not, and your boss still wants everything done, plead for him or her to find someone to help you! At least by discussing your problem you have 'signalled' that completion of every task within the agreed deadline is impossible.

Discussion point

1   Why do you think the team which is responsible for your course might *prioritise* the topics which you are taught? Make suggestions to your tutor.

2   As a group, study the following list of tasks and decide in which order you would attempt them. Then identify those you would delegate if you had an assistant. Finally, identify those tasks you would leave if you work alone and are too busy to complete all your work in one day. Compare your lists with those of other members in your group. Assume today is Monday.

   a   Typing and circulating the minutes of Friday's weekly management team meeting.
   b   Getting your filing up to date.
   c   Sending out the agenda for a safety meeting to be held the day after tomorrow.
   d   Making a reservation for your boss on a direct flight to Paris on Thursday, returning Friday.
   e   Typing a 15-page report for Wednesday's board meeting.
   f   Responding to a complaint from an important customer (your boss has handwritten a reply).
   g   Preparing slides for your boss's talk in Paris.
   h   Faxing an advert to the local paper for a new assistant administrator. Job adverts are in Wednesday's paper and the deadline for receipt of copy is noon the day before.
   i   Checking the hotline customer-answering system for messages left over the weekend.
   j   Cancelling a hotel room booked for tonight but no longer needed because the visitor had to postpone the trip to your organisation.
   k   Ordering new letter headings (stock is getting very low, and delivery normally takes seven days).
   l   Dealing with routine correspondence.
   m   Answering two e-mails – one querying the room where a meeting will be held tomorrow, the other from the health and safety officer asking if there would be any difficulties in holding a fire drill during the following week.
   n   Dealing with a request for a summary of correspondence with a customer, received directly from the managing director's secretary, for the managing director. This will take at least an hour to research and prepare.

Planning aids

Planning aids are the friends you need when you are trying to plan ahead! There are a variety of different systems you can use which help you to

- plan in advance

- record your plans

- remember what you have agreed to do.

It is a foolhardy person who uses no form of planning aid – even with the best of memories you are unlikely to remember everything unless you commit something to paper.

For instance, if a group of tutors decided on an assessment schedule for their students, they would keep a copy themselves – as they would use it for reference all year – and also issue a copy to their students. In this way, it becomes an *ongoing* planning aid to assist students to decide when to research, prepare and submit different assignments.

Making a list

You may associate lists more with buying weekly groceries than going to work! However, lists can be invaluable and are the key to remembering much of what needs to be done in an office. After all, the most sophisticated computer database system containing the names and addresses of all your customers could be described as an elaborate list!

List makers can usually be divided into three categories – compulsive, routine and sporadic.

- Compulsive list makers love writing things down and do it almost habitually. If you fall into this group, you will write down everything you need to remember and probably have little need to read the information below! Just guard against writing down so much that simply reading it makes you feel exhausted.

- Routine list makers are more selective. They make lists of things which *should* be listed – and tick off each item meticulously as it has been achieved.

- Sporadic list makers make lists as and when they are in the mood. The problem is they may neglect to list something when it really is required. The danger, if you fall into this category, lies in trying to remember things you really should have noted down.

Normally, it takes very little time to make out a list of jobs to be done at the beginning of the day. Alternatively, one very good way of ending each day can be to list the jobs to be done tomorrow. Such a list is not only invaluable but is also a psychological boost if you can tick or cross off some jobs within half an hour of walking into the office.

However, there are several dangers you should guard against.

- Do not constantly ignore jobs you dislike. (This becomes obvious if you find yourself carrying forward the same items, day after day!).

- Avoid doing the jobs in the order in which you have written them – they should be undertaken in order of priority.

- Do not forget to write down new jobs – particularly if you are given these tasks when you do not have your list or any paper with you. A tip here – carry with you a notebook and a pen which will write at all angles at all times!

- Do not fail to tick or cross off jobs as they are completed, otherwise you will have a marathon task at the end of each day updating your list.

Finally, you will be cheating if your first item is 'Make list', so that you can immediately tick this off when you have written down all the items!

Note: Many electronic diary packages include a prioritisation and listing section – see page 437.

The checklist

A checklist is a permanent list which is similar to an action plan or a set of procedures rather than a list of jobs to be done. A checklist states the activities to be undertaken for a specific, repetitive task, such as

- preparing for a meeting
- making interview arrangements
- preparing the outgoing post
- organising a sales conference.

If you have spent hours planning the activities which need to take place for a task to run smoothly, it would be foolish to throw away your 'model' and have to redo it every time it was needed.

Another way of using a checklist is to give a copy to any staff who will be involved in the task, and they can simply check off each activity as they go (hence the word 'checklist').

Discussion point

1 As a group, think of at least five other routine jobs for which a checklist would be helpful.

2 What action(s) would you take to ensure that your checklists are always up to date?

Pre-printed forms

A variation on the checklist is a pre-printed form. This is used when information is regularly requested or recorded. It can also have the dual purpose of acting as a reminder or aid to planning.

The advantage of a form is that it will record the information you need in the same order each time, which makes comparisons easier. This, of course, depends upon the form being designed properly in the first place!

A typical example of when forms may be useful is to make travel plans. If you issue forms which everyone must complete, giving details of the trip, it is far easier to make sure that you follow their requests when you are planning the arrangements.

Discussion point

1   You have been given the responsibility of planning the holiday rota for your staff – similar to task 1 in the case study on page 411.

Design a form which would obtain the information from your staff in a sensible and logical order, and compare your form with others produced by members of your group.

2   Discuss how the completed forms would assist you to plan and prepare the holiday rota for the department.

Note: The companion book to this, *Business for Advanced Secretarial Students,* discusses form design on pages 370–71.

The diary

The diary is probably the most common type of list/checklist used in an office, simply because it can be used for so many purposes. In some offices you may find there are three diaries in operation.

* The office diary – which contains appointments for various executives.

* Your own diary – which contains your boss's business appointments.

* Your boss's personal diary – which contains all his or her business and personal appointments.

The danger, of course, is that the three may not agree! You will have a particular problem if your boss makes arrangements, enters them in his or her diary and then forgets to mention them to you – unless you schedule regular 'match the diary' sessions!

There are a wide variety of diaries on the market, of different types, sizes and designs. Many organisations provide their staff with their own desk diary, often showing the company name and logo. In other organisations you may receive complimentary diaries from your suppliers or buy commercially produced diaries. Finally, of course, there are many specialist diaries on the market (particularly the pocket type) with additional information on certain topics.

You are always better to have a diary with too much space rather than too little, as – if you are so inclined – you can use the diary for lists of jobs to be done as well as appointments. Generally, allow at least one page for each day and make sure that there are sufficient time indicators for your needs, if these are pre-printed.

It is usual for appointments to be shown separately from any reminder sections (eg by using facing pages or ruling a line across the page). Certainly, it is inadvisable to mix the two. Some basic rules include the following.

- Use clear handwriting, especially if other people will need to have access to the diary.

- Write provisional appointments in pencil, until they are confirmed.

- Take down comprehensive details of appointments – including name, address, location, telephone number and reason for appointment. Keep the reason brief, particularly if the content is at all confidential. A telephone number can be essential if a meeting has to be cancelled at the last minute.

- Use different-coloured ink for your appointments and your boss's appointments – if you are using the same diary.

- Make sure regular appointments and meetings are entered throughout the year.

- Tick or cross off appointments when they have taken place – so that you can check any which are deferred or must be rearranged.

- Never be tempted to write a scribbled entry under a particular time – you then have the problem of trying to find out what you were thinking about when you made the entry!

Personal organisers

These are available in paper form (eg a Filofax) and in electronic form. The latter usually include word processing and database facilities, together with a diary and a calendar. There are a wide variety on the market and the number of facilities and amount of memory available is increasing every year.

You should note that unless your boss's personal organiser is compatible with the office computer system – and information is transferable between the two – an electronic personal organiser can present even worse problems than the personal diary. This is particularly the case if your boss uses it on business trips to make notes, jottings, change addresses, list telephone calls and appointments – and never bothers to tell you!

Don't ask me if I'm free – ask my computer!

Today many organisations operate electronic diaries. However, these often act as an adjunct to, rather than a replacement of, any paper-based diary systems.

Electronic diary systems operate across a computer network and enable people to log their appointments and meetings electronically (Figure 19.3). Other people who wish to arrange an appointment or meeting with someone can see when the person is free simply by accessing the electronic diary. They can then book a free slot and send an e-mail or note advising the person of this (sometimes automatically). This can be done for several people simultaneously, with the computer searching for 'common' free times in all the diaries.

Electronic diaries have several advantages. Routine and recurrent appointments and meetings need entering only once and can be automatically carried forward to all relevant dates simply by specifying the day and time period. Many systems have a buzzer which notifies users when appointments are due to occur. In addition, they usually include a calendar, a memo section (for making notes), a 'to do' list section in which priority actions can be entered, and a database section which can be used to store the names, addresses and telephone numbers of different customers and clients.

However, electronic diaries are not all good news! Your boss may find he or she has been booked for meetings and appointments first and is then notified later. In some cases these may be meetings which he or she may have made an excuse not to attend! In other instances, an afternoon which was required for writing an urgent report may have been 'interrupted' by someone scheduling a meeting. For that reason, if electronic diaries are regularly used to schedule people's time, it is sensible to 'book' working time (which must not be interrupted) at regular intervals throughout the working week.

Index systems and concertina files

Index systems are seen by some as rather old-fashioned but they do have their uses. They used to be very popular as 'tickler' or 'reminder' systems – particularly if the diary is over-crowded with appointments and other notes.

Quite simply, a guide card would be completed for each day of the month, each week or each month of the year. Appropriate reminders would then be placed on the appropriate card.

A variation on this system, particularly with documents which must be brought forward on certain dates, is to keep them in a concertina file where

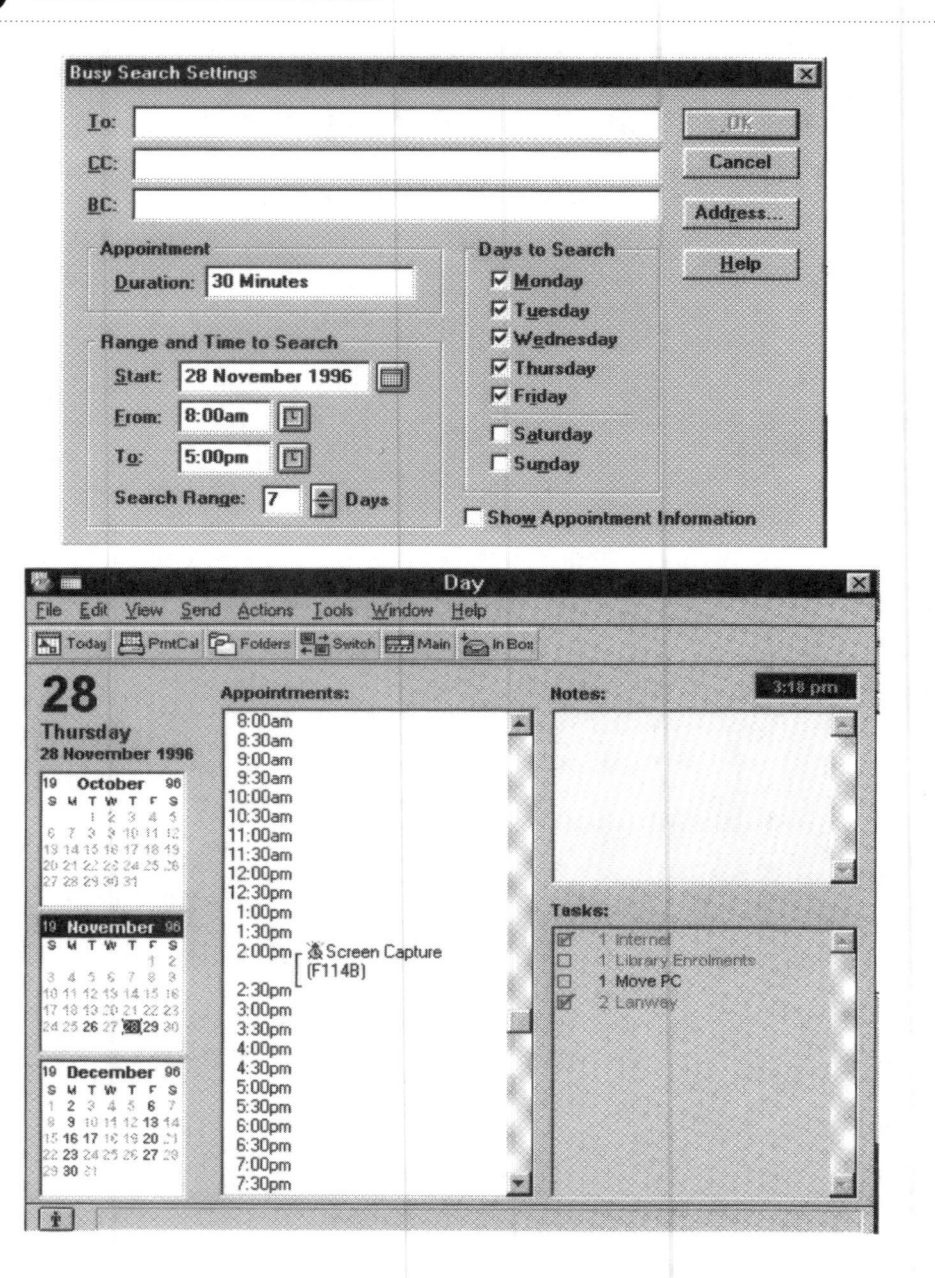

Figure 19.3 Accessing an electronic diary, to make an appointment

each compartment is allocated a different day of the month. A letter which you are asked to defer for two weeks can then simply be inserted in the correct place in the file. Similarly, if you prepare an outgoing letter which states your boss will contact someone on the 17th of the month, an alternative to entering this in the diary is to put an additional copy of the letter in the relevant compartment of the file. A practical point is that some people argue that a concertina file is no use because it has only 26 compartments, whereas there may be 30 or 31 days in the month. This is not true if you count only working days, however, when there are easily sufficient compartments!

Planners and visual aids

There are a wide variety of commercial planners on the market, which you can see by looking at any office equipment catalogue. One example is the Gantt chart, which was illustrated in Figure 13.8 on page 284. Some planners operate on a standard year of January–December, others are 'perpetual' in that they allow for a 'rolling year' where the previous month is always discarded and the next month is then added at the end.

Most of them are wall mounted and utilise a system of coloured strips which are available on magnetic rolls. You simply cut off the length you need and put this into position. You can also attach different shapes to symbolise different events – though you need to provide a key so that anyone looking at the planner will understand it!

An alternative is the white board on which you can write information. Some have pre-printed headings (such as diary-type headings), others are on a 'graph' background, many are plain, so you can use them for reminding yourself of urgent jobs which must be done.

Planners are ideal for charting regular annual or monthly events, recording progress on particular jobs (eg the Gantt chart) or for giving ongoing information/reminders to staff. Their dangers are

- too many different coloured labels and signals can become very confusing

- they can take time to set up

- those which use sticky labels are difficult to clean for re-use; those which use magnetic rubberised strips are fine provided no one knocks them off on to the floor (unless you have a paper copy of how the plan should look, which is unlikely, you may struggle to put the strips back in the correct place again)

- those which are blank and need information entering should be used properly – the idea is not to write in reminders which everyone either ignores or forgets to erase when the job has been done.

● Additional planning considerations

No matter how well you plan, things can and do go wrong! Whilst planning your own day is hard enough, trying to plan your boss's day may be even more difficult – particularly if you are the one who gets the blame if everything goes wrong! The longer you work with someone, the easier it becomes to 'second guess' their requirements for planning and scheduling.

🗨 Discussion point

1   Obtain a copy of at least one office supplies catalogue and look up the different planning aids on offer.

2   Identify which type you would purchase if you were responsible for
   a   charting the movement of six different representatives on a daily basis
   b   recording the level of sales of three different items in a small business
   c   scheduling major events, such as the AGM, annual sales conference, directors' and other regular meetings, dates for important report submissions
   d   planning sales trips abroad over the next six months
   e   planning and recording the use of six conference rooms which must be pre-booked by staff.

As a first step, however, you are advised to remember these basic principles.

• Find out how your boss prefers to spend the day. Is his or her most productive time in the morning or afternoon? Is a quiet hour preferred, either early or late in the day? Does your boss have a working lunch or prefer a regular lunch break? Is he or she in the office very early each day, or is there a marked preference for a later start and a late finish?

• Many executives prefer to schedule their day into quiet periods and busy periods. This means they have an 'open door' policy for part of the day only. In this case all the appointments will need scheduling into these times. Other people prefer to space appointments throughout the day.

• Is your boss very punctual, average, or someone who always arrives at the last minute? Use this information not only to help you to schedule appointments but also to advise other staff.

• Work out a strategy for dealing with people who overstay their welcome. Many secretaries know they should interrupt after a 10-minute overrun with a verbal reminder of a telephone call which must be made, or that the next appointment has arrived – to help speed up a tardy departure!

• *Never* overcrowd the diary or be too optimistic about the time needed for appointments, particularly if your boss is travelling. You will be very unpopular indeed if it is impossible for your boss to manage to be in all the places he or she should be to keep up with an unrealistic schedule you have prepared – particularly if several important customers have had to be kept waiting and your boss is now on his or her knees with exhaustion. In the early days of your career always overestimate, rather than underestimate, the time required.

Selecting and organising resources

20

● Introduction

The phrase 'selecting and organising resources' is not one which usually springs to the minds of aspiring secretaries and administrators when they are considering their primary duties. Frequently, resources are simply an accepted, albeit essential, feature of the job. Unless you are given the task of setting up an office from scratch, you may rarely take time to consider the resource requirements of office administration. If you were faced with a suite of empty offices, which needed furnishing and equipping with everything from desks to disk boxes and from printers to paper, you might stop for a moment to consider the dozens of items which must be constantly on hand for an office to function effectively.

Resources are, of course, a continual requirement. Whereas some items need to be replaced or renewed infrequently, others wear out or are used up on a very regular basis. Also, specific or special tasks may require additional resources. Because the cost of resources is a significant item for all organisations, any responsible administrator or secretary is expected to have a healthy respect for the whole area of resourcing – not only to keep expenditure and wastage to a minimum but also to help to monitor and control usage. This is likely to include, as well as equipment and consumable items, other key resource areas including staff and space utilisation. Wasted resources – whether they are under-employed staff, damaged paper or idle office space – all equate to higher costs, which any organisation can ill-afford.

This chapter looks at all these areas and examines the responsibilities of an administrator or secretary in relation to resource selection and organisation. It starts by examining one of the most important resources of all – time. Even with the most up-to-date and modern office environment and experienced, well-trained staff, the ability to undertake the work required to the deadlines specified often depends on the ability of those involved to manage their time effectively.

● Time management

All the techniques given in the previous chapter can usefully be labelled strategies for 'time management'. Generally, the focus of time management is *being in control* – rather than wondering where the day went to!

Time is considered to be the most important resource we have because it is the only one which is irreplaceable. Once today has gone, there is no way we can bring it back to see if we can do more. The

Americans have a phrase for free time that is used wisely – 'quality time'. The more effectively you use time which has to be spent at work (rather than working late or having to take work home with you) the more 'quality time' you have available to spend on leisure activities.

Everybody wastes time, particularly on a day when they find it difficult to concentrate or to 'get going'. However, some people are worse than others! Because they do not plan properly, are badly organised or do not focus on what they are doing, they may

- make unnecessary journeys (eg twice to the same cupboard in five minutes)

- spend ten minutes looking for a document they had an hour ago

- gossip to colleagues or chat to people on the telephone

- 'play' with papers because they cannot decide which job to do first

- prepare a completely unrealistic schedule so that they are exhausted by lunchtime and then do little for the rest of the day

- do a bit of one thing, followed by a bit of another, with nothing done properly

- use 'displacement activities' to put off doing something they do not want to do – and then panic as the deadline approaches, finish the job in a rush and make a mess of it!

The worse you are at managing time the more crises you will have and the more time you will spend trying to solve problems you have made for yourself! The whole thing then becomes a vicious circle.

Techniques for time management

To use time effectively you need to concentrate on

- planning effectively, so that you do not waste time redoing something unnecessarily and you are *prepared* for events

- being well organised (see page 447)

- prioritising work properly (see page 431)

- identifying the people who waste your time

- reducing interruptions

- developing self-discipline and control.

The people who waste your time are those who chat, gossip or think of their own priorities rather than yours. With everyone but your boss, then, you have two options.

- Keep working, answer briefly and keep your head down. Most people will drift away to find someone more receptive.

- Look up, smile and say – 'Very sorry, I've got to get this done in the next ten minutes. Perhaps we can talk later.' Then look down again. Say it firmly, not apologetically, and stay pleasant. In other words, assert your right to manage your own time.

The problem arises, of course, when it is your boss who is wasting your time! This can happen if you have a boss who likes you at his or her beck and call, or to chat when he or she has a quiet half hour. If you have a particularly demanding boss who does this every day, you would need to sit down for a talk about priorities and what he or she would like completing that day. A more frequent tactic used by many secretaries is to consider the most critical task on *their boss's* agenda and to query if this is still required urgently. For example, saying 'By the way, do you still want that fax to go to Germany before 4 o'clock?' might elicit the immediate response 'Good heavens, don't say you haven't sent it yet.' In which case you can reply that you were just completing it when he or she called you. It is highly probable that you will swiftly be sent packing to finish it!

Incidentally, the good boss/secretary relationship will include tactics for each to be able to rescue the other from time wasters. This can range from suddenly taking an 'urgently wanted file' into the next office, to having a coded knock between two adjoining rooms!

Finally, of course, you need a considerable amount of self-discipline not to waste your own time. Strategies to use include the following.

- Plan which jobs you must get through that day. You then have a clear target to achieve.

- Reduce the time you spend walking around. Group tasks which have to be done or delivered elsewhere and do them in one journey.

- Practise time and motion techniques! Never sit and wait whilst something happens (eg the photocopier does a long job). You could probably do three small jobs in that time.

- Keep 'little jobs' on one side for filling gaps. If you have none, then file half a dozen papers in the five minutes before a meeting starts.

- Treat yourself (a cup of coffee?) when you have completed an unpleasant job.

- Block out time for doing jobs on which you must concentrate, such as a complicated or long report – and divert your phone, if possible.

- Do each job properly the first time round, then you will never have to waste time redoing it.

- If you have an assistant or staff working for you, learn how to delegate. Do not always give them the boring jobs you hate doing – choose those which someone can use to learn more about the business. Remember, too, that

One job at a time?

Time management consultants often teach techniques to help people to manage their time. One is to identify key areas related to people – apparently the maximum number of key areas for sensible organisation is nine – and keep an ongoing record of what needs doing in each area. This is equivalent to having nine balls in the air, but at least knowing where they are!

Another strategy is never to hold a piece of paper without doing something productive with it. This can mean actioning it, filing it or putting it in the bin. It does not mean reading it and putting it aside! Some people also hold the view that the clearer your desk, the better – given that you can do only one job at a time there should be only one set of papers on your desk at one time. A golden rule should be to have a clear desk, with everything in folders, apart from the one item being dealt with at that moment.

If this seems extreme, do not worry! Most of us fall far short of this apparent ideal – possibly because any boss who regularly sees you with such a clear desk will immediately form the impression that you do not have enough to do – and give you ten more urgent jobs to complete!

Discussion point

1. As a group, discuss your strengths and weaknesses when 'managing time' – particularly when you have a boring job to do!

2. Practise time and motion techniques. Imagine that you have come home late – it is 7 pm – and you need to do something drastic with your hair (preferably wash it), have a shower, grab a sandwich, have a hot drink, get changed and be out of the door for 7.30 prompt! Write a brief schedule saying how you will achieve this – and compare your notes with others in your group.

ten minutes spent training the junior how to make accurate enlargements of photocopies or send faxes can eventually save hours of your time. Never be a person who says 'Everybody makes a mess of it but me.' It is often simply because no one showed them how to do it properly.

● Other resources

What other resources are required when you are planning and organising work?

Resources can be divided into

- **the space** to carry out work – how much do you need, is it a clear or cluttered area?

- **the staff** to do a job – how many people are available, when are they free, will they know what to do or do they need to be shown?

- **equipment and other items** (including stationery) – do you have everything to hand, do some items have to be ordered or bought specially, are some items shared, will you have to book any items of equipment in advance?

- **money** – if there are any resources which must be bought in or staff who must be paid overtime

- **time** – to plan and to do the job properly.

It is pointless to plan a job without considering the resources that you require. For instance, imagine that your boss wants you to send out a mailshot to 5000 customers in the next week. You prepare a checklist as follows.

Day 1: write mailshot
Day 2: have it approved
Day 3: type and print mailshot
Day 4: prepare envelopes
Day 5: insert mailshot into envelopes
Day 6: post mailshot.

You have now prepared a schedule which shows you can meet the required deadline. However, what if you have

- no customer database

- no facilities for printing the graphics on the mailshot

- insufficient envelopes in stock

- no inserting machine and insufficient staff to stuff the envelopes by hand in the time allowed

- insufficient units in the franking machine to cope with the additional items

- an already crowded office with no space available for all the boxes and papers?

Quite simply, there is no way in which you will stick to your schedule! It also means that you will not obtain any postal savings for posting in bulk, because investigation of this will soon show you that there are certain criteria to be followed – including giving notification in advance to the Royal Mail service! For these reasons, resource allocation and management is critical to good planning. Indeed, some would say it is the starting point. You should therefore look at any job and ask

- what do I need
- what have I got already
- what can I borrow
- what must I order
- how much will it cost?

You should then discuss your requirements with your boss as part of your plans to devise a schedule.

Discussion point

1   One of your colleagues is getting married and, at the last minute, your boss decides to hold a small celebration one lunchtime – drinks and nibbles as a surprise. There is a staff of 20 in your department. What resources will you need, and how much petty cash will you request? (Assume there are sufficient glasses in the cupboard!)

2   The secretarial/administrative section in your college has decided to hold an open evening for prospective students. Your group has been asked to help to plan for the event.

   What resources do you think would be needed to give a professional impression of the section? Discuss your ideas with your tutor.

● Workplace organisation and workflow

As an administrator or secretary, you have two aspects of organisation to consider. First, you should be well organised yourself, in terms of your own working habits. Secondly, you should make sure that the area in which you work is also well organised and that everything is set out to minimise delays and problems and maximise efficient **workflow.**

Workflow can be defined as the 'through-put' of work through an office. In just the same way as goods are produced in a factory, documents are produced in an office. Anything which delays the 'flow' of goods on a production line causes problems – bottlenecks, machine breakdowns, rejects or labour shortages. Anything which delays the production of work in an office reduces workflow and causes delays.

One person holding up a job is the equivalent of a bottleneck (the person might be lazy, or overwhelmed with a backlog of work to clear). Machine breakdowns can equate to computer failure, photocopier problems or – a more minor but very common problem – the printer playing up or the cartridge running out at a critical moment (very critical indeed if you have forgotten to get any more cartridges!). Rejects on a production line equate to poor or shoddy work which has to be returned to be redone (eg through poor proof-reading skills). Labour shortages occur when staff are off ill, sent on training courses or have to do too much at once.

Good organisational skills, coupled with good planning, practical office design, effective layout and well-trained staff help to avoid all these problems.

Organisational strategies

Personally, *you* need to be the epitome of good organisation! You can hardly expect everyone else to be well organised if you are in a constant muddle.

Upon your arrival

- If you are well organised, you should arrive early in the morning – not at the last minute! Top PAs usually try to arrive before their bosses but you may not find this practical particularly if he or she likes to start work very early.

- Many people like to make a slow start and relax with a cup of coffee first thing. This is ideal 'thinking time', when you can go through your lists for the day and perhaps even get a few routine jobs out of the way before the office gets busy. You may decide to greet your boss with a cup of coffee but if you do, be prepared to make this a regular habit!

- Make any routine checks which are your responsibility – these can include checking the fax machine, your e-mail and your boss's e-mail, and listening to messages left on the answering machine.

- Check that the offices are clean, tidy and warm enough. Change any calendars as appropriate.

- Check your diary and that of your boss. Warn reception if any visitors are expected (unless, being well organised, you sent them a list or e-mail the day before).

- Open or sort the mail as it arrives. Look out relevant files.

- See your boss to discuss the day's programme.

During the day

Use your organisational skills, wherever possible, to make light work of the jobs you have to do.

- Have a place for every piece of paper which lands on your desk – either in your in-tray, pending tray, filing tray, an active (correctly labelled) file folder or the wastepaper bin!

  Resist the temptation to make your pending tray an extended version of the wastepaper bin, ie putting in papers simply because you do not know what to do with them and then throwing them away two months later!

If papers arrive when you are busy with a task, put them in your in-tray. Put in there, too, any notes or reminders for yourself (eg on Post-it notes) as well as telephone messages. Regularly, look through this and sort into 'very urgent', 'urgent' and 'non–urgent'. Bear in mind that this sorting needs doing every day because today's non-urgent items may be critical in three days' time!

- Keep your desk drawers clean and tidy with a place for everything and everything in its place! This includes stationery you use regularly, pencils and pens, scissors, ruler, punch, stapler, sticky tape and other items. If you choose to keep some of these on your desk top, try to keep them to a minimum – so that your working area remains as free from clutter as possible.

- Have one master list/planner/diary that contains all the information and prompts you need – multiple systems often mean something is missed or forgotten.

- Keep key information close to hand. This includes
  - internal/external telephone lists
  - facts and reference numbers which you regularly need
  - schedules for holidays and other events.

  It is easier if these are pinned on a noticeboard above your desk for rapid reference.

- Print out a directory for your floppy disks or directories on your hard disk. This makes it easier to find a document quickly.

- Learn to create documents at the keyboard. This is much quicker than writing by hand and then typing it up (and a lot easier!).

At the end of the day
- Check your unfinished/carried forward jobs and list or prioritise these for tomorrow.

- Check the diary for the following day – highlight any priorities.

- Look out any documents which will be required first thing tomorrow, eg for a meeting or appointment.

- Make security checks to ensure equipment has been switched off, confidential papers are secured. Make sure the fax machine and telephone answering machine are left on.

- If your boss is staying on to work late, you could make yourself popular by offering him or her a cup of coffee before you go!

Office design

Offices may be open plan, landscaped or individual. An open-plan office is a large area in which several people work together, often in 'cells' or cubicles which comprise sound-proof screens. These give a degree of privacy as well as reducing the noise. A landscaped office is one where the design has been undertaken by professionals and there are colour coordinated carpets, blinds and screens. The area has a 'unified' look with specific spaces for different types of work. If the design has been carefully conceived, considerable thought will have been given to the flow of work through the office and the needs of different people to be able to contact others frequently. Such people will be sited close together to assist communication.

Many older office buildings comprise smaller individual units. In this case you may even have an office of your own – or a shared facility – adjacent to your boss. It is not sensible for an administrator or secretary to be located very far away from his or her boss as this wastes time with one having to make constant journeys to see the other.

Usually, people work better if their working area is adequately lit, heated, ventilated and air-conditioned where necessary. There should be blinds at the windows and a good, clear clock on the wall (showing the right time!). Minimum requirements of health and safety legislation should be met. A bonus is an office which is well decorated and furnished, particularly if it is attractive and colourful. The area also needs to be clean and tidy, and quiet enough for people to be able to concentrate. This can be difficult if telephones are ringing, visitors are arriving and people are constantly moving about. Noise levels are reduced if equipment such as the photocopier and fax machine are in an adjacent area and printers are fitted with acoustic hoods if they are noisy in operation.

Office layout

The layout of the office needs to be considered carefully to reduce time-wasting activities and assist maximum efficiency. This means everyone should have the following.

- A desk or workstation which is as large as possible so that there is sufficient room for working papers, paper trays, etc. An L-shaped desk is often ideal for a secretary or administrator who undertakes clerical work as well as keyboarding tasks.

- His or her own telephone – even if there is a shared line so the phones ring simultaneously. This saves having to get up and down to answer a ringing phone on someone else's desk.

- Easy access to filing cabinets used regularly.

- Enough desk accessories to store items easily.

- A comfortable chair which conforms to health and safety requirements with an adjustable back, seat and a swivel action.

A critical factor is the amount of space available. There should be easy movement between the different areas – particularly allowing for natural walkways through an office. It is very irritating to try to work with people brushing past you or leaning over you to reach something! People will also not work efficiently if

- there is insufficient storage space – so that papers are piled on top of cabinets and desks

- there is a back-log of filing – so no one can find anything

- they are separated from colleagues with whom they are working on a particular job

- their desks are poorly positioned, eg close to windows, radiators or doors (so that they are too hot, too cold or constantly in a draught)

- they are trying to do detailed or complicated work in a busy area

- they have insufficient space in which to work.

It is usually the case that the best people to decide on the most effective layout are the staff themselves. They have a vested interest in

Sick building syndrome

Some buildings are actually found to cause illnesses in staff – ranging from skin ailments, headaches, dizziness and nausea to constant fatigue, respiratory problems and eye irritation. .

The problem is caused by a variety of factors – often more noticeable in old buildings which have been 'modernised' for office use by lowering ceilings, sealing windows and restricting ventilation. This is exacerbated by chemical emissions from photocopiers and laser printers, the dust build-up in synthetic carpets and soft furnishing, fluorescent lighting, chemicals in cleaning products and radiation from monitors.

Practical steps can include repositioning the equipment, installing an efficient air-conditioning system, installing filters and using humidifiers and ionisers to purify the atmosphere. However, in some cases a whole building has had to be declared unfit and staff moved elsewhere.

Today, architects are designing buildings which maximise natural light and fresh air – in addition to building in all the wires and cabling required for modern computer systems. Therefore the purpose-built new office block is far less likely to be 'sick' or create as many problems for staff.

making life easier for themselves – which means they will do their jobs more easily and be more efficient, as well as more motivated. An additional motivator is being able to contribute to making the area pleasant to work in – by the addition of plants, posters or pictures.

Discussion point

Your company has expanded considerably over the past few years and office space is at a premium. Your boss has decided that one way round the problem is for you to move in to his office. As a group, discuss the advantages and disadvantages of this idea.

● Monitoring and controlling work

In Chapter 19 you learned that a major reason for using systems and procedures was to help monitor and control work which is undertaken by various people. However, you also need to monitor and control other tasks which are being undertaken – both by yourself and any staff in an office for which you have responsibility for workflow.

It is perfectly possible to plan a job properly, ascertain and obtain the resources required, and be extremely well organised but for something to go wrong. Whilst the more organised you are the less likely this is to happen, you still need to develop systems to enable you to monitor and control what is happening. Some of these may be formal, others less so.

Imagine, that in one morning

1   you see a disgruntled visitor leaving reception

2   your boss asks you for his flight ticket for Paris tomorrow – you have not got it

3   an important document is mislaid

4   three people telephone you to find out which room a meeting is in

5   the office junior asks you to check the contents of a letter you thought had been posted two days ago

6   you suddenly realise that you have not photocopied the job applications for the interview panel this afternoon. At this point the photocopier is out of order and the engineer has most of it in bits on the floor.

What has gone wrong? So far as you know you have an efficient visitor system. You know the travel agent confirmed the Paris flight. You thought the filing system was excellent and kept up to date. You notified everyone about the meeting yesterday and you explicitly asked the junior to type the letter urgently. You also follow a standard checklist for interview preparations.

Saying it is not your fault is simply unacceptable for anyone in a responsible job or with one eye on promotion! Identifying where problems might have occurred is one thing; solving them is another. The most critical thing is to reduce the probability of them recurring. You can never guarantee that no problems will arise – but at least you can have the systems in place to minimise their likelihood!

Looking at each problem in turn will help you to consider what to do – both in the short term and the long term.

1   The visitor may be disgruntled for no apparent reason, or because she could not be helped *or* because the person who dealt with her was unhelpful or discourteous. You have two choices. You could ask the visitor if she has a problem – then assess the situation. Or you could ask the staff (though their answer may be somewhat different).

    You then need to work out whether anything could be done about the problem. Is it a service you could offer and do not? Was the problem unavoidable? Does someone need more training on customer service skills? Simply enquiring into the matter – and letting staff see you are alert in this respect – is usually enough to keep high standards of service. However, if you are particularly concerned about this area, you could instigate a system where staff automatically report to you situations where a customer or visitor could not be assisted – so that you can discuss these with your boss.

2   In this case the travel agent has forgotten to send the ticket. Your follow-up systems are at fault here. You should have checked that the documentation had arrived – not depended upon other people to deliver it.

3   Whether you like it or not, your filing systems are obviously not excellent! If the problem is a 'one-off' you may think no more about it, particularly if the document is quickly found. If the situation recurs, then you need to review the filing system. Keeping one eye on the effectiveness of current systems is a key requirement of good administrators and secretaries.

4   In this case you have probably made a simple mistake and omitted to include the room number. Everyone makes mistakes on occasion, particularly when they are very busy. If you find, however, that you are regularly making mistakes, you need to review your own systems of working. Do you try to do jobs too quickly? Are you easily distracted? Are you overloaded and do you need assistance? Are you lazy when it comes to proof reading and checking your own work? Whatever the reason you need a time of quiet reflection on your methods of operation and to make a few resolutions for the future!

5   One of the most common problems is to give someone a job to do and then forget about it! If you have also handed over the documents relating to the task, then you may have nothing tangible to remind you. You need either to develop an excellent memory for work outstanding or – a far safer system – to record such items as 'work in progress'. You can either add these to your list or keep a work-in-progress file. Whichever way, this job should not have been crossed off your list until it was finalised and the letter posted!

6   It is Murphy's Law that if you do forget something, something else will go wrong to make the problem worse. The situation should be relatively easy to rectify as in most organisations there is usually more than one photocopier (or an agency nearby). Otherwise you will have to apologise and ask the panel to share the one form for each candidate.

The system to develop here is again related to work in progress. You may have been working through a checklist for those interviews but you had not come to the end! A useful tip is to photocopy the checklist, write on it the particular job being done (eg interviews for assistant administrator), tick things off as you go and keep the checklist in your work-in-progress file until you have finished everything.

As you become more experienced you will develop your own ways of working and your own systems to remind yourself what is happening and to jog your memory. It does not matter which system you use, so long as it works. The golden rule is not to forget current jobs until they have been completed. You will also gain a formidable reputation if you regularly remind other people of items they 'owe' you, ie those which you have asked for but have not yet received.

A final tip in the modern office – use e-mail to make your requests in writing and do not delete them until you have received the item or reminded the person concerned. Simply scrolling through your outgoing messages each day is a reminder in itself – print out important ones and put them in your work-in-progress file!

● Dealing with problems

On page 451 and above you looked at dealing with problems – and considered how best to prevent them occurring and to rectify them when they happen. However, problems do not happen only because you have overloaded your boss's diary or because people have forgotten to respond to one of your requests for information or documentation. A main area where problems can occur is when priorities change at the last minute or the unforeseen arises.

Discussion point

As a group, discuss what you would do if

a you go to prepare a conference room for an important meeting to find it has been double-booked and another meeting is in progress

b the night before an important conference, the guest speaker rings to say he has flu

c an important customer arrives, demanding to see your boss immediately, five minutes after she has left on a business trip

Coping in a crisis

There are no specifically right and wrong answers to the above problems. However, there are coping strategies you can learn. The first is not to panic. The second is to keep a clear head (it's amazing how many problems right themselves if you just wait a few minutes – the power, the fire evacuation) and to *think* through as many possible options as you can. In other cases you have to do all you can to accommodate the changes – booking travel for the managing director, locating another room, finding someone to help with the visitor. However, on other occasions, no matter what you do, you may not be able to rescue the situation. You may not be able to get another speaker or another meeting room or rearrange the remaining interviews to 'tighten' the schedule. In this case everyone will just have to accept the inevitable. All you – and your boss – need to know is that you did the best that could be expected under the circumstances.

Revision practice

Short-answer questions

1 State three advantages of implementing a system to control working practices.

2 Explain the importance of undertaking a feasibility study before implementing a new system.

3 Give two advantages and two disadvantages of consulting staff about a proposed new system.

4 Briefly explain the importance of prioritising.

5 Identify three planning aids used in an office and give one example of when each would be used.

6 State three strategies you would use to 'manage' time more effectively.

7 Identify four resources you would require if you were organising the preparation of a complex report to be sent to an important client.

8 Identify four techniques you could use to improve your personal organisation skills.

9 Give three reasons why it is important that administrators monitor work produced by staff.

10 Briefly explain
   a why it is important for administrators and secretaries to stay calm when a crisis occurs
   b the strategies you would use to help you to cope in this situation.

Essay questions

1 **a** Explain the advantages and disadvantages of operating a computerised diary system.
   b What strategies would you use if your boss had a personal electronic diary into which he entered appointments without telling you?

2 Your department is moving to new offices. You have been given the option of either taking an office adjacent to the main office area or being down the corridor but next to your boss.
   a What factors would you take into consideration when arranging for the siting of the equipment and furniture in the new main office?
   b Discuss the advantages and disadvantages of both of your possible new locations. Which would you choose, and why?

3 You have been asked to return to your college to give a talk to the students on the importance of planning for administrators and secretaries. What points would you include and why?

4 You have been asked to investigate the use of a wall-mounted planner to schedule important events.
   a Identify the advantages and disadvantages of using such a system.
   b Explain two other planning methods which are used to schedule work and operate as reminder systems.

5 You work in an office with one other secretary. Between you, you cope with the work of three directors. One morning you are concerned to discover that your colleague has had an accident which, whilst not serious, will keep her off work for the next three weeks. You have been asked to cover the work until a suitable temporary secretary can be found.

List the points you would take into consideration to enable you to maximise your use of time and organisational skills to cope with your increased workload.

Case study

Your boss, Cathryn Winters, has recently voiced her concern about the standard of customer service in your organisation. The number of complaints received has increased rapidly since Easter, when three new staff were appointed in the main office. This office is responsible for dealing with visitors and receiving telephone enquiries. In particular, the complaints have concerned

a no response to enquiries for information – despite repeated telephone calls

b a poor appointments system so that people are kept waiting for too long or the person they have arranged to see is not available

c outdated or incorrect literature being given on products – or, even worse, none available at all.

Both you and Cathryn Winters are aware that all staff are issued with telephone message pads. There is an appointments book in reception and all the executives are supposed to operate a diary system through their secretaries. A wide range of literature is kept in the stock room. This should be replenished regularly in reception and, when stocks are getting low, leaflets can be reordered centrally through the printing department. It would appear that none of these aids or facilities is being used properly.

As a result of the problem, Cathryn Winters has asked you to prepare a report in which you

1 outline a suitable customer service system which would prevent these problems recurring

2 identify the resources you would require to set up the system

3 include a brief cost–benefit analysis for the system you have suggested

4 attach draft set(s) of procedures which would have to be followed by all main office staff when
   a receiving telephone enquiries
   b receiving visitors (both with and without an appointment)
   c maintaining the reception area

5 state how you would monitor the new system to evaluate its effectiveness.

● Introduction

The aim of this book has been to give you an insight into the responsibilities of today's administrator or secretary. The types of tasks which have been described are relatively general – given that you might work in a wide variety of organisations, all with different working practices, systems and procedures. It is impossible to examine, in depth, all the variations which you may meet in your working life, but a good basic knowledge of the fundamental requirements, together with the practical ability to apply this knowledge, is the key to success.

A major requirement for senior administrators and secretaries is the ability to cope with problematic or difficult situations as well as day-to-day duties. These non-routine tasks may include

- suggesting and implementing more effective methods of working or new systems and procedures

- solving problems – often in an emergency

- planning for complex and important events

- planning and coordinating the input of several colleagues involved in a specific task.

In each case – apart from responding in an emergency – the administrator or secretary is expected to be **proactive** rather than reactive. This means thinking ahead, making sensible, logical and – best of all – creative suggestions, considering the implications of various courses of action and thinking of any possible problems which may occur. It also involves considering the effect of different courses of action on staff and other people involved – and how to communicate about difficult tasks or unwelcome duties in the most effective way in order to gain their cooperation.

You will find that these abilities are not only required by most employers today but are also tested regularly by awarding bodies who are assessing your potential to do the job properly!

In the first section of this book, you were introduced to the value of 'second sight' (see page 17). A way of describing this is the ability to plan for success. This means that you can analyse a problem or a complex request and follow this process through to the point where you can make clear, effective and comprehensive suggestions to your boss. This brief section has been written to help you to develop a technique for coping in this type of situation, so that you not only gain high marks in any written assignments or examinations based upon your study of this book, but also develop the technique of logical and analytical thinking to help you to develop and progress in your chosen career.

21

Planning skills

● Introduction

Your skills as an administrator or secretary will be most evident when you are involved in the detailed work of deciding on and planning a course of action and taking responsibility for its implementation. It is usually fairly evident to your boss (or to an examiner) if you have been able to 'think through' a problem thoroughly and have planned so well that you will be successful. A sketchy, partially developed idea, which is poorly communicated and which takes little account of timing, people or resources, is almost bound to fail. One which has been carefully considered, analysed in detail, logically developed, and where potential or possible problems have been identified at the outset, is far more likely to succeed.

● Developing expertise

Before you start to develop your own expertise in this area, it is important to reflect upon some of the basic requirements of all good administrators and secretaries.

The basics

You will usually find that it is taken for granted that you

- clearly understand the importance of **accuracy** and **attention to detail** – no one should ever need to check your work in this regard

- have a keen eye for **presentation** and **layout** – and are able to determine the most visually effective way of displaying information

- are able to **communicate** clearly, concisely and in the correct 'tone' for the occasion

- have a comprehensive knowledge of the different aspects of office work which relate to your own job (or the content of any assessment or examination you are taking).

This means that you can consider how any task should be performed and what resources would be required (in terms of staff, time and physical resources), and in what sequence if you are devising an action plan.

Moving on a stage

As you gain in experience and knowledge you will quickly learn that there is often not *one* correct solution to any problem but several. For that reason it can often be useful to consider several alternatives and then try to work out the possible implications of each – both in terms of the task itself and the people involved. You may then be able to make several suggestions, each showing the assumptions you made at each stage and your rationale in each case.

Becoming an expert

Experts realise that even the best-laid plans can go awry! For that reason, even though they may have devised a suggested plan of action which takes into account all the important factors, they still realise that various checks will have to be made to ensure that everything is going 'according to plan'. They will also have identified, *in advance,* those factors which are under their own control and those which are not – and developed contingency plans in case something goes wrong at the last minute. If a sudden crisis *does* occur, then the expert is the last to panic! The adept administrator or secretary knows when to take decisive action to rescue the situation – even if this means having to 'make do' with a second-best alternative. If this results in an event that appears to run smoothly, this is better than chaos at a critical moment!

 Test yourself

Try some elementary contingency planning yourself! In each case below identify

a the problems you *should* have foreseen were possible
b what contingency plans you *could* have made
c what you would do to rescue the situation at the last minute, assuming you'd never thought that anything could go wrong!

Discuss your answers with your group and with your tutor.

1 Your boss has been struggling to arrange a meeting with an important American client who is visiting this country for two weeks. Unfortunately, the visit clashes with your boss's trip to Australia. They have therefore arranged to meet in the executive lounge at Heathrow airport on the day your boss returns to this country – there is a three-hour 'window' before the client leaves for Chicago.

2 Your company, which produces cosmetics and beauty products, has been struggling to survive in an increasingly competitive market. In mid-January there is to be a major launch of a new product range to which all the press have been invited, as well as customers and potential customers. A celebrity has also been booked to attend. Because the event is important for public relations, all administrative staff are expected to be present to ensure it runs smoothly.

● Planning – a stage at a time

A useful step-by-step check to use when planning is given below. However, there are no 'right' and 'wrong' answers to problem solving. Therefore the list below is given to you for guidance only. Either you or your tutor may wish to amend or customise this to suit your individual needs or particular types of problems.

- Clearly state your **aim** or **objective**. What are you trying to achieve?

- Decide **what needs to be done**. This can take the form of a list of tasks, an action plan or a series of ideas at this stage.

- **Develop** and **refine** your list, plan or ideas, identifying problems or potential difficulties. Think about any people involved, their knowledge, expertise and possible reactions. Make a note of any area outside your own control.

- Identify the **resources** you have and the resources you will need. Specify any shortfall.

- Work out a draft **schedule of action** to take. Make it clear when you are planning to take an action which is **dependent** upon something else having been done. Give the reasons or rationale behind your suggestions. Give an alternative where appropriate.

- Work out how you will **communicate** your suggestions to those involved, again giving a reason for your suggestions. Include **examples of documentation** you would use, eg forms for recording information or a checklist.

- Decide what **checks** and **follow-up systems** would be needed to ensure everything is running smoothly and going to plan.

- Decide what **contingency plans** may be needed in case something goes wrong at the last minute. This usually means trying to identify potential problems before they happen!

Practical examples

It is easier for you to see how to approach this through an example. Below are given three different scenarios where you, as administrator or secretary, have been asked to consider a complex situation and to use your knowledge, experience and creativity to suggest a method of operation or plan of action.

The first scenario is then developed for you to see how the question has been attempted. Do bear in mind that other suggestions may be equally valid – in this type of situation, there is never just *one* right answer! It is suggested that, as a group or individually, you work through the other scenarios to develop your technique. Your tutor may wish the group first to brainstorm different suggestions. By the time you attempt the final scenario you may be working individually. At all times, however, you will benefit from comparing your own suggestions with those made by others. This will enable you to view the situation from a different perspective than your own – which is a very useful way of developing and broadening your own method of working.

Example scenarios

1 JT Systems Ltd is a computer consultancy which provides specialist support to complex computer installations. It has grown rapidly over the past four years and now employs 10 consultants, all of whom have a

company car for travelling to clients' premises. The terms of the agreement for use of a company car are that the car is for unlimited business use and up to 500 personal miles a month. Above that figure representatives should be charged for use at the rate of 15p a mile. The cars are leased and it is the responsibility of each representative to make certain that the car used is regularly maintained and serviced by notifying you, as office administrator, when the car is approaching the specified mileage.

Two problems have been encountered. Firstly, representatives are not informing you of their mileage to clients' premises. This not only prevents clients being billed properly for journeys undertaken on their behalf, but also means you have no way of checking personal usage of any cars. Secondly, most representatives are ignoring the servicing requirements and simply wait until their car breaks down before notifying you of a problem. This not only creates obvious operational difficulties but is also against the terms of the leasing agreement.

Your boss, Andrecz Sikorsky, has written you a memo asking you to suggest a procedure which can be implemented to solve the problem.

2 You work for an organisation which makes electronic components used as part of the control system of computerised production processes. Your boss is Marian Lewis, marketing director.

Today Marian has been informed by the MD, Bob Cryer, that a party of Japanese business people will be visiting the UK in a month's time and would like to visit the factory. There are several VIPs in the group – which is likely to number about 30 in all. The initial plan, which was discussed at today's board meeting, was that the party will arrive about 10 am on day 1 and will leave at 3 pm on day 2. Within that time frame they wish to have a tour of the factory, in addition to visiting one of your customers 15 miles away to see how your company's components have been used to improve production control.

Bob Cryer also wants to arrange for an hour-long presentation in the company's seminar room which will introduce the visitors to the product range and its applications. He thinks that a final review session should be arranged too, in relatively informal surroundings, so that marketing staff can follow up any queries at the end of the visit.

Marian Lewis is keen to give the visitors VIP treatment throughout their stay and has asked you to undertake all the following tasks.

a Devise a suggested itinerary for the two days including all meals and other events with recommended timings.

b Make a list of all the arrangements which you consider will need to be made before the event.

c Draw up an action plan to show the order in which the tasks should be undertaken.

3 You work as administrator/secretary for Dilip Patel, the managing director of Accessories Unlimited, which controls a chain of 65 leather and accessory shops. You share an office with Sarah, secretary to the marketing director, and Andrew, the trainee financial accountant. Next door are the individual offices of Mark Taylor, George McLaren the financial accountant and Jodie Stott the marketing director, together with the general office area in which are located six administrative and clerical staff and two word processor operators. These offices are situated above one of the busiest shops in the group, although access is from a separate entrance at street level.

Dilip Patel has become very concerned about security in and around the office area, particularly as quite large amounts of cash from the shop below may be held on the premises overnight. Last week he was shocked to find that a rear window had been left unlocked all night, and yesterday a shop customer was found wandering around the office area. Staff routinely leave personal items lying around and quite sensitive documents are left on their desks when they go to lunch.

Dilip Patel has asked for your suggestions as to what could be done to improve security in general and what further precautions, if any, should be taken given that from this year all customer records will be held on the company computer system. He has also requested a draft action plan which would show how new procedures could be introduced to be in force by the end of next month.

Stage 1
Define the aim or objective.

In scenario 1, the aim is two-fold:

a to improve the monitoring and recording of motoring costs so that these may be apportioned correctly between client and representative

b to ensure that all company vehicles are serviced and maintained in accordance with the terms of the leasing agreement.

You should note at this stage that when there is more than one aim or objective you may not necessarily be able to satisfy them all by introducing just one procedure!

Stage 2
Decide what needs to be done.

• Check any forms or methods of recording mileage in operation at present. Why are these procedures not used? Are they too complex, or just being ignored? Note that it is usually better to have a fresh start than to try to force people to use a procedure they have previously rejected.

- Check the terms of the leasing agreement to find out the required frequency of services.

- Find out how much notification must be given to the garage when booking a service.

- Decide whether you wish to use a manual (paper) system to record information or whether it would be easier to do it on computer (and the benefits and drawbacks of this).

- Consider suitable recording systems and form design.

- Decide the type of data which should be collected, and how often.

- Decide how you are going to charge representatives for personal usage (a bill, or a deduction from salary?) and how often.

- Review working practices (eg staff 'habits' and attitudes.) It is likely that the representatives will not welcome a system which more closely controls car usage – and for that reason it would be sensible if all instructions were given in the name of your boss, rather than yourself, with a clear rationale for introducing the system.

Stage 3
Develop or refine your ideas.

At this stage you need to consider possible form design for recording car details and mileage. A list of possible headings with some rationale as to why you are including certain types of information is required. An example could be as follows.

Name of representative

Make and model of car

Car registration number } Car details useful for garage bookings

Mileage at start of lease

Date lease agreement started

Current date column – (suggest information collected monthly, see below)

Current mileage column (running total) (= A)

Apportionment for business usage (this month) (= B)

Apportionment for personal usage (this month) (= C)

The form could include a column for noting service history/next due date (see below). (At this point you would gain extra marks by showing your draft design).

Rationale and comments

Obviously B plus C will equal A. For that reason you may recommend using a spreadsheet package to enter, record and check the data automatically.

Collecting information monthly will mean that the frequency is not so great as to irritate representatives, but enough to retain control. They could be asked to complete and submit a brief form each month giving current information. (Again, you could include an example of your proposed form.)

The date for submission could be set to be, say, a week before the invoices are prepared so that clients can be billed promptly. This would also give a clear rationale to the representatives for introducing the system. However, the drawback would be that representatives would have to keep a monthly record of their car usage, and those who forget may be tempted to 'invent' information. For that reason, one suggestion may be that all representatives telephone or e-mail the office with a weekly return on mileage. Reminder e-mails could be sent two days before until they got into the habit of providing the information.

Representatives should be billed for personal usage – this is likely to be best undertaken on a monthly basis. An alternative is for personal usage to be included on their expense claim forms. Another option is to deduct the money automatically from salary at the end of the following month. This would be decided by your boss, as the latter policy may be resented even though it would resolve any problem of late payments or unpaid bills.

Service history should be recorded on the same form. This could be done by a separate column at one side which simply shows the next mileage at which the car should be serviced. When the recorded mileage is within 300 miles of the next service figure, a booking is made for the car and the representative is informed of the date in good time. A check will need to be made as to whether this figure is appropriate, as the weekly mileage on cars differs considerably. A high user may need longer notification and a low user shorter notification.

Stage 4
Decide resources required.

In this case the resources required are minimal. You need time to obtain approval for your draft form layout and for the form requesting information – if this is the method decided. Alternatively you may need time to set up the spreadsheet on computer.

Sensibly you would then allocate time for the representatives to receive the instructions and query anything they do not understand. You should arrange a date for implementation which allows for this. You could recommend that the system should be up and running a week after receiving approval from your boss.

In a more complex or 'resource-heavy' scenario, you would need to give a range of suggestions. In each case be prepared to describe the advantages and disadvantages of each – together with the cost. Bear in mind that the greater the cost, the greater the number of advantages which should accrue!

You would also need to consider what else you will need to make your plan work – including examples of any documented procedures or information on any training sessions you would hold for staff. In this instance the representatives would be very unlikely to need any training at all – except to follow the procedures according to instructions!

At this point try to work your ideas around any time frame suggested by your boss.

Stage 5
Devise a schedule of action.

To prepare this you will have to make some assumptions. In this case you would have to assume that

- your form design/idea was accepted
- your boss agreed to inform the representatives.

You then need to decide whether your action plan will assume you are using a spreadsheet or a manual system and whether you are asking for information weekly or monthly.

Test yourself

> Draw up a schedule of action over the next week which will show how you would develop and introduce this procedure. Check your work with your tutor.

Stage 6
Identify essential communications.

The major communications are from you to your boss, explaining your ideas and how you think they should be put into operation. You could write an informal report or a simple memo – the format is up to you, provided it is clear, grammatical and well presented. The other key communication is from your boss to the representatives. You may find many employers would welcome your suggested draft, which they can amend if they wish. Certainly this would be useful to include in an examination or an assignment, as it gives further proof of your own skills!

Stage 7
Checks and follow-up systems

Issuing instructions and information or devising a schedule is only the first stage in setting up a procedure or planning an event. You would then need to check that everything was going to plan. Obvious checks in this case include making sure that returns are received from representatives and that they are accurate. It is normal for organisations to specify standard mileage for common journeys and not to accept claims above this figure. It is also normal to issue staff with a copy of such information.

You will need some follow-up system – particularly at the beginning – to make sure that you receive information, and you would need your boss's backing to chase up any particularly forgetful staff! However, the idea of reminding representatives beforehand that a return is required, to get them into the habit, should work in most cases. You will also need a follow-up system to check that bills issued for personal mileage have been paid.

Stage 8
Allowing for contingencies

In this case think of things which could go wrong! Examples are staff who fail to follow procedures (what do you suggest is done – and why?), emergencies which give people a good reason to argue the procedure is too rigid, and so on. In this case possible weaknesses may include the following.

- Difficulties for representatives on the day their car is serviced – they may not be able to arrange their visits around this date if there is an emergency. Could you check if the garage could supply a courtesy car?

- Special arrangements with certain representatives made by your boss, eg for extended personal mileage, or extended payment of the bills. You need to check you are informed about such arrangements.

- Mistakes on returns – you need to check these carefully, particularly where clients will be billed for the charge.

A useful method of showing that you have considered these aspects is to suggest a trial period during which the procedure will be implemented. Adjustments can then be made if problems are regularly encountered in a particular area.

Test yourself

You may have had further ideas yourself to add to those above. If not – and if you are struggling to follow all the arguments – do not worry. The answer above is very comprehensive. Practice, however, does help!

As a first stage, it is suggested you practise your communication skills by drafting an informal report to your boss outlining your proposals for the procedure along the lines given above. If you prefer, you could write a memo instead, but it will be clearer and easier to read if you include headings, sub-headings and list the ideas as numbered points.

Then go on to tackle the other scenarios in the manner suggested earlier in this chapter.

A final word

Finally, if you will be taking the RSA Diploma in Secretarial and Administrative Procedures, your tutor might like to note that a tutor's pack is available giving practice on tackling assignments from the simple and straightforward to the complex and more integrated. You can use these practice assignments to refine your skills at the same time as you develop and revise your knowledge.

Appendix: major sources of reference

List 1: books about reference sources
Books about books
British National Bibliography
The Bookseller (published weekly and published quarterly in *Whitaker's Cumulative Book List*)
Directory of Information Sources in the UK
Current British Directories
Management Bibliographies and Reviews

Books about periodicals and newspapers
British Humanities Index
Guide to Reference Material (Library Association)
British Sources of Information (Jackson P)
Facts in Focus (Office for National Statistics)
ANBAR Abstracts (various)
Willing's Press Guide
Ulrich's International Periodical Directory

List 2: general reference books
Telephone directories
The Phone Book
Yellow Pages
Business to Business Directories

Transmission guides and directories
Royal Mail Guide
British Telecom Guide
UK Fax Directory

General
Whitaker's Almanac
Keesing's Record of World Events
Encyclopaedia Britannica

List 3: books about people
Famous names
Who's Who (plus specialised versions, eg *Who's Who in Art, Who's Who in the City* and *Who was Who*)
Chambers Biographical Dictionary

The aristocracy
Debrett's Peerage, Baronetage, Knightage and Companionage / Burke's Landed Gentry / Kelly's Handbook

Government and the Civil Service

Vacher's Parliamentary Companion / The Times Guide to the House of Commons / Dod's Parliamentary Companion
Diplomatic Service List / Civil Service Year Book

Specialist professions

The Army List / Navy List / Air Force List / Law List / Scottish Law Directory
The Medical Register / The Dentists' Register
Kemp's International Music and Recording Industry Yearbook
Retail Directory / Insurance Directory and Year Book

List 4: books about English usage

Dictionary

A **good** desk dictionary, eg *Oxford English Dictionary* or *Chambers*

Specialised dictionaries

Chambers Dictionary of Science and Technology / Dictionary of Economics and Commerce / Black's Medical Dictionary / Dictionary of Legal Terms

English usage, grammar and vocabulary

Pears Cyclopaedia
Roget's Thesaurus / Webster's New Dictionary of Synonyms
Modern English Usage (Fowler)/*Usage and Abusage* (Partridge)/*The Hamlyn Guide to English Usage / An ABC of English Usage* (Treble & Vallins)
The Complete Plain Words (Gower)/*The Spoken Word – a BBC Guide*
Dictionary of Acronyms and Abbreviations / British Initials and Abbreviations / Word Guide to Abbreviations of Organisations / British Qualifications

List 5: books about travel

Atlas and Gazetteer
AA Members' Handbook / RAC Guide and Handbook / Michelin Guides
AA Guide to Hotels and Restaurants in GB and Ireland / Hotels and Restaurants in GB
National Express Service Guide / ABC Railway Guide / ABC World Airways Guide / ABC Shipping Guide / ABC Air / Rail Europe.Cook's International Timetable
Travel Trade Directory
World Calendar of Holidays

List 6: books about British businesses

Directory of Directors
Stock Exchange Official Yearbook / Guide to Key British Enterprises (Dun and Bradstreet) / Kompass UK
Federation of British Industries Register of British Manufacturers
Kelly's Business Directory

British Rate and Data (BRAD) (published monthly)
Who Owns Whom
UK Trade Names / Patents, Designs and Trade Marks
Croner's A–Z of Business Information Sources

List 7: books about overseas business

Statesman's Yearbook
Jane's Major Companies of Europe
Croner's European Business Information Source
Kelly's Business Directory
Yearbook of International Organisations / A Yearbook of the
    Commonwealth / Europa Yearbook: A World Survey
Croner's Reference Book for Exporters / Croner's Reference Book for
    Importers / Exporters' Yearbook / Exporters' Encyclopaedia
British Exports
Trade Directories of the World / Anglo-American Trade Directory

List 8: government publications

Parliamentary papers

Individual reports of Royal Commissions and other inquiries and statements
    of government policy
Votes and proceedings in the House of Commons and Minutes of Proceedings
    of the House of Lords/verbatim reports of parliamentary debates
    (published in *Hansard*)
House of Commons papers
Reports of House of Lords Committees
Acts of Parliament, eg Health and Safety at Work Act 1974

Non-parliamentary papers

Civil Service Year Book
Britain: An Official Handbook
Individual government department publications
Publications by international organisations, eg United Nations Organisation
Catalogues of government publications

Statistics

Government Statistics – a Brief Guide to Resources
Annual Abstract of Statistics
Business Monitors
Employment Gazette
Statistical Yearbook
National Income and Expenditure / Family Expenditure Survey
Economic Trends / Social Trends
Monthly Digest of Statistics / Financial Statistics / Statistical News

Index